HERITAGE
AFRICAN AMERICAN READINGS FOR WRITING

Joyce M. Jarrett
Hampton University

Doreatha Drummond Mbalia
University of Wisconsin at Milwaukee

Margaret Giles Lee
Hampton University

PRENTICE HALL   Upper Saddle River, New Jersey 07458

Library of Congress Cataloging-in-Publication Data

Heritage, African American readings for writing / [selected by] Joyce
M. Jarrett, Doreatha Drummond Mbalia, Margaret Giles Lee,
    p. cm.
  Includes bibliographical references and index.
  ISBN 0-13-291303-8 (pbk.)
    1. Readers—Afro-Americans.   2. Afro-Americans—Civilization—
Problems, exercises, etc.   3. English language—Readers.
4. College readers.   I. Jarrett, Joyce M.   II. Mbalia, Doreatha D.
III. Lee, Margaret Giles.
  PE1127.B55H47   1997
  808′.0427′08996073—dc20   96-2955
                                                        CIP

TO AFRICAN AMERICAN WRITERS
who through their artistic endeavors
committed themselves
to preserving the heritage
of people of African descent

Editorial/Production Supervision
  and Interior Design: **Joan E. Foley**
Editorial Director: **Charlyce Jones Owen**
Acquisitions Editor: **Maggie Barbieri**
Editorial Assistant: **Joan Polk**
Marketing Manager: **Gina Sluss**
Interior and Cover Art: **Maria Piper**
Prepress and Manufacturing Buyer: **Mary Ann Gloriande**

For permission to use copyrighted material, grateful
acknowledgment is made to the copyright holders on
pages 469–474, which are hereby made part of this copyright page.

This book was set in 10/12 ITC Bookman Light by Digitype,
and was printed and bound by Courier Companies, Inc.
The cover was printed by Phoenix Color Corp.

Printed in the United States of America
10 9 8 7 6 5 4 3 2 1

ISBN 0-13-291303-8

Prentice-Hall International (UK) Limited, *London*
Prentice-Hall of Australia Pty., Limited, *Sydney*
Prentice-Hall Canada Inc., *Toronto*
Prentice-Hall Hispanoamericana, S.A., *Mexico*
Prentice-Hall of India Private Limited, *New Delhi*
Prentice-Hall of Japan, Inc., *Tokyo*
Simon & Schuster Asia Pte. Ltd., *Singapore*
Editora Prentice-Hall do Brasil, Ltda., *Rio de Janeiro*

Contents

Rhetorical Contents

Description

Illustration

Classification

Definition

Cause and Effect

Preface

Heritage, a collection of fiction, poetry, drama, and nonfiction by and about African Americans, is a writing text, designed to appeal to writers who are interested in African American culture and the extent to which it touches every facet of American society. To emphasize that African American culture is not monolithic, we have chosen a wide range of subjects that reflect its diversity. Believing that thought-provoking writing is often the result of an inspired beginning, we have selected readings less for their use as models and more for their potential to spark the mind or touch the soul of the reader.

Our text, unlike other ethnic, multi-cultural anthologies used in writing classes, provides students with more than inviting selections; it is also an excellent writing guide. The integration of reading and writing is woven throughout. Having included nearly one hundred engaging selections, each followed by probing questions and stimulating writing assignments, we hope not only to illustrate the beauty and power of the canon, but also to motivate students, particularly through their written discourse, to discover the individual, yet universal significance of the literature.

Unlike the more generic writing texts, ours focuses on the quality of writing rather than on just form. *Heritage* has been designed to help students write more substantively, not by presenting superficial topics, but by allowing students to use provocative readings as a springboard for exploring meaningful issues and for developing their own voice. Even though there is a separate writing review section, writing is shifted from its often intimidating prominence to a means through which writers discover more about themselves and society. Readings have been chosen with writers in mind, with consideration given to interest level, vocabulary, length, readability, as well as to intrinsic literary value.

ORGANIZATION

This text is divided into two parts. Part I, "Planning Writing," provides users with a succinct but clear writing guide. In this section readers are given a writing inventory to help them understand their own writing habits and preferences.

Writing as a process is presented from an unstructured and structured approach, showing writing in various stages from paragraph to essay. Prewriting, drafting, revising/editing, and organizational strategies are also reviewed.

Part II consists of the actual readings. Each selection is introduced with a biographical sketch of the author and definitions of potentially difficult terms. At the end of the selection, the reader will find discussion questions and writing suggestions. Professional and student works represent all genres, with subjects spanning gender, generational, and philosophical lines. Thematically organized, readings range from such subjects as *Slavery, Family,* and *Civil Rights,* to those on *Reading/Writing/Education, Arts/Sciences/Media* and *Intraracial Prejudice* and *Interracial Prejudice.* At the end of Part II, are five supplemental readings that are more in-depth and challenging.

In addition to the two major divisions, the text provides other helpful sections: a glossary of literary and writing terms, a suggested bibliography for those wishing to explore a subject more fully, and a video list for readers and instructors to supplement text selections.

An *Instructor's Manual* contains answers to discussion questions.

ACKNOWLEDGMENTS

We wish to thank the following individuals: Maggie Barbieri, Prentice Hall English editor and Joan Foley, project manager, for their guidance and encouragement throughout the completion of this text; our students, with whom we worked and through whom we were inspired for permitting us to use their compositions; and the following reviewers for their sound advice: William Chapman, Prairie View A&M University; Dennis Gabriel, Cuyahoga Community College; and Brian Reed, Bethune-Cookman College.

                                        Joyce M. Jarrett
                                        Doreatha Drummond Mbalia
                                        Margaret Giles Lee

1

Planning Writing

Writing is a form of communication, and to communicate effectively, you, like all writers, must continuously work on sharpening your skills. You probably spend more time than you would like trying to write more effectively and more easily. There is, however, only one sure secret to successful writing: your willingness to work hard at it. Accepting the following facts should help you approach writing more positively, which, in turn, will likely help you communicate your ideas more effectively.

1. Writing requires both effort and discipline. Although you may jot down your thoughts fairly quickly at first, you must later work at making your writing clear and interesting to your reader.

2. There is no set procedure (recipe) that, if followed, will lead to acceptable writing. Often an individual writing task will dictate a particular approach. Not only is there no single method, you will find that even the steps you develop in responding to a particular task will need to be revisited. After completing your draft, you may find it necessary to revise the thesis or the outline. Don't worry. Going back to revise is normal. Writing is recursive, which means that even though you may complete one stage of writing, you may return to it. It is not unusual to go back and forth until the job is done.

3. Papers with correct form and without grammatical errors may not necessarily prove to be worthwhile reading. Clear purpose, focus, and interesting content are what will define your paper's worth, not its form or grammatical correctness.

Before you can become an effective writer, you must clarify your own views on writing. Answering the following questions will help you learn more about your attitudes toward writing so you can choose the approach that works best for you. Check all responses that apply.

Writing Inventory

1. Generally, which word or words best describe(s) your attitude about writing?
   a. exciting
   b. enjoyable
   c. a chore
   d. _____

2. What types of writing do you like best?
   a. letter writing
   b. diary writing
   c. essay writing
   d. research writing
   e. _____

3. When do you do your best writing?
   a. morning
   b. afternoon
   c. evening
   d. late night
   e. _____

4. Where do you prefer to write?
   a. the library
   b. your own room
   c. _____

5. What kind of atmosphere do you prefer for writing?
   a. totally quiet and in the library
   b. alone and quiet
   c. alone with music
   d. in a room with others
   e. _____

6. What happens when you begin writing?
   a. thoughts flow freely
   b. thoughts come and go
   c. thoughts come too slowly
   d. _____

Interpretation of Inventory

1. The way you feel about writing will affect how you approach the task. If you enjoy writing, you will find your job easier; if you think writing is a chore, writing will be more difficult. Just re-

member that it takes longer to do things you don't like. Plan accordingly.

2. You have probably already discovered the pleasure of developing the types of writing you enjoy. If one of your assignments requires a type of writing that you enjoy less or are less familiar with, you should allow additional time.

3. Learn those times of the day or night when you are at your best. Schedule particularly demanding writing tasks when your energy level is highest.

4. Choose a place where you are most productive. Try to establish a particular location that will become your all-business-no-fun-and-games place. Retreat to such a place, especially for demanding assignments.

5. Just as it is important for you to know the right work location, you must also know the ideal atmosphere you need to get your work done. You may even discover that music helps you work better. However, if you are someone who usually works best in silence, seek it, even if it means changing your location.

6. If your thoughts come and go when you are drafting, allow adequate time for those unproductive periods. Allow even *more* time if you often find writing painstaking. Even if writing comes easily, you must still be cautious. Allow enough time so that if your writing does not flow freely, you are not thrown into panic, because writing lapses are normal. Usually, they last only a short while, and sometimes they are important parts of the writing process, since they can give you the much needed opportunity to mull over an idea.

SELECTING A TOPIC

Writing, after all, begins with ideas. Understanding both your own views about writing and your approach to writing tasks will help you in planning how to present your ideas in your paper. There are several strategies that will help you first to explore your ideas and then to narrow them down so you can select a topic which can adequately be discussed in your paper. Freewriting, brainstorming, and asking questions are techniques that can help you select an essay topic.

Freewriting is the process of writing down your thoughts in a continuous flow, free of worry about grammar, spelling, or structure. The purpose of freewriting is to force you to begin the writing process. The procedure is simple: (1) Think of a particular topic and write it at the top of your paper. (2) For a set period, write as much as you can about that subject. (3) Don't give in to writing blocks—

write until the designated time is up, even if that means writing, "I can't think of anything else to say—let's see. . . . "

Freewriting can be unfocused or focused. With unfocused freewriting, you simply write whatever comes to mind. With focused freewriting, on the other hand, you focus on a particular topic and write about it continuously. Focused freewriting works particularly well in helping you discover how much you know about a chosen topic.

Note the following examples.

Unfocused Freewriting

> I am glad the semester is nearly over. I have learned a lot, but this term was really demanding. Mr. Jones told our African American history class that we could select our own topic for the final paper. That's a real challenge. Though I have not selected the topic, I do know that I need to begin working on it now. I can't afford not to put my best effort into this project. Darn, it seems as if I am faced with one challenge after another.

Focused Freewriting

Challenges

> It's scary being a first-generation college student. I feel so much family pressure to make good. My parents have worked so hard to get me to college. I wonder—I forgot what I was going to say . . . Well, I don't think that they mean to make me feel this way. What else do I want to say about challenges? I know, I need to remind myself that I'm up to the challenge of college because I *am*!

Brainstorming, unlike freewriting, is the process of listing and grouping words and phrases as quickly as they come to you. Once you have listed them, you may want to put related ideas together by grouping them.

A brainstorming example follows:

challenges

do well in calculus and French
organize my time
know as much as I can about my heritage
get carburetor rebuilt
submit my final paper by Nov. 30
complete my house chores on time
read the Sunday *Times* to Aunt Bebe

Grouping, like brainstorming, also involves listing ideas. However, unlike brainstorming, grouping is the process of arranging related ideas together so you can better determine the extent to which your ideas are related. Notice how the previous items that appeared under brainstorming have been grouped.

personal challenges	school challenges	home challenges
1. organize time	1. do well in calculus & French	1. complete chores on time
2. learn more about heritage	2. submit paper by Nov. 30	2. read to Aunt Bebe
3. get carburetor rebuilt		

Asking questions can also help you narrow a topic. Become a reporter: Begin by asking the journalists' questions—who, when, what, why, where, and how. Then jot down every question you can think of about your topic. This strategy is particularly good in helping you see how complex the topic can be.

challenges

1. What makes tasks challenging?
2. Why do I feel pressured to succeed just because I'm a first-generation college student?
3. How can I better organize my time?
4. Where can I learn more about my heritage?
5. What can I do to learn more about it?
6. When will I be up to the financial challenge of getting my carburetor rebuilt?
7. Who can I get to repair my carburetor cheaply?

CONSIDERING YOUR PURPOSE AND UNDERSTANDING YOUR AUDIENCE

Two other important steps in the writing process are considering your purpose and understanding your audience. In considering your purpose, you must decide whether you are communicating with the reader or if you are writing to inform, to persuade, or to express yourself. Once you have established your purpose, consider your audience. Doing so will guide you in gathering information on your topic and deciding how you will present it. Although an instructor will, of course, read your paper, you should always try to write for a real audience. Ask yourself who else would be interested in or would need to know about the information in your paper. Additionally, ask yourself the following questions: (1) Is my audience a specialized group with interests in a given field, for example, doctors, teachers, police officers, or is it a general audience? and (2) What type of tone (your attitude toward the subject) should I use with my audience? Will I be excited, angry, happy, and so on?

DEVELOPING THE THESIS

You probably remember being told by your writing instructors that in order to write a strong essay, you must start with a thesis. But what exactly does that mean? Simply put, a thesis should be a single, specific idea on which you base your entire essay. Although the thesis is often found in the beginning of your essay, it can appear anywhere in your paper, or can even be implied. The thesis must be narrow enough to be discussed thoroughly in your essay.

Note the following example:

General Thesis

African American youth should have a better understanding of their heritage.

The preceding example is too broad; it does not guide the writer or reader in a specific direction. It would be possible to write a book on such a general idea. Reading the sample sentence we are left to wonder—What does "understanding heritage" mean? What specific areas are crucial in our understanding of heritage? Why is awareness of heritage by youth so important?

Specific Thesis

African American youth must know the contributions their ancestors have made to civilization before they can better appreciate their heritage.

Notice that with the specific thesis the essay will address the relationship of the awareness of cultural contributions to one's appreciation of heritage, rather than discussing heritage in general. The writer using the specific thesis has a clear direction for the essay.

SUPPORTING THE THESIS

Once you have a specific thesis, you will need to support it with details to make your point understood. Think of your audience. What type of example(s) does your audience need in order to understand and appreciate the points you are making? There are several ways through which you can develop details. The approach you take will depend on how much or how little you know about your subject. Consider the following tips:

1. Freewrite, brainstorm, ask questions.
2. Read as much as you can about the subject.
3. Talk informally with others to get ideas.
4. Talk informally with professionals who have specific information on the topic. (This will help you clarify information you are discovering.)

Using examples is effective in explaining your subject. Abstract topics—such as pride, fear, anger—are best understood through the use of concrete examples.

ORGANIZATIONAL STRATEGIES

Once you have narrowed your thesis and thought about specific ways of supporting it, decide on the overall organizational strategy you will use in your paper. In other words, decide what approach you will take to get your point across.

Think of the following organizational strategies as structures that will give you options in how you present your ideas. Let your thesis guide you in selecting what method(s) will work best in the development of your paper. While an essay will usually have a dominant organization, that organization is often complemented by others. You will discover in considering these strategies that they work together. Don't be reluctant to use as many of them as you need in order to make your paper clear and easy to follow. You will want to consider the following organizational strategies:

1. Illustration—Using a series of examples to support a given point. These examples are usually presented in some type of logical order, for example, from least important to most or from most important to least.

If you were considering illustration as the organizational strategy for the previous sample thesis on African American youths and their appreciation of heritage, you would give examples to illustrate how youths' knowledge of specific contributions heighten their appreciation of heritage.

2. Description and Narration—Using vivid details and/or a story to make a point. In using these strategies (which are often used together) you can paint pictures with your carefully chosen words. Don't be reluctant to use description freely. Generally, the more details you provide, the clearer your writing will be. In using narration, you must be careful not to let the story dominate. Remember, the story only reinforces your main point. An advantage of using storytelling is that readers are often drawn to stories. In the story only details relevant to the main idea should be included.

If you use description and narration to develop the sample thesis, you would recount a descriptive story showing how someone's knowledge of cultural contributions increased his or her appreciation of heritage.

3. Process—Writing to tell the reader how to do something or to explain how something has been done. In this type of organization the procedure is as important as the end result.

If you were organizing the sample thesis in this way, you would focus on explaining how youth might learn more about contributions of their ancestors, perhaps even showing specifically how such awareness leads to greater appreciation of heritage.

4. Comparison and Contrast—Pointing out the similarities and/or differences between two subjects. In using this type of organization, you must use common elements in comparing or contrasting subjects.

If you use comparison and contrast to develop the sample thesis, you might decide to contrast the cultural unawareness of one group to the cultural awareness of another in order to show how one leads to greater appreciation of heritage.

5. Classification—Placing something into discrete and separate categories. The greatest challenge in using this type of organization

is making sure that each of the categories is distinct so each group is clearly distinguishable from the other.

If you use this form of organization in developing the sample thesis, you may decide to focus on youth with different types of attitudes about heritage. For example, you could show how various attitudes about heritage lead to a greater or lesser appreciation of it.

6. Cause and Effect—Examining the reasons for a certain condition or event (causes) or evaluating the results that a certain condition or event has had on something or someone else (effects).

If you were to use this form of organization in developing the sample thesis, you could look at what has caused many African American youth not to have more appreciation for heritage. Another approach could focus on the effect of increased appreciation of heritage on today's African American youth.

7. Definition—Relying on meaning to explain a word, phrase, or action. There are three basic ways of giving the definition of a word: (1) giving a synonym, (2) giving a formal (dictionary-type) definition, and (3) giving an extended definition (giving several examples of what a word means).

If you choose to use definition in developing the sample thesis, you may want to define *heritage* before exploring how one develops a greater appreciation of it. After defining the word, you might also use illustration or some other type of organizational strategies in making your point.

8. Persuasion—Attempting to persuade your reader to accept (or at least to consider) your point of view. This type of organization is nearly always used with other types of strategies, because much of what we write is written to persuade. In convincing others, you may choose to give illustrations, compare and contrast, clarify terms, tell a story. Let your thesis guide you in selecting what methods will work best in the development of the paper.

If you use persuasion in developing the sample thesis, you should be able to convince your reader that learning about cultural contributions will increase appreciation of heritage among African American youth.

OTHER ORGANIZATIONAL TIPS

Once you have your thesis and have selected the overall structure for your paper, you must *organize ideas* in such a way that the reader can effortlessly understand your thoughts and can readily see how those thoughts relate to one another and to the thesis. A formal outline may not always be necessary, but some type of plan is helpful in enabling you to order primary points and to determine ideas you want to place first, second, and so on. Your essay must also have *coherence*, a logical order in which ideas are arranged. This type of ordering helps the reader better understand how information is related.

Organizing your paper in this way will help you maintain essay *unity*, including only those points that are relevant to the thesis. To decide if information is relevant, ask yourself if the details you have included expand the reader's understanding of the subject. If additional details don't add to the subject, leave them out. More is not necessarily better.

Not only is good organization helpful to the reader, but a guiding plan will also keep you focused as you write your paper. You are less likely to distract your reader by taking unnecessary detours or by circling an issue when you really need to forge ahead.

2

Writing the First Draft

Once you have developed a specific thesis and have organized your ideas in a general plan, you are ready to write the first draft. Although some of us can remember when we had to conform to the same writing pattern, most of us now know that writing methods can be as varied as nature. In fact, if we had just consulted with the professional writers, the ones who write for a living (novelists, poets, journalists), these experts would have straightened us out a long time ago.

Toni Morrison, the Nobel Prize winning novelist, once said that she "wrote" while washing the dishes! Of course, Morrison used the word *write* to describe that mental process of thinking about ideas which occur whenever we are assigned a piece of writing or whenever we decide we are going to write. With so many obligations that demand our time and attention, the time spent "sitting" to write may not be sufficient. We may have to "stand" to write or "walk" to write or "drive" to write. Once we have mentally composed our ideas, then we can physically write them on a sheet of paper or type them on the computer when it is convenient for us to do so. What is important is that writers—whether beginning writers or professional writers—choose the approach that works best for them.

Even when you have chosen the method you think is best suited for you, there are times when your thoughts will not flow freely. Sometimes you may find yourself staring at the blank page or the computer screen. As you prepare to write the first draft of your essay, you may find it helpful to do one of the following:

1. Review your organizing plan.
2. Go back to look at your brainstorming list or your freewriting.
3. Freewrite or brainstorm again, if necessary.
4. Write an entry in your diary or journal.
5. Write a letter to a friend or a relative.
6. Take a walk or do a chore.

DRAFTING TIPS

Once you begin writing, the following drafting tips may prove helpful:

1. Use different pages for each main point of your plan. Using one
   page for each of the main points allows you to write about parts
   of your essay out of sequence. It also leaves you room to add
   ideas as you go along.
2. Write your thesis and the part of the plan you are working on at
   the top of each sheet of paper. This procedure will help you stay
   focused on your thesis statement and thus help you avoid getting
   off your topic.
3. Double-space if you are typing or skip every other line if you are
   writing. Double-spacing or skipping lines is helpful to writers
   who want to come back and add ideas. Some writers, however,
   simply choose to leave wide margins.
4. Try not to interrupt the flow of your ideas by worrying about
   paragraph development, unity and coherence, or grammar,
   spelling, and mechanics. The main concern you should have in
   composing the draft is recording your ideas. Often, when writers
   stop to check spelling or grammar, the flow of ideas is interrupted. Instead of interrupting the writing process, why not circle
   or underline the word or words you want to check? After you've
   completed your draft (or during a writing break), you can check
   for these concerns.

BEGINNINGS AND ENDINGS

Sometimes a writer may know only the thesis statement of the essay
before writing the first draft. For some students, the way the paper
begins and ends is a decision that is made only after the body of the
paper is written. Other students prefer to begin writing their drafts
by starting at the beginning. Whatever your choice, remember that
the beginning of the essay (the introduction) and the ending of the

essay (the conclusion) are just as important as any other part of the essay.

Give both the introduction and the conclusion considerable thought. Don't forget that first and last impressions are important. Think of your reader (audience), for example, your instructor, the admissions officer of a graduate or law school, or a prospective employer. The introduction to your essay may give the reader an immediately favorable or unfavorable opinion of you that can last throughout the essay, if indeed he or she chooses to complete it after reading the introduction.

You may find these questions helpful in planning your introduction and conclusion: What is my writing purpose? Who is my audience?

Ways of Beginning Your Essay

In considering ways of introducing your subject, think about the kind of general information that would most likely help the reader clearly see what your thesis statement will be about. You must also compose an introduction that blends in with your thesis. Ask yourself the following question: What is the most effective way of introducing my subject to my reader?

The following ways of beginning your essay may prove helpful to you:

1. Tell a short story (anecdote). An anecdote may help set the tone for your essay.
2. Present an interesting piece of data. An interesting statistic, for example, that may be unknown to your readers, helps prepare them for the discussion in the body of your essay.
3. Use a direct quotation. A direct quotation from an authoritative source helps convince the reader of your point of view.
4. Define a term. A definition of a term that is important to your discussion will help the reader better understand your essay.
5. Offer the pros or cons of an argument. An introduction that begins with a point of view that is the opposite of your own gives the reader a sense of fair play.

Ways of Ending Your Essay

The conclusion to your paper is just as important as your introduction, perhaps even more so, since it gives the reader a final impression of your subject. It is similar to eating a bowl of butter pecan ice cream: After a scrumptious feast, a bad nut in your last spoonful leaves an unpleasant taste in your mouth.

Consider the following ways of ending your paper:

1. Make a prediction. If you have written an essay about the high content of lead found in the drinking water in the inner cities of the United States, you may want to make a prediction concerning equality in relation to health.

2. Ask a question. If you have discussed racial or gender discrimination, you may want to end your essay by asking whether or not freedom exists in a society that discriminates against a segment of its population.

3. Call for action. If you are writing a letter to an editor of a newspaper about some issue you feel has gone unaddressed in your community, a call for action is an appropriate conclusion.

4. Make recommendations. If you have pointed out problems such as trespassing and robberies that exist in your community, you may want to make recommendations for solving them.

5. Summarize main points. If you are writing a long essay, such as a research paper, your reader may need to be reminded of the main points of your discussion.

THE FIRST DRAFT

A plan and a draft of the sample thesis statement presented in "Planning Your Paper" follow. These examples may prove helpful in showing you how informal a plan can be as well as how unfinished a first draft may look.

Essay Plan

Thesis Statement:	African American youths must know the contributions their ancestors have made to civilization in order to better appreciate their heritage.
Point 1:	—Problems caused by not knowing contributions low self-esteem
	eyes
	hair
	nose
	crime
	drugs
Point 2:	—Contributions made to civilization before the fifteenth century (before the slave trade) first people first language

Point 3:

father of medicine
pyramids
University of Timbuktu
—Contributions made to civilization after the
fifteenth century
labor of African Americans
inventors
slave heroes and heroines
political activists

Point 4:

—Upliftment caused by knowing contributions

(Notice that in this first draft the introduction is incomplete and the conclusion is omitted; it also includes grammar, punctuation, and spelling errors.)

To Know One's History Is to Know and Appreciate Oneself

1   African American youths must know the contributions their ancestors have made to civilization in order to better appreciate their heritage.

2   The problems caused by not knowing these contributions are numerous. The most serious perhaps being lack of self-esteem. African American youth are wearing blue and green contact lenses because they have been taught that blue and green eyes are prettier than brown eyes. Some youths are lightning their skin color. Others are pressing, gerri curling and finger waving their hair because they have been taught that the quality of their hair is inferior to that of white Americans. Plastic surgery is performed on noses that are thought to be too big (wide?). Plastic surgery can be expensive. In addition, the murders committed by African American youth against each other may also be a sign of low self-esteem. If you don't think much of yourself, your looks or your accomplishments, how can you respect the lives of others who look just like you?

3   African American youth can take pride in the fact that African people was the first people on earth. They contributed the first and second languages to humankind: the Nubian language of Meroe and the hieroglyphs of Egypt. The father of medicine, Imhotep, was born in Africa around 2980 B.C., the pyramids were designed and built by Africans. The famous University of Timbucktu was founded in West Africa during the Ghana-Mali-Songhai dynasty. Scholars from all over the world came to study at

this University. Before the slave trade, African people made tools such as the plow, axe, and hoe, and manufactured cloth and leather goods. An agricultural people, Africans' primary principal was working for the benefit of the group, and giving everyone, weather old, young, male, or female, an equal chance to grow in society.

4   During the slave trade, Africans continued to make impressive contributions, though many did not receive credit for them. After the Civil War, Lewis Latimer invented the first electric light with a carbon filament; Garrett Morgan invented the gas mask and the automatic traffic light; and George Washington Carver invented over three hundred products from the peanut. Moreover, the political activism of Marcus Garvey, Ida B. Wells, Malcolm X, and Martin Luther King, Jr. made it possible for African Americans to survive in the U.S. with a measure of dignity. Such slave heroes as Frederick Douglass, Harriet Tubman, David Walker, Sojourner Truth, and Nat Turner risked their own lives to free their people.

3

Revising and Editing

Revising and editing are perhaps the most important steps in the writing process, for it is in these steps that your draft is transformed from a crude, unsophisticated, and perhaps illogical and undeveloped early attempt at expression to a more refined and polished draft that represents the best that you, the writer, can produce at the time. Revising and editing are interdependent processes that involve careful review and analysis of the draft, with the writer often going back and forth within the essay in order to improve its overall quality.

It is said that "writing is revision." Revision is the act of "seeing again" or "re-envisioning" the essay, that is, looking at it with the goal of improving the organization and development of the essay. This procedure includes reexamining the purpose and audience, changing the thesis if necessary, rearranging sentences and paragraphs for unity and coherence, and reassessing the quantity and quality of supporting details.

After making necessary revisions to the draft, you are ready to begin cleaning up the essay by editing—making grammatical, punctuation, spelling, mechanical, and word choice improvements. Editing provides a finishing touch to the essay.

PRACTICAL GUIDES FOR REVISING AND EDITING

Here are some practical guides you may find helpful as you go through the revising and editing processes.

1. Give yourself enough time to write your essay, to put it aside (for at least a day), and to review it thoroughly before submitting it. Sufficient time allows you to come back to the essay with a fresh perspective.
2. Make sure your point is developed sufficiently. You may need to write additional drafts to carry out the purpose of the essay.
3. Read the essay aloud. Reading aloud helps you hear possible problem areas.
4. Ask someone, perhaps a friend, to read the essay. A second reader can give you another perspective on the essay. Also, having someone read the essay aloud to you can accomplish the same goal.
5. Pay special attention to problem areas that your instructor or others have pointed out in previous essays. Doing so helps you be more alert to your specific writing weaknesses.
6. Concentrate first on the larger elements—thesis, purpose, audience, arrangement of ideas, and supporting details. These elements should be your first concern because they represent the core of the writing and serve to carry out your intentions for the essay.
7. Examine later the grammar, punctuation, spelling, mechanics, and style of the essay. Making corrections and changes in these elements is the final step toward polishing the essay.

REVISING AND EDITING GUIDE

When reviewing your essay in preparation for revising and editing it, consider the following five aspects in writing:

Revision

> Organization: I have examined the following:
>   Purpose
>   Audience
>   Introduction
>   Thesis sentence
>   Relevance of ideas
>   Logical order of ideas
>   Use of transitions
>   Conclusion

Development:	I have included the following: Enough details to support the main idea Specific details to support the main idea

Editing

Grammar:	I have reviewed the essay for the following: Fragments Comma splices Fused sentences Subject-verb agreement Pronoun-antecedent agreement Pronoun usage Verb form Verb tense Adjective or adverb usage
Mechanics:	I have reviewed the essay for the following: Punctuation: comma, semicolon, colon, apostrophe Spelling Capitalization
Style:	I have reviewed the essay for the following: Appropriate tone and language Correct word choices Effective sentence types, variety, and length Wordiness

REVISING AND EDITING EXAMPLE

The following revised and rewritten drafts illustrate the revising and editing process of the essay on the importance of African American youth developing greater appreciation of themselves through studying their heritage. You may want to review the first draft of this essay, which appears at the end of Chapter 2.

Revision Comments

After careful review of the first draft, the student determined that the following revisions were necessary:

Refocusing the thesis statement: The original thesis sentence was, "African American youths must know the contributions their ancestors have made to civilization in order to better appreciate *their heritage*." After reconsidering this thesis in relation to the content of the essay, as well as to its title, the student decided to replace the words *their heritage* with the word *themselves* to have the thesis state, "African American youths must know the contributions their ancestors have made to civilization in order to better appreciate *themselves.*"

Insufficient Details: The beginning of the essay (the introduction) needs more details to provide background information for the thesis and to make clear the purpose of the essay. A short story about the writer's own observations regarding the portrayal of African Americans may accomplish this.

Lack of Unity: In the second paragraph, the sentence "Plastic surgery can be expensive" is not directly related to the main idea of the essay. Therefore, it should be omitted.

Lack of Coherence: In the fourth paragraph, the sentence about the slave heroes Douglass, Tubman, and so on, is out of logical order. It should be placed before the "Civil War" sentence, since these heroes worked to abolish slavery before the Civil War ended slavery.

Lack of Ending: The essay needs an ending (a conclusion) to leave the reader with a final thought about the main idea of the essay. A call for action or prediction may accomplish this.

Editing Comments

After careful review of the draft, the student also determined that the following editing changes were necessary.

Misspelled Words: In the second paragraph, the word *lightning* should be lightening, and the word *gerri* should be spelled *jheri.* In the third paragraph, the word *Timbucktu* should be spelled *Timbuktu.*

Fragment: In the second paragraph, the second group of words, "The most serious perhaps being lack of self-esteem" is a fragment. It should be connected to the first sentence by replacing the period with a comma: "The problems caused by not knowing these contributions are numerous, the most serious perhaps being lack of self-esteem."

Subject-Verb Agreement Error: In the third paragraph, the first sentence should read "African American youth can take pride in the fact that African people *were* the first people on earth."

Comma Splice: In the third paragraph, the comma that separates the "The father of medicine" sentence from the "the pyramids" sentence should be replaced with a period to form two separate sentences: "The father of medicine, Imhotep, was born in Africa around 2980 B.C. The pyramids were . . . "

Word Choice Errors: In the last sentence in the third paragraph, the word *principal* should be replaced with the word *principle;* in this same sentence, the word *weather* should be replaced with the word *whether.*

REVISED AND EDITED DRAFT

The following draft illustrates the student's revising and editing notes based on the preceding revising and editing comments.

To Know One's History is to Know and
Appreciate Oneself

1   African American youths must know the contributions their ancestors have made to civilization
in order to better appreciate their heritage.

Refocus thesis— change "their heritage" to "themselves"

Add background info.- story about my experiences

2   The problems caused by not knowing these contributions are numerous. The most serious perhaps
being lack of self-esteem. African American
youths are wearing blue and green contact lenses
because they have been taught that blue and green
eyes are prettier than brown eyes. Some youths
are lightening their skin color. Others are pressing, jheri curling and finger waving their hair
because they have been taught that the quality of
their hair is inferior to that of white
Americans. Plastic surgery is performed on noses
that are thought to be too big (wide?). Plastic
surgery can be expensive. In addition, the murders committed by African American youths against
each other may also be a sign of low self-esteem.

(irrelevant)

If you don't think much of yourself, your looks‸ or your accomplishments, how can you respect the lives of others who look just like you?

3   African American youths can take pride in the fact that African people ~~was~~ **were** the first people on earth. They contributed the first and second languages to humankind: the Nubian language of Meroe and the hieroglyphs of Egypt. The father of medicine, Imhotep, was born in Africa around 2980 B.C. ⊙ **T**he pyramids were designed and built by Africans. The famous University of ~~Timbucktu~~ **Timbuktu** was founded in West Africa during the Ghana-Mali-Songhai dynasty. Scholars from all over the world came to study at this University. Before the slave trade, African people made tools such as the plow, axe, and hoe, and manufactured cloth and leather goods. An agricultural people, Africans' primary ~~principal~~ **principle** was to work for the benefit of the group, and giving everyone, **whether** ~~weather~~ old, young, male, or female, an equal chance to grow in society.

4   During the slave trade, Africans continued to make impressive contributions, though many did not receive credit for them. After the Civil War, Lewis Latimer invented the first electric light with a carbon filament; Garrett Morgan invented the gas mask and the automatic traffic light; and George Washington Carver invented over three hundred products from the peanut.

Moreover, the political activism of Marcus
Garvey, Ida B. Wells, Malcolm X, and Martin
Luther King, Jr.⌃made it possible for African
Americans to survive in the U.S. with a measure
of dignity.⌈Such slave heroes as Frederick
Douglass, Harriet Tubman, David Walker,   **Place**
Sojourner Truth, and Nat Turner risked their own   **before**
Add a   lives to free their people.   **"Civil**
conclusion   **War"**
perhaps a   **sentence**
summary,
or prediction

SECOND (REWRITTEN) DRAFT

The following is the student's second draft, written to include the preceding revising and editing changes.

To Know One's History Is to Know and Appreciate Oneself

1   I wonder what percentage of African American youths perceives a positive image of themselves. In public school, for example, I can remember that in February, "Black History Month," our teachers devoted some time to discussing Martin Luther King, Jr., and Harriet Tubman. But that was about the extent of African American history that we received. Until I got to college, the overwhelming message I received from television commercials to news broadcasts was that African Americans, youths in particular, were either imitators of white society or criminals. Once I discovered the many positive ways in which people of African descent have influenced the world, I felt an indescribable pride in myself and for my people. Therefore, I have come to the firm conclusion that African American youths must know the contributions their ancestors have made to civilization in order to better appreciate themselves.
2   The problems caused by not knowing these contributions are numerous, the most serious perhaps being lack

of self-esteem. African American youths are wearing blue and green contact lenses because they have been taught that blue and green eyes are prettier than brown eyes. Some youths are lightening their skin color. Others are pressing, jheri curling, and finger waving their hair because they have been taught that the quality of their hair is inferior to that of white Americans. Plastic surgery is performed on noses that are thought to be too wide. In addition, the murders committed by African American youths against each other may also be a sign of low self-esteem. If you don't think much of yourself, your looks, or your accomplishments, how can you respect the lives of others who look just like you?

3   African American youths can take pride in the fact that African people were the first people on earth. They contributed the first and second languages to humankind: the Nubian language of Meroe and the hieroglyphs of Egypt. The father of medicine, Imhotep, was born in Africa around 2980 B.C. The pyramids were designed and built by Africans. The famous University of Timbuktu was founded in West Africa during the Ghana-Mali-Songhai dynasty. Scholars from all over the world came to study at this university. Before the slave trade, African people made tools such as the plow, axe, and hoe, and manufactured cloth and leather goods. An agricultural people, Africans' primary principle was to work for the benefit of the group, and giving everyone, whether old, young, male, or female, an equal chance to grow in society.

4   During the slave trade, Africans continued to make impressive contributions, though many did not receive credit for them. Such slave heroes as Frederick Douglass, Harriet Tubman, David Walker, Sojourner Truth, and Nat Turner risked their own lives to free their people. After the Civil War, Lewis Latimer invented the first electric light with a carbon filament; Garrett Morgan invented the gas mask and the automatic traffic light; and George Washington Carver invented over three hundred products from the peanut. Moreover, the political activism of Marcus Garvey, Ida B. Wells, Malcolm X, and Martin Luther King, Jr., made it possible for African Americans to survive in the U.S. with a measure of dignity.

5   The impact that this information has had on my life is absolutely amazing. I see myself as the offspring of a race of giants who were not just capable of surviving under extreme pressure, but were also capable of making great strides in spite of overwhelming odds. Other African American youth cannot help but to be uplifted as I was, once they know about the contributions of our ancestors.

4

Slavery

HOW BUCK WON HIS FREEDOM

Anonymous

African American folktales, often remembered for their humor and/or cleverness, played an important role in cultural history. These anonymous crafty tales, passed on from person to person and from one generation to the next, helped slaves in the United States preserve their humanity in oppression. The following folktale demonstrates the extent to which slaves had to resort to trickery to "right" the wrongs of an unjust system.

Buck was the shrewdest slave on the big Washington plantation. He could steal things almost in front of his master's eyes without being detected. Finally, after having had his chickens and pigs stolen until he was sick, Master Henry Washington called Buck to him one day and said, "Buck, how do you manage to steal without getting caught?"

"Dat's easy, Massa," replied Buck, "dat's easy. Ah kin steal yo' clo'es right tonight, wid you aguardin' 'em."

"No, no," said the master, "you may be a slick thief, but you can't do that. I will make a proposition with you: If you steal my

suit of clothes tonight, I will give you your freedom, and if you
fail to steal them, then you will stop stealing my chickens."

"Aw right, Massa, aw right," Buck agreed. "Dat's uh go."   4

That night about nine o'clock the master called his wife   5
into the bedroom, got his Sunday suit of clothes, laid it out on
the table, and told his wife about the proposition he had made
with Buck. He got on one side of the table and had his wife get
on the other side, and they waited. Pretty soon, through a window that was open, the master heard the mules and the horses
in the stable lot running as if someone were after them.

"Here wife," said he, "you take this gun and keep an eye on   6
this suit. I am going to see what's the matter with those animals."

Buck, who had been out to the horse lot and started the   7
stampede to attract the master's attention, now approached the
open window. He was a good mimic, and in tones that sounded
like his master's he called out, "Ol' lady, ol' lady, ol' lady, you
better hand me that suit. That damn thief might steal it while
I'm gone."

The master's wife, thinking that it was her husband ask-   8
ing for his suit, took it from the table and handed it out the
window to Buck. This is how Buck won his freedom.

Discussion Questions

1. How did Buck win his freedom?

2. What does this tale reveal about the lives of slaves?

3. To what extent does Buck's use of language reveal that he wears
a mask in front of his master?

4. What does the folktale tell you about Buck?

5. How does this tale serve as evidence that the creativity of African
Americans was not destroyed in slavery?

6. Although this folktale relies primarily on narration in recounting
the story, what other method of organization is used?

7. What is the lesson of the folktale?

Writing Assignments

1. Write a short tale using a younger person as your audience, and
teach him or her a lesson.

2. Write an essay describing a time when you or someone you know
outsmarted someone else.

3. Write an essay describing the process by which you finally
achieved a goal that you had hoped to achieve for some time.

BURY ME IN A FREE LAND

Frances Ellen Watkins Harper

Born free in Baltimore, Frances Ellen Watkins Harper (1825–1911) is one of the best known antislavery poets of the antebellum period. Her notable works include a short story, "The Two Offers" (1859); her narrative Moses, A Story of the Nile *(1870); a very popular volume of poetry,* Poems on Miscellaneous Subjects *(1874), from which the following selection is taken; and a novel* Iola LeRoy *(1892). The following poem reflects the extent to which slaves must have longed for "free land," even in death.*

Vocabulary

galling   (stanza 5)   irritating

Make me a grave where'er you will,   1
In a lowly plain, or a lofty hill;
Make it among earth's humblest graves,
But not in a land where men are slaves.

I could not rest if around my grave   2
I heard the steps of a trembling slave;
His shadow above my silent tomb
Would make it a place of fearful gloom.

I could not rest if I heard the tread   3
Of a coffle gang[1] to the shambles led,
And the mother's shriek of wild despair
Rise like a curse on the trembling air.

I could not sleep if I saw the lash   4
Drinking her blood at each fearful gash,
And I saw her babes torn from her breast,
Like trembling doves from their parent nest.

I'd shudder and start if I heard the bay   5
Of bloodhounds seizing their human prey,
And I heard the captive plead in vain
As they bound afresh his galling chain.

[1]coffle gang   (stanza 3)   A train of slaves fastened together.

If I saw young girls from their mothers' arms　　　　6
Bartered and sold for their youthful charms,
My eye would flash with a mournful flame,
My death-paled cheek grow red with shame.

I would sleep, dear friends, where bloated might　　7
Can rob no man of his dearest right;
My rest shall be calm in any grave
Where none can call his brother a slave.

I ask no monument, proud and high,　　　　　　　　8
To arrest the gaze of the passers-by;
All that my yearning spirit craves,
Is bury me not in a land of slaves.

Discussion Questions

1. Why does the writer want to be buried in a free land?
2. According to the poem, what kind of injustices did slaves suffer?
3. What are some of the reasons the speaker gives for not wishing to be buried in a land where "men" were slaves?
4. In the sixth stanza, why were girls "bartered and sold"?
5. What is the tone of the poem?
6. What does the title of the poem tell you about the speaker?
7. In what way does description help the poet make her point?
8. Study the structure of the poem. How has the poet chosen to organize her ideas? Is that organization effective? Why or why not?

Writing Assignments

1. The institution of slavery glaringly revealed one people's inhumanity to another. Write an essay in which you provide a current example of such inhumanity.
2. Write an essay about some societal problems that you do not believe will be corrected in your lifetime. Explain why you feel as you do.
3. Write an essay focusing on the negative effects that some inconsiderate act has had on you or someone you know.

THE SLAVE MISTRESS

Linda Brent

Born Harriet Ann Jacobs, the author (1813–1897) lived in a slave state for twenty-seven years. Upon arriving in Philadelphia, she was encouraged to publish Incidents in the Life of a Slave Girl *(1860), a sketch of her life, and she did so under the name of Linda Brent. She wrote not "to attract attention" to herself, but to show the people of the free states the "deep and dark and foul . . . abominations" of slavery. The following selection from* Incidents *describes a condition of slavery peculiar to the slave woman.*

Vocabulary

malevolence	(paragraph 2)	hostility
vigilance	(paragraph 2)	attention
asylum	(paragraph 2)	institution
buoyant	(paragraph 2)	happy
vile	(paragraph 3)	hateful

I would ten thousand times rather that my children should be the half-starved paupers of Ireland than to be the most pampered among the slaves of America. I would rather drudge out my life on a cotton plantation, till the grave opened to give me rest, than to live with an unprincipled master and a jealous mistress. The felon's home in a penitentiary is preferable. He may repent, and turn from the error of his ways, and so find peace; but it is not so with a favorite slave. She is not allowed to have any pride of character. It is deemed a crime in her to wish to be virtuous.

Mrs. Flint possessed the key to her husband's character before I was born. She might have used this knowledge to counsel and to screen the young and the innocent among her slaves; but for them she had no sympathy. They were the objects of her constant suspicion and malevolence. She watched her husband with unceasing vigilance; but he was well practised in means to evade it. What he could not find opportunity to say in words he manifested in signs. He invented more than were ever thought of in a deaf and dumb asylum. I let them pass, as if I did not understand what he meant; and many were

1

2

the curses and threats bestowed on me for my stupidity. One day he caught me teaching myself to write. He frowned, as if he was not well pleased; but I suppose he came to the conclusion that such an accomplishment might help to advance his favorite scheme. Before long, notes were often slipped into my hand. I would return them, saying, "I can't read them, sir." "Can't you?" he replied; "then I must read them to you." He always finished the reading by asking, "Do you understand?" Sometimes he would complain of the heat of the tea room, and order his supper to be placed on a small table in the piazza. He would seat himself there with a well-satisfied smile, and tell me to stand by and brush away the flies. He would eat very slowly, pausing between mouthfuls. These intervals were employed in describing the happiness I was so foolishly throwing away, and in threatening me with the penalty that finally awaited my stubborn disobedience. He boasted much of the forbearance he had exercised towards me, and reminded me that there was a limit to his patience. When I succeeded in avoiding opportunities for him to talk to me at home, I was ordered to come to his office, to do some errand. When there, I was obliged to stand and listen to such language as he saw fit to address to me. Sometimes I so openly expressed my contempt for him that he would become violently enraged, and I wondered why he did not strike me. Circumstanced as he was, he probably thought it was better policy to be forbearing. But the state of things grew worse and worse daily. In desperation I told him that I must and would apply to my grandmother for protection. He threatened me with death, and worse than death, if I made any complaint to her. Strange to say, I did not despair. I was naturally of a buoyant disposition, and always I had a hope of somehow getting out of his clutches. Like many a poor, simple slave before me, I trusted that some threads of joy would yet be woven into my dark destiny.

I had entered my sixteenth year, and every day it became more apparent that my presence was intolerable to Mrs. Flint. Angry words frequently passed between her and her husband. He had never punished me himself, and he would not allow any body else to punish me. In that respect, she was never satisfied; but, in her angry moods, no terms were too vile for her to bestow upon me. Yet I, whom she detested so bitterly, had far more pity for her than he had, whose duty it was to make her life happy. I never wronged her, or wished to wrong her; and one word of kindness from her would have brought me to her feet.

Discussion Questions

1. What kind of experiences does Linda have with Mr. Flint? With Mrs. Flint?
2. How does Mr. Flint harass Linda?
3. What life does Linda see as preferable to her life as a slave?
4. The narrator says that a favorite slave is not allowed to have any pride of character. What do you think she means?
5. Why is Mrs. Flint jealous of Linda?
6. Specifically, what is Linda's dilemma? What does her response to her situation tell you about her?
7. What details in particular make Linda Brent's narrative believable?
8. What is the theme of the story?

Writing Assignments

1. Write an essay discussing a problem that women confront today in the workplace.
2. In an essay describe a time when you had to use trickery in addressing a problem rather than dealing with it directly.
3. Write an essay focusing on the idea of "powerlessness."

HOW A SLAVE WAS MADE A MAN

Frederick Douglass

An ex-slave, Frederick Douglass (1817–1895) fled North at an early age and became a powerful orator and writer who provided leadership and guidance in fighting the institution of slavery. He is said to have been influential in President Lincoln's "Great Emancipation" efforts as well as a force in the passage of the Fourteenth and Fifteenth Amendments. Douglass published three accounts of his slave struggles: The Narrative of the Life of Frederick Douglass *(1845), from which the following selection is taken;* My Bondage and My Freedom *(1855); and* The Life and Times of Frederick Douglass *(1881). In the selection that follows you can see the courage Douglass exhibited even in slavery.*

Vocabulary

languished	(1)	faded
shrouded	(3)	veiled
moorings	(4)	docks
turbid	(4)	unclean
goaded	(5)	angered
sundry	(7)	various
quailed	(7)	snapped

If at any one time of my life more than another, I was made to drink the bitterest dregs of slavery, that time was during the first six months of my stay with Mr. Covey. We were worked in all weathers. It was never too hot or too cold; it could never rain, blow, hail, or snow, too hard for us to work in the field. Work, work, work, was scarcely more the order of the day than of the night. The longest days were too short for him, and the shortest nights too long for him. I was somewhat unmanageable when I first went there, but a few months of this discipline tamed me. Mr. Covey succeeded in breaking me. I was broken in body, soul, and spirit. My natural elasticity was crushed, my intellect languished, the disposition to read departed, the cheerful spark that lingered about my eye died; the dark night of slavery closed in upon me; and behold a man transformed into a brute!

Sunday was my only leisure time. I spent this in a sort of   2
beast-like stupor, between sleep and wake, under some large
tree. At times I would rise up, a flash of energetic freedom
would dart through my soul, accompanied with a faint beam of
hope, that flickered for a moment, and then vanished. I sank
down again, mourning over my wretched condition. I was
sometimes prompted to take my life, and that of Covey, but was
prevented by a combination of hope and fear. My sufferings on
this plantation seem now like a dream rather than a stern reality.

Our house stood within a few rods of the Chesapeake Bay,   3
whose broad bosom was ever white with sails from every quarter of the habitable globe. Those beautiful vessels, robed in
purest white, so delightful to the eye of freemen, were to me so
many shrouded ghosts, to terrify and torment me with
thoughts of my wretched condition. I have often, in the deep
stillness of a summer's Sabbath, stood all alone upon the lofty
banks of that noble bay, and traced, with saddened heart and
tearful eye, the countless number of sails moving off to the
mighty ocean. The sight of these always affected me powerfully.
My thoughts would compel utterance; and there, with no audience but the Almighty, I would pour out my soul's complaint,
in my rude way, with an apostrophe to the moving multitude of
ships:—

"You are loosed from your moorings and are free; I am fast   4
in my chains, and am a slave! You move merrily before the gentle gale, and I sadly before the bloody whip! You are freedom's
swift-winged angels, that fly round the world; I am confined in
bands of iron! O that I were free! O, that I were on one of your
gallant decks, and under your protecting wing! Alas! betwixt
me and you, the turbid waters roll. Go on, go on. O that I could
also go! Could I but swim! If I could fly! O, why was I born a
man, of whom to make a brute! The glad ship is gone; she
hides in the dim distance. I am left in the hottest hell of unending slavery. O God, save me! God, deliver me! Let me be free! Is
there any God? Why am I a slave? I will run away. I will not
stand it. Get caught, or get clear, I'll try it. I had as well die
with ague as the fever. I have only one life to lose. I had as well
be killed running as die standing. Only think of it; one hundred
miles straight north, and I am free! Try it? Yes! God helping me,
I will. It cannot be that I shall live and die a slave. I will take to
the water. This very bay shall yet bear me into freedom. The
steamboats steered in a north-east course from North Point. I

will do the same; and when I get to the head of the bay, I will turn my canoe adrift, and walk straight through Delaware into Pennsylvania. When I get there, I shall not be required to have a pass; I can travel without being disturbed. Let but the first opportunity offer, and, come what will, I am off. Meanwhile, I will try to bear up under the yoke. I am not the only slave in the world. Why should I fret? I can bear as much as any of them. Besides, I am but a boy, and all boys are bound to some one. It may be that my misery in slavery will only increase my happiness when I get free. There is a better day coming."

Thus I used to think, and thus I used to speak to myself; goaded almost to madness at one moment, and at the next reconciling myself to my wretched lot. 5

I have already intimated that my condition was much worse, during the first six months of my stay at Mr. Covey's, than in the last six. The circumstances leading to the change in Mr. Covey's course toward me form an epoch in my humble history. You have seen how a man was made a slave; you shall see how a slave was made a man. On one of the hottest days of the month of August, 1833, Bill Smith, William Hughes, a slave named Eli, and myself, were engaged in fanning wheat.[1] Hughes was clearing the fanned wheat from before the fan. Eli was turning, Smith was feeding, and I was carrying wheat to the fan. The work was simple, requiring strength rather than intellect; yet, to one entirely unused to such work, it came very hard. About three o'clock of that day, I broke down; my strength failed me; I was seized with a violent aching of the head, attended with extreme dizziness; I trembled in every limb. Finding what was coming, I nerved myself up, feeling it would never do to stop work. I stood as long as I could stagger to the hopper with grain. When I could stand no longer, I fell, and felt as if held down by an immense weight. The fan of course stopped; every one had his own work to do; and no one could do the work of the other, and have his own go on at the same time. 6

Mr. Covey was at the house, about one hundred yards from the treading-yard where we were fanning. On hearing the fan stop, he left immediately, and came to the spot where we were. He hastily inquired what the matter was. Bill answered that I was sick, and there was no one to bring wheat to the fan. 7

[1]fanning wheat   (6)   Driving away the outer covering of grain by means of air current.

I had by this time crawled away under the side of the post and rail-fence by which the yard was enclosed, hoping to find relief by getting out of the sun. He then asked where I was. He was told by one of the hands. He came to the spot, and, after looking at me awhile, asked me what was the matter. I told him as well as I could, for I scarce had strength to speak. He then gave me a savage kick in the side, and told me to get up. I tried to do so, but fell back in the attempt. He gave me another kick, and again told me to rise. I again tried, and succeeded in gaining my feet; but, stooping to get the tub with which I was feeding the fan, I again staggered and fell. While down in this situation, Mr. Covey took up the hickory slat with which Hughes had been striking off the half-bushel measure, and with it gave me a heavy blow upon the head, making a large wound, and the blood ran freely; and with this again told me to get up. I made no effort to comply, having now made up my mind to let him do his worst. In a short time after receiving this blow, my head grew better. Mr. Covey had now left me to my fate. At this moment I resolved, for the first time, to go to my master, enter a complaint and ask his protection. In order to do this, I must that afternoon walk seven miles; and this, under the circumstances, was truly a severe undertaking. I was exceedingly feeble; made so as much by the kicks and blows which I received, as by the severe fit of sickness to which I had been subjected. I, however, watched my chance, while Covey was looking in an opposite direction, and started for St. Michael's. I succeeded in getting a considerable distance on my way to the woods, when Covey discovered me, and called after me to come back, threatening what he would do if I did not come. I disregarded both his calls and his threats, and made my way to the woods as fast as my feeble state would allow; and thinking I might be overhauled by him if I kept the road, I walked through the woods, keeping far enough from the road to avoid detection, and near enough to prevent losing my way. I had not gone far before my little strength again failed me. I could go no farther. I fell down, and lay for a considerable time. The blood was yet oozing from the wound on my head. For a time I thought I should bleed to death; and think now that I should have done so, but that the blood so matted my hair as to stop the wound. After lying there about three quarters of an hour, I nerved myself up again, and started on my way, through bogs and briers, barefooted and bareheaded, tearing my feet sometimes at nearly every step; and after a journey of about seven miles, occupying some five hours to perform it, I arrived at master's store. I then presented an appearance enough to affect any but a heart of iron. From the crown of my head to my feet, I was covered with blood. My hair was all clotted with dust and blood; my shirt was stiff with blood. My legs and feet were torn in sundry places with briers and thorns, and were also covered with blood. I suppose I looked like a man who had escaped a den of wild beasts, and barely escaped them. In this state I appeared before my master, humbly entreating him to interpose his authority for my protection. I told him all the circumstances as well as I could, and it seemed, as I spoke, at times to affect him. He would then walk the floor, and seek to justify Covey by saying he expected I deserved it. He asked me what I wanted. I told him, to let me get a new home; that as sure as I lived with Mr. Covey again, I should live with but to die with him; that Covey would surely kill me; he was in a fair way for it. Master Thomas ridiculed the idea that there was any danger of Mr. Covey's killing me, and said that he knew Mr. Covey; that he was a good man, and that he could not think of taking me from him; that, should he do so, he would lose the whole year's wages; that I belonged to Mr. Covey for one year, and that I must go back to him, come what might; and that I must not trouble him with any more stories, or that he would himself *get hold of me.* After threatening me thus, he gave me a very large dose of salts, telling me that I might remain in St. Michael's that night, (it being quite late,) but that I must be off back to Mr. Covey's early in the morning; and that if I did not, he would *get hold of me,* which meant that he would whip me. I remained all night, and according to his orders, I started off to Covey's in the morning, (Saturday morning,) wearied in body and broken in spirit. I got no supper that night, or breakfast that morning. I reached Covey's about nine o'clock; and just as I was getting over the fence that divided Mrs. Kemp's fields from ours, out ran Covey with his cowskin, to give me another whipping. Before he could reach me, I succeeded in getting to the cornfield; and as the corn was very high, it afforded me the means of hiding. He seemed very angry, and searched for me a long time. My behavior was altogether unaccountable. He finally gave up the chase, thinking, I suppose, that I must come home for something to eat; he would give himself no further trouble in looking for me. I spent that day mostly in the woods, having the alternative before me,—to go home and be whipped to death, or stay in the woods and be starved to death. That night, I fell in with Sandy Jenkins, a slave with whom I was somewhat acquainted. Sandy had a free wife who lived about four miles from Mr. Covey's; and it being Saturday, he was on his way to see her. I told him my circumstances, and he very kindly invited me to go home with him. I went home with him, and talked this whole matter over, and got his advice as to what course it was best for me to pursue. I found Sandy an old adviser. He told me, with great solemnity, I must go back to Covey; but that before I went, I must go with him into another part of the woods, where there was a certain *root*, which, if I would take some of it with me, carrying it *always on my right side*, would render it impossible for Mr. Covey, or any other white man, to whip me. He said he had carried it for years; and since he had done so, he had never received a blow, and never expected to while he carried it. I at first rejected the idea, that the simple carrying of a root in my pocket would have any such effect as he had said, and was not disposed to take it; but Sandy impressed the necessity with much earnestness, telling me it could do no harm, if it did no good. To please him, I at length took the root, and, according to his direction, carried it upon my right side. This was Sunday morning. I immediately started for home; and upon entering the yard gate, out came Mr. Covey on his way to meeting. He spoke to me very kindly, bade me drive the pigs from a lot near by, and passed on towards the church. Now, this singular conduct of Mr. Covey really made me begin to think that there was something in the *root* which Sandy had given me; and had it been on any other day than Sunday, I could have attributed the conduct to no other cause than the influence of that root; and as it was, I was half inclined to think the *root* to be something more than I at first had taken it to be. All went well till Monday morning. On this morning, the virtue of the *root* was fully tested. Long before daylight, I was called to go and rub, curry, and feed, the horses. I obeyed, and was glad to obey. But whilst thus engaged, whilst in the act of throwing down some blades from the loft, Mr. Covey entered the stable with a long rope; and just as I was half out of the loft, he caught hold of my legs, and was about tying me. As soon as I found what he was up to, I gave a sudden spring, and as I did so, he holding to my legs, I was brought sprawling on the stable floor. Mr. Covey seemed now to think he had me, and could do what he pleased; but at this moment—from whence came the spirit I don't know—I resolved to fight; and, suiting my action to the resolution, I seized Covey hard by the throat; and as I did so, I rose. He held on to me, and I to him. My resistance was so entirely unexpected, that Covey seemed taken all aback. He trembled like a leaf. This gave me assurance, and I held him uneasy, causing the blood to run where I touched him with the ends of my fingers. Mr. Covey soon called out to Hughes for help. Hughes came, and, while Covey held me, attempted to tie my right hand. While he was in the act of doing so, I watched my chance, and gave him a heavy kick close under the ribs. This kick fairly sickened Hughes, so that he left me in the hands of Mr. Covey. This kick had the effect of not only weakening Hughes, but Covey also. When he saw Hughes bending over with pain, his courage quailed. He asked me if I meant to persist in my resistance. I told him I did, come what might; that he had used me like a brute for six months, and that I was determined to be used so no longer. With that, he strove to drag me to a stick that was lying just out of the stable door. He meant to knock me down. But just as he was leaning over to get the stick, I seized him with both hands by his collar, and brought him by a sudden snatch to the ground. By this time, Bill came. Covey called upon him for assistance. Bill wanted to know what he could do. Covey said, "Take hold of him, take hold of him!" Bill said his master hired him out to work, and not to help to whip me; so he left Covey and myself to fight our own battle out. We were at it for nearly two hours. Covey at length let me go, puffing and blowing at a great rate, saying that if I had not resisted, he would not have whipped me half so much. The truth was, that he had not whipped me at all. I considered him as getting entirely the worst end of the bargain; for he had drawn no blood from me, but I had from him. The whole six months afterwards, that I spent with Mr. Covey, he never laid the weight of his finger upon me in anger. He would occasionally say, he didn't want to get hold of me again. "No," thought I, "you need not; for you will come off worse than you did before."

This battle with Mr. Covey was the turning-point in my career as a slave. It rekindled the few expiring embers of freedom, and revived within me a sense of my own manhood. It recalled the departed self-confidence, and inspired me again with a determination to be free. The gratification afforded by the triumph was a full compensation for whatever else might follow, even death itself. He only can understand the deep satisfaction which I experienced, who has himself repelled by force the bloody arm of slavery. I felt as I never felt before. It was a glori-

8

ous resurrection, from the tomb of slavery, to the heaven of freedom. My long-crushed spirit rose, cowardice departed, bold defiance took its place; and I now resolved that, however long I might remain a slave in form, the day had passed forever when I could be a slave in fact. I did not hesitate to let it be known of me, that the white man who expected to succeed in whipping, must also succeed in killing me.

From this time I was never again what might be called   9
fairly whipped, though I remained a slave four years afterwards. I had several fights, but was never whipped.

Discussion Questions

1. Douglass states, "You have seen how a man was made a slave. You shall see how a slave was made a man." How is a man made into a slave? How is a slave made into a man?
2. Why did Mr. Covey kick Douglass when Covey was told of Douglass's illness?
3. How did Douglass's first six months with Covey differ from his last?
4. Why did Douglass's master send him back to Covey?
5. How was Douglass's battle with Covey a turning point in his life as a slave?
6. How does Douglass's use of cause and effect help you better understand the dilemma that Douglass faced?
7. For what audience has Douglass written his narrative?

Writing Assignments

1. Write an essay describing a time when you resisted someone or something that threatened you.
2. In an essay contrast the way you were before some significant event occurred in your life and the way you were after that event.
3. Write an essay recalling an event that has changed your life.

Student Essay:
FRUITS OF LABOR, FRUITS OF SORROW, FRUITS OF LOVE

Hakimah Alim Gregory

Vocabulary

chattel   (3)   personal, moveable property
succession (3)   sequence

One of the most effective methods that the white slave master
employed to transform an African woman into a slave was to
destroy her family unit. In doing so, the slave master destroyed
the African woman's most sacred source of value and liveli-
hood, thus effectively weakening her resistance.

    The African mother learned soon after her arrival in Amer-
ica that neither her body nor the bodies of her children, present and unborn, belonged to her. She learned that the life and
death of African women and children were at the mercy of the
slave trader. He had two evil methods of securing the obedience
of the slaves. There was the breaking-in process, which was
used by the slave traders to break the slaves' spirits by molding
the captives into accepting their lowly position. This was often
achieved by forcing the slaves to either endure or watch grave
acts of cruelty that were committed against themselves or fellow slaves. One cruel ritual involved tying a naked pregnant
African woman to a tree. A slave trader then plunged a knife
into her belly, cut it, and ripped her unborn child from her
womb. As the victim struggled with death, the fetus was held
before the faces of the horrified audience and eventually
thrown onto the ground.

    During slavery, Africans were not classified as human, but
treated as chattel by the slave owner. This made it easier for
him to use the African as he would a piece of machinery, to be
used, sold, and discarded at his will. Therefore, while the
African woman was defined in terms of her breeding capacity,
the concept of motherhood and the care for her children were
minimized. The master's primary interest in the slave woman
was the potential increase in wealth that each new African
birth represented. It was not uncommon for slave women to be
forced to conceive up to ten children, each in dangerously rapid

1

2

3

succession. Profit from these births would be gained by either selling the child, once he or she reached a certain age, or by integrating the child into the owner's labor force. Because the slave master's desire to profit preceded any respectful, humane responsibility, many marriages, when they were allowed to occur at all, were done for purposes of breeding and were not recognized or protected by law. Many times, however, the slave master did not bother to mate Africans to bear children. Instead, he and his white hired help impregnated African slave women themselves. Throughout the era of slavery, the African woman was raped and sexually exploited more than any other woman in history.

Physically, the African woman was continually subjected to   4
brutal labor throughout her pregnancy and childbirth. After her child was born, the new mother was given little, if any, time to recover. The mother often returned to the fields with a child as young as two weeks fastened to her back and placed underneath a nearby tree. She used the few periods granted for break to nurse her child, giving up her only opportunity to relieve herself or refresh herself with a drink of water. Once the child was past nursing age, the mother had to leave the child with an "Auntie," usually an older African woman no longer considered profitable in the fields, who was appointed to care for the young children while their parents labored from "can't see in the morning to can't see at night." Although the house slave sometimes found her physical conditions better than those of the field slave, she was always forced to put the care of the master's household and children before the care of her own.

The conditions under which the African woman was forced   5
to maintain a family called for her to make sacrifices without any guarantee of results. Despite the great odds, the African mother often extended herself in any way possible to make the survival of her children probable and their living conditions just a bit more bearable. The African mother suffered through infant mortality and forced abortions to produce children for the survival of her family in the United States.

Discussion Questions

1. What was the "breaking-in" process?
2. What was the slave master's primary interest in the slave woman?
3. Why were marriages allowed between slaves?

4. How was the slave woman treated during her pregnancy and after childbirth?
5. Who was the "Auntie" on the slave plantation?
6. What rhetorical strategy (or strategies) has the writer used to develop her essay?
7. Does the writer give sufficient details to support her thesis? Support your answer.

Writing Assignments

1. Write an essay in which you discuss racist methods used to discriminate against an oppressed race or culture.
2. Write an essay in which you discuss sacrifices made by your mother or grandmother in an attempt to protect your family.

5

African American Women

THE SKY IS GRAY

Ernest J. Gaines

Ernest J. Gaines (1933–   ) was born in Oscar, Louisiana. He received his B.A. degree in 1957 from San Francisco State College and then studied fiction writing at Stanford University. Among his works of fiction are The Autobiography of Miss Jane Pittman *(1971) and "A Gathering of Old Men" (1983). Much of his fiction, including the following selection taken from* Bloodline *(1968), examines the struggle of African Americans to survive in poor rural areas of Louisiana.*

"Fasten that coat, let's go," Mama says.   1

"You don't have to leave," the lady says.   2

Mama don't answer the lady, and we right out in the cold   3
again. I'm warm right now—my hands, my ears, my feet—but I
know this ain't go'n last too long. It done sleet so much now
you got ice everywhere you look.

We cross the railroad tracks, and soon's we do, I get cold.   4
That wind goes through this little old coat like it ain't even
there. I got on a shirt and a sweater under the coat, but that

44

wind don't pay them no mind. I look up and I can see we got a long way to go. I wonder if we go'n make it 'fore I get too cold.

We cross over to walk on the sidewalk. They got just one   5
sidewalk back here, and it's over there.

After we go just a little piece, I smell bread cooking. I look,   6
then I see a baker shop. When we get closer, I can smell it more better. I shut my eyes and make 'tend I'm eating. But I keep them shut too long and I butt up 'gainst a telephone post. Mama grabs me and see if I'm hurt. I ain't bleeding or nothing and she turns me loose.

I can feel I'm getting colder and colder, and I look up to   7
see how far we still got to go. Uptown is 'way up yonder. A half mile more, I reckon. I try to think of something. They say think and you won't get cold. I think of that poem, "Annabel Lee." I ain't been to school in so long—this bad weather—I reckon they done passed "Annabel Lee" by now. But passed it or not, I'm sure Miss Walker go'n make me recite it when I get there. That woman don't never forget nothing. I ain't never seen nobody like that in my life.

I'm still getting cold, "Annabel Lee" or no "Annabel Lee,"   8
I'm still getting cold. But I can see we getting closer. We getting there gradually.

Soon 's we turn the corner, I see a little old white lady up   9
in front of us. She's the only lady on the street. She's all in black and she's got a long black rag over her head.

"Stop," she says.   10

Me and Mama stop and look at her. She must be crazy to   11
be out in all this bad weather. Ain't got but a few other people out there, and all of them's men.

"Y'all done ate?" she says.   12

"Just finish," Mama says.   13

"Y'all must be cold then?" she says.   14

"We headed for the dentist," Mama says. "We'll warm up   15
when we get there."

"What dentist?" the old lady says. "Mr. Bassett?"   16

"Yes, ma'am," Mama says.   17

"Come on in," the old lady says. "I'll telephone him and tell   18
him y'all coming."

Me and Mama follow the old lady in the store. It's a little   19
bitty store, and it don't have much in there. The old lady takes off her head rag and folds it up.

"Helena?" somebody calls from the back.   20

"Yes, Alnest?" the old lady says.   21

"Did you see them?"   22

"They're here. Standing beside me."   23
"Good. Now you can stay inside."   24
The old lady looks at Mama. Mama's waiting to hear what   25
she brought us in here for. I'm waiting for that, too.
"I saw y'all each time you went by," she says. "I came out   26
to catch you, but you were gone."
"We went back of town," Mama says.   27
"Did you eat?"   28
"Yes, ma'am."   29
The old lady looks at Mama a long time, like she's thinking   30
Mama might be just saying that. Mama looks right back at her.
The old lady looks at me to see what I have to say. I don't say
nothing. I sure ain't going 'gainst my mama.
"There's food in the kitchen," she says to Mama. "I've been   31
keeping it warm."
Mama turns right round and starts for the door.   32
"Just a minute," the old lady says. Mama stops. "The boy'll   33
have to work for it. It isn't free."
"We don't take no handout," Mama says.   34
"I'm not handing out anything," the old lady says. "I need   35
my garbage moved to the front. Ernest has a bad cold and can't
go out there."
"James'll move it for you," Mama says.   36
"Not unless you eat," the old lady says. "I'm old, but I have   37
my pride, too, you know."
Mama can see she ain't go'n beat this old lady down, so   38
she just shakes her head.
"All right," the old lady says. "Come into the kitchen."   39
She leads the way with that rag in her hand. The kitchen   40
is a little bitty little old thing, too. The table and the stove just
'bout fill it up. They got a little room to the side. Somebody in
there laying 'cross the bed—cause I can see one of his feet.
Must be the person she was talking to: Ernest or Alnest—
something like that.
"Sit down," the old lady says to Mama. "Not you," she says   41
to me. "You have to move the cans."
"Helena?" the man says in the other room.   42
"Yes, Alnest?" the old lady says.   43
"Are you going out there again?"   44
"I must show the boy where the garbage is, Alnest," the   45
old lady says.
"Keep that shawl over your head," the old man says.   46

"You don't have to remind me. Alnest. Come, boy," the old
lady says.   47

We go out in the yard. Little old back yard ain't no bigger   48
than the store or the kitchen. But it can sleet here just like it
can sleet in any big back yard. And 'fore you know it, I'm trembling.

"There," the old lady says, pointing to the cans. I pick up   49
one of the cans and set it right back down. The can's so light,
I'm go'n see what's inside of it.

"Here," the old lady says. "Leave that can alone."   50

I look back at her standing there in the door. She's got   51
that black rag wrapped round her shoulders, and she's pointing one of her little old fingers at me.

"Pick it up and carry it to the front," she says. I go by her   52
with the can, and she's looking at me all the time. I'm sure the
can's empty. I'm sure she could've carried it herself—maybe
both of them at the same time. "Set it on the sidewalk by the
door and come back for the other one," she says.

I go and come back, and Mama looks at me when I pass   53
her. I get the other can and take it to the front. It don't feel a bit
heavier than that first one. I tell myself I ain't go'n be nobody's
fool, and I'm go'n look inside this can to see just what I been
hauling. First, I look up the street, then down the street. Nobody coming. Then I look over my shoulder toward the door.
That little old lady done slipped up there quiet 's mouse, watching me again. Look like she knowed what I was go'n do.

"Ehh, Lord," she says. "Children, children. Come in here,   54
boy, and go wash your hands."

I follow her in the kitchen. She points toward the bath-   55
room, and I go in there and wash up. Little bitty old bathroom,
but it's clean, clean. I don't use any of her towels; I wipe my
hands on my pants legs.

When I come back in the kitchen, the old lady done dished   56
up the food. Rice, gravy, meat—and she even got some lettuce
and tomato in a saucer. She even got a glass of milk and a
piece of cake there, too. It looks so good, I almost start eating
'fore I say my blessing.

"Helena?" the old man says.   57
"Yes, Alnest?"   58
"Are they eating?"   59
"Yes," she says.   60
"Good," he says. "Now you'll stay inside."   61

The old lady goes in there where he is and I can hear them 62
talking. I look at Mama. She's eating slow like she's thinking. I
wonder what's the matter now. I reckon she's thinking 'bout
home.

The old lady comes back in the kitchen. 63

"I talked to Dr. Bassett's nurse," she says. "Dr. Bassett will 64
take you as soon as you get there."

"Thank you, ma'am," Mama says. 65

"Perfectly all right," the old lady says. "Which one is it?" 66

Mama nods toward me. The old lady looks at me real sad. 67
I look sad, too.

"You're not afraid, are you?" she says. 68

"No, ma'am," I say. 69

"That's a good boy," the old lady says. "Nothing to be 70
afraid of. Dr. Bassett will not hurt you."

When me and Mama get through eating, we thank the old 71
lady again.

"Helena, are they leaving?" the old man says. 72

"Yes, Alnest." 73

"Tell them I say good-bye." 74

"They can hear you, Alnest." 75

"Good-bye both mother and son," the old man says. "And 76
may God be with you."

Me and Mama tell the old man good-bye, and we follow the 77
old lady in the front room. Mama opens the door to go out, but
she stops and comes back in the store.

"You sell salt meat?" she says. 78

"Yes." 79

"Give me two bits worth." 80

"That isn't very much salt meat," the old lady says. 81

"That's all I have," Mama says. 82

The old lady goes back of the counter and cuts a big piece 83
off the chunk. Then she wraps it up and puts it in a paper
bag.

"Two bits," she says. 84

"That looks like awful lot of meat for a quarter," Mama 85
says.

"Two bits," the old lady says. "I've been selling salt meat 86
behind this counter twenty-five years. I think I know what I'm
doing."

"You got a scale there," Mama says. 87

"What?" the old lady says. 88

"Weigh it," Mama says. 89

"What?" the old lady says. "Are you telling me how to run 90
my business?

"Thanks very much for the food," Mama says. 91

"Just a minute," the old lady says. 92

"James," Mama says to me. I move toward the door. 93

"Just one minute, I said," the old lady says. 94

Me and Mama stop again and look at her. The old lady takes 95
the meat out of the bag and unwraps it and cuts 'bout half of it
off. Then she wraps it up again and juggs it back in the bag and
gives the bag to Mama. Mama lays the quarter on the counter.

"Your kindness will never be forgotten," she says. "James," 96
she says to me.

We go out, and the old lady comes to the door to look at 97
us. After we go a little piece I look back, and she's still there
watching us.

The sleet's coming down heavy, heavy now, and I turn up 98
my coat collar to keep my neck warm. My mama tells me turn
it right back down.

"You not a bum," she says. "You a man." 99

Discussion Questions

1. What type of mother is Octavia?
2. Do you think that James understands his mother's intentions? What indications is the reader given to suggest that James understands his mother's actions?
3. In what ways does the mother try to prepare her son for life?
4. Do you think that Octavia should have taken the larger portion of meat? Why or why not?
5. What do you think is the meaning of the title?
6. Why do you think that Gaines chooses to have young James narrate the story?
7. What is the author's purpose in creating a mother whose voice is heard only on rare, necessary occasions?

Writing Assignments

1. Write an essay about an incident when a person seemed to have had too little or too much pride.
2. Write an essay about someone who has tried to set an example for you.
3. Write an essay discussing someone you know who sacrifices her or his own needs or wishes on behalf of others.

I AM A BLACK WOMAN

Mari Evans

Born in Toledo, Ohio, Mari Evans wrote and printed her first story in the fourth grade in a school newspaper and has been writing ever since. She has taught African American literature at several universities since 1969. Evans is most widely known for her poetry, which reflects her concern for African Americans. She once said, ". . . when I write, I write according to the title of poet Margaret Walker's classic: 'for my people'." The following poem reflects Evans's commitment. It is taken from her book of poetry, I Am a Black Woman *(1970).*

Vocabulary

arpeggio	(1)	musical chords played in rapid succession
canebrake	(2)	a dense growth of cane plants
assailed	(3)	assaulted, attacked with violent blows, verbally attacked
impervious	(3)	not open to, incapable of being penetrated or affected

I am a black woman   1
the music of my song
some sweet arpeggio of tears
is written in a minor key
and I
can be heard humming in the night
Can be heard
                    humming
in the night

I saw my mate leap screaming to the sea   2
and I/with these hands/cupped the lifebreath
from my issue in the canebrake
I lost Nat's swinging body in a rain of tears
and heard my son scream all the way from Anzio[1]

---

[1]Anzio (2)   A town and port on the western coast of Italy; the site of a World War II beachhead (January 1944).

for Peace he never knew. . . . I
learned Da Nang[2] and Pork Chop Hill[3]
in anguish
Now my nostrils know the gas
and these trigger tire/d fingers
seek the softness in my warrior's beard

I   3
am a black woman
tall as a cypress
strong
beyond all definition still
defying place
and time
and circumstance
  assailed
    impervious
      indestructible
Look
  on me and be
renewed

Discussion Questions

1. Specifically, how would you characterize the speaker in the poem?
2. Who does the "I" represent in the poem?
3. How does the poem help us understand African American history?
4. What is the significance of the last line?
5. Why do you think the poet omits punctuation marks and shifts words to the right of the page?
6. What image of the black woman do you visualize from the poet's use of descriptive words and phrases?
7. Why do you think Evans chooses to begin her stanzas with the same sentence pattern: the personal pronoun plus the verb?

[2]Da Nang   (2)   Site of one of the battles during the Vietnam War.
[3]Pork Chop Hill   (2)   Site of a major battle during the Korean War.

Writing Assignments

1. Write an essay describing a woman who influences or has influenced your life.
2. Write an essay describing something you do to forget your pain.
3. In an essay, discuss the various ways African American women have been depicted on television shows.

THOSE "SUPER STRONG" BLACK WOMEN

Tansey Thomas

The following excerpt was written as a letter to an editor of a newspaper in 1974. It describes some of the myths of the African American woman.

Vocabulary

hypertension	(6)	high blood pressure
abject	(7)	disgusting, wretched
jibes	(11)	agrees with (informal English)

To the Editor:

The past three years have been very significant for black women, both nationally and on the campus. 1

On campus, the women are prouder, surer of themselves, friendlier and more hopeful. Oh, there are still the notes of despair, but watch their actions and you will find determination to get where they want to be, which is born of hope. 2

Needless to say, we are far from being out of the woods. We still have the problems of racism and poverty, but I would like to attack some of the myths about black women. 3

1. The myth of the nagging, castrating black woman. Most studies show that black women complain much less than their white counterparts although black women suffer much more deprivation. 4

2. The myth of the strong super women. It seems apparent that many people regard a black woman like a black cat— she has nine lives and therefore you can treat her any kind of way and she will survive. Toss her off a 10 story building and she will land on her feet every time. She needs no help. This flies in the face of the facts of the high mortality rate of black women, at some ages twice the rate of white women; the high maternal death rate; the fact that a black woman is eight times more likely to get raped than a white woman. 5

Seventeen times more black women suffer from hypertension than white women. The person most fearful for her personal safety in this country is the black woman. Yet, she needs nothing? 6

3. The myth of the free black woman. There is this ridicu-   7
lous myth that black women have always been so much freer
than black men; you know, so much less oppressed. This is believed by many black women, also. They are free to be raped,
free to be murdered, free to be insulted, free to live in abject
poverty, free to be prostitutes. In other words, free for the worst
this society has to offer. How else can you explain the fact that
we are at the bottom of the social and economic heap? Being
defenseless and vulnerable has been mistaken for freedom.

I would like to see some role reversals, or at least, in some   8
of the rhetoric.

Like black men should stand by their women; black men   9
should be more understanding and supportive of their women.

I would like to see some conferences by black men on the   10
needs of black women and children. And don't say "let's deal
with black people" because it has been noted that black "people" usually means black men.

Yes, these past three years have been very significant for   11
black women, especially the younger ones. There have been increased interest in and opportunities for them, token though
they may be. This jibes with the recent report of a tremendous
decrease in the birth rate among low-income black women during the 60s. It also marks a move of a large segment of low-
income black women from the domestic job market to clerical
and sales jobs during the 60s. The hopes of black women are
even higher for the 70s. Right on!

Discussion Questions

1. What are some of the myths about black women that Thomas
cites? Can you think of others?

2. What are the role reversals that Thomas wants to see in U.S. society?

3. According to Thomas, how were the 1960s different from the
1970s for black women?

4. Have conditions changed for African American women today? Offer evidence to support your answer.

5. What is the tone of this letter?

6. Do you think the letter is persuasive? Why or why not?

7. What is Thomas's purpose in using comparison and contrast in
the letter?

8. Is the author's numbering of the myths in this letter effective or
ineffective? Explain your answer.

Writing Assignments

1. Write an essay in which you attack myths of some ethnic group or some occupation, for example, white males, lawyers, doctors, the disabled.
2. In an essay, describe a race or group of people other than your own that you feel has been misunderstood. Explain why you feel this way.
3. Write an essay in which you discuss another group (to which you do not belong) that is perceived as strong (or a group that is perceived as weak).

SLAVERY AND WOMANHOOD

Angela Y. Davis

Angela Yvonne Davis (1944–) was born in Birmingham, Alabama. On August 18, 1970, Davis, professor of philosophy at the University of California-Los Angeles, was placed on the Federal Bureau of Investigation's ten-most-wanted list for owning guns used to commit a crime. Cries of "Free Angela" were heard throughout the world, and eventually she was found innocent of all charges. Since that time, Angela Davis has written and published numerous works, including Women, Race and Class *(1983), from which the following selection on the abuse of slave women is taken.*

Vocabulary

chattel	(1)	an item of movable personal property
ideology	(1)	a body of ideas that influences a person or a group
anomalies	(1)	irregular or abnormal things
diametrical	(2)	exactly opposite; contrary
expediency	(4)	self interests
appraised	(5)	considered, valued
exaltation	(5)	praise or honor
coercion	(7)	the use of force
exploitation	(8)	selfish of unethical use
orthodox	(8)	following established traditions or beliefs

1   The slave system defined Black people as *chattel*. Since women, no less than men, were viewed as profitable labor-units, they might as well have been genderless as far as the slaveholders were concerned. In the words of one scholar, "the slave woman was first a full-time worker for her owner, and only incidentally a wife, mother and homemaker." Judged by the evolving nineteenth-century ideology of femininity, which emphasized women's roles as nurturing mothers and gentle companions and housekeepers for their husbands, Black women were practically anomalies.

2   Though Black women enjoyed few of the dubious benefits of the ideology of womanhood, it is sometimes assumed that the typical female slave was a houseservant—either a cook, maid, or mammy for the children in the "big house." Uncle Tom

and Sambo have always found faithful companions in Aunt Jemima and the Black Mammy—stereotypes which presume to capture the essence of the Black woman's role during slavery. As is so often the case, the reality is actually the diametrical opposite of the myth. Like the majority of slave men, slave women, for the most part, were field workers. While a significant proportion of border-state slaves may have been house-servants, slaves in the Deep South—the real home of the slaveocracy—were predominantly agricultural workers. Around the middle of the nineteenth century, seven out of eight slaves, men and women alike, were field workers.

Just as the boys were sent to the fields when they came of age, so too were the girls assigned to work the soil, pick the cotton, cut the cane, harvest the tobacco. An old woman interviewed during the 1930s described her childhood initiation to field work on an Alabama cotton plantation: 3

> We had old ragged huts made out of poles and some of the cracks chinked up with mud and moss and some of them wasn't. We didn't have no good beds, just scaffolds nailed up to the wall out of poles and the old ragged bedding throwed on them. That sure was hard sleeping, but even that felt good to our weary bones after them long hard days' work in the field. I 'tended to the children when I was a little gal and tried to clean house just like Old Miss tells me to. Then as soon as I was ten years old, Old Master, he say, "Git this here nigger to that cotton patch."

Jenny Proctor's experience was typical. For most girls and women, as for most boys and men, it was hard labor in the fields from sunup to sundown. Where work was concerned, strength and productivity under the threat of the whip outweighed considerations of sex. In this sense, the oppression of women was identical to the oppression of men.

But women suffered in different ways as well, for they were victims of sexual abuse and other barbarous mistreatment that could only be inflicted on women. Expediency governed the slaveholders' posture toward female slaves: when it was profitable to exploit them as if they were men, they were regarded, in effect, as genderless, but when they could be exploited, punished and repressed in ways suited only for women, they were locked into their exclusively female roles. 4

When the abolition of the international slave trade began to threaten the expansion of the young cotton-growing industry, the slaveholding class was forced to rely on natural reproduction as the surest method of replenishing and increasing 5 the domestic slave population. Thus a premium was placed on the slave woman's reproductive capacity. During the decades preceding the Civil War, Black women came to be increasingly appraised for their fertility (or for the lack of it): she who was potentially the mother of ten, twelve, fourteen or more became a coveted treasure indeed. This did not mean, however, that as mothers, Black women enjoyed a more respected status than they enjoyed as workers. Ideological exaltation of motherhood—as popular as it was during the nineteenth century—did not extend to slaves. In fact, in the eyes of the slaveholders, slave women were not mothers at all; they were simply instruments guaranteeing the growth of the slave labor force. They were "breeders"—animals, whose monetary value could be precisely calculated in terms of their ability to multiply their numbers.

Since slave women were classified as "breeders" as opposed to "mothers," their infant children could be sold away from them like calves from cows. One year after the importation of Africans was halted, a South Carolina court ruled that female slaves had no legal claims whatever on their children. Consequently, according to this ruling, children could be sold away from their mothers at any age because "the young of slaves . . . stand on the same footing as other animals."

As females, slave women were inherently vulnerable to all forms of sexual coercion. If the most violent punishments of men consisted of floggings and mutilations, women were flogged and mutilated, as well as raped. Rape, in fact, was an uncamoflaged expression of the slaveholder's economic mastery and the overseer's control over Black women as workers.

The special abuses inflicted on women thus facilitated the ruthless economic exploitation of their labor. The demands of this exploitation caused slaveowners to cast aside their orthodox sexist attitudes except for purposes of repression. If Black women were hardly "women" in the accepted sense, the slave system also discouraged male supremacy in Black men. Because husbands and wives, fathers and daughters were equally subjected to the slavemasters' absolute authority, the promotion of male supremacy among the slaves might have prompted a dangerous rupture in the chain of command. Moreover, since Black women as workers could not be treated as the "weaker sex" or the "housewife," Black men could not be candidates for the figure of "family head" and certainly not for "family provider." After all, men, women and children alike were all "providers" for the slaveholding class.

In the cotton, tobacco, corn and sugar-cane fields, women 9
worked alongside their men. In the words of an ex-slave:

> The bell rings at four o'clock in the morning and they have half
> an hour to get ready. Men and women start together, and the
> breeders must work as steadily as the men and perform the
> same work as the men.

Most slaveowners established systems of calculating their slaves'
yield in terms of the average rates of productivity they demanded.
Children, thus, were frequently rated as quarter hands. Women,
it was generally assumed, were full hands—unless they had been
expressly assigned to be "breeders" or "sucklers," in which case
they sometimes ranked as less than full hands.

Slaveowners naturally sought to ensure that their "breed- 10
ers" would bear children as often as biologically possible. But
they never went so far as to exempt pregnant women and
mothers with infant children from work in the fields. While
many mothers were forced to leave their infants lying on the
ground near the area where they worked, some refused to leave
them unattended and tried to work at the normal pace with
their babies on their backs. An ex-slave described such a case
on the plantation where he lived:

> One young woman did not, like the others, leave her child at the
> end of the row, but had contrived a sort of rude knapsack, made
> of a piece of coarse linen cloth, in which she fastened her child,
> which was very young, upon her back; and in this way carried it
> all day, and performed her task at the hoe with the other people.

On other plantations, the women left their infants in the care of
small children or older slaves who were not able to perform
hard labor in the fields. Unable to nurse their infants regularly,
they endured the pain caused by their swollen breasts. In one
of the most popular slave narratives of the period, Moses
Grandy related the miserable predicament of slave mothers:

> On the estate I am speaking of, those women who had sucking
> children suffered much from their breasts becoming full of milk,
> the infants being left at home. They therefore could not keep up
> with the other hands: I have seen the overseer beat them with raw
> hide, so that the blood and milk flew mingled from their breasts.

Pregnant women were not only compelled to do the normal 11
agricultural work, they could also expect the floggings workers
normally received if they failed to fulfill their day's quota or if
they "impudently" protested their treatment.

> A woman who gives offense in the field, and is large in a family
> way, is compelled to lie down over a hole made to receive her cor-
> pulency, and is flogged with the whip or beat with a paddle,
> which has holes in it; at every stroke comes a blister. One of my
> sisters was so severely punished in this way, that labor was
> brought on, and the child was born in the field. This very over-
> seer, Mr. Brooks, killed in this manner a girl named Mary. Her
> father and mother were in the field at that time.

On those plantations and farms where pregnant women were
dealt with more leniently, it was seldom on humanitarian
grounds. It was simply that slaveholders appreciated the value
of a slave child born alive in the same way that they appreciated the value of a newborn calf or colt.

    When timid attempts at industrialization were made in the   12
pre-Civil War South, slave labor complemented—and frequently
competed with—free labor. Slaveowning industrialists used
men, women and children alike, and when planters and farmers hired out their slaves, they found women and children in as
great demand as men.

Discussion Questions

1. Describe the lifestyle of the typical slave woman.
2. Why was the slave mother not allowed to be a mother to her children?
3. What was the slave woman's relationship to her husband?
4. What evidence does Davis give to support her argument that men
   and women were equal in slavery?
5. What were problems peculiar to the slave woman and not to the
   slave man?
6. How effective is Davis's use of illustration and persuasion in this
   essay?
7. What is the thesis of Davis's essay? Is it implied or written?

Writing Assignments

1. Write an essay comparing the role of today's woman to the role of
   the slave woman.
2. Using evidence from the essay, argue that gender did not protect
   the woman from the horrors of slavery.
3. Write an essay describing the kind of problems women face today.

Student Essay:
ISLAM AND AFRICAN AMERICAN WOMEN

Vernell Munadi

Vocabulary

regimen (3) habit

The African American woman suffers from a double oppres- 1
sion. First, because some African American males lack the ability
or interest in fulfilling their duties as husbands and fathers,
many African American women are forced to assume the responsibilities of mother, father, homemaker, and breadwinner. Sec-
ondly, because of her acceptance of the Western lifestyle, the
African American woman has also been oppressed both mentally
and physically, keeping her at the lowest levels of society. She is
often looked upon as a sex object or an ignorant person who receives welfare. Therefore, through the practice of the universal religion of Islam, the African woman is saved from this double oppression and elevated to her rightful place in society.

Islam is the fastest growing religious community in North 2
America, particularly among African Americans. Many women
in this country are realizing the realities of gender oppression
and wearing their hijab[1] as a symbol of liberation. While many
outside of the Islamic faith may feel that Muslim women are
oppressed, Muslim women feel that Islam encourages intellec-
tualism and education of women. Many of these women would
argue that if they were as oppressed as their critics suggest,
then why are there so many Western-educated women being
attracted to Islam?

It is evident that the African American community of the 3
United States is in trouble because of the fundamental break-
down of the basic family unit and the African American male-female relationship. Some attribute the trouble to African American men, some of whom have no code of ethics to control their
behavior and no fear of punishment for their actions. Islam gives
the man and the woman a specific purpose and disciplines them
both by charging them with five daily prayers, dietary restrictions

[1]hijab (2)   The veil; the Islamic woman's adherence to acceptable dress:
covering everything except her face and hands.

(no pork, a scientifically proven killer), forbiddance of alcohol and other drugs, and a regimen of personal hygiene.

The goal of Islam in terms of the woman, through protec- 4
tion and financial maintenance, is to elevate her by allowing her to fulfill her role as the center of the community. From the time she is a girl, she lives in the house of her father who provides for her. If her father is deceased, then her uncle or older brother takes on this responsibility.

When a women is married, she moves into her husband's 5
home and from that point, she becomes sole manager of that house; it belongs to her. She runs it the way she sees fit because it is where she will raise her children. If her husband can afford it, she is also entitled to a housekeeper, especially when housecleaning becomes so burdensome that it interferes with the time spent with her children and husband.

A Muslim woman is totally liberated from the preoccupa- 6
tion of food, clothing, and shelter. Her husband is responsible for providing them. In the event that he becomes unemployed, he cannot ask his wife to work, since working is not her responsibility. However, if she does decide to help him temporarily, it must be her decision and it is a charity to him because she is temporarily relieving him of his responsibility. Even if she decides not to work, there is relief available from the Islamic community. If a wife wishes to work and her working does not interfere with the rearing of her children or with managing the household and her husband agrees to it, she may work.

In Islam, it is the woman who is placed in the midst of the 7
children, to educate them, to train them, and to nurture them. It is the children in any society who carry the society's traditions into the future. In controlling the development of the children, it is the Muslim woman who quietly, but firmly controls the Islamic community because "the hand that rocks the cradle, rules the world." As an Islamic woman, I only wish that more African American women would come to see the benefits of this religion.

Discussion Questions

1. What are the roles of the African American male and female in the Muslim family?
2. In what way can the beliefs of the Islamic faith strengthen the husband-wife relationship?

3. How does the author argue against the notion of Islam as a religion that oppresses women?
4. What does Islam offer the African American male?
5. Under what condition is the Islamic woman permitted to work?
6. To what extent do you feel that the author's use of comparison and contrast in her essay is an effective organizational strategy?
7. "Therefore" is used to introduce the last sentence of the first paragraph. What other transition(s) could be used? Explain your substitution.

Writing Assignments

1. Write an essay discussing major challenges of male-female relationships today.
2. Write an essay in which you discuss the husband-wife relationship as dictated by some other religion.

6

African American Men

A FLING ON THE TRACK

Bill Cosby

William H. Cosby, Jr. (1937–) was born in Germantown, Pennsylvania. He earned a B.A. degree from Temple University and both the M.A. and the Ed.D. degrees from the University of Massachusetts. He was the first African American co-star of a television dramatic series, I Spy, *and was the star and producer of the popular 1980s sitcom,* The Cosby Show. *Winner of eight Grammy and four Emmy awards, and the NAACP Image Award, Cosby is the author of* The Wit and Wisdom of Fat Albert *(1973),* Bill Cosby's Personal Guide to Power Tennis *(1986), and* Love and Marriage *(1989), from which this essay is taken. Here Cosby recounts his adolescent breakup with a girlfriend.*

Vocabulary

sentimentalist (3) one who has or shows emotions
token (17) reminder

During my last year of high school, I fell in love so hard   1
with a girl that it made my love for Sarah McKinney seem like a
stupid infatuation with a teacher. Charlene Gibson was the

Real Thing and she would be Mrs. Charlene Cosby, serving me hot dogs and watching me drive to the hoop and giving me the full-court press for the rest of my life.

In tribute to our great love, I was moved to give Charlene something to wear. A Temple T-shirt didn't seem quite right and neither did my Truman button. What Charlene needed was a piece of jewelry; and I was able to find the perfect one, an elegant pin, in my mother's dresser drawer. 2

Ten days after I made this grand presentation, Charlene dumped me; but, sentimentalist that she was, she kept the pin. When I confessed my dark deed to my mother, she didn't throw a brick at me, she merely wanted to have the pin back, a request that I felt was not unreasonable since I had stolen it. Moreover, retrieving the pin was important to *me*, but for a romantic notion: I wanted to punish Charlene. Paying back the person with whom you have recently been in love is one of life's most precious moments. 3

"I want that pin back," I said to Charlene on the phone. 4

"I can't do that," she replied. 5

"Why not?" 6

"You *lost* it?" 7

"That's what I just said." 8

"How could you *lose* it?" 9

"Easy. First I had it, then I didn't." 10

And so, I went to her house, where her mother said she wasn't home. Nervously I told her mother why I needed the pin returned and she understood without saying I had done anything wrong. Of course, she didn't have the world's sharpest judgment because she still thought I was a wonderful person. In fact, *all* the mothers of the girls who rejected me thought I was a wonderful person; I would have made a fine father to those girls. 11

"Mrs. Gibson," I said, "Charlene told me she lost the pin. I'm not saying I don't believe her, but I don't." 12

"Just one minute, William," she said, and she turned and went upstairs. Moments later, she returned with the pin. And then I went home and waited for the satisfaction of Charlene calling me to say: 13

How dare you go to my house and ask my mother for that pin! 14

But no call from her came. 15

Probably because she's ashamed of lying to me, I told myself; *but maybe because she truly likes me and wants to keep the pin for that reason.* 16

I was convincing myself that Charlene wanted to have an   17
elegant token of me and that now I should call *her* to rekindle
this wondrous love-hate relationship, for Charlene and I had
been meant for each other: she was a liar and I was a thief.
Two such people, who had been so deeply in love, should have
had a chance to keep torturing each other. We once had kissed
for almost three hours, inhaling each other and talking about
how many children we should have. True, she was the kind of
girl who might be having children by other men too, but there
was still a softness about her I liked, a softness that matched
the one in my head. We had been too close for our relationship
to end with her dumping me. We had to get back together so I
could dump *her*.

Discussion Questions

1. Why did Cosby want to "punish" Charlene?
2. What do you think Cosby means by his statement that "I would
   have made a wonderful father to those girls"?
3. Do you believe that Cosby was still in love with Charlene after
   their breakup? Explain your answer.
4. What is the tone of this essay?
5. What are some characteristics of narration that are particularly
   effective in this story?
6. Why do you think Cosby chose to give his story this title?

Writing Assignments

1. Write an essay about a time when you fell in or out of love.
2. Write an essay about a time when you or someone you know got
   revenge for a hurtful act.
3. Write an essay about a time when you or someone you know was
   the target of revenge.

BLACKS IN VIETNAM

Robert Mullen

*Robert W. Mullen (1937–   ) is professor of speech at North-
ern Kentucky University. He earned his B.S. and M.S. degrees from Emerson College and his Ph.D. from Ohio State
University. He is the author of* Blacks in America's Wars
(1973), from which this excerpt is taken; Rhetorical Strategies of Black America *(1980); and* Blacks and Vietnam
*(1981). In this excerpt, Mullen describes the impact of the
Vietnam War on the African Americans who participated in
it.*

Vocabulary

defoliate	(2)	to cause the leaves to fall off, especially by the use of a chemical spray or dust
cynicism	(4)	an attitude of questioning the sincerity of someone's motives or actions
rationales	(4)	justifications
succinct	(4)	brief, concise
disaffection	(5)	withdrawal of affection or loyalty
ameliorate	(23)	improve

The Vietnam War, probably more than any other single   1
event in decades, demonstrated to Black Americans that the
reason for their lack of material progress was not so much this
society's lack of financial and material resources to improve
housing, education, and job opportunities as its lack of willingness to *commit* the resources to those uses.

The government's prosecution of the war at the cost of   2
tens of billions of dollars a year, and its willingness to ultimately invest the manpower of several million GIs to carry it
out, showed that the resources were indeed available. But it
also showed that the government was willing to mobilize these
resources to kill National Liberation Front fighters in Vietnam,
to bomb the countryside of North and South Vietnam, to burn
villages, defoliate crops and forests, to take many innocent
lives, and to create millions of refugees, while it was not willing
to mobilize those resources to replace slum housing or improve
ghetto education.

By 1969, according to the [previously cited] *Newsweek* 3
poll, Blacks were already persuaded by a margin of seven to
one that "Vietnam is directly pinching the homefront war on
poverty."

In a very basic sense, the massive opposition of Afro- 4
Americans to U.S. policy in Vietnam reflected the growth of
cynicism about American society. Old rationales no longer were
taken as good coin. Earlier feelings that if Blacks could only
prove themselves American society would open up to them
were replaced by a feeling that American society was not closed
to them out of misunderstanding but through conscious policy.
Perhaps the most succinct expression of the cynicism about
the United States was contained in the comment of one Afro-
American who was heavily involved in the civil rights struggle
in Mississippi. "Our criticism of Vietnam policy," he said, "does
not come from what we know of Vietnam, but from what we
know of America."

The widespread opposition of Afro-Americans to the Viet- 5
nam War and their unwillingness to accept manifestations of
racism in the armed forces resulted in much disaffection
among Black GIs. As a 1971 NAACP report stated, "an uncomfortable number of young Black servicemen are disenchanted,
alienated and have lost faith in the capacity and the will of the
armed forces to deal honestly with their problems."

This lack of faith in the capacity and willingness of the 6
armed forces to change the prevailing racism led GIs to feel
that they themselves must protest against racism and act
against it. The common oppression of Blacks forged a tremendous bond between them in Vietnam. As one Black GI put it:
"In Vietnam, whenever you saw a brother and gave him the
power sign he gave it right back."

There was little feeling among the troops that their own 7
demands for equality should be subordinated to the war effort.
This was especially true since most GIs, Black and white, did
not feel that the war had anything to do with their interests. As
Aaron Cross, a young Black GI observed: "I didn't want to go to
Vietnam. I didn't think I had anything to fight for. I don't think
anyone knew why I was over there. . . . I often wondered what
they would have told my parents if I had been killed. That I
died for my country?"

The new spirit of the Black GIs often threw their white offi- 8
cers into a panic. Officers in Vietnam began to develop a para-
noic fear of giving direct orders to Afro-American GIs for fear of

getting "fragged." The number of actual cases of "fragging," throwing a fragmentation grenade into an officer's tent, was probably exaggerated. But enough cases did take place to keep many officers on edge. And the practice was not restricted to Black GIs. White GIs in Vietnam, who were also affected by antiwar sentiment at home and by a realization that the war had nothing to do with their interests, also engaged in the practice.

But much more significant than fragging was the development of organized groups resisting racism and opposing the war in the armed forces. These groups probably reached their high point in 1970 in Germany. General Michael S. Davison, the commander of the Seventh Army, acknowledged that in that year "Black dissident organizations could turn out 1500 soldiers for a demonstration." It is estimated that there were twenty such organizations in ten cities in Germany. These groups held rallies and protest marches and published underground newspapers. Some of their activities were coordinated with German radical student groups, like the July 4, 1970, rally at the University of Heidelberg attended by over 1000 GIs, most of them Black.

Perhaps the action by Black GIs in Germany that most embarrassed the army was a petition signed by over 100 Black GIs from the Berlin area, 60 from Frankfurt, and 56 from Darmstad addressed to Soviet and East German authorities asking them, as parties with some say over the international administration of West Berlin, to act against the discrimination against Black GIs in West Berlin by the American and West German authorities.

Organized activity, however, was not restricted to Germany. In the United States there were also numerous demonstrations, rallies, and groups formed by Black and white GIs. One of the earliest of such occurrences was the case of the Fort Hood 43. In August 1968, at the time of the Chicago Democratic National Convention, units at Fort Hood, Texas, were put on alert for possible use in Chicago for "riot control" duty. Several hundred Black GIs gathered to protest this assignment, and forty-three were arrested and court martialed.

In early 1969, Black GIs at Fort Jackson, South Carolina, organized an antiwar group called GIs United Against the War in Vietnam. It was organized by a Black GI, Joe Miles, a member of the Young Socialist Alliance and Socialist Workers Party. Miles began GIs United by playing tape recordings of Malcolm X's speeches in his barracks. GIs United later expanded its membership to white antiwar GIs as well as Blacks, Puerto Ricans, and Chicanos. From January to May 1969 GIs United was able to hold regular meetings of fifty or more GIs on base. In May, the army arrested eight of the leaders of the group and placed them in the stockade. Due to a national defense campaign, however, the Army was unable to successfully court-martial the GIs, and charges against them were dropped.

At Fort McClellan, Alabama, on November 15, 1971, seventy-one Black GIs and sixty-eight Black WACs were arrested after a series of demonstrations and mass meetings on post opposing racial discrimination. Most eventually had the charges against them dropped or were discharged from the armed forces. [13]

But it was in the navy that some of the most dramatic incidents involving Blacks took place. The navy has had the smallest percentage of Blacks of any of the services, with only 6.9 percent of the enlisted men, 4 percent of the noncommissioned officers, and 0.9 percent of the officers being Afro-Americans. [14]

Two of the largest incidents in the navy took place in the same week in October 1972 on the aircraft carriers *Kitty Hawk* and *Constellation.* On the *Kitty Hawk,* fights between Black and white seamen lasted for fifteen hours and resulted in the hospitalization of forty whites and six Blacks. [15]

Four days later, racial turmoil resulted in the cancellation of a training exercise on the *Constellation* and forced the ship to return to port. Upon arriving in port, 122 Black sailors and 8 white sailors staged a dockside sitdown, raised clenched fist salutes, and refused to reboard the vessel. [16]

Within the month of these two incidents, clashes were reported between Blacks and whites aboard the assault ship *USS Sumpter* and a battle took place on the *USS Hassayampa* in the Philippines. Major battles on Midway Island and in Norfolk, Virginia, took place a month later. [17]

In all these incidents, 196 men, almost all Black, were arrested. Of these, 147 received "non-judicial punishment," and 15 had charges dropped or were found not guilty. [18]

These clashes were the result of the Black sailors' unwillingness to accept racist insults, and their protest against the discrimination in assignments and promotions in the Navy. [19]

In conclusion, history indicates that white America generally restricted Black participation in the armed forces until emergency situations forced the use of Black manpower. But, at the same time, the Black American traditionally viewed his military record as proof of his loyalty and as a claim to full citizenship. Seeking participation in America's wars, he held the hope that his sacrifices would bring the reward of increased rights to America's biggest minority. It was this optimism that had been one of the major factors behind his loyalty from the Revolutionary War to Korea. 20

But even as early as 1766, some Blacks counseled that it was inconsistent for them to fight for American independence while the country adhered to the tenets of slavery. In later wars this sentiment was expressed in terms of an unwillingness to forget that the real enemy was at home in America. 21

At the end of the war, Black veterans returned to their inferior status in American society, either as slaves or as separate and unequal citizens, the recipients of inferior education, the worst jobs, and white violence, North and South. 22

During the course of the Vietnam War, the majority of Afro-Americans and most Afro-American political groups opposed the war, seeing it as a waste of Black youth, a waste of resources that could be better used to ameliorate the conditions of America's poor, and often a racist war against a colored people struggling for self-determination. 23

For the first time, the great majority of Blacks, inside and outside the military, were unwilling to defer their demands until the end of the war. They felt they did not have to *prove* their right to citizenship through military service, but rather that they should not be forced to fight and possibly die for a society unwilling to grant them full civil and human rights. 24

Discussion Questions

1. Why did some black Americans oppose the Vietnam War?
2. What was the purpose of the black GIs' and sailors' protests and demonstrations during the war?
3. Why did some black GIs feel that "the real enemy was at home in America"?
4. Why have blacks traditionally sought participation in America's wars?

5. To what conditions did black American veterans return after the war?

6. How does Mullen use illustration to show that black Americans who participated in the war formed a "tremendous bond"?

7. For what audience do you think this excerpt is written? Explain your answer.

Writing Assignments

1. Write an essay that describes a current problem that you feel would justify protest or demonstration.

2. Interview someone you know who participated in a war, and write an essay illustrating that person's experiences.

3. Write an essay discussing one of the following terms: "cynicism," "discrimination," "hatred," "deceit," "loyalty," or a similar term of your choice.

BLACK MEN AND PUBLIC SPACE

Brent Staples

Brent Staples (1951–   ) received his Ph.D. degree in psychology from the University of Chicago. He has written for several magazines and newspapers, including the Chicago Sun-Times, *and* The New York Times *where he writes about politics and culture for the editorial board. His works include "Parallel Time" (1994). This essay, originally entitled "Just Walk on By: A Black Man Ponders His Power to Alter Public Space," was first published in* Ms. magazine in *September 1986. In this excerpt, Staples describes his feelings about how people, especially white women, react when they encounter him on the street late at night.*

Vocabulary

uninflammatory	(1)	not causing excitement or anger
unwieldy	(2)	hard to manage, troublesome
quarry	(2)	anything being hunted or pursued
wayfarers	(2)	persons who travel on foot
errant	(2)	wandering
taut	(4)	tense
berth	(7)	distance, space
skittish	(7)	nervous, frightened
congenial	(7)	friendly
constitutionals	(8)	walks for health

My first victim was a woman—white, well dressed, probably in 1 her early twenties. I came upon her late one evening on a deserted street in Hyde Park, a relatively affluent neighborhood in an otherwise mean, impoverished section of Chicago. As I swung onto the avenue behind her, there seemed to be a discreet, uninflammatory distance between us. Not so. She cast back a worried glance. To her, the youngish black man—a broad six feet two inches with a beard and billowing hair, both hands shoved into the pockets of a bulky military jacket—seemed menacingly close. After a few more quick glimpses, she picked up her pace and was soon running in earnest. Within seconds she disappeared into a cross street.

That was more than a decade ago. I was twenty-two years 2 old, a graduate student newly arrived at the University of

Chicago. It was in the echo of that terrified woman's footfalls that I first began to know the unwieldy inheritance I'd come into—the ability to alter public space in ugly ways. It was clear that she thought herself the quarry of a mugger, a rapist, or worse. Suffering a bout of insomnia, however, I was stalking sleep, not defenseless wayfarers. As a softy who is scarcely able to take a knife to a raw chicken—let alone hold it to a person's throat—I was surprised, embarrassed, and dismayed all at once. Her flight made me feel like an accomplice in tyranny. It also made it clear that I was indistinguishable from the muggers who occasionally seeped into the area from the surrounding ghetto. That first encounter, and those that followed, signified that a vast, unnerving gulf lay between nighttime pedestrians—particularly women—and me. And I soon gathered that being perceived as dangerous is a hazard in itself. I only needed to turn a corner into a dicey situation, or crowd some frightened, armed person in a foyer somewhere, or make an errant move after being pulled over by a policeman. Where fear and weapons meet—and they often do in urban America—there is always the possibility of death.

In that first year, my first away from my hometown, I was to become thoroughly familiar with the language of fear. At dark, shadowy intersections in Chicago, I could cross in front of a car stopped at a traffic light and elicit the *thunk, thunk, thunk, thunk* of the driver—black, white, male, or female—hammering down the door locks. On less traveled streets after dark, I grew accustomed to but never comfortable with people who crossed to the other side of the street rather than pass me. Then there were the standard unpleasantries with police, doormen, bouncers, cab drivers, and others whose business it is to screen out troublesome individuals *before* there is any nastiness.   3

I moved to New York nearly two years ago and I have remained an avid night walker. In central Manhattan, the near-constant crowd cover minimizes tense one-on-one street encounters. Elsewhere—visiting friends in SoHo,[1] where sidewalks are narrow and tightly spaced buildings shut out the sky—things can get very taut indeed. . . . "   4

The fearsomeness mistakenly attributed to me in public places often has a perilous flavor. The most frightening of these   5

[1] Soho (4)   A district of lower Manhattan.

confusions occurred in the late 1970s and early 1980s when I worked as a journalist in Chicago. One day, rushing into the office of a magazine I was writing for with a deadline story in hand, I was mistaken for a burglar. The office manager called security and, with an ad hoc posse, pursued me through the labyrinthine halls, nearly to my editor's door. I had no way of proving who I was. I could only move briskly toward the company of someone who knew me.

Another time I was on assignment for a local paper and killing time before an interview. I entered a jewelry store on the city's affluent Near North Side. The proprietor excused herself and returned with an enormous red Doberman pinscher straining at the end of a leash. She stood, the dog extended toward me, silent to my questions, her eyes bulging nearly out of her head. I took a cursory look around, nodded, and bade her good night. Relatively speaking, however, I never fared as badly as another black male journalist. He went to nearby Waukegan, Illinois, a couple of summers ago to work on a story about a murderer who was born there. Mistaking the reporter for the killer, police hauled him from his car at gunpoint and but for his press credentials would probably have tried to book him. Such episodes are not uncommon. Black men trade tales like this all the time. . . .

I began to take precautions to make myself less threatening. I move about with care, particularly late in the evening. I give a wide berth to nervous people on subway platforms during the wee hours, particularly when I have exchanged business clothes for jeans. If I happen to be entering a building behind some people who appear skittish, I may walk by, letting them clear the lobby before I return, so as not to seem to be following them. I have been calm and extremely congenial on those rare occasions when I've been pulled over by the police.

And on late-evening constitutionals along streets less traveled by, I employ what has proved to be an excellent tension-reducing measure: I whistle melodies from Beethoven and Vivaldi and the more popular classical composers. Even steely New Yorkers hunching toward nighttime destinations seem to relax, and occasionally they even join in the tune. Virtually everybody seems to sense that a mugger wouldn't be warbling bright, sunny selections from Vivaldi's *Four Seasons.* It is my equivalent of the cowbell that hikers wear when they know they are in bear country.

Discussion Questions

1. What is the main idea of Staples's essay?
2. What examples does Staples use to support his main idea?
3. What is the tone of the essay?
4. Why are black men generally seen as "criminals" in U.S. society?
5. How does Staples feel about his "power to alter public space"?
6. What precautions does Staples take to make himself "less threatening"?
7. How effective is Staples's use of description? Explain your answer.
8. How did Staples choose to begin his essay? What are some other options?

Writing Assignments

1. Write an essay about a time when you or someone you know felt threatened in a particular situation.
2. Write an essay about a time when you or someone you know was misunderstood or mistreated in a particular situation because of preconceived ideas about you or that person.
3. Write an essay that illustrates a stereotypical perception held by some people about a particular segment of society, for example, the elderly or women.

RESPECT ON THE STREETS

Elijah Anderson

Elijah Anderson is the Charles and William Day Professor of Social Sciences at the University of Pennsylvania. A sociologist, Anderson studies urban society, specifically life in the inner cities. He is the author of A Place on the Corner *(1978),* Streetwise: Race, Class and Change in the Urban Community *(1990), and* "The Code of the Streets" *(1994), which first appeared in the* Atlantic Monthly *and from which this excerpt is taken. Here Anderson describes the desperate search for respect by African American young men in poor inner-city communities.*

Vocabulary

deter	(2)	prevent, discourage
tatters	(3)	pieces, shreds
intricately	(3)	bound up with
circumscribed	(3)	limited
prerogatives	(4)	rights, privileges
ruthlessness	(4)	cruelty
existential	(4)	based on experience
implicit	(5)	implied, understood
incomprehensible	(6)	unable to be understood
demeanor	(6)	behavior
alluring	(6)	tempting, fascinating
internalized	(8)	taken inside oneself
imminent	(8)	about to occur
compunctions	(8)	feelings of guilt
quid pro quo	(8)	equal exchange
deferential	(8)	courteous, respectful

Among young people, whose sense of self-esteem is particularly 1
vulnerable, there is an especially heightened concern with being disrespected. Many inner-city young men in particular crave respect to such a degree that they will risk their lives to attain and maintain it.

The issue of respect is thus closely tied to whether a per- 2
son has an inclination to be violent, even as a victim. In the wider society people may not feel required to retaliate physically after an attack, even though they are aware that they

have been degraded or taken advantage of. They may feel a
great need to defend themselves *during* an attack, or to behave
in such a way as to deter aggression (middle-class people certainly can and do become victims of street-oriented youths),
but they are much more likely than street-oriented people to
feel that they can walk away from a possible altercation with
their self-esteem intact. Some people may even have the
strength of character to flee, without any thought that their
self-respect or esteem will be diminished.

   In impoverished inner-city black communities, however,   3
particularly among young males and perhaps increasingly
among females, such flight would be extremely difficult. To run
away would likely leave one's self-esteem in tatters. Hence people often feel constrained not only to stand up and at least attempt to resist during an assault but also to "pay back"—to
seek revenge—after a successful assault on their person. This
may include going to get a weapon or even getting relatives involved. Their very identity and self-respect, their honor, is often
intricately tied up with the way they perform on the streets
during and after such encounters. This outlook reflects the cir-
cumscribed opportunities of the inner-city poor. Generally people outside the ghetto have other ways of gaining status and regard, and thus do not feel so dependent on such physical
displays.

By Trial of Manhood

On the street, among males these concerns about things and   4
identity have come to be expressed in the concept of "manhood." Manhood in the inner city means taking the preroga-
tives of men with respect to strangers, other men, and
women—being distinguished as a man. It implies physicality
and a certain ruthlessness. Regard and respect are associated
with this concept in large part because of its practical application: if others have little or no regard for a person's manhood,
his very life and those of his loved ones could be in jeopardy.
But there is a chicken-and-egg aspect to this situation: one's
physical safety is more likely to be jeopardized in public *because* manhood is associated with respect. In other words, an
existential link has been created between the idea of manhood
and one's self-esteem, so that it has become hard to say which
is primary. For many inner-city youths, manhood and respect
are flip sides of the same coin; physical and psychological well-

being are inseparable, and both require a sense of control, of being in charge.

The operating assumption is that a man, especially a real man, knows what other men know—the code of the streets. And if one is not a real man, one is somehow diminished as a person, and there are certain valued things one simply does not deserve. There is thus believed to be a certain justice to the code, since it is considered that everyone has the opportunity to know it. Implicit in this is that everybody is held responsible for being familiar with the code. If the victim of a mugging, for example, does not know the code and so responds "wrong," the perpetrator may feel justified even in killing him and may feel no remorse. He may think, "Too bad, but it's his fault. He should have known better."

So when a person ventures outside, he must adopt the code—a kind of shield, really—to prevent others from "messing with" him. In these circumstances it is easy for people to think they are being tried or tested by others even when this is not the case. For it is sensed that something extremely valuable is at stake in every interaction, and people are encouraged to rise to the occasion, particularly with strangers. For people who are unfamiliar with the code—generally people who live outside the inner city—the concern with respect in the most ordinary inter-actions can be frightening and incomprehensible. But for those who are invested in the code, the clear object of their demeanor is to discourage strangers from even thinking about testing their manhood. And the sense of power that attends the ability to deter others can be alluring even to those who know the code without being heavily invested in it—the decent inner-city youths. Thus a boy who has been leading a basically decent life can, in trying circumstances, suddenly resort to deadly force.

Central to the issue of manhood is the widespread belief that one of the most effective ways of gaining respect is to man-ifest "nerve." Nerve is shown when one takes another person's possessions (the more valuable the better), "messes with" someone's woman, throws the first punch, "gets in someone's face," or pulls a trigger. Its proper display helps on the spot to check others who would violate one's person and also helps to build a reputation that works to prevent future challenges. But since such a show of nerve is a forceful expression of disrespect toward the person on the receiving end, the victim may be greatly offended and seek to retaliate with equal or greater force. A display of nerve, therefore, can easily provoke a life-threatening response, and the background knowledge of that possibility has often been incorporated into the concept of nerve.

True nerve exposes a lack of fear of dying. Many feel that it is acceptable to risk dying over the principle of respect. In fact, among the hard-core street-oriented, the clear risk of violent death may be preferable to being "dissed" by another. The youths who have internalized this attitude and convincingly display it in their public bearing are among the most threatening people of all, for it is commonly assumed that they fear no man. As the people of the community say, "They are the baddest dudes on the street." They often lead an existential life that may acquire meaning only when they are faced with the possibility of imminent death. Not to be afraid to die is by implication to have few compunctions about taking another's life. Not to be afraid to die is the quid pro quo of being able to take somebody else's life—for the right reasons, if the situation demands it. When others believe this is one's position, it gives one a real sense of power on the streets. Such credibility is what many inner-city youths strive to achieve, whether they are decent or street-oriented, both because of its practical defensive value and because of the positive way it makes them feel about themselves. The difference between the decent and the street-oriented youth is often that the decent youth makes a conscious decision to appear tough and manly; in another setting—with teachers, say, or at his part-time job—he can be polite and differential. The street-oriented youth, on the other hand, has made the concept of manhood a part of his very identity; he has difficulty manipulating it—it often controls him.

Discussion Questions

1. According to Anderson, why do many inner-city young men crave respect to such a great degree?
2. What is the relationship between self-respect and violence in the inner city?
3. What does the concept of "manhood" mean in the inner city?
4. According to Anderson, what is considered "true nerve" among hard-core inner-city youth?
5. What is the difference between the "decent and the street-oriented youth"?

6. How does Anderson use definition to develop this excerpt?

7. What is the thesis of this excerpt?

Writing Assignments

1. Write an essay that discusses your concept of one of the following: respect, honor, self-esteem, nerve, manhood (or womanhood).

2. Write an essay in which you describe the "code" of your neighborhood or community.

3. Write an essay in which you or someone you know was affected by violence of some kind.

Student Essay:
ARE BLACK MALES BECOMING AN ENDANGERED SPECIES?

Dwayne Griffin

Vocabulary

verge   (1)   edge
imminent (5)   immediate

To say today that a specific group of people is on the verge   1
of extinction is something some might find unbelievable. However, it is true. The black male, since his arrival in the Americas, has been through years of oppression—slavery, racism,
and stereotypes. Today, black men are a group at risk. Steps
must be taken to reverse this plague that has our black men on
the verge of extinction.

One of, if not the most, detrimental causes of turmoil is a   2
short life expectancy. The most disturbing fact of the black
male's life expectancy is that it is shorter than any other race
or sex. The young black male, according to numerous news reports, has a much higher death rate than a white youth, primarily because the greatest causes of death among black
youths are homicide, drug abuse, suicide, and accidents
whereas accidents and cardiovascular disease are the primary
causes of death among white youth.

Another factor affecting the existence of the black male is
physical health and illnesses. Many members of the black community, especially men, receive inadequate health-care services. This problem has long been a contributing factor to the
short life span of black males. Even today with improved health
services, black men still have a higher rate of cancer compared
to any other group in the United States. Reports indicate that
the most prevalent form of cancer found in black males—lung
cancer—is one of the most difficult forms of cancer to cure and
the easiest to prevent.

However, today the stereotype associating black males   3
with crime and violence has sadly become a reality. Just last
week my friend, who is a sociology major, gave me a shocking
statistic: "Even though Black men account for only about 7

percent of the population, they make up half the population of males in local, state, and federal jails and penitentiaries." Crime in the black community and among black males is at an all-time high. Black males account for the majority of Americans killed in crime-related incidents each year. Blacks for the most part aren't just killing members of other races but, in fact, are killing one another. Black-on-black crime is on the rise as are drug and gang-related homicides. There is no end in sight.

Alcohol and drug abuse are also threats to the black   4
man's health. Alcohol abuse is a more serious problem for black men than it is for white men, white women, and black women. The consequences of alcohol abuse, which affects both the personal and social lives of black men, include substantial increases in the rates of homicides, arrests, accidents, assaults, and physical illnesses. The alcohol problems among black men are further compounded by obstacles that make treatment of the disease difficult. These obstacles include few alcohol treatment centers in black communities, lack of drug and alcohol education, and the lack of funding for treatment.

The most publicized danger to the black male's existence   5
is that of unemployment. This is the issue concerning black males on which the media focus. Unemployment is so widespread among black males that they are twice as likely to be jobless as their white counterparts. Since it may contribute to crime and violence or to health-related problems, unemployment poses the most imminent and devastating threat to the black man and his family.

The black male is in grave danger. Answers must be found   6
to address the many conditions that threaten not only his survival, but the survival of the African American family.

Discussion Questions

1. According to Griffin, what are major threats to the African American male?
2. The author has his own ranking of these problems. Which do you feel is the greatest threat? Support your answer.
3. Why does the author consider black males an endangered species?
4. What are some of the greatest causes of death among black youth?
5. What are health concerns that affect black men?

6. To what extent does the author's use of illustration increase the essay's credibility?
7. Why do you think the author chose to use a question as his title? Would a statement have been a better choice? Why or why not?

Writing Assignments

1. Write an essay responding to the following sentence: _____ is becoming an endangered species.
2. Write an essay in which you disprove some misconception regarding the African American male.

7

Childhood • Adolescence
Growing Up

GORILLA, MY LOVE

Toni Cade Bambara

Born Toni Cade, Bambara (1939–95), who grew up in New York City, attended Queens College and City College of New York. She edited two short story anthologies before publishing two collections of her own: Gorilla, My Love *(1972) and* The Sea Birds Are Still Alive *(1977). The Salt Eaters (1980), a remarkable first novel, was acclaimed in the* New Yorker *as "a book full of marvels." In the following selection, the title story of her 1972 collection, Bambara shows us a young girl's struggle with disappointment.*

That was the year Hunca Bubba changed his name. Not a change up, but a change back, since Jefferson Winston Vale was the name in the first place. Which was news to me cause he'd been my Hunca Bubba my whole lifetime, since I couldn't manage Uncle to save my life. So far as I was concerned it was a change completely to somethin soundin very geographical weatherlike to me, like somethin you'd find in a almanac. Or somethin you'd run across when you sittin in the navigator seat with a wet thumb on the map crinkly in your lap, watchin

1

the roads and signs so when Granddaddy Vale say "Which way, Scout," you got sense enough to say take the next exit or take a left or whatever it is. Not that Scout's my name. Just the name Granddaddy call whoever sittin in the navigator seat. Which is usually me cause I don't feature sittin in the back with the pecans. Now, you figure pecans all right to be sittin with. If you thinks so, that's your business. But they dusty sometime and make you cough. And they got a way of slidin around and dippin down sudden, like maybe a rat in the buckets. So if you scary like me, you sleep with the lights on and blame it on Baby Jason and, so as not to waste good electric, you study the maps. And that's how come I'm in the navigator seat most times and get to be called Scout.

So Hunca Bubba in the back with the pecans and Baby   2
Jason, and he in love. And we got to hear all this stuff about this woman he in love with and all. Which really ain't enough to keep the mind alive, though Baby Jason got no better sense than to give his undivided attention and keep grabbin at the photograph which is just a picture of some skinny woman in a countrified dress with her hand shot up to her face like she shame fore cameras. But there's a movie house in the background which I ax about. Cause I am a movie freak from way back, even though it do get me in trouble sometime.

Like when me and Big Brood and Baby Jason was on our   3
own last Easter and couldn't go to the Dorset cause we'd seen all the Three Stooges they was. And the RKO Hamilton was closed readying up for the Easter Pageant that night. And the West End, the Regun and the Sunset was too far, less we had grownups with us which we didn't. So we walk up Amsterdam Avenue to the Washington and *Gorilla, My Love* playin, they say, which suit me just fine, though the "my love" part kinda drag Big Brood some. As for Baby Jason, shoot, like Granddaddy say, he'd follow me into the fiery furnace if I say come on. So we go in and get three bags of Havmore potato chips which not only are the best potato chips but the best bags for blowin up and bustin real loud so the matron come trottin down the aisle with her chunky self, flashin that flashlight dead in your eye so you can give her some lip, and if she answer back and you already finish seein the show anyway, why then you just turn the place out. Which I love to do, no lie. With Baby Jason kickin at the seat in front, egging me on, and Big Brood mumblin bout what fiercesome things we goin do. Which means me. Like when the big boys come up on us talkin

bout Lemme a nickel. It's me that hide the money. Or when the bad boys in the park take Big Brood's Spaudeen[1] way from him. It's me that jump on they back and fight awhile. And it's me that turns out the show if the matron get too salty.

So the movie come on and right away it's this churchy   4
music and clearly not about no gorilla. Bout Jesus. And I am ready to kill, not cause I got anything gainst Jesus. Just that when you fixed to watch a gorilla picture you don't wanna get messed around with Sunday School stuff. So I am mad. Besides, we see this raggedy old brown film *King of Kings* every year and enough's enough. Grownups figure they can treat you just anyhow. Which burns me up. There I am, my feet up and my Havmore potato chips really salty and crispy and two jawbreakers in my lap and the money safe in my shoe from the big boys, and here comes this Jesus stuff. So we all go wild. Yellin, booin, stompin and carryin on. Really to wake the man in the booth up there who musta went to sleep and put on the wrong reels. But no, cause he holler down to shut up and then he turn the sound up so we really gotta holler like crazy to even hear ourselves good. And the matron ropes off the children section and flashes her light all over the place and we yell some more and some kids slip under the rope and run up and down the aisle just to show it take more than some dusty ole velvet rope to tie us down. And I'm flingin the kid in front of me's popcorn. And Baby Jason kickin seats. And it's really somethin. Then here come the big and bad matron, the one they let out in case of emergency. And she totin that flashlight like she gonna use it on somebody. This here the colored matron Brandy and her friends call Thunderbuns. She do not play. She do not smile. So we shut up and watch the simple ass picture.

Which is not so simple as it is stupid. Cause I realize that   5
just about anybody in my family is better than this god they always talkin about. My daddy wouldn't stand for nobody treatin any of us that way. My mama specially. And I can just see it now, Big Brood up there on the cross talking bout Forgive them Daddy cause they don't know what they doin. And my Mama say Get on down from there you big fool, whatcha think this is, playtime? And my Daddy yellin to Granddaddy to get him a ladder cause Big Brood actin the fool, his mother side of the family showin up.

---

[1]Spaudeen (3)   Probably from "Spaulding," the sporting goods company, makers of rubber balls.

And my mama and her sister Daisy jumpin on them Romans beatin them with they pocketbooks. And Hunca Bubba tellin them folks on they knees they better get out the way and go get some help or they goin to get trampled on. And Granddaddy Vale sayin Leave the boy alone, if that's what he wants to do with his life we ain't got nothin to say about it. Then Aunt Daisy givin him a taste of that pocketbook, fussin bout what a damn fool old man Granddaddy is. Then everybody jumpin in his chest like the time Uncle Clayton went in the army and come back with only one leg and Granddaddy say somethin stupid about that's life. And by this time Big Brood off the cross and in the park playin handball or skully or somethin. And the family in the kitchen throwin dishes at each other, screamin bout if you hadn't done this I wouldn't had to do that. And me in the parlor trying to do my arithmetic yellin Shut it off.

Which is what I was yellin all by myself which make me a   6
sittin target for Thunderbuns. But when I yell We want our money back, that gets everybody in chorus. And the movie windin up with this heavenly cloud music and the smart-ass up there in his hole in the wall turns up the sound again to drown us out. Then there comes Bugs Bunny which we already seen so we know we been had. No gorilla my nuthin. And Big Brood say Awwww sheeet, we goin to see the manager and get our money back. And I know from this we business. So I brush the potato chips out of my hair, which is where Baby Jason like to put em, and I march myself up the aisle to deal with the manager who is a crook in the first place for lying out there sayin *Gorilla, My Love* playin. And I never did like the man cause he oily and pasty at the same time like the bad guy in the serial, the one that got a hideout behind a push-button bookcase and play "Moonlight Sonata" with gloves on. I knock on the door and I am furious. And I am alone, too. Cause Big Brood suddenly got to go so bad even though my mama told us bout goin in them nasty bathrooms. And I hear him sigh like he disgusted when he get to the door and see only a little kid there. And now I'm really furious cause I get so tired grownups messin over kids just cause they little and can't take em to court. What is it, he say to me like I lost my mittens or wet on myself or am somebody's retarded child. When in reality I am the smartest kid P.S. 186 ever had in its whole lifetime and you can ax anybody. Even them teachers that don't like me cause I won't sing them Southern songs or back off when they tell me my questions are out of order. And cause my Mama come up

there in a minute when them teachers start playin the dozens behind colored folks. She stalk in with her hat pulled down bad and that Persian lamb coat draped back over one hip on account of she got her fist planted there so she can talk that talk which gets us all hypnotized, and teacher be comin undone cause she know this could be her job and her behind cause Mama got pull with the Board and bad by her own self anyhow.

So I kick the door open wider and just walk right by him   7 and sit down and tell the man about himself and that I want my money back and that goes for Baby Jason and Big Brood too. And he still trying to shuffle me out the door even though I'm sitting which shows him for the fool he is. Just like them teachers do fore they realize Mama like a stone on that spot and ain't backin up. So he ain't gettin up off the money. So I was forced to leave, takin the matches from under his ashtray, and set a fire under the candy stand, which closed the raggedy ole Washington down for a week. My Daddy had the suspect it was me cause Big Brood got a big mouth. But I explained right quick what the whole thing was about and I figured it was even-steven. Cause if you say Gorilla, My Love, you suppose to mean it. Just like when you say you goin to give me a party on my birthday, you gotta mean it. And if you say me and Baby Jason can go South pecan haulin with Granddaddy Vale, you better not be comin up with no stuff about the weather look uncertain or did you mop the bathroom or any other trickified business. I mean even gangsters in the movies say My word is my bond. So don't nobody get away with nothin far as I'm concerned. So Daddy put his belt back on. Cause that's the way I was raised. Like my Mama say in one of them situations when I won't back down, Okay Badbird, you right. Your point is well-taken. Not that Badbird my name, just what she say when she tired arguin and know I'm right. And Aunt Jo, who is the hardest head in the family and worse even than Aunt Daisy, she say, You absolutely right Miss Muffin, which also ain't my real name but the name she gave me one time when I got some medicine shot in my behind and wouldn't get up off her pillows for nothin. And even Granddaddy Vale—who got no memory to speak of, so sometime you can just plain lie to him, if you want to be like that—he say, Well if that's what I said, then that's it. But this name business was different they said. It wasn't like Hunca Bubba had gone back on his word or anything. Just that he was thinkin bout gettin married and was usin his real name now. Which ain't the way I saw it at all.

So there I am in the navigator seat. And I turn to him and   8
just plain ole ax him. I mean I come right on out with it. No
sense goin all around that barn the old folks talk about. And
like my mama say, Hazel—which is my real name and what she
remembers to call me when she bein serious—when you got
somethin on your mind, speak up and let the chips fall where
they may. And if anybody don't like it, tell em to come see your
mama. And Daddy look up from the paper and say, You hear
your mama good, Hazel. And tell em to come see me first. Like
that. That's how I was raised.

So I turn clear round in the navigator seat and say, "Look   9
here, Hunca Bubba or Jefferson Windsong Vale or whatever
your name is, you gonna marry this girl?"

"Sure am," he say, all grins.   10

And I say, "Member that time you was baby-sittin me   11
when we lived at four-o-nine and there was this big snow and
Mama and Daddy got held up in the country so you had to stay
for two days?"

And he say, "Sure do."   12

"Well. You remember how you told me I was the cutest   13
thing that ever walked the earth?"

"Oh, you were real cute when you were little," he say,   14
which is suppose to be funny. I am not laughin.

"Well. You remember what you said?"   15

And Granddaddy Vale squintin over the wheel and axin   16
Which way, Scout. But Scout is busy and don't care if we all
get lost for days.

"Watcha mean, Peaches?"   17

"My name is Hazel. And what I mean is you said you were   18
going to marry *me* when I grew up. You were going to wait.
That's what I mean, my dear Uncle Jefferson." And he don't say
nuthin. Just look at me real strange like he never saw me before in life. Like he lost in some weird town in the middle of
night and looking for directions and there's no one to ask. Like
it was me that messed up the maps and turned the road posts
round. "Well, you said it, didn't you?" And Baby Jason lookin
back and forth like we playin ping-pong. Only I ain't playin. I'm
hurtin and I can hear that I am screamin. And Granddaddy
Vale mumblin how we never gonna get to where we goin if I
don't turn around and take my navigator job serious.

"Well, for cryin out loud, Hazel, you just a little girl. And I   19
was just teasin."

" 'And I was just teasin,' " I say back just how he said it so he can hear what a terrible thing it is. Then I don't say nuthin. And he don't say nuthin. And Baby Jason don't say nuthin nohow. Then Granddaddy Vale speak up. "Look here, Precious, it was Hunca Bubba what told you them things. This here, Jefferson Winston Vale." And Hunca Bubba say, "That's right. That was somebody else. I'm a new somebody." 20

"You a lyin dawg," I say, when I meant to say treacherous dog, but just couldn't get hold of the word. It slipped away from me. And I'm crying and crumplin down in the seat and just don't care. And Granddaddy say to hush and steps on the gas. And I'm losin my bearins and don't even know where to look on the map cause I can't see for cryin. And Baby Jason cryin too. Cause he is my blood brother and understands that we must stick together or be forever lost, what with grownups playin change-up and turnin you round every which way so bad. And don't even say they sorry. 21

Discussion Questions

1. How would you characterize the narrator?
2. Why is the narrator upset with Hunca Bubba?
3. How is the narrator's movie problem similar to her problem with Hunca Bubba?
4. Are you surprised by the narrator's reaction at the end of the story? Explain your answer.
5. Why does Bambara entitle her story "Gorilla, My Love"?
6. To what extent is Bambara's use of description an effective means of organization for her story?
7. What is the theme of the story?

Writing Assignments

1. Write an essay about a time when you felt betrayed by an adult.
2. Write an essay about a time when what you were promised was not what you received.
3. In an essay, describe an incident when a minor occurrence opened up a wound and caused you to overreact.

ALICE

Paulette Childress White

Paulette Childress White (1948–   ), the mother of five sons, was born and continues to live in Detroit. White has used that city as the setting of her poetry and short stories. She wrote Love Poems to a Black Junkie *(1975) and* The Watermelon Dress: Portrait of a Woman: Poems and Illustrations *(1984). In 1977, White published in* Essence *magazine her first short story, "Alice," which appears here. Notice that the story, which shows how perceptions change as one grows, is like a long poem with its rhythms and movement.*

Vocabulary

bellowing   (5)   shouting

Alice. Drunk Alice. Alice of the streets. Of the party. Of the 1
house of dark places. From whom without knowing I hid love
all my life behind remembrances of her house where I went
with Momma in the daytime to borrow things, and we found
her lounging in the front yard on a dirty plastic lawn chair
drinking warm beer from the can in a little brown bag where
the flies buzzed in and out of the always-open door of the
house as we followed her into the cool, dim rank-smelling
rooms for what it was we'd come. And I fought frowns as my
feet caught on the sticky gray wooden floor but looked up to
smile back at her smile as she gave the dollar or the sugar or
the coffee to Momma who never seemed to notice the floor or
the smell or Alice.

Alice, tall like a man, with soft wooly hair spread out in 2
tangles like a feathered hat and her face oily and her legs ashy,
whose beauty I never quite believed because she valued it so
little but was real. Real like wild flowers and uncut grass, real
like the knotty sky-reach of a dead tree. Beauty of warm brown
eyes in a round dark face and of teeth somehow always white
and clean and of lips moist and open, out of which rolled the
voice and the laughter, deep and breathless, rolling out the
strong and secret beauty of her soul.

Alice of the streets. Gentle walking on long legs. Close- 3
kneed. Careful. Stopping sometimes at our house on her way to

unknown places and other people. She came wearing loose, flowered dresses and she sat in our chairs rubbing the too-big knees that sometimes hurt, and we gathered, Momma, my sisters and I, to hear the beautiful bad-woman talk and feel the rolling laughter, always sure that she left more than she came for. I accepted the tender touch of her hands on my hair or my face or my arms like favors I never returned. I clung to the sounds of her words and the light of her smiles like stolen fruit.

Alice, mother in a house of dark places. Of boys who fought each other and ran cursing through the wild back rooms where I did not go alone but sometimes with Alice when she caught them up and knuckled their heads and made them cry or hugged them close to her saying funny things to tease them into laughter. And of the oldest son, named for his father, who sat twisted into a wheelchair by sunny windows in the front where she stayed with him for hours giving him her love, filling him with her laughter and he sat there—his words strained, difficult but soft and warm like the sun from the windows. 4

Alice of the party. When there was not one elsewhere she could make one of the evenings when her husband was not storming the dim rooms in drunken fits or lying somewhere in darkness filling the house with angry grunts and snores before the days he would go to work. He sat near her drinking beer with what company was there—was always sure to come— greedy for Alice and her husband, who leaned into and out of each other, talking hard and laughing loud and telling lies and being real. And there were rare and wondrously wicked times when I was caught there with Daddy who was one of the greedy ones and could not leave until the joy-shouting, table-slapping arguments about God and Negroes, the jumping up and down, the bellowing "what about the time" talks, the boasting and reeling of people drunk with beer and laughter and the ache of each other was over and the last ones sat talking sad and low, sick with themselves and too much beer. I watched Alice growing tired and ill and thought about the boys who had eaten dinners of cake and soda pop from the corner store, and I struggled to despise her for it against the memory of how, smiling they'd crept off to their rooms and slept in peace. And later at home I, too, slept strangely safe and happy, hugging the feel of that sweet fury in her house and in Alice of the party. 5

Alice, who grew older as I grew up but stayed the same while I grew beyond her, away from her. So far away that once, 6 on a clear early morning in the spring, when I was eighteen and smart and clean on my way to work downtown in the high-up office of my government job, with eyes that would not see I cut off her smile and the sound of her voice calling my name. When she surprised me on a clear spring morning, on her way somewhere or from somewhere in the streets and I could not see her beauty, only the limp flowered dress and the tangled hair and the face puffy from too much drinking and no sleep, I cut off her smile. I let my eyes slide away to say without speaking that I had grown beyond her. Alice, who had no place to grow in but was deep in the soil that fed me.

It was eight years before I saw Alice again and in those 7 eight years Alice had buried her husband and one of her boys and lost the oldest son to the county hospital where she traveled for miles to take him the sun and her smiles. And she had become a grandmother and a member of the church and cleaned out her house and closed the doors. And in those eight years I had married and become the mother of sons and did not always keep my floors clean or my hair combed or my legs oiled and I learned to like the taste of beer and how to talk bad-woman talk. In those eight years life had led me to the secret laughter.

Alice, when I saw her again, was in black, after the funeral 8 of my brother, sitting alone in an upstairs bedroom of my mother's house, her face dusted with brown powder and her gray-streaked hair brushed back into a neat ball and her wrinkled hands rubbing the tight-stockinged, tumor-filled knees and her eyes quiet and sober when she looked at me where I stood at the top of the stairs. I had run upstairs to be away from the smell of food and the crowd of comforters come to help bury our dead when I found Alice sitting alone in black and was afraid to smile remembering how I'd cut off her smile when I thought I had grown beyond her and was afraid to speak because there was too much I wanted to say.

Then Alice smiled her same smile and spoke my name in 9 her same voice and rising slowly from the tumored knees said, "Come on in and sit with me." And for the very first time I did.

Discussion Questions

1. How does the narrator's childhood image of Alice change from her adult image of Alice?

2. The narrator presents several descriptive snapshots of Alice. What are her positive and negative characteristics?

3. The author uses many similes (comparisons using *like* or *as*). What are two similes that you think are particularly effective? Explain your answer.

4. How does the narrator grow "beyond and away from" Alice?

5. Why does the narrator say that Alice was "deep in the soil that fed" her?

6. Why does the narrator at the end of the story say that she sat with Alice for the first time?

7. What is a cause-and-effect relationship illustrated in this story?

8. White begins many paragraphs with fragments. Why do you think the author uses the fragments rather than complete sentences? What is your assessment of her stylistic choice?

Writing Assignments

1. Write an essay in which you describe how your childhood perceptions of someone changed once you became an adult.

2. Write an essay in which you describe something that you do less well as an adult than you did as a child.

3. Write an essay about someone who has had an indirect, but substantial influence on your life.

LIVING JIM CROW

Richard Wright

Born in Natchez, Mississippi, and educated in the Chicago public school system, Richard Wright (1908–1960) is probably best known for his well-received novel Native Son *(1940). Wright wrote three other novels, a book of short stories, and four nonfiction works. In the following selection from* Black Boy *(1945), an autobiographical work, Wright recounts some of his humiliating experiences through which he gained his Jim Crow education.*

Vocabulary

cinders	(1)	hot coals
appalling	(2)	disgusting
barrage	(2)	attack
fortifications	(2)	barriers
profusely	(2)	freely
delirious	(7)	mentally wandering, confused
chamois	(61)	cotton cloth

I

My first lesson in how to live as a Negro came when I was quite small. We were living in Arkansas. Our house stood behind the railroad tracks. Its skimpy yard was paved with black cinders. Nothing green ever grew in that yard. The only touch of green we could see was far away, beyond the tracks, over where the white folks lived. But cinders were good enough for me and I never missed the green growing things. And anyhow cinders were fine weapons. You could always have a nice hot war with huge black cinders. All you had to do was crouch behind the brick pillars of a house with your hands full of gritty ammunition. And the first woolly black head you saw pop out from behind another row of pillars was your target. You tried your very best to knock it off. It was great fun.

I never fully realized the appalling disadvantages of a cinder environment till one day the gang to which I belonged found itself engaged in a war with the white boys who lived beyond the tracks. As usual we laid down our cinder barrage,

1

2

thinking that this would wipe the white boys out. But they replied with a steady bombardment of broken bottles. We doubled our cinder barrage, but they hid behind trees, hedges, and the sloping embankments of their lawns. Having no such fortifications, we retreated to the brick pillars of our homes. During the retreat a broken milk bottle caught me behind the ear, opening a deep gash which bled profusely. The sight of blood pouring over my face completely demoralized our ranks. My fellow-combatants left me standing paralyzed in the center of the yard, and scurried for their homes. A kind neighbor saw me and rushed me to a doctor, who took three stitches in my neck.

I sat brooding on my front steps, nursing my wound and waiting for my mother to come from work. I felt that a grave injustice had been done me. It was all right to throw cinders. The greatest harm a cinder could do was leave a bruise. But broken bottles were dangerous; they left you cut, bleeding, and helpless. 3

When night fell, my mother came from the white folks' kitchen. I raced down the street to meet her. I could just feel in my bones that she would understand. I knew she would tell me exactly what to do next time. I grabbed her hand and babbled out the whole story. She examined my wound, then slapped me. 4

"How come yuh didn't hide?" she asked me. "How come yuh awways fightin'?" 5

I was outraged, and bawled. Between sobs I told her that I didn't have any trees or hedges to hide behind. There wasn't a thing I could have used as a trench. And you couldn't throw very far when you were hiding behind the brick pillars of a house. She grabbed a barrel stave, dragged me home, stripped me naked, and beat me till I had a fever of one hundred and two. She would smack my rump with the stave, and, while the skin was still smarting, impart to me gems of Jim Crow[1] wisdom. I was never to throw cinders any more. I was never to fight any more wars. I was never, never, under any conditions, to fight *white* folks again. And they were absolutely right in clouting me with the broken milk bottle. Didn't I know she was working hard every day in the hot kitchens of the white folks to make money to take care of me? When was I ever going to learn to be a good boy? She couldn't be bothered with my fights. She 6

[1]Jim Crow (6)   Systematic practice of segregating, suppressing, and discriminating against African Americans.

finished by telling me that I ought to be thankful to God as long as I lived that they didn't kill me.

All that night I was delirious and could not sleep. Each time I closed my eyes I saw monstrous white faces suspended from the ceiling, leering at me.   7

From that time on, the charm of my cinder yard was gone. The green trees, the trimmed hedges, the cropped lawns grew very meaningful, became a symbol. Even today when I think of white folks, the hard, sharp outlines of white houses surrounded by trees, lawns, and hedges are present somewhere in the background of my mind. Through the years they grew into an over-reaching symbol of fear.   8

It was a long time before I came in close contact with white folks again. We moved from Arkansas to Mississippi. Here we had the good fortune not to live behind the railroad tracks, or close to white neighborhoods. We lived in the very heart of the local Black Belt. There were black churches and black preachers; there were black schools and black teachers; black groceries and black clerks. In fact, everything was so solidly black that for a long time I did not even think of white folks, save in remote and vague terms. But this could not last forever. As one grows older one eats more. One's clothing costs more. When I finished grammar school I had to go to work. My mother could no longer feed and clothe me on her cooking job.   9

There is but one place where a black boy who knows no trade can get a job, and that's where the houses and faces are white, where the trees, lawns, and hedges are green. My first job was with an optical company in Jackson, Mississippi. The morning I applied I stood straight and neat before the boss, answering all his questions with sharp yessirs and nosirs. I was very careful to pronounce my *sirs* distinctly, in order that he might know that I was polite, that I knew where I was, and that I knew he was a *white* man. I wanted that job badly.   10

He looked me over as though he were examining a prize poodle. He questioned me closely about my schooling, being particularly insistent about how much mathematics I had had. He seemed very pleased when I told him I had had two years of algebra.   11

"Boy, how would you like to try to learn something around here?" he asked me.   12

"I'd like it fine, sir," I said, happy. I had visions of "working my way up." Even Negroes have those visions.   13

"All right," he said. "Come on." 14

I followed him to the small factory. 15

"Pease," he said to a white man of about thirty-five, "this is 16
Richard. He's going to work for us."

Pease looked at me and nodded. 17

I was then taken to a white boy of about seventeen. 18

"Morrie, this is Richard, who's going to work for us." 19

"Whut yuh sayin' there, boy!" Morrie boomed at me. 20

"Fine!" I answered. 21

The boss instructed these two to help me, teach me, give 22
me jobs to do, and let me learn what I could in my spare time.

My wages were five dollars a week. 23

I worked hard, trying to please. For the first month I got 24
along O.K. Both Pease and Morrie seemed to like me. But one
thing was missing. And I kept thinking about it. I was not
learning anything and nobody was volunteering to help me.
Thinking they had forgotten that I was to learn something
about the mechanics of grinding lenses, I asked Morrie one day
to tell me about the work. He grew red.

"Whut yuh tryin' t' do, nigger, git smart?" he asked. 25

"Naw; I ain't tryin' t' git smart," I said. 26

"Well, don't, if yuh know whut's good for yuh!" 27

I was puzzled. Maybe he just doesn't want to help me, I 28
thought. I went to Pease.

"Say, are yuh crazy, you black bastard?" Pease asked me, 29
his gray eyes growing hard.

I spoke out, reminding him that the boss had said I was to 30
be given a chance to learn something.

"Nigger, you think you're *white,* don't you?" 31

"Naw, sir!" 32

"Well, you're acting mighty like it!" 33

"But, Mr. Pease, the boss said . . . " 34

Pease shook his fist in my face. 35

"This is a *white* man's work around here, and you better 36
watch yourself!"

From then on they changed toward me. They said good- 37
morning no more. When I was just a bit slow in performing
some duty, I was called a lazy black son-of-a-bitch.

Once I thought of reporting all this to the boss. But the 38
mere idea of what would happen to me if Pease and Morrie
should learn that I had "snitched" stopped me. And after all,
the boss was a white man too. What was the use?

The climax came at noon one summer day. Pease called 39

me to his work-bench. To get to him I had to go between two
narrow benches and stand with my back to a wall.

"Yes, sir," I said.   40

"Richard, I want to ask you something," Pease began   41
pleasantly, not looking up from his work.

"Yes, sir," I said again.   42

Morrie came over, blocking the narrow passage between   43
the benches. He folded his arms, staring at me solemnly.

I looked from one to the other, sensing that something was   44
coming.

"Yes, sir," I said for the third time.   45

Pease looked up and spoke very slowly.   46

"Richard, *Mr.* Morrie here tells me you call me *Pease.*"   47

I stiffened. A void seemed to open up in me. I knew this   48
was the show-down.

He meant that I had failed to call him *Mr.* Pease. I looked   49
at Morrie. He was gripping a steel bar in his hands. I opened
my mouth to speak, to protest, to assure Pease that I had never
called him simply *Pease,* and that I had never had any intentions of doing so, when Morrie grabbed me by the collar, ram-
ming my head against the wall.

"Now, be careful, nigger!" snarled Morrie, baring his teeth.   50
"I heard yuh call 'im *Pease!* 'N' if yuh say yuh didn't, yuh're
callin' me a *lie,* see?" He waved the steel bar threateningly.

If I had said: No, sir, Mr. Pease, I never called you *Pease,* I   51
would have been automatically calling Morrie a liar. And if I
had said: Yes, sir Mr. Pease, I called you *Pease,* I would have
been pleading guilty to having uttered the worst insult that a
Negro can utter to a southern white man. I stood hesitating,
trying to frame a neutral reply.

"Richard, I asked you a question!" said Pease. Anger was   52
creeping into his voice.

"I don't remember calling you *Pease,* Mr. Pease," I said   53
cautiously. "And if I did, I sure didn't mean . . . "

"You black son-of-a-bitch! You called me *Pease,* then!" he   54
spat, slapping me till I bent sideways over a bench. Morrie was
on top of me, demanding:

"Didn't yuh call 'im *Pease?* If yuh say yuh didn't, I'll rip yo'   55
gut string loose with this bar, yuh black granny dodger! Yuh
can't call a white man a lie 'n' git erway with it, you black son-
of-a-bitch!"

I wilted. I begged them not to bother me. I knew what they   56
wanted. They wanted me to leave.

"I'll leave," I promised. "I'll leave right *now.*"   57

They gave me a minute to get out of the factory. I was   58
warned not to show up again, or tell the boss.

I went.   59

When I told the folks at home what had happened, they   60
called me a fool. They told me that I must never again attempt
to exceed my boundaries. When you are working for white
folks, they said, you got to "stay in your place" if you want to
keep working.

II

My Jim Crow education continued on my next job, which was   61
portering in a clothing store. One morning, while polishing
brass out front, the boss and his twenty-year-old son got out of
their car and half dragged and half kicked a Negro woman into
the store. A policeman standing at the corner looked on,
twirling his nightstick. I watched out of the corner of my eye,
never slackening the strokes of my chamois upon the brass. After a few minutes, I heard shrill screams coming from the rear
of the store. Later the woman stumbled out, bleeding, crying,
and holding her stomach. When she reached the end of the
block, the policeman grabbed her and accused her of being
drunk. Silently, I watched him throw her into a patrol wagon.

When I went to the rear of the store, the boss and his son   62
were washing their hands at the sink. They were chuckling.
The floor was bloody and strewn with wisps of hair and clothing. No doubt I must have appeared pretty shocked, for the
boss slapped me reassuringly on the back.

"Boy, that's what we do to niggers when they don't want to   63
pay their bills," he said, laughing.

His son looked at me and grinned.   64

"Here, hava cigarette," he said.   65

Not knowing what to do, I took it. He lit his and held the   66
match for me. This was a gesture of kindness, indicating that
even if they had beaten the poor old woman, they would not
beat me if I knew enough to keep my mouth shut.

"Yes, sir," I said, and asked no questions.   67

After they had gone, I sat on the edge of a packing box and   68
stared at the bloody floor till the cigarette went out.

That day at noon, while eating in a hamburger joint, I told   69
my fellow Negro porters what had happened. No one seemed
surprised. One fellow, after swallowing a huge bite, turned to
me and asked:

"Huh! Is tha' all they did t' her?"   70

"Yeah. Wasn't tha' enough?" I asked.   71

"Shucks! Man, she's a lucky bitch!" he said, burying his   72
lips deep into a juicy hamburger. "Hell, it's a wonder they didn't
lay her when they got through."

III

I was learning fast, but not quite fast enough. One day, while I   73
was delivering packages in the suburbs, my bicycle tire was
punctured. I walked along the hot, dusty road, sweating and
leading my bicycle by the handle-bars.

A car slowed at my side.   74

"What's the matter boy?" a white man called.   75

I told him my bicycle was broken and I was walking back   76
to town.

"That's too bad," he said. "Hop on the running board."   77

He stopped the car. I clutched hard at my bicycle with one   78
hand and clung to the side of the car with the other.

"All set?"   79

"Yes, sir," I answered. The car started.   80

It was full of young white men. They were drinking. I   81
watched the flask pass from mouth to mouth.

"Wanna drink, boy?" one asked.   82

I laughed as the wind whipped my face. Instinctively obey-   83
ing the freshly planted precepts of my mother, I said:

"Oh, no!"   84

The words were hardly out of my mouth before I felt some-   85
thing hard and cold smash me between the eyes. It was an
empty whisky bottle. I saw stars, and fell backwards from the
speeding car into the dust of the road, my feet becoming entangled in the steel spokes of my bicycle. The white men piled out
and stood over me.

"Nigger, ain't yuh learned no better sense'n tha' yet?"   86
asked the man who hit me. "Ain' yuh learned t' say *sir* t' a
white man yet?"

Dazed, I pulled to my feet. My elbows and legs were bleed-   87
ing. Fists doubled, the white man advanced, kicking my bicycle
out of the way.

"Aw, leave the bastard alone. He's got enough," said one.   88

They stood looking at me. I rubbed my shins, trying to   89
stop the flow of blood. No doubt they felt a sort of contemptu-
ous pity, for one asked:

"Yuh wanna ride t' town now, nigger? Yuh reckon yuh   90
know enough t' ride now?"

"I wanna walk," I said, simply.   91
Maybe it sounded funny. They laughed.   92
"Well, walk, yuh black son-of-a-bitch!"   93
When they left they comforted me with: 94
"Nigger, yuh sho better be damn glad it wuz us yuh talked   95
t' tha' way. Yuh're a lucky bastard, 'cause if yuh'd said tha' t'
somebody else, yuh might've been a dead nigger now."

Discussion Questions

1. What is the significance of the title?
2. Why does Pease and Morrie's behavior change toward the narrator? In what way does the question they ask the narrator in paragraph 50 reflect their behavioral change?
3. What does "stay in your place" mean in the context of the story?
4. Why do the store boss and son invite the narrator to have a cigarette with them after the woman leaves?
5. Why do the young white men offer the narrator a ride the first time?
6. What lessons did Wright learn from his Jim Crow education?
7. Why is the author's use of process important to our understanding of Wright's Jim Crow education?
8. Why do you think Wright chose to divide this essay into three parts?

Writing Assignments

1. Write an essay that describes lessons about life you learned while growing up.
2. Write an essay recounting an incident that you considered a no-win situation.
3. Write an essay in which you discuss some lesson that must be experienced rather than taught.

MARGUERITE'S GRADUATION

Maya Angelou

Author, poet, playwright, political activist, singer, profes-
sional stage and screen performer, the talented Maya An-
gelou (1928–   ) was born Marguerite Johnson in St. Louis,
Missouri. Angelou is best known for her autobiographical
books, which include the following: I Know Why the Caged
Bird Sings *(1969),* Gather Together in My Name *(1974),*
Singin' and Swingin' and Gettin' Merry Like Christmas
(1976), The Heart of a Woman *(1982), and* Maya Angelou
Boxed *(1994). The following selection from* I Know Why the
Caged Bird Sings *recounts Angelou's bitter disappointment*
at her graduation.

Vocabulary

reprieve	(2)	delayed punishment
presentiment	(12)	indication, hunch
dais	(13)	platform, stage
piqued	(13)	aroused
bootblack	(23)	one who shines shoes
penance	(23)	compensation for an offense
constrained	(24)	held back, restricted
decasyllabic	(26)	having ten syllables
farcical	(27)	laughable, ridiculous
presumptuous	(27)	bold, overconfident
abomination	(29)	anything disgusting
perfunctory	(31)	thoughtless, automatic
palpable	(32)	real, visible
elocution	(36)	style or manner of speaking
auctioned	(44)	sold to the highest bidder

Amazingly the great day finally dawned and I was out of bed   1
before I knew it. I threw open the back door to see it more
clearly, but Momma said, "Sister, come away from that door
and put your robe on."

I hoped the memory of that morning would never leave   2
me. Sunlight was itself young, and the day had none of the in-
sistence maturity would bring it in a few hours. In my robe and
barefoot in the backyard, under cover of going to see about my
new beans, I gave myself up to the gentle warmth and thanked

God that no matter what evil I had done in my life He had allowed me to live to see this day. Somewhere in my fatalism I had expected to die, accidentally, and never have the chance to walk up the stairs in the auditorium and gracefully receive my hard-earned diploma. Out of God's merciful bosom I had won reprieve.

Bailey[1] came out in his robe and gave me a box wrapped 3 in Christmas paper. He said he had saved his money for months to pay for it. It felt like a box of chocolates, but I knew Bailey wouldn't save money to buy candy when we had all we could want under our noses.

He was as proud of the gift as I. It was a soft-leather- 4 bound copy of a collection of poems by Edgar Allan Poe, or, as Bailey and I called him, "Eap." I turned to "Annabel Lee" and we walked up and down the garden rows, the cool dirt between our toes, reciting the beautifully sad lines.

Momma made a Sunday breakfast although it was only 5 Friday. After we finished the blessing, I opened my eyes to find the watch on my plate. It was a dream of a day. Everything went smoothly and to my credit, I didn't have to be reminded or scolded for anything. Near evening I was too jittery to attend to chores, so Bailey volunteered to do all before his bath.

Days before, we had made a sign for the Store, and as we 6 turned out the lights Momma hung the cardboard over the doorknob. It read clearly: CLOSED. GRADUATION.

My dress fitted perfectly and everyone said that I looked 7 like a sunbeam in it. On the hill, going toward the school, Bailey walked behind with Uncle Willie, who muttered, "Go on, Ju." He wanted him to walk ahead with us because it embarrassed him to have to walk so slowly. Bailey said he'd let the ladies walk together, and the men would bring up the rear. We all laughed nicely.

Little children dashed by out of the dark like fireflies. 8 Their crepe-paper dresses and butterfly wings were not made for running and we heard more than one rip, dryly, and the regretful "uh uh" that followed.

The school blazed without gaiety. The windows seemed 9 cold and unfriendly from the lower hill. A sense of ill-fated timing crept over me, and if Momma hadn't reached for my hand I would have drifted back to Bailey and Uncle Willie, and possi-

---

[1]Bailey (3)   The author's brother.

bly beyond. She made a few slow jokes about my feet getting cold, and tugged me along to the now-strange building.

Around the front steps, assurance came back. There were   10
my fellow "greats," the graduating class. Hair brushed back, legs oiled, new dresses and pressed pleats, fresh pocket hand-kerchiefs and little handbags, all homesewn. Oh, we were up to snuff, all right. I joined my comrades and didn't even see my family go in to find seats in the crowded auditorium.

The school band struck up a march and all classes filed in   11
as had been rehearsed. We stood in front of our seats, as as-signed, and on a signal from the choir director, we sat. No sooner had this been accomplished than the band started to play the national anthem. We rose again and sang the song, af-ter which we recited the pledge of allegiance. We remained standing for a brief minute before the choir director and the principal signaled to us, rather desperately I thought, to take our seats. The command was so unusual that our carefully re-hearsed and smooth-running machine was thrown off. For a full minute we fumbled for our chairs and bumped into each other awkwardly. Habits change or solidify under pressure, so in our state of nervous tension we had been ready to follow our usual assembly pattern: the American national anthem, then the pledge of allegiance, then the song every Black person I knew called the Negro National Anthem. All done in the same key, with the same passion and most often standing on the same foot.

Finding my seat at last, I was overcome with a presenti-   12
ment of worse things to come. Something unrehearsed, un-planned, was going to happen, and we were going to be made to look bad. I distinctly remember being explicit in the choice of pronoun. It was "we," the graduating class, the unit, that con-cerned me then.

The principal welcomed "parents and friends" and asked   13
the Baptist minister to lead us in prayer. His invocation was brief and punchy, and for a second I thought we were getting on the high road to right action. When the principal came back to the dais, however, his voice had changed. Sounds always af-fected me profoundly and the principal's voice was one of my favorites. During the assembly it melted and lowed weakly into the audience. It had not been in my plan to listen to him, but my curiosity was piqued and I straightened up to give him my attention.

He was talking about Booker T. Washington, our "late   14
great leader," who said we can be as close as the fingers on the
hand, etc. . . . . Then he said a few vague things about friendship and the friendship of kindly people to those less fortunate
than themselves. With that his voice nearly faded, thin, away.
Like a river diminishing to a stream and then to a trickle. But
he cleared his throat and said, "Our speaker tonight, who is
also our friend, came from Texarkana to deliver the commence-
ment address, but due to the irregularity of the train schedule,
he's going to, as they say, 'speak and run.' " He said that we
understood and wanted the man to know that we were most
grateful for the time he was able to give us and then something
about how we were willing always to adjust to another's program, and without more ado—"I give you Mr. Edward Donleavy."

Not one but two white men came through the door off-   15
stage. The shorter one walked to the speaker's platform, and
the tall one moved to the center seat and sat down. But that
was our principal's seat, and already occupied. The dislodged
gentleman bounced around for a long breath or two before the
Baptist minister gave him his chair, then with more dignity
than the situation deserved, the minister walked off the stage.

Donleavy looked at the audience once (on reflection, I'm   16
sure that he wanted only to reassure himself that we were really there), adjusted his glasses and began to read from a sheaf
of papers.

He was glad "to be here and to see the work going on just   17
as it was in the other schools."

At the first "Amen" from the audience I willed the offender   18
to immediate death by choking on the word. But Amens and
Yes, sir's began to fall around the room like rain through a
ragged umbrella.

He told us of the wonderful changes we children in   19
Stamps[2] had in store. The Central School (naturally, the white
school was Central) had already been granted improvements
that would be in use in the fall. A well-known artist was coming
from Little Rock to teach art to them. They were going to have
the newest microscopes and chemistry equipment for their lab-
oratory. Mr. Donleavy didn't leave us long in the dark over who

---

[2]Stamps   (19)   Town in Arkansas.

made these improvements available to Central High. Nor were we to be ignored in the general betterment scheme he had in mind.

He said that he had pointed out to people at a very high   20
level that one of the first-line football tacklers at Arkansas Agricultural and Mechanical College had graduated from good old Lafayette County Training School. Here fewer Amen's were heard. Those few that did break through lay dully in the air with the heaviness of habit.

He went on to praise us. He went on to say how he had   21
bragged that "one of the best basketball players at Fisk sank his first ball right here at Lafayette County Training School."

The white kids were going to have a chance to become   22
Galileos and Madame Curies and Edisons and Gauguins, and our boys (the girls weren't even in on it) would try to be Jesse Owenses and Joe Louises.

Owens and the Brown Bomber were great heroes in our   23
world, but what school official in the white-goddom[3] of Little Rock had the right to decide that those two men must be our only heroes? Who decided that for Henry Reed to become a scientist he had to work like George Washington Carver, as a bootblack, to buy a lousy microscope? Bailey was obviously always going to be too small to be an athlete, so which concrete angel glued to what country seat had decided that if my brother wanted to become a lawyer he had to first pay penance for his skin by picking cotton and hoeing corn and studying correspondence books at night for twenty years?

The man's dead words fell like bricks around the audito-   24
rium and too many settled in my belly. Constrained by hard-learning manners I couldn't look behind me, but to my left and right the proud graduating class of 1940 had dropped their heads. Every girl in my row had found something new to do with her handkerchief. Some folded the tiny squares into love knots, some into triangles, but most were wadding them, then pressing them flat on their yellow laps.

On the dais, the ancient tragedy was being replayed. Pro-   25
fessor Parsons sat, a sculptor's reject, rigid. His large, heavy body seemed devoid of will or willingness, and his eyes said he was no longer with us. The other teachers examined the flag (which was draped stage right) or their notes, or the windows which opened on our now-famous playing diamond.

[3]white-goddom (23)   Top white policy makers.

Graduation, the hush-hush magic time of frills and gifts   26
and congratulations and diplomas, was finished for me before
my name was called. The accomplishment was nothing. The
meticulous maps, drawn in three colors of ink, learning and
spelling decasyllabic words, memorizing the whole of *The Rape
of Lucrece* [4]—it was for nothing. Donleavy had exposed us.

We were maids and farmers, handymen and washer-   27
women, and anything higher that we aspired to was farcical
and presumptuous.

Then I wished that Gabriel Prosser and Nat Turner [5] had   28
killed all whitefolks in their beds and that Abraham Lincoln
had been assassinated before the signing of the Emancipation
Proclamation, and that Harriet Tubman [6] had been killed by
that blow on her head and Christopher Columbus had drowned
in the *Santa Maria*.

It was awful to be a Negro and have no control over my   29
life. It was brutal to be young and already trained to sit quietly
and listen to charges brought against my color with no chance
of defense. We should all be dead. I thought I should like to see
us all dead, one on top of the other. A pyramid of flesh with the
whitefolks on the bottom, as the broad base, then the Indians
with their silly tomahawks and teepees and wigwams and
treaties, the Negroes with their mops and recipes and cotton
sacks and spirituals sticking out of their mouths. The Dutch
children should all stumble in their wooden shoes and break
their necks. The French should choke to death on the
Louisiana Purchase (1803) while silkworms ate all the Chinese
with their stupid pigtails. As a species, we were an abomina-
tion. All of us.

Donleavy was running for election, and assured our par-   30
ents that if he won we could count on having the only colored
paved playing field in that part of Arkansas. Also—he never
looked up to acknowledge the grunts of acceptance—also, we
were bound to get some new equipment for the home economics building and the workshop.

He finished, and since there was no need to give any more   31
than the most perfunctory thank-you's, he nodded to the men
on the stage, and the tall white man who was never introduced

---

[4]*The Rape of Lucrece* (26)   Long narrative poem by William Shakespeare.
[5]Gabriel Prosser and Nat Turner (28)   Leaders of slave rebellion in the
early 1800s in Virginia.
[6]Harriet Tubman (28)   Popular Underground Railroad leader who led over
three hundred slaves to freedom.

joined him at the door. They left with the attitude that now they were off to something really important. (The graduation ceremonies at Lafayette County Training School had been a mere preliminary.)

The ugliness they left was palpable. An uninvited guest who wouldn't leave. The choir was summoned and sang a modern arrangement of "Onward, Christian Soldiers," with new words pertaining to graduates seeking their place in the world. But it didn't work. Elouise, the daughter of the Baptist minister, recited "Invictus"[7] and I could have cried at the impertinence of "I am the master of my fate, I am the captain of my soul." 32

My name had lost its ring of familiarity and I had to be nudged to go and receive my diploma. All my preparations had fled. I neither marched up to the stage like a conquering Amazon, nor did I look in the audience for Bailey's nod of approval. Marguerite Johnson, I heard the name again, my honors were read, there were noises in the audience of appreciation, and I took my place on the stage as rehearsed. 33

I thought about colors I hated: ecru, puce, lavender, beige and black. 34

There was shuffling and rustling around me, then Henry Reed was giving his valedictory address, "To Be or Not to Be." Hadn't he heard the whitefolks? We couldn't *be*, so the question was a waste of time. Henry's voice came out clear and strong. I feared to look at him. Hadn't he got the message? There was no "nobler in the mind" for Negroes because the world didn't think we had minds, and they let us know it. "Outrageous fortune"? Now, that was a joke. When the ceremony was over I had to tell Henry Reed some things. That is, if I still cared, Not "rub," Henry, "erase." "Ah, there's the erase." Us. 35

Henry had been a good student in elocution. His voice rose on tides of promise and fell on waves of warnings. The English teacher had helped him to create a sermon winging through Hamlet's soliloquy. To be a man, a doer, a builder, a leader, or to be a tool, an unfunny joke, a crusher of funky toadstools. I marveled that Henry could go through with the speech as if we had a choice. 36

I had been listening and silently rebutting each sentence with my eyes closed; then there was a hush, which in an audience warns that something unplanned is happening. I looked 37

[7]"Invictus" (32)   Poem by William Ernest Henley.

up and saw Henry Reed, the conservative, the proper, the A student, turn his back to the audience and turn to us (the proud graduating class of 1940) and sing, nearly speaking,

> "Lift ev'ry voice and sing
> Till earth and heaven ring
> Ring with the harmonies of Liberty . . . "

It was the poem written by James Weldon Johnson. It was the music composed by J. Rosamond Johnson. It was the Negro National Anthem. Out of habit we were singing it.

Our mothers and fathers stood in the dark hall and joined   38
the hymn of encouragement. A kindergarten teacher led the small children onto the stage and the buttercups and daisies and bunny rabbits marked time and tried to follow:

> "Stony the road we trod
> Bitter the chastening rod
> Felt in the days when hope, unborn, had died.
> Yet with a steady beat
> Have not our weary feet
> Come to the place for which our fathers sighed?"

Each child I knew had learned that song with his ABC's   39
and along with "Jesus Loves Me This I Know." But I personally had never heard it before. Never heard the words, despite the thousands of times I had sung them. Never thought they had anything to do with me.

On the other hand, the words of Patrick Henry had made   40
such an impression on me that I had been able to stretch myself tall and trembling and say, "I know not what course others may take, but as for me, give me liberty or give me death."

And now I heard, really for the first time: 41

> "We have come over a way that with tears
> has been watered,
> We have come, treading our path through
> the blood of the slaughtered."

While echoes of the song shivered in the air, Henry Reed   42
bowed his head, said "Thank you," and returned to his place in the line. The tears that slipped down many faces were not wiped away in shame.

We were on top again. As always, again. We survived. The   43
depths had been icy and dark, but now a bright sun spoke to
our souls. I was no longer simply a member of the proud graduating class of 1940; I was a proud member of the wonderful,
beautiful Negro race.

Oh, Black known and unknown poets, how often have   44
your auctioned pains sustained us? Who will compute the
lonely nights made less lonely by your songs, or the empty pots
made less tragic by your tales?

If we were a people much given to revealing secrets, we   45
might raise monuments and sacrifice to the memories of our
poets, but slavery cured us of that weakness. It may be
enough, however, to have it said that we survive in exact relationship to the dedication of our poets (include preachers, musicians and blues singers).

Discussion Questions

1. How is Marguerite different at the end of the graduation speech
than she is at the beginning of the ceremony?
2. To what extent does Mr. Donleavy's "promised gift" reflect his
racist views?
3. How does Mr. Donleavy's speech spoil the hopes and dreams of
the graduates and their families?
4. How appropriate to the occasion is Henry Reed's valedictory address?
5. Why does the singing of "Lift Every Voice and Sing" renew the
graduates' hopes and lift their spirits?
6. What does Marguerite mean when she says that she had never
heard the song even though she had sung it a thousand times?
7. Angelou uses many rhetorical strategies—narration, comparison-
contrast, cause and effect, and description—to make her point.
How does each contribute to the reader's understanding and appreciation of the story?
8. What do you think is a major theme of the story?

Writing Assignments

1. Write an essay in which you contrast a mood of anticipation that
you have experienced with a later one of disappointment.
2. Write an essay describing something memorable about your
graduation.
3. Write an essay about a time when something or someone caused
you to feel better about something that had previously depressed
you.

Student Essay:
STONE CITY

Jerome Mason

Vocabulary

forged	(4)	walked slowly, but steadily
synchronized	(6)	harmonized, blended

Being successful can mean different things to different people. To some people it can mean getting a great job, or accumulating a large sum of money; to others it can mean achieving some other goal that a person feels is important. In ·my life, I have had as many successes as failures, some big and some small. The most important things that I have accomplished are very personal things that give meaning to my life, such as being admitted to the University of Wisconsin-Milwaukee (UWM). It meant more to me than just being able to further my educational horizons; it was a fulfillment of a childhood dream.

Most of my childhood was spent living in a house on the east side of Milwaukee, a little over a mile away from the university in a section of town now called Riverwest. The area has lots of parks and trails alongside the Milwaukee River. When I was about nine, I used to go to those nearby parks with my older brother and his friends when they would let me go with them. We would hike up and down the trails as if we were on an expedition into the wild of some far-off country. Mostly, we would end up down by the river catching frogs or turtles or whatever we could find. We would always stay on the west side of the Locust Street Bridge because our mother would not allow us to go on the other side by ourselves. Of course, I often crossed the bridge in the family car, but I had never gone over it on foot.

Then one morning on the way to school, my buddy suggested that we go to the other side of the bridge. I had never skipped school, but the idea of going on an adventure sounded much more exciting than school. We took an alternate route to school so that none of the other kids would see us as we set out to see just what lay ahead on the other side of that bridge.

We forged across the long bridge, which, at the time, seemed like the link to another world. It felt as if we were exploring strange new territories, discovering a new land unknown to the rest of the world. In a childlike way, we were doing just that. Just on the other side of the bridge was a long concrete trail close to the river. We wandered down the trail for a while and then decided to climb up the riverbank to see what was at the top.

When we reached the peak, not too far off in the distance,   5
we spotted three huge stone buildings towering over the tops of the neighboring houses. There was no question that this was the direction in which we wanted to head. To keep a low profile, we stuck to the back streets and alleys as much as possible. When we reached the street where the huge buildings stood, we came upon an awesome sight: a large isolated community, which seemed to us to be a stone city. We had to investigate and find out more about this mysterious place. We explored a couple of the buildings and saw people in large classrooms that looked like movie theaters. The doors to all the buildings were open, so we just roamed around, going from building to building.

One of the buildings was more like a shopping mall with-   6
out the department stores; it had lots of restaurants and offices, and there was even a recreation room and a bowling alley in the basement. This is the building where we found lots of people "hanging out." They seemed to be coming from every direction. Some were studying big books, and others were eating and talking. The motion of the people appeared almost chaotic, yet synchronized. Everything they were doing seemed to be important, exciting; they just seemed to be enjoying themselves as if they were at a carnival or something. I was feeding on the intensity of it all. I felt like there was an electric current flowing through my veins. It was as if I was in the place where the people ran the world. This was living!

No one said anything to us, and we figured that we were   7
safe, since we were far from anybody who would recognize us. We were wrong. Someone had recognized us. A student teacher who had recently completed his field placement in our classroom came over and asked us why we were not in school. We were caught! The adventure was over. We told him the truth in hopes that he wouldn't take us back to school to be punished.

He didn't take us back to the school, but he told us that   8
he was going to telephone later to see if we had made it without him. On the way back, I was worried about facing the consequences, but I was also glad we had found out what a univer-

sity was like. I had become enlightened. I had discovered a whole other world on the far side of that bridge that I never even knew existed.

This experience greatly influenced me. After my adventure, 9 I became fascinated with the university. Every chance I could get to go over there, I took. I found out that the university offered summer youth programs, which I attended every year after that while I was in grade school. Being involved in these activities was important to me because it made me feel connected to the university. In my mind, UWM was the place to be if you wanted to be more than just average; it was the place to be if you wanted to be great.

In the community where I grew up, there wasn't a strong 10 emphasis on education at the college level. I didn't know of any professional people in my neighborhood outside of my teachers at school who had careers that required a college degree. Sadly, as time passed, I began to feel that it was unrealistic for me to think that I would ever be able to have a chance to do something like go to college. I started to feel as though college, careers, and things like that were only for privileged, well-to-do white people. They were not for a fairly average, everyday young black male like me. Therefore, I started losing interest in school and had lost interest completely by the time I was midway through high school. I stopped thinking about ever going to college; it seemed way beyond my reach.

I eventually dropped out of high school and ended up go- 11 ing to an alternative school where I received my general equivalency diploma (G.E.D.). By the time I had turned eighteen, all of my childhood dreams of going to college one day and becoming successful had completely faded.

When I entered the work force, I had no direction, nor did 12 I have any idea of what kind of work I wanted to do. I just took whatever jobs were offered to me, even though not one of those jobs seemed to satisfy or replace the feeling of being connected to something important, like that feeling I had as a child visiting the great stone city.

After several years of going through life's ups and downs, I 13 decided that it was time for me to pursue what was really important to me. It was time to fulfill my life's dreams. At twenty-five, I enrolled in the human services program at the Milwaukee Area Technical College. When I completed my studies there, I transferred to the social welfare program at the University of Wisconsin-Milwaukee. When I was accepted at the university, it was like a dream come true. Although I do plan to graduate and go on to do other things, I have already achieved personal success. To me, being successful is achieving your own personal dreams, whatever they may be.

Discussion Questions

1. Why were the writer's descriptions of the stone city particularly effective? To what extent did the author's first time experience affect his description of it?

2. What were the circumstances that led the author to UWM for the first time?

3. What fascinated the author about the university?

4. Some people reading this story would say that skipping school may have saved the narrator's life. Would you agree with such an assessment? Why or why not?

5. Why did the author's hopes of attending the university fade as he grew older and entered high school?

6. What do you learn about the narrator as a result of the decisions that he made?

7. What predominant rhetorical strategies does the writer use in developing his essay?

8. What type of beginning does Mason use to introduce his essay?

Writing Assignments

1. Write an essay in which you show how the decisions that some of us make reveal much about the kind of people we are.

2. Write an essay discussing a fulfilled (or unfulfilled) childhood dream.

8

Family

MOTHER TO SON

Langston Hughes

Langston Hughes (1902–1967) was born in Joplin, Missouri. As an undergraduate, he attended both Columbia University and Lincoln University. In 1921, he published in the Crisis *his famous poem, "The Negro Speaks of Rivers." He published his first book of poetry,* The Weary Blues, *in 1926 and his second volume,* Fine Clothes to the Jew, *in 1927. In the 1940s, he created the memorable Jesse B. Semple, a humorous character who speaks straightforwardly about the African American experience. The following selection, from Langston Hughes's* Selected Poems *(1926), offers sound advice to youth in any generation: Life is a constant struggle.*

Well, son, I'll tell you:
Life for me ain't been no crystal stair.
It's had tacks in it,
And splinters,
And boards torn up,   5
And places with no carpet on the floor—
Bare.

> But all the time
> I'se been a-climbin' on,
> And reachin' landin's,   10
> And turnin' corners,
> And sometimes goin' in the dark
> Where there ain't been no light.
> So boy, don't you turn back.
> Don't you set down on the steps   15
> 'Cause you finds it's kinder hard.
> Don't you fall now—
> For I'se still goin', honey.
> I'se still climbin',
> And life for me ain't been no crystal stair.   20

Discussion Questions

1. Other than the obvious relationship between mother and son, what other relationship(s) does the poem suggest?
2. Why do you think the author uses a colon in the first line?
3. How do the images of crystal stairs and torn-up stairs symbolize one's struggle in life?
4. What is the mother's advice to the son?
5. How is the mother a role model for her son?
6. How does the mother feel about facing obstacles?
7. How does Hughes use comparison and contrast in the poem?
8. Do you think the author's use of dialect is effective? Why or why not?

Writing Assignments

1. In an essay, write about an image, such as a river or a tree, that helps describe your life.
2. In an essay, discuss some useful advice you once received from your mother or from some other elder.
3. In an essay, describe a time when you decided not to follow the advice of one of your parents. Also discuss the consequences of your decision.

SUCH A PARADISE THAT I LIVED

Jamaica Kincaid

Jamaica Kincaid (1949–   ) was born in St. John's, Antigua, to a Carib-Indian mother from Dominica. In 1966, she came to the United States to complete her education and decided to stay. She has written for such magazines as Ms., *the* New Yorker, Rolling Stone, *and* Paris Review. *Her works include* At the Bottom of the River *(1983) and her most recent novel is* Lucy *(1991). The following excerpt, taken from her second book* Annie John *(1985), is a semi-autobiographical account of the warm and loving relationship that exists among a young girl, her mother, and her father.*

Vocabulary

chemise   (1)   a loose-fitting dress

From time to time, my mother would fix on a certain place in our house and give it a good cleaning. If I was at home when she happened to do this, I was at her side, as usual. When she did this with the trunk, it was a tremendous pleasure, for after she had removed all the things from the trunk, and aired them out, and changed the camphor balls,[1] and then refolded the things and put them back in their places in the trunk, as she held each thing in her hand she would tell me a story about myself. Sometimes I knew the story first hand, for I could remember the incident quite well; sometimes what she told me had happened when I was too young to know anything; and sometimes it happened before I was even born. Whichever way, I knew exactly what she would say, for I had heard it so many times before, but I never got tired of it. For instance, the flowers on the chemise, the first garment I wore after being born, were not put on correctly, and that is because when my mother was embroidering them I kicked so much that her hand was unsteady. My mother said that usually when I kicked around in her stomach and she told me to stop I would, but on that day I paid no attention at all. When she told me this story, she

[1] camphor balls   (1)   Crystalline balls used to keep away insects.

119

would smile at me and say, "You see, even then you were hard to manage." It pleased me to think that, before she could see my face, my mother spoke to me in the same way she did now. On and on my mother would go. No small part of my life was so unimportant that she hadn't made a note of it, and now she would tell it to me over and over again. I would sit next to her and she would show me the very dress I wore on the day I bit another child my age with whom I was playing. "Your biting phase," she called it. Or the day she warned me not to play around the coal pot, because I liked to sing to myself and dance around the fire. Two seconds later, I fell into the hot coals, burning my elbows. My mother cried when she saw that it wasn't serious, and now, as she told me about it, she would kiss the little black patches of scars on my elbows.

As she told me the stories, I sometimes sat at her side,   2
leaning against her, or I would crouch on my knees behind her back and lean over her shoulder. As I did this, I would occasionally sniff at her neck, or behind her ears, or at her hair. She smelled sometimes of lemons, sometimes of sage, sometimes of roses, sometimes of bay leaf. At times I would no longer hear what it was she was saying; I just liked to look at her mouth as it opened and closed over words, or as she laughed. How terrible it must be for all the people who had no one to love them so and no one whom they loved so, I thought. My father, for instance. When he was a little boy, his parents, after kissing him goodbye and leaving him with his grandmother, boarded a boat and sailed to South America. He never saw them again, though they wrote to him and sent him presents—packages of clothes on his birthday and at Christmas. He then grew to love his grandmother, and she loved him, for she took care of him and worked hard at keeping him well fed and clothed. From the beginning, they slept in the same bed, and as he became a young man they continued to do so. When he was no longer in school and had started working, every night, after he and his grandmother had eaten their dinner, my father would go off to visit his friends. He would then return home at around midnight and fall asleep next to his grandmother. In the morning, his grandmother would awake at half past five or so, a half hour before my father, and prepare his bath and breakfast and make everything proper and ready for him, so that at seven o'clock sharp he stepped out the door off to work. One morning, though, he overslept, because his grandmother didn't wake him up. When he awoke, she was still lying next to

him. When he tried to wake her, he couldn't. She had died lying next to him sometime during the night. Even though he was overcome with grief, he built her coffin and made sure she had a nice funeral. He never slept in that bed again, and shortly afterward he moved out of that house. He was eighteen years old then.

When my father first told me this story, I threw myself at 　3 him at the end of it, and we both started to cry—he just a little, I quite a lot. It was a Sunday afternoon; he and my mother and I had gone for a walk in the botanical gardens. My mother had wandered off to look at some strange kind of thistle, and we could see her as she bent over the bushes to get a closer look and reach out to touch the leaves of the plant. When she returned to us and saw that we had both been crying, she started to get quite worked up, but my father quickly told her what had happened and she laughed at us and called us her little fools. But then she took me in her arms and kissed me, and she said that I needn't worry about such a thing as her sailing off or dying and leaving me all alone in the world. But if ever after that I saw my father sitting alone with a faraway look on his face, I was filled with pity for him. He had been alone in the world all that time, what with his mother sailing off on a boat with his father and his never seeing her again, and then his grandmother dying while lying next to him in the middle of the night. It was more than anyone should have to bear. I loved him so and wished that I had a mother to give him, for, no matter how much my own mother loved him, it could never be the same.

When my mother got through with the trunk, and I had 　4 heard again and again just what I had been like and who had said what to me at what point in my life, I was given my tea—a cup of cocoa and a buttered bun. My father by then would return home from work, and he was given his tea. As my mother went around preparing our supper, picking up clothes from the stone heap, or taking clothes off the clothesline, I would sit in a corner of our yard and watch her. She never stood still. Her powerful legs carried her from one part of the yard to the other, and in and out of the house. Sometimes she might call out to me to go and get some thyme or basil or some other herb for her, for she grew all her herbs in little pots that she kept in a corner of our little garden. Sometimes when I gave her the herbs, she might stoop down and kiss me on my lips and then on my neck. It was in such a paradise that I lived.

Discussion Questions

1. How does cleaning become a time of bonding for Annie and her mother?
2. What kind of relationship exists among Annie, her mother, and her father?
3. How does the story of Annie's paternal great-grandmother relate to the rest of the story?
4. Why does Annie admire her mother?
5. What strategy (or strategies) does Kincaid use to convince her readers that she lived in a paradise as a young child?
6. How effective is Kincaid's placement of her thesis as the last sentence in the essay?

Writing Assignments

1. Write an essay about a special time in your childhood.
2. In an essay, recount a special bonding time between you and someone you love.
3. Write an essay about a memorable cbject that belongs to you or your family.

THOSE WINTER SUNDAYS

Robert Hayden

Born in Detroit, Michigan, Robert Hayden (1913–1980) attended Wayne State University as an undergraduate and received his M.A. from the University of Michigan. He taught English at Fisk University and at the University of Michigan. Hayden published the following books of poetry: Heart-Shape in the Dust *(1940),* A Ballad of Remembrance *(1962),* Selected Poems *(1966), and* Words in the Mourning Time *(1971). Some of his most memorable poems are those concerning slavery that appear in the 1966 volume: "Runagate Runagate," "Middle Passage," and "Frederick Douglass." The following selection, first published in* Angels and Accents: New and Selected Poems *(1975), recounts an African American youth's recollection of his harsh, but loving childhood environment.*

Vocabulary

chronic (9)   occurring frequently, continuing for long periods of time

austere (14)   strict or harsh

> Sundays too my father got up early
> and put his clothes on in the blueblack cold,
> then with cracked hands that ached
> from labor in the weekday weather made
> banked fires blaze. No one ever thanked him.   5
> I'd wake and hear the cold splintering, breaking.
> When the rooms were warm, he'd call,
> and slowly I would rise and dress,
> fearing the chronic angers of that house,
> Speaking indifferently to him,   10
> who had driven out the cold
> and polished my good shoes as well.
> What did I know, what did I know
> of love's austere and lonely offices?

Discussion Questions

1. What is the relationship between the speaker of the poem (the persona) and his father?

2. What kind of man is the persona's father?

3. What is the meaning of the line, "speaking indifferently to him"?

4. What is the meaning of the speaker's statement, "I would rise and dress, fearing the chronic angers of that house"?

5. What does the speaker realize now that he did not realize as a young child?

6. How is illustration used effectively to show the father's love is one that is demonstrated, not stated?

7. How effective is Hayden's use of a question to end his poem?

Writing Assignments

1. Often, appreciation for others' good deeds on your behalf comes well after the deeds are done. Write an essay discussing this idea.

2. Think of a pleasant time in your past and write an essay describing it.

3. In an essay, discuss the feelings you have (or once had) about an idol or role model.

INTEGRATED HOUSING: AN EXPLODED DREAM?

Lorraine Hansberry

Born in Chicago, Illinois, Lorraine Hansberry (1930–1965) became interested in the theatre while still in high school. She studied stage design and drama from 1948 to 1950 at the University of Wisconsin. Her first play, A Raisin in the Sun, *from which the following selection is taken, won the New York Drama Critics' Circle Award for best play of 1959. She was the first African American playwright to win this award. In 1973, the play was revived as a musical and won a Tony Award. Her other play,* The Sign in Sidney Brustein's Window, *was produced in 1965. Hansberry died of cancer at the young age of 34. "Integrated Housing: An Exploded Dream?" concerns the Younger family's joyous anticipation of moving to a better neighborhood, but this joy is dampened by the news that the "better neighborhood" does not want "Negroes" living there.*

Vocabulary

exuberant	(5)	joyous
burlesque	(67)	comic theatrical entertainment
pantomime	(86)	communication by means of facial and body gestures

Act II, Scene 3

TIME *Saturday, moving day, one week later.*

Before the curtain rises, RUTH's *voice, a strident, dramatic church alto, cuts through the silence.*

It is, in the darkness, a triumphant surge, a penetrating statement of expectation: "Oh, Lord, I don't feel no ways tired! Children, oh, glory hallelujah!"

As the curtain rises we see that RUTH *is alone in the living room, finishing up the family's packing. It is moving day. She is nailing crates and tying cartons.* BENEATHA *enters, carrying a guitar case, and watches her exuberant sister-in-law.*

RUTH HEY!
BENEATHA (*Putting away the case*) Hi.

RUTH (*Pointing at a package*) Honey—look in that package there and see what I found on sale this morning at the South Center. (RUTH *gets up and moves to the package and draws out some curtains*) Lookahere—hand-turned hems!

BENEATHA How do you know the window size out there?

RUTH (*Who hadn't thought of that*) Oh—Well, they bound to fit   5
something in the whole house. Anyhow, they was too good a bargain to pass up. (RUTH *slaps her head, suddenly remembering something*) Oh, Bennie—I meant to put a special note on that carton over there. That's your mama's good china and she wants 'em to be very careful with it.

BENEATHA I'll do it.

(BENEATHA *finds a piece of paper and starts to draw large letters on it*)

RUTH You know what I'm going to do soon as I get in that new house?

BENEATHA What?

RUTH Honey—I'm going to run me a tub of water up to here . . . (*With her fingers practically up to her nostrils*) And I'm going to get in it—and I am going to sit . . . and sit . . . and sit in that hot water and the first person who knocks to tell *me* to hurry up and come out—

BENEATHA Gets shot at sunrise.   10

RUTH (*Laughing happily*) You said it, sister! (*Noticing how large* BENEATHA *is absent-mindedly making the note*) Honey, they ain't going to read that from no airplane.

BENEATHA (*Laughing herself*) I guess I always think things have more emphasis if they are big, somehow.

RUTH (*Looking up at her and smiling*) You and your brother seem to have that as a philosophy of life. Lord, that man—done changed so 'round here. You know—you know what we did last night? Me and Walter Lee?

BENEATHA What?

RUTH (*Smiling to herself*) We went to the movies. (*Looking at*   15
BENEATHA *to see if she understands*) We went to the movies. You know the last time me and Walter went to the movies together?

BENEATHA No.

RUTH Me neither. That's how long it been. (*Smiling again*) But we went last night. The picture wasn't much good, but that didn't seem to matter. We went—and we held hands.

BENEATHA Oh, Lord!

RUTH We held hands—and you know what?   20

BENEATHA What?

RUTH   When we come out of the show it was late and dark and all the stores and things was closed up . . . and it was kind of chilly and there wasn't many people on the streets . . . and we was still holding hands, me and Walter.

BENEATHA   You're killing me.

(WALTER *enters with a large package. His happiness is deep in him; he cannot keep still with his new-found exuberance. He is singing and wiggling and snapping his fingers. He puts his package in a corner and puts a phonographic record, which he has brought in with him, on the record player. As the music comes up he dances over to* RUTH *and tries to get her to dance with him. She gives in at last to his raunchiness and in a fit of giggling allows herself to be drawn into his mood and together they deliberately burlesque an old social dance of their youth)*

BENEATHA   (*Regarding them a long time as they dance, then drawing in her breath for a deeply exaggerated comment which she does not particularly mean*) Talk about—olddddddddddd-fashionedddddddd—Negroes!

WALTER   (*Stopping momentarily*) What kind of Negroes?

(*He says this in fun. He is not angry with her today, nor with anyone. He starts to dance with his wife again*)

BENEATHA   Old-fashioned.   25

WALTER   (*As he dances with* RUTH) You know, when these *New Negroes* have their convention—(*Pointing at his sister*)—that is going to be the chairman of the Committee on Unending Agitation. (*He goes on dancing, then stops*) Race, race, race! . . . Girl, I do believe you are the first person in the history of the entire human race to successfully brainwash yourself. (BE-NEATHA *breaks up and he goes on dancing. He stops again, enjoying his tease*) Damn, even the N double A C P takes a holiday sometimes! (BENEATHA *and* RUTH *laugh. He dances with* RUTH *some more and starts to laugh and stops and pantomimes someone over an operating table*) I can just see that chick someday looking down at some poor cat on an operating table before she starts to slice him, saying . . . (*Pulling his sleeves back maliciously*) "By the way what are your views on civil rights down there? . . ."

He laughs at her again and starts to dance happily. The bell sounds)

BENEATHA   Sticks and stones may break my bones but . . . words will never hurt me!

(BENEATHA *goes to the door and opens it as* WALTER *and* RUTH *go on with the clowning.* BENEATHA *is somewhat surprised to see a quiet-looking middle-aged white man in a business suit holding his hat and a briefcase in his hand and consulting a small piece of paper)*

MAN   Uh—how do you do, miss. I am looking for a Mrs.—*(He looks at the slip of paper)* Mrs. Lena Younger?

BENEATHA   *(Smoothing her hair with slight embarrassment)* Oh—yes, that's my mother. Excuse me. *(She closes the door and turns to quiet the other two)* Ruth! Brother! Somebody's here. *(Then she opens the door. The man casts a curious quick glance at all of them)* Uh—come in please.

MAN   *(Coming in)* Thank you.   30

BENEATHA   My mother isn't here just now. Is it business?

MAN   Yes . . . well, of a sort.

WALTER   *(Freely, the Man of the House)* Have a seat. I'm Mrs. Younger's son. I look after most of her business matters.

*(*RUTH *and* BENEATHA *exchange amused glances)*

MAN   *(Regarding* WALTER, *and sitting)* Well—My name is Karl Lindner . . .

WALTER   *(Stretching out his hand)* Walter Younger. This is my   35
wife—*(*RUTH *nods politely)*—and my sister.

LINDNER   How do you do.

WALTER   *(Amiably, as he sits himself easily on a chair, leaning with interest forward on his knees and looking expectantly into the newcomer's face)* What can we do for you, Mr. Lindner!

LINDNER   *(Some minor shuffling of the hat and briefcase on his knees)* Well—I am a representative of the Clybourne Park Improvement Association—

WALTER   *(Pointing)* Why don't you sit your things on the floor?

LINDNER   Oh—yes. Thank you. *(He slides the briefcase and hat   40
under the chair)* And as I was saying—I am from the Clybourne Park Improvement Association and we have had it brought to our attention at the last meeting that you people—or at least your mother—has bought a piece of residential property at—*(He digs for the slip of paper again)*—four o six Clybourne Street . . .

WALTER   That's right. Care for something to drink? Ruth, get Mr. Lindner a beer.

LINDNER   *(Upset for some reason)* Oh—no, really. I mean thank you very much, but no thank you.

RUTH   *(Innocently)* Some coffee?

LINDNER   Thank you, nothing at all.

*(*BENEATHA *is watching the man carefully)*

LINDNER Well, I don't know how much you folks know about   45
our organization. (*He is a gentle man; thoughtful and somewhat
labored in his manner*) It is one of these community organizations set up to look after—oh, you know, things like block up-
keep and special projects and we also have what we call our
New Neighbors Orientation Committee . . .
BENEATHA (*Drily*) Yes—and what do they do?
LINDNER (*Turning a little to her and then returning the main
force to* WALTER) Well—it's what you might call a sort of welcoming committee, I guess. I mean they, we, I'm the chairman of
the committee—go around and see the new people who move
into the neighborhood and sort of give them the lowdown on
the way we do things out in Clybourne Park.
BENEATHA (*With appreciation of the two meanings, which escape* RUTH *and* WALTER) Un-huh.
LINDNER And we also have the category of what the association
calls—(*He looks elsewhere*)—uh—special community problems . . .
BENEATHA Yes—and what are some of those?   50
WALTER Girl, let the man talk.
LINDNER (*With understated relief*) Thank you. I would sort of
like to explain this thing in my own way. I mean I want to ex-
plain to you in a certain way.
WALTER Go ahead.
LINDNER Yes. Well, I'm going to try to get right to the point. I'm
sure we'll all appreciate that in the long run.
BENEATHA Yes.   55
WALTER Be still now!
LINDNER Well—
RUTH (*Still innocently*) Would you like another chair—you don't
look comfortable.
LINDNER (*More frustrated than annoyed*) No, thank you very
much. Please. Well—to get right to the point I—(*A great breath,
and he is off at last*) I am sure you people must be aware of
some of the incidents which have happened in various parts of
the city when colored people have moved into certain areas—
(BENEATHA *exhales heavily and starts tossing a piece of fruit up
and down in the air*) Well—because we have what I think is going to be a unique type of organization in American community
life—not only do we deplore that kind of thing—but we are trying to do something about it. (BENEATHA *stops tossing and turns
with a new and quizzical interest to the man*) We feel—(*Gaining

confidence in his mission because of the interest in the faces of the people he is talking to)—we feel that most of the trouble in this world, when you come right down to it—(*He hits his knee for emphasis*)—most of the trouble exists because people just don't sit down and talk to each other.

RUTH   (*Nodding as she might in church, pleased with the*   60
remark) You can say that again, mister.

LINDNER   (*More encouraged by such affirmation*) That we don't try hard enough in this world to understand the other fellow's problem. The other guy's point of view.

RUTH   Now that's right.

(BENEATHA *and* WALTER *merely watch and listen with genuine interest*)

LINDNER   Yes—that's the way we feel out in Clybourne Park. And that's why I was elected to come here this afternoon and talk to you people. Friendly like, you know, the way people should talk to each other and see if we couldn't find some way to work this thing out. As I say, the whole business is a matter of *caring* about the other fellow. Anybody can see that you are a nice family of folks, hard working and honest I'm sure. (BENEATHA *frowns slightly, quizzically, her head tilted regarding him*) Today everybody knows what it means to be on the outside of *something.* And of course, there is always somebody who is out to take the advantage of people who don't always understand.

WALTER   What do you mean?

LINDNER   Well—you see our community is made up of people   65
who've worked hard as the dickens for years to build up that little community. They're not rich and fancy people; just hard-working, honest people who don't really have much but those little homes and a dream of the kind of community they want to raise their children in. Now, I don't say we are perfect and there is a lot wrong in some of the things they want. But you've got to admit that a man, right or wrong, has the right to want to have the neighborhood he lives in a certain kind of way. And at the moment the overwhelming majority of our people out there feel that people get along better, take more of a common interest in the life of the community, when they share a common background. I want you to believe me when I tell you that race prejudice simply doesn't enter into it. It is a matter of the people of Clybourne Park believing, rightly or wrongly, as I say, that for the happiness of all concerned that our Negro families are happier when they live in their own communities.

BENEATHA (*With a grand and bitter gesture*) This, friends, is the Welcoming Committee!

WALTER (*Dumfounded, looking at* LINDNER) Is this what you came marching all the way over here to tell us?

LINDNER Well, now we've been having a fine conversation. I hope you'll hear me all the way through.

WALTER (*Tightly*) Go ahead, man.

LINDNER You see—in the face of all things I have said, we are   70 prepared to make your family a very generous offer . . .

BENEATHA Thirty pieces and not a coin less!

WALTER Yeah?

LINDNER (*Putting on his glasses and drawing a form out of the briefcase*) Our association is prepared, through the collective effort of our people, to buy the house from you at a financial gain to your family.

RUTH Lord have mercy, ain't this the living gall!

WALTER All right, you through?   75

LINDNER Well, I want to give you the exact terms of the financial arrangement—

WALTER We don't want to hear no exact terms of no arrangements. I want to know if you got any more to tell us 'bout getting together?

LINDNER (*Taking off his glasses*) Well—I don't suppose that you feel . . .

WALTER Never mind how I feel—you got any more to say 'bout how people ought to sit down and talk to each other? . . . Get out of my house, man.

(*He turns his back and walks to the door*)

LINDNER (*Looking around at the hostile faces and reaching and*   80 *assembling his hat and briefcase*) Well—I don't understand why you people are reacting this way. What do you think you are going to gain by moving into a neighborhood where you just aren't wanted and where some elements—well—people can get awful worked up when they feel that their whole way of life and everything they've ever worked for is threatened.

WALTER Get out.

LINDNER (*At the door, holding a small card*) Well—I'm sorry it went like this.

WALTER Get out.

LINDNER (*Almost sadly regarding* WALTER) You just can't force people to change their hearts, son.

(*He turns and puts his card on a table and exits.* WALTER *pushes*

the door to with stinging hatred, and stands looking at it. RUTH
just sits and BENEATHA *just stands. They say nothing.*

. . . .

[*Later* WALTER's *friend* BOBO *visits and brings disturbing news.*]   85
RUTH   Why don't you answer the door, man?
WALTER   (*Suddenly bounding across the floor to her*) 'Cause
sometimes it hard to let the future begin! (*Stooping down in her
face*)
I got wings! You got Wings!
All God's children got wings!
(*He crosses to the door and throws it open. Standing there is a
very slight little man in a not too prosperous business suit and
with haunted frightened eyes and a hat pulled down tightly,
brim up, around his forehead.* WALTER *leans deep in the man's
face, still in his jubilance*)
When I get to heaven gonna put on my wings,
Gonna fly all over God's heaven . . .
(*The little man just stares at him*)
Heaven—
(*Suddenly he stops and looks past the little man into the empty
hallway*) Where's Willy, man?
BOBO   He ain't with me.
WALTER   (*Not disturbed*) Oh—come on in. You know my wife.
BOBO   (*Dumbly, taking off his hat*) Yes—h'you, Miss Ruth.
RUTH   (*Quietly, a mood apart from her husband already, seeing*   90
BOBO) Hello, Bobo.
WALTER   You right on time today . . . Right on time. That's the
way! (*He slaps* BOBO *on his back*) Sit down . . . lemme hear.
(RUTH *stands stiffly and quietly in back of them, as though some-
how she senses death, her eyes fixed on her husband*)
BOBO   (*His frightened eyes on the floor, his hat in his hands*)
Could I please get a drink of water, before I tell you about it,
Walter Lee?
(WALTER *does not take his eyes off the man.* RUTH *goes blindly to
the tap and gets a glass of water and brings it to* BOBO)
WALTER   There ain't nothing wrong, is there?
BOBO   Lemme tell you—
WALTER   Man—didn't nothing go wrong?   95
BOBO   Lemme tell you—Walter Lee. (*Looking at* RUTH *and talk-
ing to her more than to* WALTER) You know how it was. I got to tell
you how it was. I mean first I got to tell you how it was all the
way . . . I mean about the money I put in, Walter Lee . . .

WALTER (*With taut agitation now*) What about the money you put in?

BOBO Well—it wasn't much as we told you—me and Willy—(*He stops*) I'm sorry, Walter. I got a bad feeling about it. I got a real bad feeling about it . . .

WALTER Man, what you telling me about all this for? . . . Tell me what happened in Springfield . . .

BOBO Springfield.

RUTH (*Like a dead woman*) What was supposed to happen in Springfield?

BOBO (*To her*) This deal that me and Walter went into with Willy—Me and Willy was going to go down to Springfield and spread some money 'round so's we wouldn't have to wait so long for the liquor license . . . That's what we were going to do. Everybody said that was the way you had to do, understand, Miss Ruth?

WALTER Man—what happened down there?

BOBO (*A pitiful man, near tears*) I'm trying to tell you, Walter.

WALTER (*Screaming at him suddenly*) THEN TELL ME, GOD-DAMMIT . . . WHAT'S THE MATTER WITH YOU?

BOBO Man . . . I didn't go to no Springfield, yesterday.

WALTER (*Halted, life hanging in the moment*) Why not?

BOBO (*The long way, the hard way to tell*) 'Cause I didn't have no reasons to . . .

WALTER Man, what are you talking about!

BOBO I'm talking about the fact that when I got to the train station yesterday morning—eight o'clock like we planned . . . Man—*Willy didn't never show up.*

WALTER Why . . . where was he . . . where is he?

BOBO That's what I'm trying to tell you . . . I don't know . . . I waited six hours . . . (*Breaking into tears*) That was all the extra money I had in the world . . . (*Looking up at* WALTER *with the tears running down his face*) Man, *Willy is gone.*

WALTER Gone, what you mean Willy is gone? Gone where? You mean he went by himself. You mean he went off to Springfield by himself—to take care of getting the license—(*Turns and looks anxiously at* RUTH) You mean maybe he didn't want too many people in on the business down there? (*Looks to* RUTH *again, as before*) You know Willy got his own ways. (*Looks back to* BOBO) Maybe you was late yesterday and he just went on down there without you. Maybe—maybe—he's been callin' you at home tryin' to tell you what happened or something. Maybe—maybe—he just got sick. He's somewhere—he's got to be somewhere. We just got to find him—me and you got to find him. (*Grabs* BOBO *senselessly by the collar and starts to shake him*) We got to!

BOBO (*In sudden angry, frightened agony*) What's the matter with you, Walter! *When a cat take off with your money he don't leave you no maps!*

WALTER (*Turning madly, as though he is looking for* WILLY *in the very room*) Willy! . . . Willy . . . don't do it . . . Please don't do it . . . Man, not with that money . . . Man, please not with that money . . . Oh, God . . . Don't let it be true . . . (*He is wandering around, crying out for* WILLY *and looking for him or perhaps for help from God*) Man . . . I trusted you . . . Man, I put my life in your hands . . . (*He starts to crumble down on the floor as* RUTH *just covers her face in horror,* MAMA *opens the door and comes into the room, with* BENEATHA *behind her*) Man . . . (*He starts to pound the floor with his fists, sobbing wildly*) *That money is made out of my father's flesh* . . . 115

BOBO (*Standing over him helplessly*) I'm sorry, Walter . . . (*Only* WALTER'S *sobs reply.* BOBO *puts on his hat*) I had my life staked on this deal, too . . .

(*He exits*)

MAMA (*To* WALTER) Son—(*She goes to him, bends down to him, talks to his bent head*) Son . . . Is it gone? Son, I gave you sixty-five hundred dollars. Is it gone? All of it? Beneatha's money too?

WALTER (*Lifting his head slowly*) Mama . . . I never . . . went to the bank at all . . .

MAMA (*Not wanting to believe him*) You mean . . . your sister's school money . . . you used that too . . . Walter?

WALTER Yessss! . . . All of it . . . It's all gone . . . 120

(*There is total silence,* RUTH *stands with her face covered with her hands;* BENEATHA *leans forlornly against a wall, fingering a piece of red ribbon from the mother's gift.* MAMA *stops and looks at her son without recognition and then, quite without thinking about it, starts to beat him senselessly in the face.* BENEATHA *goes to them and stops it*)

BENEATHA Mama!

(MAMA *stops and looks at both of her children and rises slowly and wanders vaguely, aimlessly away from them*)

MAMA I seen . . . him . . . night after night . . . come in . . . and look at that rug . . . and then look at me . . . the red showing in his eyes . . . the veins moving in his head . . . I seen him grow thin and old before he was forty . . . working

and working and working like somebody's old horse . . .
killing himself . . . and you—you give it all away in a day . . .
BENEATHA Mama—
MAMA Oh, God . . . (*She looks up at Him*) Look down here—
and show me the strength.
BENEATHA Mama—
MAMA (*Folding over*) Strength . . .
BENEATHA (*Plaintively*) Mama . . .   125
MAMA Strength!

CURTAIN

Discussion Questions

1. What is the mood of the Younger family before Mr. Lindner's visit?
   Use specific examples from the play to support your answer.
2. What is the Clybourne Park Improvement Association?
3. What proposal does Mr. Lindner have for the Younger family?
4. What are the two strategies Mr. Lindner uses to persuade the
   Younger family not to move?
5. How do Ruth, Walter, and Beneatha react to Mr. Lindner's offer?
6. What bad news does Bobo give Walter Lee?
7. To develop her theme, Hansberry uses many rhetorical strategies, including illustration, comparison and contrast, and cause
   and effect. How can you argue that cause and effect is the dominant strategy?
8. How would a poem or short story about the Younger family differ
   from this play?

Writing Assignments

1. Write an essay describing a time when you had planned for
   something and, at the last minute, your plans were ruined.
2. Write an essay describing the differences between two neighborhoods in your city.
3. In an essay, recount an incident when some type of discrimination prevented you from realizing your dream.

Student Essay:
THE POSITIVE ENVIRONMENT IN BLACK FEMALE-HEADED FAMILIES

Camille Gray

In recent years, there has been a substantial increase in the number of families headed by single black females. This increase can be attributed to social factors such as divorce, separation, a shortage of eligible black men to marry, and an increase in the number of single women with children. Much negative attention, mostly from the media, has been given to families headed by black females. The negative images displayed on television and in newspapers and magazines tend to concentrate on poor black families who are either receiving some form of assistance from a federal or state agency or who are living well below the U.S. poverty level. All too often these negative images dominate how the black female-headed family is viewed. However, what the media fails to acknowledge are the positive aspects of black female-headed households. 1

The current trend of females heading families in the black community can be looked at as a method of adaptability and survival for black families in the United States. In many cases, this survival strategy has had positive results. For example, contrary to popular belief, the majority of black female-headed families offer nurturing and supportive environments for the children who are in them. Evidence shows that even though a male is not present in the home, children can be and are socialized to function effectively in mainstream American society. 2

Natural support systems help make the black female-headed family environment one that is nurturing and supportive. A natural support system can be both inside and outside of the household. The functions of this support system include, but are not limited to, the socialization of the children, providing care for younger children, disciplining children, and teaching age and sex roles to children. This natural support system consists of, but is not limited to, close and distant relatives, extended family, and close friends. This type of arrangement is beneficial to both the mother and the children for several reasons. For the child, the support system often provides role models who provide guidance in areas such as education and 3 religion. For the mother, this arrangement often provides much needed child care so that she can secure gainful employment to provide for her family.

Another important positive aspect of child-rearing prac-   4
tices within the context of the black female-headed household is the bonding between the mother and the children. This bonding is crucial because it has a tremendous impact on a child's behavior inside and outside of the home. Despite the claim made by some studies that there is a relationship between the number of parents in the household, parent-child bonding, and juvenile delinquency, children who are raised by hard-working black mothers are often well behaved, close to and protective of their mothers, and very responsible. For example, many children of eight and up fulfill responsibilities around the house that help the family function smoothly. Usually, the responsibilities are assigned according to a child's age and ability, not according to his or her gender.

Too often, black female-headed households are negatively   5
portrayed. However, instead of stereotyping these types of families and the mothers who run them, the media should commend black females who head households by working hard and raising disciplined and responsible children.

Discussion Questions

1. How are black female-headed families portrayed in the media?
2. In many of these families, what is the relationship between the mother and her children?
3. How do the children function in these families?
4. What is a "natural support system"?
5. How does the author think the media should portray black female-headed families?
6. How does Gray use both illustration and persuasion to support her thesis?
7. What type of ending does the author choose? What other ways could Gray have ended her essay?

Writing Assignments

1. Write an essay describing the type of family you grew up in.
2. In an essay, discuss whether or not you think there should be one type of family that serves as the model family for us all.

9

Male-Female Relationships

LIKE A WINDING SHEET

Ann Petry

Ann Petry (1911–), novelist and short story writer, was born in Old Saybrook, Connecticut. She is the author of a novella, In Darkness and Confusion *(1949); a children's book,* The Drugstore Cat *(1949); and three novels,* The Street *(1946),* Country Place *(1947), and* The Narrows *(1953). Most of her works contrast the city and the small town. "Like a Winding Sheet," (1945), one of her best known short stories, is about a man's struggle to control his rage.*

Vocabulary

enmeshed (85)   entangled

He had planned to get up before Mae did and surprise her by fixing breakfast. Instead he went back to sleep and she got out of bed so quietly he didn't know she wasn't there beside him until he woke up and heard the queer soft gurgle of water running out of the sink in the bathroom.   1

He knew he ought to get up but instead he put his arms across his forehead to shut the afternoon sunlight out of his eyes, pulled his legs up close to his body, testing them to see if the ache was still in them. 2

Mae had finished in the bathroom. He could tell because she never closed the door when she was in there and now the sweet smell of talcum powder was drifting down the hall and into the bedroom. Then he heard her coming down the hall. 3

"Hi, babe," she said affectionately. 4

"Hum," he grunted, and moved his arms away from his head, opened one eye. 5

"It's a nice morning." 6

"Yeah," he rolled over and the sheet twisted around him, outlining his thighs, his chest. "You mean afternoon, don't ya?" 7

Mae looked at the twisted sheet and giggled. 8

"Looks like a winding sheet," she said. "A shroud—." Laughter tangled with her words and she had to pause for a moment before she could continue. "You look like a huckle-berry—in a winding sheet—" 9

"That's no way to talk. Early in the day like this," he protested. 10

He looked at his arms silhouetted against the white of the sheets. They were inky black by contrast and he had to smile in spite of himself and he lay there smiling and savouring the sweet sound of Mae's giggling. 11

"Early?" She pointed a finger at the alarm clock on the table near the bed, and giggled again. "It's almost four o'clock. And if you don't spring up out of there you're going to be late again." 12

"What do you mean 'again'?" 13

"Twice last week. Three times the week before. And once the week before and—" 14

"I can't get used to sleeping in the day time," he said fret-fully. He pushed his legs out from under the covers experimen-tally. Some of the ache had gone out of them but they weren't really rested yet. "It's too light for good sleeping. And all that standing beats the hell out of my legs." 15

"After two years you oughtta be used to it," Mae said. 16

He watched her as she fixed her hair, powdered her face, slipping into a pair of blue denim overalls. She moved quickly and yet she didn't seem to hurry. 17

"You look like you'd had plenty of sleep," he said lazily. He had to get up but he kept putting the moment off, not wanting 18

to move, yet he didn't dare let his legs go completely limp because if he did he'd go back to sleep. It was getting later and
later but the thought of putting his weight on his legs kept him
lying there.

When he finally got up he had to hurry and he gulped his   19
breakfast so fast that he wondered if his stomach could possibly use food thrown at it at such a rate of speed. He was still
wondering about it as he and Mae were putting their coats on
in the hall.

Mae paused to look at the calendar. "It's the thirteenth,"   20
she said. Then a faint excitement in her voice. "Why it's Friday
the thirteenth." She had one arm in her coat sleeve and she
held it there while she stared at the calendar. "I oughtta stay
home," she said. "I shouldn't go otta the house."

"Aw don't be a fool," he said. "To-day's payday. And pay-   21
day is a good luck day everywhere, any way you look at it." And
as she stood hesitating he said, "Aw, come on."

And he was late for work again because they spent fifteen   22
minutes arguing before he could convince her she ought to go
to work just the same. He had to talk persuasively, urging her
gently and it took time. But he couldn't bring himself to talk to
her roughly or threaten to strike her like a lot of men might
have done. He wasn't made that way.

So when he reached the plant he was late and he had to   23
wait to punch the time clock because the day shift workers
were streaming out in long lines, in groups and bunches that
impeded his progress.

Even now just starting his work-day his legs ached. He   24
had to force himself to struggle past the out-going workers,
punch the time clock, and get the little cart he pushed around
all night because he kept toying with the idea of going home
and getting back in bed.

He pushed the cart out on the concrete floor, thinking that   25
if this was his plant he'd make a lot of changes in it. There
were too many standing up jobs for one thing. He'd figure out
some way most of 'em could be done sitting down and he'd put
a lot more benches around. And this job he had—this job that
forced him to walk ten hours a night, pushing this little cart,
well, he'd turn it into a sitting down job. One of those little
trucks they used around railroad stations would be good for a
job like this. Guys sat on a seat and the thing moved easily,
taking up little room and turning in hardly any space at all,
like on a dime.

He pushed the cart near the foreman. He never could re- 26
member to refer to her as the forelady even in his mind. It was
funny to have a woman for a boss in a plant like this one.

She was sore about something. He could tell by the way 27
her face was red and her eyes were half shut until they were
slits. Probably been out late and didn't get enough sleep. He
avoided looking at her and hurried a little, head down, as he
passed her though he couldn't resist stealing a glance at her
out of the corner of his eyes. He saw the edge of the light colored slacks she wore and the tip end of a big tan shoe.

"Hey, Johnson!" the woman said. 28

The machines had started full blast. The whirr and the 29
grinding made the building shake, made it impossible to hear
conversations. The men and women at the machines talked to
each other but looking at them from just a little distance away
they appeared to be simply moving their lips because you
couldn't hear what they were saying. Yet the woman's voice cut
across the machine sounds—harsh, angry.

He turned his head slowly. "Good Evenin', Mrs. Scott," he 30
said and waited.

"You're late again." 31

"That's right. My legs were bothering me." 32

The woman's face grew redder, angrier looking. "Half this 33
shift comes in late," she said. "And you're the worst one of all.
You're always late. Whatsa matter with ya?"

"It's my legs," he said. "Somehow they don't ever get 34
rested. I don't seem to get used to sleeping days. And I just
can't get started."

"Excuses. You guys always got excuses," her anger grew 35
and spread. "Every guy comes in here late always has an excuse. His wife's sick or his grandmother died or somebody in
the family had to go to the hospital," she paused, drew a deep
breath. "And the niggers are the worse. I don't care what's
wrong with your legs. You get in here on time. I'm sick of you
niggers—"

"You got the right to get mad," he interrupted softly. "You 36
got the right to cuss me four ways to Sunday but I ain't letting
nobody call me a nigger."

He stepped closer to her. His fists were doubled. His lips 37
were drawn back in a thin narrow line. A vein in his forehead
stood out swollen, thick.

And the woman backed away from him, not hurriedly but 38
slowly—two, three steps back.

"Aw, forget it," she said. "I didn't mean nothing by it. It   39
slipped out. It was a accident." The red of her face deepened
until the small blood vessels in her cheeks were purple. "Go on
and get to work," she urged. And she took three more slow
backward steps.

He stood motionless for a moment and then turned away   40
from the red lipstick on her mouth that made him remember
that the foreman was a woman. And he couldn't bring himself
to hit a woman. He felt a curious tingling in his fingers and he
looked down at his hands. They were clenched tight, hard,
ready to smash some of those small purple veins in her face.

· He pushed the cart ahead of him, walking slowly. When he   41
turned his head, she was staring in his direction, mopping her
forehead with a dark blue handkerchief. Their eyes met and
then they both looked away.

He didn't glance in her direction again but moved past the   42
long work benches, carefully collecting the finished parts, going
slowly and steadily up and down, back and forth the length of
the building and as he walked he forced himself to swallow his
anger, get rid of it.

And he succeeded so that he was able to think about what   43
had happened without getting upset about it. An hour went by
but the tension stayed in his hands. They were clenched and
knotted on the handles of the cart as though ready to aim a
blow.

And he thought he should have hit her anyway, smacked   44
her hard in the face, felt the soft flesh of her face give under the
hardness of his hands. He tried to make his hands relax by offering them a description of what it would have been like to
strike her because he had the queer feeling that his hands were
not exactly a part of him any more—they had developed a separate life of their own over which he had no control. So he dwelt
on the pleasure his hands would have felt—both of them cracking at her, first one and then the other. If he had done that his
hands would have felt good now—relaxed, rested.

And he decided that even if he'd lost his job for it he   45
should have let her have it and it would have been a long time,
maybe the rest of her life before she called anybody else a nigger.

The only trouble was he couldn't hit a woman. A woman   46
couldn't hit back the same way a man did. But it would have
been a deeply satisfying thing to have cracked her narrow lips
wide open with just one blow, beautifully timed and with all his

weight in back of it. That way he would have gotten rid of all the energy and tension his anger had created in him. He kept remembering how his heart had started pumping blood so fast he had felt it tingle even in the tips of his fingers.

With the approach of night, fatigue nibbled at him. The corner of his mouth dropped, the frown between his eyes deepened, his shoulders sagged; but his hands stayed tight and tense. As the hours dragged by he noticed that the women workers had started to snap and snarl at each other. He couldn't hear what they said because of the sound of machines but he could see the quick lip movements that sent words tumbling from the sides of their mouths. They gestured irritably with their hands and scowled as their mouths moved.   47

Their violent jerky motions told him that it was getting close on to quitting time but somehow he felt that the night still stretched ahead of him, composed of endless hours of steady walking on his aching legs. When the whistle finally blew he went on pushing the cart, unable to believe that it had sounded. The whirring of the machines died away to a murmur and he knew then that he'd really heard the whistle. He stood still for a moment filled with a relief that made him sigh.   48

Then he moved briskly, putting the cart in the store room, hurrying to take his place in the line forming before the paymaster. That was another thing he'd change, he thought. He'd have the pay envelopes handed to the people right at their benches so there wouldn't be ten or fifteen minutes lost waiting for the pay. He always got home about fifteen minutes late on payday. They did it better in the plant where Mae worked, brought the money right to them at their benches.   49

· He stuck his pay envelope in his pants' pocket and followed the line of workers heading for the subway in a slow moving stream. He glanced up at the sky. It was a nice night, the sky looked packed full to running over with stars. And he thought if he and Mae would go right to bed when they got home from work they'd catch a few hours of darkness for sleeping. But they never did. They fooled around—cooking and eating and listening to the radio and he always stayed in a big chair in the living room and went almost but not quite to sleep and when they finally got to bed it was five or six in the morning and daylight was already seeping around the edges of the sky.   50

He walked slowly, putting off the moment when he would have to plunge into the crowd hurrying toward the subway. It   51

was a long ride to Harlem and to-night the thought of it appalled him. He paused outside an all-night restaurant to kill
time, so that some of the first rush of workers would be gone
when he reached the subway.

The lights in the restaurant were brilliant, enticing. There   52
was life and motion inside. And as he looked through the window he thought that everything within range of his eyes
gleamed—the long imitation marble counter, the tall stools, the
white porcelain topped tables and especially the big metal coffee urn right near the window. Steam issued from its top and a
gas flame flickered under it—a lively, dancing, blue flame.

A lot of the workers from his shift—men and women—were   53
lining up near the coffee urn. He watched them walk to the
porcelain topped tables carrying steaming cups of coffee and he
saw that just the smell of the coffee lessened the fatigue lines
in their faces. After the first sip their faces softened, they
smiled, they began to talk and laugh.

On a sudden impulse he shoved the door open and joined   54
the line in front of the coffee urn. The line moved slowly. And as
he stood there the smell of the coffee, the sound of the laughter
and of the voices, helped dull the sharp ache in his legs.

He didn't pay any attention to the girl who was serving the   55
coffee at the urn. He kept looking at the cups in the hands of
the men who had been ahead of him. Each time a man stepped
out of the line with one of the thick white cups the fragrant
steam got in his nostrils. He saw that they walked carefully so
as not to spill a single drop. There was a froth of bubbles at the
top of each cup and he thought about how he would let the
bubbles break against his lips before he actually took a big
deep swallow.

Then it was his turn. "A cup of coffee," he said, just as he   56
had heard the others say.

The girl looked past him, put her hands up to her head   57
and gently lifted her hair away from the back of her neck, tossing her head back a little. "No more coffee for awhile," she said.

He wasn't certain he'd heard her correctly and he said,   58
"What?" blankly.

"No more coffee for awhile," she repeated.   59

There was silence behind him and then uneasy movement.   60
He thought someone would say something, ask why or protest,
but there was only silence and then a faint shuffling sound as
though the men standing behind him had simultaneously
shifted their weight from one foot to the other.

He looked at her without saying anything. He felt his hands 61
begin to tingle and the tingling went all the way down to his finger tips so that he glanced down at them. They were clenched
tight, hard, into fists. Then he looked at the girl again. What he
wanted to do was hit her so hard that the scarlet lipstick on her
mouth would smear and spread over her nose, her chin, out toward her cheeks, so hard that she would never toss her head
again and refuse a man a cup of coffee because he was black.

He estimated the distance across the counter and reached 62
forward, balancing his weight on the balls of his feet, ready to
let the blow go. And then his hands fell back down to his sides
because he forced himself to lower them, to unclench them and
make them dangle loose. The effort took his breath away because his hands fought against him. But he couldn't hit her.
He couldn't even now bring himself to hit a woman, not even
this one, who had refused him a cup of coffee with a toss of her
head. He kept seeing the gesture with which she had lifted the
length of her blond hair from the back of her neck as expres-
sive of her contempt for him.

When he went out the door he didn't look back. If he had 63
he would have seen the flickering blue flame under the shiny
coffee urn being extinguished. The line of men who had stood
behind him lingered a moment to watch the people drinking
coffee at the tables and then they left just as he had without
having had the coffee they wanted so badly. The girl behind the
counter poured water in the urn and swabbed it out and as she
waited for the water to run out she lifted her hair gently from
the back of her neck and tossed her head before she began
making a fresh lot of coffee.

But he walked away without a backward look, his head 64
down, his hands in his pockets, raging at himself and whatever
it was inside of him that had forced him to stand quiet and still
when he wanted to strike out.

The subway was crowded and he had to stand. He tried 65
grasping an overhead strap and his hands were too tense to
grip it. So he moved near the train door and stood there swaying back and forth with the rocking of the train. The roar of the
train beat inside his head, making it ache and throb, and the
pain in his legs clawed up into his groin so that he seemed to
be bursting with pain and he told himself that it was due to all
that anger-born energy that had piled up in him and not been
used and so it had spread through him like a poison—from his
feet and legs all the way up to his head.

Mae was in the house before he was. He knew she was   66
home before he put the key in the door of the apartment. The
radio was going. She had it tuned up loud and she was singing
along with it.

"Hello, Babe," she called out as soon as he opened the   67
door.

He tried to say "hello" and it came out half a grunt and   68
half sigh.

"You sure sound cheerful," she said.   69

She was in the bedroom and he went and leaned against   70
the door jamb. The denim overalls she wore to work were carefully draped over the back of a chair by the bed. She was
standing in front of the dresser, tying the sash of a yellow
housecoat around her waist and chewing gum vigorously as
she admired her reflection in the mirror over the dresser.

"Whatsa matter?" she said. "You get bawled out by the   71
boss or somep'n?"

"Just tired," he said slowly. "For God's sake do you have to   72
crack that gum like that?"

"You don't have to lissen to me," she said complacently.   73
She patted a curl in place near the side of her head and then
lifted her hair away from the back of her neck, ducking her
head forward and then back.

He winced away from the gesture. "What you got to be al-   74
ways fooling with your hair for?" he protested.

"Say, what's the matter with you, anyway?" she turned   75
away from the mirror to face him, put her hands on her hips.
"You ain't been in the house two minutes and you're picking on
me."

He didn't answer her because her eyes were angry and he   76
didn't want to quarrel with her. They'd been married too long
and got along too well and so he walked all the way into the
room and sat down in the chair by the bed and stretched his
legs out in front of him, putting his weight on the heels of his
shoes, leaning way back in the chair, not saying anything.

"Lissen," she said sharply. "I've got to wear those overalls   77
again tomorrow. You're going to get them all wrinkled up leaning against them like that."

He didn't move. He was too tired and his legs were throb-   78
bing now that he had sat down. Besides the overalls were already wrinkled and dirty, he thought. They couldn't help but be
for she'd worn them all week. He leaned further back in the
chair.

"Come on, get up," she ordered.   79

"Oh, what the hell," he said wearily and got up from the   80
chair. "I'd just as soon live in a subway. There'd be just as
much place to sit down."

He saw that her sense of humor was struggling with her   81
anger. But her sense of humor won because she giggled.

"Aw, come on and eat," she said. There was a coaxing note   82
in her voice. "You're nothing but a old hungry nigger trying to
act tough and—" she paused to giggle and then continued,
"You—"

He had always found her giggling pleasant and deliber-   83
ately said things that might amuse her and then waited, listening for the delicate sound to emerge from her throat. This time
he didn't even hear the giggle. He didn't let her finish what she
was saying. She was standing close to him and that funny tingling started in his finger tips, went fast up his arms and sent
his fist shooting straight for her face.

There was the smacking sound of soft flesh being struck   84
by a hard object and it wasn't until she screamed that he realized he had hit her in the mouth—so hard that the dark red
lipstick had blurred and spread over her full lips, reaching up
toward the tip of her nose, down toward her chin, out toward
her cheeks.

The knowledge that he had struck her seeped through him   85
slowly and he was appalled but he couldn't drag his hands
away from her face. He kept striking her and he thought with
horror that something inside him was holding him, binding
him to this act, wrapping and twisting about him so that he
had to continue it. He had lost all control over his hands. And
he groped for a phrase, a word, something to describe what
this thing was like that was happening to him and he thought
it was like being enmeshed in a winding sheet—that was it—
like a winding sheet. And even as the thought formed in his
mind his hands reached for her face again and yet again.

Discussion Questions

1. What type of person does Johnson appear to be at the beginning
   of the story?
2. What is the relationship between Johnson and Mrs. Scott, the
   forelady?
3. Why does Johnson refrain from hitting the two white women
   even though he wants to do so very much?

4. Why does Johnson beat his wife? Why is he unable to stop beating her once he starts? Does this behavior surprise you? Why or why not?

5. Is there evidence to suggest that Johnson's behavior is out of character? Why or why not?

6. What is the significance of the story's title?

7. How does Petry use comparison and contrast in this story?

8. What are some of the transitions that help the reader move smoothly through the story?

Writing Assignments

1. Write an essay describing the consequences of your (or someone else's) uncontrolled anger.

2. Write an essay describing a time when you or someone you know did something completely out of character. Discuss what you feel caused such an action.

3. Write an essay discussing anger, stress, frustration, abuse, or violence.

A SUMMER TRAGEDY

Arna Bontemps

Arna Wendell Bontemps (1902–1973), one of the leading figures of the Harlem Renaissance and the first African American historical novelist, was born in Alexandria, Louisiana. His works include a romantic novel, God Sends Sunday *(1931), which he and Countee Cullen adapted for Broadway in 1946 as "Saint Louis Woman";* Black Thunder *(1936) with Langston Hughes;* The Poetry of the Negro: 1746–1946 *(1949);* Book of Negro Folklore *(1958); a collection of poetry,* Personals *(1963); and a book of stories and essays,* The Old South *(1973). In this short story, "A Summer Tragedy," a couple works together to find a solution to their problems.*

Vocabulary

obstinate	(1)	difficult to manage
gnarled	(5)	twisted
negligible	(5)	barely existing, having little value
semblance	(8)	likeness
stupor	(25)	daze
fodder	(72)	straw and hay used as food for horses and cattle
anguish	(105)	great mental or physical pain
cavernous	(106)	hollow

Old Jeff Patton, the black share farmer, fumbled with his bow   1
tie. His fingers trembled and the high, stiff collar pinched his
throat. A fellow loses his hand for such vanities after thirty or
forty years of simple life. Once a year, or maybe twice if there's
a wedding among his kinfolks, he may spruce up; but generally
fancy clothes do nothing but adorn the wall of the big room
and feed the moths. That had been Jeff Patton's experience. He
had not worn his stiff-bosomed shirt more than a dozen times
in all his married life. His swallow-tailed coat[1] lay on the bed
beside him, freshly brushed and pressed, but it was as full of
holes as the overalls in which he worked on weekdays. The

---

[1] swallow-tailed coat (1)   A man's full-dress coat that tapers down in two long tails in the back.

moths had used it badly. Jeff twisted his mouth into a hideous toothless grimace as he contended with the obstinate bow. He stamped his good foot and decided to give up the struggle.

"Jennie," he called.   2

"What's that, Jeff?" His wife's shrunken voice came out of   3
the adjoining room like an echo. It was hardly bigger than a whisper.

"I reckon you'll have to he'p me wid this heah bow tie,   4
baby," he said meekly. "Dog if I can hitch it up."

Her answer was not strong enough to reach him, but   5
presently the old woman came to the door, feeling her way with a stick. She had a wasted, dead-leaf appearance. Her body, as scrawny and gnarled as a string bean, seemed less than nothing in the ocean of frayed and faded petticoats that surrounded her. These hung an inch or two above the tops of her heavy unlaced shoes and showed little grotesque piles where the stockings had fallen down from her negligible legs.

"You oughta could do a heap mo' wid a thing like that'n   6
me—beingst as you got yo' good sight."

"Looks like I oughta could," he admitted. "But my fingers   7
is gone democrat on me. I get all mixed up in the looking glass an' can't tell wicha way to twist the devilish thing."

Jennie sat on the side of the bed, and old Jeff Patton got   8
down on one knee while she tied the bow knot. It was a slow and painful ordeal for each of them in this position. Jeff's bones cracked, his knee ached, and it was only after a half dozen attempts that Jennie worked a semblance of a bow into the tie.

"I got to dress maself now," the old woman whispered.   9
"These is ma old shoes an' stockings, and I ain't so much as unwrapped ma dress."

"Well, don't worry 'bout me no mo', baby," Jeff said. "That   10
'bout finishes me. All I gotta do now is slip on that old coat 'n ves' an' I'll be fixed to leave."

Jennie disappeared again through the dim passage into   11
the shed room. Being blind was no handicap to her in that black hole. Jeff heard the cane placed against the wall beside the door and knew that his wife was on easy ground. He put on his coat, took a battered top hat from the bed post, and hobbled to the front door. He was ready to travel. As soon as Jennie could get on her Sunday shoes and her old black silk dress, they would start.

Outside the tiny log house, the day was warm and mellow   12
with sunshine. A host of wasps were humming with busy excitement in the trunk of a dead sycamore. Gray squirrels were
searching through the grass for hickory nuts, and blue jays were
in the trees hopping from branch to branch. Pine woods
stretched away to the left like a black sea. Among them were
scattered scores of log houses like Jeff's, houses of black share
farmers.[2] Cows and pigs wandered freely among the trees. There
was no danger of loss. Each farmer knew his own stock and
knew his neighbor's as well as he knew his neighbor's children.

Down the slope to the right were the cultivated acres on   13
which the colored folks worked. They extended to the river,
more than two miles away, and they were today green with the
unmade cotton crop. A tiny thread of a road, which passed directly in front of Jeff's place, ran through these green fields like
a pencil mark.

Jeff, standing outside the door, with his absurd hat in his   14
left hand, surveyed the wide scene tenderly. He had been forty-
five years on these acres. He loved them with the unexplained
affection that others have for the countries to which they belong.

The sun was hot on his head, his collar still pinched his   15
throat, and the Sunday clothes were intolerably hot. Jeff transferred the hat to his right hand and began fanning with it. Suddenly the whisper that was Jennie's voice came out of the shed
room.

"You can bring the car round front whilst you's waitin'," it   16
said feebly. There was a tired pause; then it added, "I'll soon be
fixed to go."

"A'right, baby," Jeff answered. "I'll get it in a minute."   17

But he didn't move. A thought struck him that made his   18
mouth fall open. The mention of the car brought to his mind,
with new intensity, the trip he and Jennie were about to take.
Fear came into his eyes; excitement took his breath. Lord, Jesus!

"Jeff. . . . O Jeff," the old woman's whisper called.   19

He awakened with a jolt. "Hunh, baby?"   20

"What you doin'?"   21

"Nuthin. Jes studyin'. I jes been turnin' things round 'n   22
round in ma mind."

---

[2] share farmers (12)   Farmers who work the land for a share of the crop.

"You could be gettin' the car," she said.   23

"Oh yes, right away, baby."   24

He started round to the shed, limping heavily on his bad   25
leg. There were three frizzly chickens in the yard. All his other
chickens had been killed or stolen recently. But the frizzly
chickens had been saved somehow. That was fortunate indeed,
for these curious creatures had a way of devouring "poison"
from the yard and in that way protecting against conjure and
black luck and spells. But even the frizzly chickens seemed
now to be in a stupor. Jeff thought they had some ailment; he
expected all three of them to die shortly.

The shed in which the old T-model Ford stood was only a   26
grass roof held up by four corner poles. It had been built by
tremulous hands at a time when the little rattletrap car had
been regarded as a peculiar treasure. And miraculously, despite wind and downpour, it still stood.

Jeff adjusted the crank and put his weight upon it. The   27
engine came to life with a sputter and bang that rattled the old
car from radiator to tail light. Jeff hopped into the seat and put
his foot on the accelerator. The sputtering and banging increased. The rattling became more violent. That was good. It
was good banging, good sputtering and rattling, and it meant
that the aged car was still in running condition. She could be
depended on for this trip.

Again Jeff's thought halted as if paralyzed. The suggestion   28
of the trip fell into the machinery of his mind like a wrench. He
felt dazed and weak. He swung the car out into the yard, made
a half turn, and drove around to the front door. When he took
his hands off the wheel, he noticed that he was trembling violently. He cut off the motor and climbed to the ground to wait
for Jennie.

A few minutes later she was at the window, her voice rat-   29
tling against the pane like a broken shutter.

"I'm ready, Jeff."   30

He did not answer, but limped into the house and took her   31
by the arm. He led her slowly through the big room, down the
step, and across the yard.

"You reckon I'd oughta lock the do'?" he asked softly.   32

They stopped and Jennie weighed the question. Finally   33
she shook her head.

"Ne' mind the do'," she said. "I don't see no cause to lock   34
up things."

"You right," Jeff agreed. "No cause to lock up."   35

Jeff opened the door and helped his wife into the car. A   36
quick shudder passed over him. Jesus! Again he trembled.

"How come you shaking so?" Jennie whispered.   37

"I don't know," he said.   38

"You mus' be scairt, Jeff."   39

"No, baby, I ain't scairt."   40

He slammed the door after her and went around to crank   41
up again. The motor started easily. Jeff wished that it had not
been so responsive. He would have liked a few more minutes in
which to turn things around in his head. As it was, with Jennie
chiding him about being afraid, he had to keep going. He
swung the car into the little pencilmark road and started off toward the river, driving very slowly, very cautiously.

Chugging across the green countryside, the small battered   42
Ford seemed tiny indeed. Jeff felt a familiar excitement, a thrill,
as they came down the first slope to the immense levels on
which the cotton was growing. He could not help reflecting that
the crops were good. He knew what that meant, too; he had
made forty-five of them with his own hands. It was true that he
had worn out nearly a dozen mules, but that was the fault of
old man Stevenson, the owner of the land. Major Stevenson
had the odd notion that one mule was all a share farmer
needed to work a thirty-acre plot. It was an expensive notion,
the way it killed mules from overwork, but the old man held to
it. Jeff thought it killed a good many share farmers as well as
mules, but he had no sympathy for them. He had always been
strong, and he had been taught to have no patience with weakness in men. Women or children might be tolerated if they were
puny, but a weak man was a curse. Of course, his own children—

Jeff's thought halted there. He and Jennie never men-   43
tioned their dead children any more. And naturally, he did not
wish to dwell upon them in his mind. Before he knew it, some
remark would slip out of his mouth and that would make Jennie feel blue. Perhaps she would cry. A woman like Jennie
could not easily throw off the grief that comes from losing five
grown children within two years. Even Jeff was still staggered
by the blow. His memory had not been much good recently. He
frequently talked to himself. And, although he had kept it a secret, he knew that his courage had left him. He was terrified by
the least unfamiliar sound at night. He was reluctant to ven-
ture far from home in the daytime. And that habit of trembling
when he felt fearful was now far beyond his control. Sometimes

he became afraid and trembled without knowing what had frightened him. The feeling would just come over him like a chill.

The car rattled slowly over the dusty road. Jennie sat erect   44
and silent with a little absurd hat pinned to her hair. Her useless eyes seemed very large, very white in their deep sockets.
Suddenly Jeff heard her voice, and he inclined his head to
catch the words.

"Is we passed Delia Moore's house yet?" she asked.   45

"Not yet," he said.   46

"You must be drivin' mighty slow, Jeff."   47

"We just as well take our time, baby."   48

There was a pause. A little puff of steam was coming out   49
of the radiator of the car. Heat wavered above the hood. Delia
Moore's house was nearly half a mile away. After a moment
Jennie spoke again.

"You ain't really scairt, is you, Jeff?"   50

"Nah, baby, I ain't scairt."   51

"You know how we agreed—we gotta keep on goin'."   52

Jewels of perspiration appeared on Jeff's forehead. His   53
eyes rounded, blinked, became fixed on the road.

"I don't know," he said with a shiver. "I reckon it's the only   54
thing to do."

"Hm."   55

A flock of guinea fowls, pecking in the road, were scattered   56
by the passing car. Some of them took to their wings; others
hid under bushes. A blue jay, swaying on a leafy twig, was an-
noying a roadside squirrel. Jeff held an even speed till he came
near Delia's place. Then he slowed down noticeably.

Delia's house was really no house at all, but an aban-   57
doned store building converted into a dwelling. It sat near a
crossroads, beneath a single black cedar tree. There Delia, a
cattish old creature of Jennie's age, lived alone. She had been
there more years than anybody could remember, and long ago
had won the disfavor of such women as Jennie. For in her
young days Delia had been gayer, yellower, and saucier than
seemed proper in those parts. Her ways with menfolks had
been dark and suspicious. And the fact that she had had as
many husbands as children did not help her reputation.

"Yonder's old Delia," Jeff said as they passed.   58

"What she doin'?"   59

"Jes sittin' in the do'," he said.   60

"She see us?"   61

"Hm," Jeff said. "Musta did."   62

That relieved Jennie. It strengthened her to know that her 63
old enemy had seen her pass in her best clothes. That would
give the old she-devil something to chew her gums and fret
about. Jennie thought. Wouldn't she have a fit if she didn't find
out? Old evil Delia! This would be just the thing for her. It
would pay her back for being so evil. It would also pay her,
Jennie thought, for the way she used to grin at Jeff—long ago,
when her teeth were good.

The road became smooth and red, and Jeff could tell by 64
the smell of the air that they were nearing the river. He could
see the rise where the road turned and ran along parallel to the
stream. The car chugged on monotonously. After a long silent
spell, Jennie leaned against Jeff and spoke.

"How many bale o' cotton you think we got standin'?" she 65
said.

Jeff wrinkled his forehead as he calculated. 66
" 'Bout twenty-five, I reckon." 67
"How many you make las' year?" 68
"Twenty-eight," he said. "How come you ask that?" 69
"I's jes thinkin'," Jennie said quietly. 70
"It don't make a speck o' difference though," Jeff reflected. 71
"If we get much or if we get little, we still gonna be in debt to
old man Stevenson when he gets through counting up agin us.
It's took us a long time to learn that."

Jennie was not listening to these words. She had fallen 72
into a trance-like meditation. Her lips twitched. She chewed
her gums and rubbed her gnarled hands nervously. Suddenly,
she leaned forward, buried her face in the nervous hands, and
burst into tears. She cried aloud in a dry, cracked voice that
suggested the rattle of fodder on dead stalks. She cried aloud
like a child, for she had never learned to suppress a genuine
sob. Her slight old frame shook heavily and seemed hardly able
to sustain such violent grief.

"What's the matter, baby?" Jeff asked awkwardly. 73
"Why you cryin' like all that?" 74
"I's jes thinkin'," she said. 75
"So you the one what's scairt now, hunh?" 76
"I ain't scairt, Jeff. I's jes thinkin' 'bout leavin' eve'thing 77
like this—eve'thing we been used to. It's right sad-like."

Jeff did not answer, and presently Jennie buried her face 78
again and cried.

The sun was almost overhead. It beat down furiously on 79
the dusty wagon-path road, on the parched roadside grass and
the tiny battered car. Jeff's hands, gripping the wheel, became

wet with perspiration; his forehead sparkled. Jeff's lips parted. His mouth shaped a hideous grimace. His face suggested the face of a man being burned. But the torture passed and his expression softened again.

"You mustn't cry, baby," he said to his wife. "We gotta be   80
strong. We can't break down."

Jennie waited a few seconds, then said, "You reckon we   81
oughta do it, Jeff? You reckon we oughta go 'head an' do it, really?"

Jeff's voice choked; his eyes blurred. He was terrified to   82
hear Jennie say the thing that had been in his mind all morning. She had egged him on when he had wanted more than anything in the world to wait, to reconsider, to think things over a little longer. Now she was getting cold feet. Actually, there was no need of thinking the question through again. It would only end in making the same painful decision once more. Jeff knew that. There was no need of fooling around longer.

"We jes as well to do like we planned," he said. "They ain't   83
nothin' else for us now—it's the bes' thing."

Jeff thought of the handicaps, the near impossibility, of   84
making another crop with his leg bothering him more and more each week. Then there was always the chance that he would have another stroke, like the one that had made him lame. Another one might kill him. The least it could do would be to leave him helpless. Jeff gasped—Lord, Jesus! He could not bear to think of being helpless, like a baby, on Jennie's hands. Frail, blind Jennie.

The little pounding motor of the car worked harder and   85
harder. The puff of steam from the cracked radiator became larger. Jeff realized that they were climbing a little rise. A moment later the road turned abruptly, and he looked down upon the face of the river.

"Jeff."   86

"Hunh?"   87

"Is that the water I hear?"   88

"Hm. Tha's it."   89

"Well, which way you goin' now?"   90

"Down this-a way," he said. "The road runs 'long 'side o'   91
the water a lil piece."

She waited a while calmly. Then said she, "Drive faster."   92

"A'right, baby," Jeff said.   93

The water roared in the bed of the river. It was fifty or sixty   94
feet below the level of the road. Between the road and the water

there was a long smooth slope, sharply inclined. The slope was dry, the clay hardened by prolonged summer heat. The water below, roaring in a narrow channel, was noisy and wild.

"Jeff." 95

"Hunh?" 96

"How far you goin'?" 97

"Jes a lil piece down the road." 98

"You ain't scairt, is you, Jeff?" 99

"Nah, baby," he said trembling. "I ain't scairt." 100

"Remember how we planned it, Jeff. We gotta do it like we 101 said. Brave-like."

"Hm." 102

Jeff's brain darkened. Things suddenly seemed unreal, 103 like figures in a dream. Thoughts swam in his mind foolishly, hysterically, like little blind fish in a pool within a dense cave. They rushed again. Jeff soon because dizzy. He shuddered violently and turned to his wife.

"Jennie, I can't do it. I can't." His voice broke pitifully. 104

She did not appear to be listening. All the grief had gone 105 from her face. She sat erect, her unseeing eyes wide open, strained and frightful. Her glossy black skin had become dull. She seemed as thin, as sharp and bony, as a starved bird. Now, having suffered and endured the sadness of tearing herself away from beloved things, she showed no anguish. She was absorbed with her own thoughts, and she didn't even hear Jeff's voice shouting in her ear.

Jeff said nothing more. For an instant there was light in 106 his cavernous brain. The great chamber was, for less than a second, peopled by characters he knew and loved. They were simple, healthy creatures, and they behaved in a manner that he could understand. They had quality. But since he had already taken leave of them long ago, the remembrance did not break his heart again. Young Jeff Patton was among them, the Jeff Patton of fifty years ago who went down to New Orleans with a crowd of country boys to the Mardi Gras doings. The gay young crowd, boys with candy-striped shirts and rouged brown girls in noisy silks, was like a picture in his head. Yet it did not make him sad. On that very trip Slim Burns had killed Joe Beasley—the crowd had been broken up. Since then Jeff Patton's world had been the Greenbriar Plantation. If there had been other Mardi Gras carnivals, he had not heard of them. Since then there had been no time; the years had fallen on him like waves. Now he was old, worn out. Another paralytic stroke (like the one he had already suffered) would put him on his back for keeps. In that condition, with a frail blind woman to look after him, he would be worse off than if he were dead.

Suddenly Jeff's hands became steady. He actually felt   107
brave. He slowed down the motor of the car and carefully pulled off the road. Below, the water of the stream boomed, a soft thunder in the deep channel. Jeff ran the car onto the clay slope, pointed it directly toward the stream and put his foot heavily on the accelerator. The little car leaped furiously down the steep incline toward the water. The movement was nearly as swift and direct as a fall. The two old black folks, sitting quietly side by side, showed no excitement. In another instant the car hit the water and dropped immediately out of sight.

A little later it lodged in the mud of a shallow place. One   108
wheel of the crushed and upturned little Ford became visible above the rushing water.

Discussion Questions

1. How does Bontemps convey the idea that the Pattons are about to go on an important trip?

2. What images of poverty does Bontemps present in the story?

3. What kind of relationship exists between Jeff and Jennie?

4. What physical and economic factors influence Jeff and Jennie's decision to take their journey? Is their decision a well-thought-out one? Support your answer.

5. What are the couple's feelings as they approach the river, especially in paragraph 106?

6. Do you believe that Jeff and Jennie take the courageous or the cowardly way to solve their problems? Explain your answer.

7. How effective is Bontemps's use of description in developing this story? Explain your answer.

8. How does the opening paragraph set the tone for the story?

Writing Assignments

1. Write an essay describing your feelings as you prepared to do something you anticipated with great joy or great fear.

2. Write an essay relating a time when economic or physical conditions forced you to do something drastic.

3. Write an essay in which you agree or disagree with the following statement: "There is no such thing as a hopeless situation."

JUST DON'T NEVER GIVE UP ON LOVE

Sonia Sanchez

Sonia Sanchez (1934–) was born in Birmingham, Alabama. An activist, poet, playwright, editor, and teacher, she is the author of several works, including her first book of poetry, Homecoming *(1969),* It's a New Day *(1971),* A Blues Book for Blue Black Magical Women *(1973),* I've Been a Woman: New and Selected Poems *(1981), and* homegirls and hand grenades *(1984). In this selection, a young woman describes an unexpected encounter with an old woman in the park.*

Vocabulary

ruminating	(1)	meditating
impropriety	(6)	improper action or behavior
spunk	(13)	courage
buddah	(14)	evil, disgusting woman
crocheted keloids	(14)	raised scars having the appearance of being knitted with one hooked needle
confessionals	(15)	secrets
anticlimactic	(25)	declining in disappointing contrast to a previous rise

Feeling tired that day, I came to the park with the children. I 1
saw her as I rounded the corner, sitting old as stale beer on the
bench, ruminating on some uneventful past. And I thought,
"Hell, No rap from the roots today. I need the present. On this
day. This Monday. This July day buckling me under her summer wings, I need more than old words for my body to squeeze
into."

I sat down at the far end of the bench, draping my legs 2
over the edge, baring my back to time and time unwell spent. I
screamed to the children to watch those curves threatening
their youth as they rode their ten-speed bikes against midwestern rhythms.

I opened my book and began to write. They were coming 3
again, those words insistent as his hands had been pounding
inside me, demanding their time and place. I relaxed as my
hands moved across the paper like one possessed.

I wasn't sure just what it was I heard. At first I thought it   4
was one of the boys calling me so I kept on writing. They knew
the routine by now. Emergencies demanded a presence. A facial confrontation. No long-distance screams across trees and
space and other children's screams. But the sound pierced the
pages and I looked around, and there she was inching her
bamboo-creased body toward my back, coughing a beaded sentence off her tongue.

"Guess you think I ain't never loved, huh girl? Hee. Hee.   5
Guess that what you be thinking, huh?"

I turned. Startled by her closeness and impropriety, I stut-   6
tered, "I, I, I, Whhhaat dooooo you mean?"

"Hee. Hee. Guess you think I been old like this fo'ever,   7
huh?" She leaned toward me, "Huh? I was so pretty that mens
brought me breakfast in bed. Wouldn't let me hardly do no
hard work at all."

"That's nice, ma'am. I'm glad to hear that." I returned to   8
my book. I didn't want to hear about some ancient love that
she carried inside her. I had to finish a review for the journal. I
was already late. I hoped she would get the hint and just sit
still. I looked at her out of the corner of my eyes. She quit and I
continued my work.

"He could barely keep hisself in changing clothes. But he   9
was pretty. My first husband looked like the sun. I used to say
his name over and over again till it hung from my ears like dia-
monds. Has you ever loved a pretty man, girl?"

I raised my eyes, determined to keep a distance from this   10
woman disturbing my day.

"No ma'am. But I've seen many a pretty man. I don't like   11
them though cuz they keep their love up high in a linen closet
and I'm too short to reach it."

Her skin shook with laughter.   12

"Girl you gots some spunk about you after all. C'mon over   13
here next to me. I wants to see yo' eyes up close. You looks so
uneven sittin over there."

Did she say uneven? Did this old buddah splintering   14
death say uneven? Couldn't she see that I had one eye shorter
than the other; that my breath was painted on porcelain; that
one breast crocheted keloids under this white blouse?

I moved toward her though. I scooped up the years that   15
had stripped me to the waist and moved toward her. And she
called to me to come out, come out wherever you are young
woman, playing hide and go seek with scarecrow men. I gathered myself up at the gateway of her confessionals.

"Do you know what it mean to love a pretty man girl?" She 16
crooned in my ear. "You always running behind a man like that
girl while he cradles his privates. Ain't no joy in a pretty yellow
man, cuz he always out pleasurin' and givin' pleasure."

I nodded my head as her words sailed in my ears. Here 17
was the pulse of a woman whose black ass shook the world
once.

She continued. "A woman crying all the time is pitiful. Piti- 18
ful I says. I wuz pitiful sitting by the window every night like a
cow in the fields chewin' on cud. I wanted to cry out, but not
even God hisself could hear me. I tried to cry out till my mouth
wuz split open at the throat. I 'spoze there is a time all womens
has to visit the slaughter house. My visit lasted five years."

Touching her hands, I felt the summer splintering in 19
prayer; touching her hands, I felt my bones migrating in red
noise. I asked, "When did you see the butterflies again?"

Her eyes wandered like quicksand over my face. Then she 20
smiled, "Girl don't you know yet that you don't never give up on
love? Don't you know you has in you the pulse of winds? The
noise of dragon flies?" Her eyes squinted close and she said,
"One of them mornings he woke up callin' me and I wuz gone. I
wuz gone running with the moon over my shoulders. I looked
no which way at all. I had inside me 'nough knives and spoons
to cut/scoop out the night. I wuz a tremblin' as I met the
mornin'."

She stirred in her eighty-four-year-old memory. She 21
stirred up her body as she talked. "They's men and mens.
Some good. Some bad. Some breathing death. Some breathing
life. William wuz my beginnin'. I come to that man spittin'
metal and he just pick me up and fold me inside him. I wuz
christen' with his love."

She began to hum. I didn't recognize the song; it was a 22
prayer. I leaned back and listened to her voice rustling like silk.
I heard cathedrals and sonnets; I heard tents and revivals and
a black woman spilling black juice among her ruins.

"We all gotta salute death one time or 'nother girl. Death 23
be waitin' outdoors trying to get inside. William died at his job.
Death just turned 'round and snatched him right off the
street."

Her humming became the only sound in the park. Her 24
voice moved across the bench like a mutilated child. And I
cried. For myself. For this woman talkin' about love. For all the
women who have ever stretched their bodies out anticipating
civilization and finding ruins.

The crashing of the bikes was anticlimactic. I jumped up, 25
rushed toward the accident. Man. little man. Where you bicy-
cling to so very fast? Man. Second little man. Take it slow. It all
passes so fast any how.

As I walked the boys and their bikes toward the bench, I 26
smiled at this old woman waiting for our return.

"I want you to meet a great lady, boys." 27

"Is she a writer, too, ma?" 28

"No honey. She's a lady who has lived life instead of writ- 29
ing about it."

"After we say hello can we ride a little while longer? 30
Please!"

"Ok. But watch your manners now and your bones after- 31
wards."

"These are my sons, ma'am." 32

"How you do sons? I'm Mrs. Rosalie Johnson. Glad to 33
meet you."

The boys shook her hand and listened for a minute to her 34
words. Then they rode off, spinning their wheels on a city neutral with pain.

As I stood watching them race the morning, Mrs. Johnson 35
got up.

"Don't go," I cried. "You didn't finish your story." 36

"We'll talk by-and-by. I comes out here almost everyday. I 37
sits here on the same bench everyday. I'll probably die sittin'
here one day. As good a place as any I 'magine."

"May I hug you, ma'am? You've helped me so much today. 38
You've given me strength to keep on looking."

"No. Don't never go looking for love girl. Just wait. It'll 39
come. Like the rain fallin' from the heaven, it'll come. Just
don't never give up on love."

We hugged; then she walked her eighty-four-year-old walk 40
down the street. A black woman. Echoing gold. Carrying cou-
plets from the sky to crease the ground.

Discussion Questions

1. What is the narrator's first impression of the old woman? Why
   does that impression change?
2. How would you characterize the woman? How does she differ
   from the narrator?
3. What is the old woman's philosophy of love? How have her experiences with men during her youth helped develop her philosophy?

4. Why does the narrator want to introduce the woman to her sons?
5. What is the significance of the essay's title?
6. How does Sanchez's use of description help the reader character-ize the narrator?
7. Why do you think Sanchez chose to use a double negative in her title?

Writing Assignments

1. Write an essay that illustrates one of the following statements:
   a. Experience is the best teacher.
   b. One can never judge a book by its cover.
2. Write an essay in which you describe a time when you were given helpful or interesting advice from an older person.
3. Write an essay about someone who unexpectedly made a differ-ence in your life.

TEA CAKE AND JANIE

Zora Neale Hurston

*Zora Neale Hurston (1907–1960) was born in Eatonville,
Florida, and is the author of three novels:* Jonah's Gourd
Vine *(1934),* Their Eyes Were Watching God *(1937), from
which this excerpt is taken, and* Seraph on the Suwanee
(1948). Her works also include her autobiography, Dust
Tracks on the Road *(1943), and several volumes of folklore.
This story describes the newfound love between Tea Cake
and Janie, despite disapproval from their friends and
townspeople.*

Vocabulary

step off	(26)	get married
flommuck	(29)	flop, failure
kerflommuck	(37)	announcement, important issue
stand up wid	(39)	marry

"Pheoby," Sam Watson said one night as he got in the bed, "Ah   1
b'lieve yo' buddy is all tied up with dat Tea Cake shonough.
Didn't b'lieve it at first."

"Aw she don't mean nothin' by it. Ah think she's sort of   2
stuck on dat undertaker up at Sanford."

"It's somebody 'cause she looks mighty good dese days.   3
New dresses and her hair combed a different way nearly every
day. You got to have something to comb hair over. When you
see uh woman doin' so much rakin' in her head, she's combin'
at some man or 'nother."

" 'Course she kin do as she please, but dat's uh good   4
chance she got up at Sanford. De man's wife died and he got
uh lovely place tuh take her to—already furnished. Better'n her
house Joe left her."

"You better sense her intuh things then 'cause Tea Cake   5
can't do nothing' but help her spend whut she got. Ah reckon
dat's whut he's after. Throwin' away whut Joe Starks worked
hard tuh git tuh gether."

"Dat's de way it looks. Still and all, she's her own woman.   6
She oughta know by now whut she wants tuh do."

"De men wuz talkin' 'bout it in de grove tuhday and givin'   7 her and Tea Cake both de devil. Dey figger he's spendin' on her now in order tuh make her spend on him later."

"Umph! Umph! Umph!"

8

"Oh dey got it all figgered out. Maybe it ain't as bad as they say, but they talk it and make it sound real bad on her part."

9

"Dat's jealousy and malice. Some uh dem very mens wants tuh do whut dey claim deys skeered Tea Cake is doin'."

10

"De Pastor claim Tea Cake don't 'low her tuh come tuh church only once in awhile 'cause he want dat change tuh buy gas wid. Just draggin' de woman away from church. But anyhow, she's yo' bosom friend, so you better go see 'bout her. Drop uh lil hint here and dere and if Tea Cake is tryin' tuh rob her she kin see and know. Ah laks de woman and Ah sho would hate tuh see her come up like Mrs. Tyler."

11

"Ah mah God, naw! Reckon Ah better step over dere tomorrow and have some chat wid Janie. She jus' ain't thinkin' whut she doin', dat's all."

12

The next morning Pheoby picked her way over to Janie's house like a hen to a neighbor's garden. Stopped and talked a little with everyone she met, turned aside momentarily to pause at a porch or two—going straight by walking crooked. So her firm intention looked like an accident and she didn't have to give her opinion to folks along the way.

13

Janie acted glad to see her and after a while Pheoby broached her with, "Janie, everybody's talkin' 'bout how dat Tea Cake is draggin' you round tuh places you ain't used tuh. Baseball games and huntin' and fishin'. He don't know you'se useter uh more high time crowd than dat. You always did class off."

14

"Jody classed me off. Ah didn't. Naw, Pheoby, Tea Cake ain't draggin' me off nowhere Ah don't want tuh go. Ah always did want tuh git round uh whole heap, but Jody wouldn't 'low me tuh. When Ah wasn't in de store he wanted me tuh jes sit wid folded hands and sit dere. And Ah'd sit dere wid de walls creepin' up on me and squeezin' all de life outa me. Pheoby, dese educated women got uh heap of things to sit down and consider. Somebody done tole 'em what to set down for. Nobody ain't told poor me, so sittin' still worries me. Ah wants tuh utilize mahself all over."

15

"But, Janie, Tea Cake, whilst he ain't no jail-bird, he ain't got uh dime tuh cry. Ain't you skeered he's jes after yo' money—him bein' younger than you?"

16

"He ain't never ast de first penny from me yet, and if he 17
love property he ain't no different from all de rest of us. All dese
ole men dat's settin' round me is after de same thing. They's
three mo' widder women in town, how come dey don't break
dey neck after dem? 'Cause dey ain't got nothin', dat's why."

"Folks seen you out in colors and dey thinks you ain't 18
payin' de right amount uh respect tuh yo' dead husband."

"Ah ain't grievin' so why do Ah hafta mourn? Tea Cake 19
love me in blue, so Ah wears it. Jody ain't never in his life
picked out no color for me. De world picked out black and
white for mournin', Joe didn't. So Ah wasn't wearin' it for him.
Ah was wearin' it for de rest of y'all."

"But anyhow, watch yo'self, Janie, and don't be took ad- 20
vantage of. You know how dese young men is wid older women.
Most of de time dey's after whut dey kin git, then dey's gone lak
uh turkey through de corn."

"Tea Cake don't talk dat way. He's aimin' tuh make hisself 21
permanent wid me. We done made up our mind tuh marry."

"Janie, you'se yo' own woman, and Ah hope you know 22
whut you doin'. Ah sho hope you ain't lak uh possum—de older
you gits, de less sense yuh got. Ah'd feel uh whole heap better
'bout yuh if you wuz marryin' dat man up dere in Sanford. He
got somethin' tuh put long side uh whut you got and dat make
it more better. He's endurable."

"Still and all Ah'd ruther be wid Tea Cake." 23

"Well, if yo' mind is already made up, 'tain't nothin' no- 24
body kin do. But you'se takin' uh awful chance."

"No mo' than Ah took befo' and no mo' than anybody else 25
takes when dey gits married. It always changes folks, and
sometimes it brings out dirt and meanness dat even de person
didn't know they had in 'em theyselves. You know dat. Maybe
Tea Cake might turn out lak dat. Maybe not. Anyhow Ah'm
ready and willin' tuh try 'im."

"Well, when you aim tuh step off?" 26

"Dat we don't know. De store is got tuh be sold and then 27
we'se goin' off somewhere tuh git married."

"How come you sellin' out de store?" 28

" 'Cause Tea Cake ain't no Jody Starks, and if he tried tuh 29
be, it would be uh complete flommuck. But de minute Ah marries 'im everybody is gointuh be makin' comparisons. So us is
goin' off somewhere and start all over in Tea Cake's way. Dis
ain't no business proposition, and no race after property and ti-

tles. Dis is uh love game. Ah done lived Grandma's way, now Ah means tuh live mine."

"What you mean by dat, Janie?" 30

"She was borned in slavery time when folks, dat is black 31
folks, didn't sit down anytime dey felt lak it. So sittin' on porches lak de white madam looked lak uh mighty fine thing tuh her. Dat's whut she wanted for me—don't keer whut it cost. Git up on uh high chair and sit dere. She didn't have time tuh think whut tuh do after you got up on de stool uh do nothin'. De object wuz tuh git dere. So Ah got up on de high stool lak she told me, but Pheoby, Ah done nearly languished tuh death up dere. Ah felt like de world wuz cryin' extry and Ah ain't read de common news yet."

"Maybe so, Janie. Still and all Ah'd love tuh experience it 32
for just one year. It look lak heben tuh me from where Ah'm at."

"Ah reckon so." 33

"But anyhow, Janie, you be keerful 'bout dis sellin' out 34
and goin' off wid strange men. Look whut happened tuh Annie Tyler. Took whut little she had and went off tuh Tampa wid dat boy dey call Who Flung. It's somethin' tuh think about."

"It sho is. Still Ah ain't Mis' Tyler and Tea Cake ain't no 35
Who Flung, and he ain't no stranger tuh me. We'se just as good as married already. But Ah ain't puttin' it in de street. Ah'm tellin' you."

"Ah just lak uh chicken. Chicken drink water, but he don't 36
peepee."

"Oh, Ah know you don't talk. We ain't shame faced. We 37
jus' ain't ready tuh make no big kerflommuck as yet."

"You doin' right not tuh talk it, but Janie, you'se takin' uh 38
mighty big chance."

" 'Tain't so big uh chance as it seem lak, Pheoby. Ah'm 39
older than Tea Cake, yes. But he done showed me where it's de thought dat makes de difference in ages. If people thinks de same they can make it all right. So in the beginnin' new thoughts had tuh be thought and new words said. After Ah got used tuh dat, we gits 'long jus' fine. He done taught me de maiden language all over. Wait till you see de new blue satin Tea Cake done picked out for me tuh stand up wid him in. High heel slippers, necklace, earrings, *everything* he wants tuh see me in. Some of dese mornin's and it won't be long, you gointuh wake up callin' me and Ah'll be gone."

Discussion Questions

1. Why do the townspeople disapprove of the relationship between Janie and Tea Cake?
2. How does Tea Cake differ from Joe Starks?
3. What is the relationship between Tea Cake and Janie?
4. What does Janie mean when she says she has lived "Grandma's way"? What kind of life did her grandmother want for Janie?
5. How do females' attitudes toward love and marriage today compare with those of Janie and Pheoby?
6. How does Hurston use illustration to show the love that Tea Cake and Janie have for one another?
7. Do you think that Hurston's use of black dialect and folk expressions adds to or takes away from the story? Why or why not?

Writing Assignments

1. Write an essay discussing today's views on older women-younger men relationships.
2. Write an essay describing how you get along better with an older person than with someone your own age.
3. Write an essay by completing the following statement: "I wish I had the courage to _____."

Student Essay:
POSITIVE AFFIRMATIONS AMONG AFRICAN AMERICAN MEN AND WOMEN

Jason Orr

Vocabulary

perennial	(1)	annual
insurmountable	(2)	not capable of being resolved
affirmations	(5)	positive truths

As I travel the country each summer to attend my annual family reunion, a pattern is beginning to emerge. After all the children are fed and all the prizes are given out, without fail the women of the family migrate to one corner of the park and commence to have their perennial discussion of—well, you may have guessed by now—black men. I'm sure you've seen the scene. It is the same one depicted in the novel by Terry McMillan, *Waiting to Exhale*.[1] In these conversations one million and one excuses are given why black women might stray from black men. I will give you three why they should not. 1

The first reason why black women should not seek out relationships in other races is really elementary. The fact is that there are basic cultural differences that make it difficult and sometimes even impossible for other races, especially European Americans, to relate to black people. To some extent, these differences are understandable. However, there are many rituals that are sacred to the black community and should be kept that way. Take, for instance, African American cuisine. I have not tasted any cooking that can rival the cooking of black folk, and yet outsiders frown when talking of chitterlings, cornbread, and collard greens. Another example is the African American parties and gatherings. Have you seen an outsider at a party "thrown" by blacks? It is not a sight that is pleasing to the eye. The manner in which African Americans worship God in the Baptist church is clearly different from the way white Baptists worship God. Finally, black music has a style all its own, even though today there are many white musicians who attempt to 2

[1] *Waiting to Exhale* (1)   A well-received 1992 novel by Terry McMillan that focuses on difficulties in African American male-female relationships.

imitate this style. In the end, it all comes down to the fact that there are insurmountable differences that separate black culture from others.

Another reason black women should date and marry   3
within their race is one that has to do with the future. I have seen too many products of interracial marriages grow up with identity problems. There are too many problems that face the black community already without having to worry about a person of another race raising a black child. When interracial couples have children, they are repeating the cycle of the confused black child that asks, "Mommy, am I white or black?" There is only one person that can raise a black boy or girl and that is a black man or woman.

The most important reason why black women should date   4
within their race is that there are far too many strong black men to choose from. Being a student at a predominantly black college, I stand among the top male prospects in the world. Please, do not get me wrong. College helps, but it does not make a man's education. There are lessons to be learned in the street, home, and church that will never be taught in the classroom by a professor holding the highest degree. Too many times I hear women categorizing black men: too poor, too ugly, too conceited, too humble, too dark, gay, straight, divorced, addicted to drugs. Yet, there is one category that is the largest and the most overlooked: the positive, strong, well-rounded black man.

The black man is someone to be cherished. Therefore,   5
what should be emphasized at family reunions and at the roundtable conferences that occur so frequently among black women is the positive affirmations of the black male. If not, the black community will keep turning, but it will definitely be for the worst.

Discussion Questions

1. What is Orr's principal complaint?
2. What three reasons does he give to support his argument? How valid are these reasons?
3. What do you perceive as the strength and weakness of his argument? Explain your response.
4. What kind of rituals does the author consider sacred to the black community?
5. According to the author, who can best raise a black child?

6. Does the author offer sufficient evidence to make his argument a convincing one?
7. How effective is the conclusion? Explain your answer.

Writing Assignments

1. Write an essay stating your own reasons why people should (should not) date outside of their race or culture.
2. Write an essay describing the rituals or cultural practices within your ethnic or religious group.

10

Civil Rights

WORKING FOR SNCC

David Rubel

David Rubel is a writer and journalist whose work has appeared in such publications as the Washington Post *and the* Boston Globe. *After graduating from Columbia University, he worked as a correspondent for the Pacific News Service and later became a mathematics textbook editor. Currently he is a children's book editor in New York City. In the following selection taken from* Fannie Lou Hamer: From Sharecropping to Politics *(1990), Rubel describes how Hamer and fellow Student Nonviolent Coordinating Committee (SNCC) worker Robert Moses sought to win voting rights for blacks in Ruleville, Mississippi, in the early 1960s.*

The Student Nonviolent Coordinating Committee (SNCC) wasn't like most other civil rights organizations. Because it followed a legal strategy, the National Association for the Advancement of Colored People (NAACP) rarely sent people into small, backwater towns like Ruleville. But SNCC came to Ruleville because SNCC went everywhere in the rural South.

1

Led by young staff members and volunteers, SNCC favored forceful, direct action. Grass-roots organizing was its specialty.   2

In its first few years of experience. SNCC had focused its   3
attention on the sit-ins and the other mass demonstrations. But by the summer of 1961, some SNCC staff members, particularly Robert Moses, wanted to shift SNCC resources to voter-registration drives.

Moses admitted that the sit-ins had achieved some real   4
gains. But he pointed out that the freedom to eat at a Woolworth's lunch counter was not the same as freedom from police brutality or the right to obtain a fair trial.

To win these civil rights in Mississippi, Moses argued,   5
African Americans would have to influence the sheriffs and judges of Mississippi. And the only sure way to do that, he knew, was to register and vote. The system had to be changed at its roots.

In August 1961, SNCC decided to pursue both sit-ins and   6
registration drives. Moses was picked to lead the registration effort.

Moses was the perfect man for this difficult job. He was al-   7
ready well known within the movement as a tireless and capable worker. And he was also a born leader. With large, tranquil eyes hidden behind thick, plastic-framed glasses, he spoke with a calm voice and chose his words slowly and carefully.

Perhaps Moses' style came from the time he spent as a   8
mathematics teacher, but wherever it came from, it inspired and reassured the people with whom he worked. "He could walk into a place where a lynch mob had just left and make up a bed and prepare to go to sleep, as if the situation was normal," one SNCC worker said.

Moses set up SNCC field offices all over the state of Mis-   9
sissippi because the only way he saw to register African Americans to vote was to go out into the fields and talk to those who weren't registered.

Many of the unregistered African Americans would need   10
help, of course. Like Fannie Lou Hamer herself, many didn't even know they could vote. Others would need help with the forms. Almost all of them would need help to pass the tricky literacy test.[1]

---

[1] literacy test (10)   A test to prove that people wishing to vote could read and write.

But, as Moses knew, all of this could be taught. What   11
would be more difficult to provide would be the courage each
new registrant needed to challenge Mississippi's system of
white domination. All their lives, the poor blacks of Mississippi
had lived in fear of whites. All their lives, they had been told
that whites were superior. Fannie Lou Hamer had never believed it, but she was one of the exceptions.

Most of Hamer's neighbors found it very difficult to forget   12
what the whites had taught them, particularly when so many
violent whites were happy to remind them of these lessons.

Fannie Lou Hamer returned to Ruleville that winter of   13
1962 as a field secretary for SNCC. She immediately started organizing a local poverty program. This included asking the federal government for food and clothing for the needy families of
Ruleville. She also began the work of organizing the townspeople politically. This was her most important task. In the fields
by day and in the churches by night, Hamer talked to people
about the movement and about their right to vote.

In addition to all this, Hamer even found time to cook for   14
all the SNCC workers who regularly came to town.

Fannie Lou Hamer soon became one of SNCC's most effec-   15
tive fundraisers. She often traveled north to speak to white audiences about the desperation of black Mississippians and their
desire for change. "I'm sick and tired of being sick and tired,"
Hamer would tell them.

So far there had been no repeat of the September 10   16
shootings, but the harassment continued. One morning before
daylight, two policemen came into the Hamers' bedroom with
their guns drawn. They pretended to conduct a search, but
they had no warrant. Their real purpose was to scare the
Hamers.

Another time, the Hamers received a water bill for $9,000,   17
when they didn't even have running water. Nevertheless, Pap
was arrested over this bill.

These years were very difficult ones for the Hamers,   18
though it must have helped to know that they had the movement behind them. Fannie Lou's $10-a-week SNCC salary
barely allowed the family to get by, but friends and neighbors
helped out when they could.

Still, it was difficult to keep going. After all, most SNCC   19
volunteers were much younger and much better educated than
Fannie Lou Hamer was. They also didn't have families to support. But what Fannie Lou Hamer lacked in those areas, she
more than made up for in courage and determination.

January 10, 1963, was a Thursday. It was also the day 20
that Fannie Lou Hamer, on her third try, became one of the
first of Sunflower County's 30,000 African Americans to register to vote. She had been studying sections of the Mississippi
state constitution, hoping to get one on the test that she could
interpret. She did get one, and she passed.

When election day came that fall, however, Hamer was still 21
denied her right to vote because she couldn't afford the money
to pay the Mississippi poll tax.[2]

Discussion Questions

1. Why do you think the author begins this essay by making a distinction between SNCC and the other civil rights organizations?
2. Why did Robert Moses want to shift emphasis from mass demonstrations to voter-registration drives?
3. What characteristics made Moses a "born leader"?
4. What leadership traits did Fannie Lou Hamer have?
5. What are some of the many obstacles that prevented black Mississippians from voting?
6. To what extent does the author's use of cause and effect enhance
your understanding of the civil rights struggles that Hamer and
Moses faced?
7. Why do you think the author chose to add paragraph 21 rather
than ending the essay with paragraph 20? What does that final
paragraph tell us about Hamer in particular and the civil rights
movement in general?

Writing Assignments

1. Write an essay about an extraordinary person you know.
2. Write an essay about an organization, community, or individual
that you feel has misused power. Try to also explain why this
misuse of power occurred.
3. Write an essay in which you explore the meaning of "power."

[2] poll tax (21) An unlawful tax that blacks were required to pay in order
to vote.

EMMETT TILL IS DEAD

Anne Moody

Anne Moody (1940–   ) was born in Wilkinson County,
Mississippi, a rural poverty area. After receiving a bache-
lor's degree from Tougaloo College, Moody became active in
the Civil Rights Movement and carried her activities north to
Cornell University. In the following excerpt from her autobio-
graphical novel, Coming of Age in Mississippi *(1968),*
Moody reflects on how her racial consciousness was raised
as a result of the murder of Emmett Till.

Not only did I enter high school with a new name, but also with   1
a completely new insight into the life of Negroes in Mississippi. I
was now working for one of the meanest white women in town,
and a week before school started Emmett Till[1] was killed.

Up until his death, I had heard of Negroes found floating   2
in a river or dead somewhere with their bodies riddled with bul-
lets. But I didn't know the mystery behind these killings then. I
remember once when I was only seven I heard Mama and one
of my aunts talking about some Negro who had been beaten to
death. "Just like them low-down skunks killed him they will do
the same to us," Mama had said. When I asked her who killed
the man and why, she said, "An Evil Spirit killed him. You gotta
to be a good girl or it will kill you too." So since I was seven, I
had lived in fear for that "Evil Spirit." It took me eight years to
learn what that spirit was.

I was coming from school the evening I heard about Em-   3
mett Till's death. There was a whole group of us, girls and
boys, walking down the road headed home. A group of about
six high school boys were walking a few paces ahead of me and
several other girls. We were laughing and talking about something that had happened in school that day. However, the six
boys in front of us weren't talking very loud. Usually they kept
up so much noise. But today they were just walking and talking among themselves. All of a sudden they began to shout at
each other.

---

[1] Emmett Till (1)   A black youth who was murdered in Mississippi for his
"forward" behavior toward a white woman. The white men, tried for killing Till, were
acquitted by an all-white jury.

"Man, what in the hell do you mean?"   4

"What I mean is these goddamned white folks is gonna   5
start some shit here, you just watch!"

"That boy wasn't but fourteen years old and they killed   6
him. Now what kin a fourteen-year-old boy do with a white
woman? What if he did whistle at her, he might have thought
the whore was pretty."

"Look at all these white men here that's fucking over our   7
women. Everybody knows it too and what's done about that?
Look how many white babies we got walking around in our
neighborhoods. Their mamas ain't white either. That boy was
from Chicago, shit, everybody fuck everybody up there. He
probably didn't even think of the bitch as white."

What they were saying shocked me. I knew all of those   8
boys and I had never heard them talk like that. We walked on
behind them for a while listening. Questions about who was
killed, where, and why started running through my mind. I
walked up to one of the boys.

"Eddie, what boy was killed?"   9

"Moody, where've you been?" he asked me. "Everybody   10
talking about that fourteen-year-old boy who was killed in
Greenwood by some white men. You don't know nothing that's
going on besides what's in them books of yours, huh?"

Standing there before the rest of the girls, I felt so stupid.   11
It was then that I realized I really didn't know what was going
on all around me. It wasn't that I was dumb. It was just that
ever since I was nine, I'd had to work after school and do my
lessons on lunch hour. I never had time to learn anything, to
hang around with people my own age. And you never were told
anything by adults.

That evening when I stopped off at the house on my way   12
to Mrs Burke's, Mama was singing. Any other day she would
have been yelling at Adline and Junior them to take off their
school clothes. I wondered if she knew about Emmett Till. The
way she was singing she had something on her mind and it
wasn't pleasant either.

I got a shoe, you got a shoe,
All of God's chillun got shoes;
When I get to hebben, I'm gonna put on my shoes,
And gonna tromp all over God's hebben.
When I get to hebben I'm gonna put on my shoes,
And gonna walk all over God's hebben.

Mamma was dishing up beans like she didn't know any-   13
one was home. Adline, Junior, and James had just thrown
their books down and sat themselves at the table. I didn't usually eat before I went to work. But I wanted to ask Mama about
Emmett Till. So I ate and thought of some way of asking her.

"These beans are some good, Mama," I said, trying to   14
sense her mood.

"Why is you eating anyway? You gonna be late for work.   15
You know how Miss Burke is," she said to me.

"I don't have much to do this evening. I kin get it done be-   16
fore I leave work," I said.

The conversation stopped after that. Then Mama started   17
humming that song again.

> When I get to hebben, I'm gonna put on my shoes,
> And gonna tromp all over God's hebben.

She put a plate on the floor for Jennie Ann and Jerry.

"Jennie Ann! You and Jerry sit down here and eat and   18
don't put beans all over the floor."

Ralph, the baby, started crying, and she went in the bed-   19
room to give him his bottle. I got up and followed her.

"Mama, did you hear about that fourteen-year-old Negro   20
boy who was killed a little over a week ago by some white
men?" I asked her.

"Where did you hear that?" she said angrily.   21

"Boy, everybody really thinks I am dumb or deaf or some-   22
thing. I heard Eddie them talking about it this evening coming
from school."

"Eddie them better watch how they go around here talk-   23
ing. These white folks git a hold of it they gonna be in trouble,"
she said.

"What are they gonna be in trouble about, Mama? People   24
got a right to talk, ain't they?"

"You go on to work before you is late. And don't you let on   25
like you know nothing about that boy being killed before Miss
Burke them. Just do your work like you don't know nothing,"
she said. "That boy's a lot better off in heaven than he is here,"
she continued and then started singing again.

On my way to Mrs Burke's that evening, Mama's words   26
kept running through my mind. "Just do your work like you
don't know nothing." "Why is Mama acting so scared?" I
thought. "And what if Mrs Burke knew we knew? Why must I

pretend I don't know? Why are these people killing Negroes? What did Emmett Till do besides whistle at that woman?"

By the time I got to work, I had worked my nerves up 27
some. I was shaking as I walked up on the porch. "Do your work like you don't know nothing." But once I got inside, I couldn't have acted normal if Mrs Burke were paying me to be myself.

I was so nervous, I spent most of the evening avoiding 28
them, going about the house dusting and sweeping. Everything went along fairly well until dinner was served.

"Don, Wayne, and Mama, y'all come on to dinner. Essie, 29
you can wash up the pots and dishes in the sink now. Then after dinner you won't have as many," Mrs Burke called to me.

If I had the power to mysteriously disappear at that mo- 30
ment, I would have. They used the breakfast table in the kitchen for most of their meals. The dining room was only used for Sunday dinner or when they had company. I wished they had company tonight so they could eat in the dining room while I was at the kitchen sink.

"I forgot the bread," Mrs Burke said when they were all 31
seated. "Essie, will you cut it and put it on the table for me?"

I took the cornbread, cut it in squares, and put it on a 32
small round dish. Just as I was about to set it on the table, Wayne yelled at the cat. I dropped the plate and the bread went all over the floor.

"Never mind, Essie," Mrs Burke said angrily as she got up 33
and got some white bread from the breadbox.

I didn't say anything. I picked up the cornbread from 34
around the table and went back to the dishes. As soon as I got to the sink, I dropped a saucer on the floor and broke it. Didn't anyone say a word until I had picked up the pieces.

"Essie, I bought some new cleanser today. It's setting on 35
the bathroom shelf. See if it will remove the stains in the tub," Mrs Burke said.

I went to the bathroom to clean the tub. By the time I got 36
through with it, it was snow white. I spent a whole hour scrubbing it. I had removed the stains in no time but I kept scrubbing until they finished dinner.

When they had finished and gone into the living room as 37
usual to watch TV, Mrs Burke called me to eat. I took a clean plate out of the cabinet and sat down. Just as I was putting the first forkful of food in my mouth, Mrs Burke entered the kitchen.

"Essie, did you hear about that fourteen-year-old boy who   38
was killed in Greenwood?" she asked me, sitting down in one of
the chairs opposite me.

"No, I didn't hear that," I answered, almost choking on the   39
food.

"Do you know why he was killed?" she asked and I didn't   40
answer.

"He was killed because he got out of his place with a white   41
woman. A boy from Mississippi would have known better than
that. This boy was from Chicago. Negroes up North have no respect for people. They think they can get away with anything.
He just came to Mississippi and put a whole lot of notions in
the boys' heads here and stirred up a lot of trouble," she said
passionately.

"How old are you, Essie?" she asked me after a pause.   42

"Fourteen. I will soon be fifteen though," I said.   43

"See, that boy was just fourteen too. It's a shame he had   44
to die so soon." She was so red in the face, she looked as if she
was on fire.

When she left the kitchen I sat there with my mouth open   45
and my food untouched. I couldn't have eaten now if I were
starving. "Just do your work like you don't know nothing" ran
through my mind again and I began washing the dishes.

I went home shaking like a leaf on a tree. For the first time   46
out of all her trying, Mrs Burke had made me feel like rotten
garbage. Many times she had tried to instill fear within me and
subdue me and had given up. But when she talked about Emmett Till there was something in her voice that sent chills and
fear all over me.

Before Emmett Till's murder, I had known the fear of   47
hunger, hell, and the Devil. But now there was a new fear
known to me—the fear of being killed just because I was black.
This was the worst of my fears. I knew once I got food, the fear
of starving to death would leave. I also was told that if I were a
good girl, I wouldn't have to fear the Devil or hell. But I didn't
know what one had to do or not do as a Negro not to be killed.
Probably just being a Negro period was enough, I thought.

A few days later, I went to work and Mrs Burke had about   48
eight women over for tea. They were all sitting around in the
living room when I got there. She told me she was having a
"guild meeting," and asked me to help her serve the cookies
and tea.

After helping her, I started cleaning the house. I always swept the hallway and porch first. As I was sweeping the hall, I could hear them talking. When I heard the word "nigger," I stopped and listened. Mrs Burke must have sensed this, because she suddenly came to the door.   49

"Essie, finish the hall and clean the bathroom," she said hesitantly. "Then you can go for today. I am not making dinner tonight." Then she went back in the living room with the rest of the ladies.   50

Before she interrupted my listening, I had picked up the words "NAACP" and "that organization". Because they were talking about niggers, I knew NAACP had something to do with Negroes. All that night I kept wondering what could that NAACP mean?   51

Later when I was sitting in the kitchen at home doing my lessons, I decided to ask Mama. It was about twelve-thirty. Everyone was in bed but me. When Mama came in to put some milk in Ralph's bottle, I said, "Mama, what do NAACP mean?"   52

"Where did you git that from?" she asked me, spilling milk all over the floor.   53

"Mrs Burke had a meeting tonight—"   54

"What kind of meeting?" she asked, cutting me off.   55

"I don't know. She had some women over—she said it was a guild meeting," I said.   56

"A guild meeting," she repeated.   57

"Yes, they were talking about Negroes and I heard some woman say 'that NAACP' and another 'that organization,' meaning the same thing."   58

"What else did they say?" she asked me.   59

"That's all I heard. Mrs Burke must have thought I was listening, so she told me to clean the bathroom and leave."   60

"Don't you ever mention that word around Mrs Burke or no other white person, you heah! Finish your lesson and cut that light out and go to bed," Mama said angrily and left the kitchen.   61

"With a Mama like that you'll never learn anything," I thought as I got into bed. All night long I thought about Emmett Till and the NAACP. I even got up to look up NAACP in my little concise dictionary. But I didn't find it.   62

The next day at school, I decided to ask my homeroom teacher Mrs Rice the meaning of NAACP. When the bell sounded for lunch, I remained in my seat as the other students left the room.   63

"Are you going to spend your lunch hour studying again   64
today, Moody?" Mrs Rice asked me.

"Can I ask you a question, Mrs Rice?" I asked her.   65

"You *may* ask me a question, yes, but I don't know if you   66
can or not," she said.

"What does the word NAACP mean?" I asked.   67

"Why do you want to know?"   68

"The lady I worked for had a meeting and I overheard the   69
word mentioned."

"What else did you hear?"   70

"Nothing. I didn't know what NAACP meant, that's all." I   71
felt like I was on the witness stand or something.

"Well, next time your boss has another meeting you listen   72
more carefully. NAACP is a Negro organization that was established a long time ago to help Negroes gain a few basic rights,"
she said.

"What's it gotta do with the Emmett Till murder?" I asked.   73

"They are trying to get a conviction in Emmett Till's case.   74
You see the NAACP is trying to do a lot for the Negroes and get
the right to vote for Negroes in the South. I shouldn't be telling
you all this. And don't you dare breathe a word of what I said.
It could cost me my job if word got out I was teaching my students such. I gotta go to lunch and you should go outside too
because it's nice and sunny out today," she said leaving the
room. "We'll talk more when I have time."

About a week later, Mrs Rice had me over for Sunday din-   75
ner, and I spent about five hours with her. Within that time, I
digested a good meal and accumulated a whole new pool of
knowledge about Negroes being butchered and slaughtered by
whites in the South. After Mrs Rice had told me all this, I felt
like the lowest animal on earth. At least when other animals
(hogs, cows, etc.) were killed by man, they were used as food.
But when man was butchered or killed by man, in the case of
Negroes by whites, they were left lying on a road or found floating in a river or something.

Mrs Rice got to be something like a mother to me. She told   76
me anything I wanted to know. And made me promise that I
would keep all this information she was passing on to me to
myself. She said she couldn't, rather didn't want to, talk about
these things to other teachers, that they would tell Mr Willis
and she would be fired. At the end of that year she was fired. I
never found out why. I haven't seen her since then.

Discussion Questions

1. Why was Emmett Till murdered?
2. Why does Moody's mother tell her to "do your work like you don't know nothing"?
3. How does Moody feel after hearing the news of Till's murder?
4. Why do you think Mrs. Rice is fired?
5. Why do Mrs. Burke and the other ladies in the guild talk about the NAACP?
6. In what way does the mother's desire to protect her daughter result in her hurting her?
7. To what extent does Moody's use of comparison and contrast help us understand the racial conditions in the story?
8. What is the theme of the story?

Writing Assignments

1. Write an essay illustrating a coming-of-age experience that you have had.
2. Write an essay in which you describe an event that devastated your group or community. What was your personal response?
3. Write an essay in which you recount a time when you or someone you know was encouraged to keep quiet, when speaking up should have been the thing to do.

HOWARD UNIVERSITY: A RUDE AWAKENING

Cleveland Sellers

Cleveland Sellers, Jr. (1944–   ), was born in Denmark, South Carolina. A political activist himself, he met Stokely Carmichael (Kwame Toure) while a student at Howard University. In 1965, Sellers was elected program secretary of SNCC (Student Nonviolent Coordinating Committee). He was arrested for his participation in the Orangeburg Massacre and was later released on bail so he could attend college. In the following excerpt from River of No Return *(1973), his memoirs of the civil rights movement, Sellers reveals his disappointment regarding the apathy of many college students.*

Vocabulary

expendable	(3)	unnecessary
exasperation	(9)	frustration
flamboyant	(14)	showy, flashy
bombast	(14)	egotism, airs
kooks	(19)	oddballs, weirdos
affiliate	(20)	ally, partner

Howard University was a big disappointment. I arrived on campus in September, 1962. Filled with the unbounded enthusiasm peculiar to seventeen-year-olds, I expected to see everyone, students, instructors and administrators, passionately involved in the movement. I was eager to participate in emotion-packed mass meetings, tense strategy sessions and frequent demonstrations. Unfortunately, I didn't find any of these things.

When I attempted to discuss the movement with the guys in my dormitory, they would grunt and change the subject. They were much more interested in cars, fraternities, clothes, parties and girls. They loved to sit in bull sessions for hours discussing them. They also spent a lot of time talking about the high-paying jobs they intended to get after graduating. By the end of my first semester, I felt like an outcast. I tried to discuss my feelings and interests with my instructors—I needed help from someone who understood what I was going through—but

1

2

they were harder to talk to than my classmates. Their primary concerns seemed to be their cars, their homes, their professional associations and their salaries.

The administrators were no different. They were remote men who never seemed to have enough time really to hear what students were saying. They related to us as if we were cogs in a giant machine: those cogs which did not conform to the machine's program were expendable. 3

There was a great deal of interest among almost everyone on campus in *the Howard image,* which was designed to create the impression that there were no substantial differences between Howard's students and those at elite white colleges. Students went to absurd lengths to conform to *the image.* The guys wore suits, jackets and ties everywhere—including football games and breakfasts. The girls wore stockings and heels. Many of them refused to date men whose clothes did not fit *the image.* 4

I refused to conform. I had always been a very casual dresser and saw no reason to change. I liked to wear blue jeans, sweat shirts, army jackets and sneakers. Although I did not relish the outsider-outcast role that was accorded me because of my clothes, I was determined not to change. 5

"I have the right to dress in any way I please!" I snapped at my roommate one night when he attempted to scold me for wearing blue jeans to a big dance. 6

"But, Cleve," he responded, "you'll never get a girlfriend. No girl's gonna be caught dead with you if you keep dressing like a refugee from World War I." 7

My roommate was in love with Howard. He was having a ball. He couldn't understand why I had so much trouble adjusting. 8

"Fuck it, man," he said to me one night in exasperation after I asked him if he didn't feel some responsibility to try to improve racial conditions. 9

"Don't confront me with that Martin Luther King shit. Everybody's gotta go for himself and I'm going for me. If niggas down South don't like the way they're being treated, they oughtta leave. I'm not going to join no picket lines and get the shit beat outta me by them crazy-ass Ku Klux-ers! 10

"I'm interested in four things," he added. "A degree, a good job, a good woman and a good living. That's all. You and Martin Luther King can take care of the demonstrating and protesting. I have *no* use for them!" 11

My roommate was typical. Although few stated their feel-   12
ings so bluntly, most of Howard's students shared his attitude.

I met my first real friend near mid-semester. He was a tall,   13
lanky junior with sparkling eyes and an infectious smile. Although he was from New York, we had many things in common, the most important being our intense interest in the
movement. We both had a burning passion to do something
about the plight of blacks. His name was Stokely Carmichael.

From the day we met, I considered Stokely a special   14
friend, a special person. Although he was flamboyant and extremely cocky, there was something about his manner that attracted people. Everyone on campus knew him. Few of his ad-
mirers ever got close enough to him to see what I saw: an
extremely sensitive person who generally disguised his sensitivity with bombast.

Stokely, who had worked in Mississippi for SNCC the pre-   15
vious summer, belonged to a campus organization called the
Nonviolent Action Group (NAG). It was just what I had been
looking for. I joined immediately.

NAG was organized in 1960, soon after the first sit-ins in   16
Greensboro. Some of its initial demonstrations attracted as
many as two hundred participants. One demonstration conducted during the summer of 1960 attracted five congressmen.

During its first year, NAG's members succeeded in deseg-   17
regating about twenty-five facilities, including lunch counters,
restaurants, a movie theater and Washington, D.C.'s only
amusement park. At least one hundred persons were arrested
in connection with demonstrations conducted by NAG.

The organization's name symbolized the determination of   18
its members to "nag" the conscience of Washington. The name
also reflected the theme of passive-aggressive protest that characterized that stage of the civil rights movement.

By the time I joined NAG in the winter of 1962, most of   19
Howard's students had lost interest in it. Picket lines and
demonstrations were not considered glamorous activities any-
more. The twenty-five to thirty students who belonged to the
organization were considered "kooks."

NAG was a "Friends of SNCC" affiliate. This meant that   20
those of us who belonged to it were unofficial members of
SNCC. As members of NAG, we could attend some SNCC meetings and vote in some SNCC elections. There were scores of
other Friends of SNCC groups on other campuses, especially in
the North. Most of these organizations devoted their energies to

fund-raising projects; few were actively involved in campus or community politics.

NAG was different. Although we sponsored dances and benefits for SNCC, that was not our primary task. Our primary task was demonstrating. We had a lot of good people, most of whom were Howard students—Courtland Cox, Murial Tillenez, Stokely, Stanley Wise, William (Bill) Mahoney, Ed Brown (Rap's brother) and Phil Hutchins.   21

Whenever black people in the city of Washington needed pickets, they would get in touch with NAG. It didn't matter to us if it was cold outside. If we thought we could help black people, we didn't mind demonstrating.   22

We frequently picketed various government departments. We weren't afraid of any of them. At different times the second semester, we picketed the Justice Department, Congress and the White House.   23

By the end of my second semester at Howard, I went on campus only to eat, sleep, attend classes and participate in periodic NAG rallies. I spent the rest of my time demonstrating and getting to know the people who lived in the huge black ghetto surrounding the campus. Unlike our classmates, the people in the community had a great deal of respect for those of us who belonged to NAG. We were great heroes to the young kids.   24

Discussion Questions

1. What is the "movement" to which Sellers refers in the first paragraph?

2. Why was Sellers disappointed in the students at Howard University?

3. What was the primary purpose of the NAG and SNCC organizations?

4. What were some of the contributions NAG made to the civil rights movement?

5. What type of person is Sellers? Cite specific details in the essay to support your answer.

6. Why were many of Howard's students apathetic to the "movement"?

7. What types of rhetorical organization does Sellers use in his essay?

8. What do you think is the purpose of paragraph 1?

Writing Assignments

1. Write an essay in which you discuss how an event or a place was a disappointment to you.
2. Sellers describes several activities that Howard students found interesting in 1962. Write an essay describing what many university students find interesting today.
3. Write an essay describing your university's image.

I HAVE A DREAM

Martin Luther King, Jr.

A clergyman and civil rights leader, Martin Luther King, Jr. (1929–1968), was born in Atlanta, Georgia, and was educated at Morehouse College, Crozer Theological Seminary, and Boston University. As a nonviolent advocate, Dr. King encouraged others to resist segregation. He led a boycott of blacks against the city's segregated bus system in Montgomery, Alabama (1955–1956), and in 1963 he organized a massive march on Washington during which time he delivered his famous "I Have a Dream" speech, which appears here. Among his best known works are Stride Toward Freedom *(1958), a history of the Montgomery bus boycott, and "Letter from Birmingham Jail" (1964). Although he was the 1964 Nobel Peace Prize recipient, Dr. King met a violent death. On April 4, 1968, he was assassinated in Memphis, Tennessee, while in the city to support striking sanitation workers.*

Vocabulary

manacles	(2)	chains
unalienable	(4)	that which cannot be given or taken away
inextricably	(12)	hopelessly tangled
redemptive	(16)	freeing
interposition	(22)	act of coming between parties in a dispute
nullification	(22)	act of refusing to recognize or enforce a law
prodigious	(27)	enormous, gigantic

Five score years ago, a great American, in whose symbolic shadow we stand today, signed the Emancipation Proclamation. This momentous decree came as a great beacon of light of hope to millions of Negro slaves who had been seared in the flames of withering injustice. It came as a joyous daybreak to end the long night of their captivity. 1

But one hundred years later, the Negro still is not free. One hundred years later, the life of the Negro is still sadly crippled by the manacles of segregation and the chains of discrimination. 2

One hundred years later, the Negro lives on a lonely island of poverty in the midst of a vast ocean of material prosperity. 3

One hundred years later, the Negro is still languished in the corners of American society and finds himself an exile in his own land. So we have come here today to dramatize a shameful condition.

In a sense we have come to our nation's capital to cash a   4
check. When the architects of our republic wrote the magnificent words of the Constitution and the Declaration of Independence, they were signing a promissory note to which every American was to fall heir. This note was a promise that all men, yes, black men as well as white men, would be granted the unalienable rights of life, liberty, and the pursuit of happiness.

It is obvious today that America has defaulted on this   5
promissory note insofar as her citizens of color are concerned. Instead of honoring this sacred obligation, America has given the Negro people a bad check; which has come back marked "insufficient funds."

But we refuse to believe that the bank of justice is bank-   6
rupt. We refuse to believe that there are insufficient funds in the great vaults of opportunity of this nation. So we have come to cash this check—a check that will give us upon demand the riches of freedom and the security of justice.

We have also come to this hallowed spot to remind Amer-   7
ica of the fierce urgency of now. This is no time to engage in the luxury of cooling off or to take the tranquilizing drug of gradualism. Now is the time to make real the promises of democracy. Now is the time to rise from the dark and desolate valley of segregation to the sunlit path of racial justice. Now is time to lift our nation from the quick sands of racial injustice and to the solid rock of brotherhood. Now is the time to make justice a reality for all of God's children.

It would be fatal for the nation to overlook the urgency of   8
the movement and to underestimate the determination of the Negro. This sweltering summer of the Negro's legitimate discontent will not pass until there is an invigorating autumn of freedom and equality. Nineteen sixty-three is not an end but a beginning. Those who hope that the Negro needed to blow off steam and will now be content will have a rude awakening if the nation returns to business as usual.

There will be neither rest nor tranquility in America until   9
the Negro is granted his citizenship rights. The whirlwinds of revolt will continue to shake the foundations of our nation until the bright day of justice emerges.

But there is something that I must say to my people who   10
stand on the warm threshold which leads into the palace of
justice. In the process of gaining our rightful place we must not
be guilty of wrongful deeds.

Let us not seek to satisfy our thirst for freedom by drink-   11
ing from the cup of bitterness and hatred. We must forever
conduct our struggle on the high plane of dignity and discipline. We must not allow our creative protest to degenerate into
physical violence. Again and again we must rise to the majestic
heights of meeting physical force with soul force.

The marvelous new militancy which has engulfed the Ne-   12
gro community must not lead us to a distrust of all white people, for many of our white brothers, as evidenced by their presence here today, have come to realize that their destiny is tied
up with our destiny and they have come to realize that their
freedom is inextricably bound to our freedom. This offense we
share, mounted to storm the battlements of injustice, must be
carried forth by a bi-racial army. We cannot walk alone.

And as we walk, we must make the pledge that we shall   13
always march ahead. We cannot turn back. There are those
who are asking the devotees of civil rights, "When will you be
satisfied?" We can never be satisfied as long as the Negro is the
victim of the unspeakable horrors of police brutality.

We can never be satisfied as long as our bodies, heavy   14
with fatigue of travel, cannot gain lodging in the motels of the
highways and the hotels of the cities. We cannot be satisfied as
long as the Negro's basic mobility is from a smaller ghetto to a
larger one.

We can never be satisfied as long as our children are   15
stripped of their selfhood and robbed of their dignity by signs
stating "for whites only." We cannot be satisfied as long as a
Negro in Mississippi cannot vote and a Negro in New York believes he has nothing for which to vote. No, we are not satisfied,
and we will not be satisfied until justice rolls down like waters
and righteousness like a mighty stream.

I am not unmindful that some of you have come here out   16
of excessive trials and tribulation. Some of you have come fresh
from narrow jail cells. Some of you have come from areas
where your quest for freedom left you battered by the storms of
persecution and staggered by the winds of police brutality. You
have been the veterans of creative suffering. Continue to work
with the faith that unearned suffering is redemptive.

Go back to Mississippi; go back to Alabama; go back to   17
South Carolina; go back to Georgia; go back to Louisiana; go
back to the slums and ghettoes of the Northern cities, knowing
that somehow this situation can, and will, be changed. Let us
not wallow in the valley of despair.

So I say to you, my friends, that even though we must face   18
the difficulties of today and tomorrow, I still have a dream. It is
a dream deeply rooted in the American dream that one day this
nation will rise up and live out the true meaning of its creed—
we hold these truths to be self-evident, that all men are created
equal.

I have a dream that one day on the red hills of Georgia,   19
sons of former slaves and sons of former slave-owners will be
able to sit down together at the table of brotherhood.

I have a dream that one day, even the state of Mississippi,   20
a state sweltering with the heat of injustice, sweltering with the
heat of oppression, will be transformed into an oasis of freedom
and justice.

I have a dream my four little children will one day live in a   21
nation where they will not be judged by the color of their skin
but by content of their character. I have a dream today!

I have a dream that one day, down in Alabama, with its vi-   22
cious racists, with its governor having his lips dripping with the
words of interposition and nullification, that one day, right
there in Alabama, little black boys and black girls will be able
to join hands with little white boys and white girls as sisters
and brothers. I have a dream today!

I have a dream that one day every valley shall be exalted,   23
every hill and mountain shall be made low, the rough places
shall be made plain, and the crooked places shall be made
straight and the glory of the Lord will be revealed and all flesh
shall see it together.

This is our hope. This is the faith that I go back to the   24
South with.

With this faith we will be able to bear out of the mountain   25
of despair a stone of hope. With this faith we will be able to
transform the jangling discords of our nation into a beautiful
symphony of brotherhood.

With this faith we will be able to work together, to pray to-   26
gether, to struggle together, to go to jail together, to stand up
for freedom together, knowing that we will be free one day. This
will be the day when all of God's children will be able to sing
with new meaning "my country 'tis of thee; sweet land of lib-

erty; of thee I sing; land where my fathers died, land of the pilgrim's pride; from every mountain side, let freedom ring." And if America is to be a great nation, this must become true.

So let freedom ring from the prodigious hilltops of New Hampshire.　27

Let freedom ring from the mighty mountains of New York.　28

Let freedom ring from the heightening Alleghenies of Pennsylvania.　29

Let freedom ring from the snow-capped Rockies of Colorado.　30

Let freedom ring from the curvaceous slopes of California.　31

But not only that.　32

Let freedom ring from Stone Mountain of Georgia.　33

Let freedom ring from Lookout Mountain of Tennessee.　34

Let freedom ring from every hill and molehill of Mississippi, from every mountainside, let freedom ring.　35

And when we allow freedom to ring, when we let it ring from every village and hamlet, from every state and city, we will be able to speed up that day when all of God's children—black men and white men, Jews and Gentiles, Catholics and Protestants—will be able to join hands and to sing in the words of the old Negro spiritual, "Free at last, free at last; thank God Almighty, we are free at last."　36

Discussion Questions

1. What is King's dream?
2. What examples does King offer to support his argument that there was no democracy in the 1960s for blacks in the United States?
3. What do you think King means by his statement, "We have come to the nation's capital to cash a check"?
4. King relies on his skillful use of descriptive language, such as the example in question 3, to make his points clear. What are some other examples?
5. To what extent does King's repetition of phrases such as "One hundred years later," "Now is the time," "I have a dream" enhance the effectiveness of his speech?
6. To what extent, if any, has King's dream become a reality for African Americans today?
7. To what extent does King's use of illustration and description help strengthen his argument?

8. What in the speech indicates that King has an understanding of his audience?

Writing Assignments

1. In an essay argue whether or not King's dream of an America where "all men are created equal" has become a reality.
2. Write an essay describing one of your dreams.
3. Write an essay in which you describe a society free of one of today's ills: AIDS, drugs, sexism.

Student Essay:
THE CRIMINAL JUSTICE SYSTEM AND POOR BLACKS

Marshall Mercy

Vocabulary

disproportionate (4)   mismatched

The black man's place within American society has been well   1
defined since he was forced to come here. His place within
white society is either to work hard for the white man, which
does not benefit him but does benefit his oppressor, or to be
caged in like an animal because he is believed not to be fit to
live within a "democratic society."

Prominent sociologists have proven that the criminal jus-   2
tice system is more unfairly applied to lower income people
than to higher income people. Sociologists also offer evidence
that the majority of people who are arrested, convicted, and
punished are black males. Black males are more likely to go to
prison or to have a record by the age of twenty-six than any
other ethnic group. Although blacks are the minority, only 12%
of the population of the United States, they are the majority
within the prison system. Blacks are the least likely to be
paroled and the most likely to receive capital punishment.
Blacks on death row are more likely to be executed than their
white counterparts who commit the same crimes.

It seems that ever since the black man was stolen from his   3
home, forced to work on the hot plantation fields in the South,
forced to be poor and at the very mercy of the white man, he
has been denied the privileges guaranteed to others. In the
1800s the black male was discriminated against because he
was not allowed to testify against whites, but was allowed to
testify against other blacks. In the 1960s, through the struggle
for civil rights, blacks were again discriminated against when
they were thrown in jail for marching and protesting the mistreatment they received. In the 1990s, blacks in general and
black males in particular are still suffering at the hands of the
dominant society—white males.

From police brutality, highlighted by the Rodney King   4
case, to the disproportionate numbers of blacks on death row,

the black male is subjected to prejudices on the basis of race and class. As a result, he has been forced to be always in the pursuit of equality, liberty, and justice.

Discussion Questions

1. What principal arguments does Mercy give to support her statement that the criminal justice system is less "just" toward blacks?
2. To what extent is the author's use of logical persuasion effective?
3. Why does Mercy place quotation marks around "democratic society"?
4. How does the author show the history of discrimination blacks have suffered in the United States?
5. From reading the essay, what do you know about the author?
6. Mercy chooses illustration as one of her dominant rhetorical strategies. Are her examples sufficient to support his thesis?

Writing Assignments

1. Write an essay describing your ideas of a fair criminal justice system of the future.
2. Write an essay discussing the weakness and/or strength of the U.S. criminal justice system.

11

Freedom • Equality
Unity • Protest

FREEDOM

Joyce M. Jarrett

Teacher, writer, poet, Joyce M. Jarrett (1951–   ) was born in Meridian, Mississippi. A first-generation college student, Jarrett graduated from Tennessee State University and Vanderbilt University. Currently, she is associate professor of English at Hampton University. She is a co-author of Pathways: A Text for Developing Writers *(1990) and* Heritage: African American Readings for Writing *(1996). All of her creative works have grown out of her African American experience. In the selection here, which was first published in* Between Worlds *(1986), Jarrett reflects on one of her struggles during the civil rights movement.*

Vocabulary

hordes	(2)	groups or crowds
irate	(3)	angry
denigrating	(3)	insulting and belittling
constraints	(10)	restrictions
overt	(10)	obvious, apparent
futile	(10)	useless

"Born free, as free as the wind blows, as free as the grass grows, born free to follow your heart." (Don Black)

My first illusion of freedom came in 1966, many years fol- 1
lowing the Supreme Court's decision on school desegregation.
Of course, to a fifteen-year-old girl, isolated, caged like a rodent
in the poverty-stricken plains of the Magnolia State,[1] Brown
vs. the Board of Education had no meaning. Though many
must have thought that my decision to attend the all-white city
high school that fall, along with 49 other blacks, was made in
protest or had evolved from a sense of commitment for the betterment of my people, nothing could have been further from the
truth. Like a rat finding a new passageway, I was propelled to
my new liberty more out of curiosity than out of a sense of mission.

On the first day of school, I was escorted by hordes of na- 2
tional guardsmen. Like a funeral procession, the steady stream
of official-looking cars followed me to the campus. Some patrol-
men were parked near campus gates, while others, with guns
strapped to their sides, stood near building entrances. Though
many of my escorts had given me smiles of support, still I was
not prepared for what I encountered upon entering *my* new
school.

There, I had to break through lines of irate white protes- 3
tors, spraying obscenities at me while carrying their denigrat-
ing signs: "KKK Forever," read one; "Back to Africa," said another. And as I dashed toward the school door, blinded with
fear, I nearly collided with another sign that screamed, "Nigger
Go Home."

Once inside the fortress, I was ushered by school adminis- 4
trators and plain-clothes police to and from my respective
classes. The anger and fear that I had felt outside of those walls
were numbed by the surprisingly uneventful classroom experiences—until I went to geometry, my last scheduled class for
that day.

As I sauntered into the classroom and took a seat, there 5
was a flurry of activity. When everyone had settled, I sat in the
center of the class, surrounded by empty desks—on each side,
and in front and back.

"We have a nigger in the class," someone shouted. 6

[1] Magnolia State   (1)   Mississippi.

"Let's get quiet and make the best of it," Mr. Moore smugly   7
replied. Then he proceeded with the course orientation.

Near the end of the class, I mustered up enough courage   8
to ask a question, so, nervously, I raised my hand. Keeping
silent, Mr. Moore stared, and stared, and stared at me until my
arm grew heavy and began to tremble. My heart sank, and my
picture of freedom shattered in infinite pieces as he said, "I see
that there are no questions. Class dismissed."

I have always blamed myself for that crushing moment.   9
Why did I allow myself to be overlooked? Why did I not feel
free? That painful, dehumanizing incident within itself did not
provide any answers, though it signaled the beginning of my
search. And finally, through years of disappointments, I discovered the truth—the truth that had evaded me during those
high school years.

Freedom is not a gift, but a right. Officials did not, could   10
not, award "freedom." It had to be something that I wanted,
craved, demanded. The Supreme Court had liberated me of
many external restrictions, but I had failed to liberate myself.
In some instances internal constraints can be more binding
than the overt ones. It is impossible to enslave one who has liberated oneself and futile to pry off the external chains of an internally bound person. Only when there is emancipation of
both body and soul are any of us truly *free* to follow our hearts.

Discussion Questions

1. In the first paragraph, what is the curiosity to which the narrator
   refers?
2. Why were National Guardsmen needed to escort Jarrett to the
   school?
3. How did Mr. Moore demonstrate his racism?
4. Why does the narrator blame herself for the incident in Mr.
   Moore's class? Would you have blamed yourself had you been in
   the narrator's place?
5. To what extent does the narrator's attitude change after the incident?
6. What does the narrator mean when she says, "It is impossible to
   enslave one who has liberated oneself and futile to pry off the external chains of an internally bound person"?
7. The predominant organization of the essay is definition. To what
   extent does the writer use other strategies—illustration, cause

and effect, comparison and contrast—to help the reader understand her definition of "freedom"?

8. In what way, if any, would the essay change had the writer used
her concluding paragraph as her opening paragraph? Explain
your answer.

Writing Assignments

1. Write an essay describing an incident that caused you to develop
a mature awakening.
2. Write an essay in which you define one of the following terms:
freedom, racism, discrimination, commitment, struggle.
3. Write an essay about something you did (good or bad) for the
wrong reason.

WE WEAR THE MASK

Paul Laurence Dunbar

Paul Laurence Dunbar (1872–1906) was the first nationally known African American poet. He published six volumes of poetry, four novels, and four volumes of short stories. Despite his national reputation, however, Dunbar faced a dilemma as a poet: His publishers wanted him to write poetry portraying African Americans who were always happy and content. His best and most serious poetry detailing the struggles of his people was discouraged. Dunbar solved the dilemma of being forced to write about happy African Americans content with living conditions in the United States by using dialect. He wrote his most serious poetry, including the following selection, in standard English. Published in The Complete Poems *(1913), "We Wear the Mask" is a poem whose subject is one that has been explored since slavery: African Americans must hide their true feelings in racist America.*

Vocabulary

guile	(1)	fraud, dishonesty
myriad	(1)	countless
subtleties	(1)	those things or ideas that are not obvious
vile	(3)	foul, evil

We wear the mask that grins and lies,   1
It hides our cheeks and shades our eyes,—
This debt we pay to human guile;
With torn and bleeding hearts we smile,
And mouth with myriad subtleties.

Why should the world be overwise,   2
In counting all our tears and sighs?
Nay, let them only see us, while
  We wear the mask.

We smile, but, O great Christ, our cries   3
To thee from tortured souls arise
We sing, but oh the clay is vile
Beneath our feet, and long the mile;
But let the world dream otherwise,
  We wear the mask!

Discussion Questions

1. How would you describe the mask?
2. Why does the "we" in the poem wear the mask?
3. What lies behind the mask?
4. What or who is the "world" referred to in the second stanza?
5. Is there a solution offered in the poem to the problem of mask wearing? Explain your answer.
6. How does Dunbar combine the strategies of comparison and contrast and description to explain the title of the poem?
7. How does the exclamation point at the end of the last line affect the ending of the poem?

Writing Assignments

1. Write an essay illustrating an individual or a group in our society that wears a mask.
2. Write an essay describing an incident in which you were forced to wear a mask.
3. In an essay, recount the horror you found in some incident.

IF WE MUST DIE

Claude McKay

Born in Jamaica, British West Indies, Claude McKay (1889–1948) was a well-known poet in both Jamaica and the United States. He came to the United States in 1912 and studied at Tuskegee Institute and Kansas State College. After deciding on a literary career, McKay moved to Harlem, New York, and contributed greatly to the literary period known as the Harlem Renaissance. In the United States, he published two collections of poetry, Spring in New Hampshire and Other Poems *(1920) and* Harlem Shadows *(1922). He also published four novels:* Home to Harlem *(1928),* Banjo *(1929),* Gingertown *(1932), and* Banana Bottom *(1933). "If We Must Die," first published in 1919 in the magazine* The Liberator, *is a poem written in reaction to the race riots that occurred throughout major cities in the United States during the "bloody" summer of 1919. Its message of defiance in the face of overwhelming odds has made this work the theme poem of the Harlem Renaissance.*

If we must die, let it not be like hogs   1
Hunted and penned in an inglorious spot,
While round us bark the mad and hungry dogs,
Making their mock at our accursed lot.

If we must die, O let us nobly die,   2
So that our precious blood may not be shed
In vain; then even the monsters we defy
Shall be constrained to honor us though dead!

O kinsmen! we must meet the common foe!   3
Though far outnumbered let us show us brave,
And for their thousand blows deal one
        deathblow!

What though before us lies the open grave?   4
Like men we'll face the murderous, cowardly
        pack,
Pressed to the wall, dying, but fighting back!

Discussion Questions

1. Who is the "we" in the poem? Who is the "monster"?
2. Why does the persona (speaker) think that if "we" fight back, the "monster" will honor us?
3. How significant is it that the image of "we" changes from one of hogs to men? Explain your answer.
4. How does the poem deal with death?
5. What is the tone of the poem?
6. How does McKay use persuasion as a means of convincing his audience to accept his message?
7. What is the significance of using a subordinate clause as the title of the poem?

Writing Assignments

1. In an essay, recount an instance when you acted defiantly against overwhelming odds.
2. Write an essay that explains a principle you feel is worth dying for.
3. Write an essay in which you explore the term *honor.*

THE RAP ON FREDERICK DOUGLASS

Roger Guenveur Smith

Roger Guenveur Smith is an actor and the creator of "Frederick Douglass Now," a one-man multimedia show. First published in the New York Times, *February 19, 1990, just five days after Douglass's birthday, the following rap was extracted from the one-man show.*

If there is no struggle there is no progress
That was the rap of Brother Frederick Douglass
From 1818 to 1895
Frederick Douglass is still alive
No jive: 5
In 1985 he was alive
In 1986 we threw him in the mix
In 1987 he was looking down from heaven
In 1988 he said:
Mash down Aparthate   10
Smash down Aparthate
Mash down Smash down Bash down Aparthate.
In '89 he was right on time
Now check it out while I bust this rhyme:
They love Black music but they hate Black people.   15
They love this rhythm
They love this rhyme
But when it comes to the struggle they don't have the time
They love Michael Jackson on MTV
They love Eddie Murphy and Mr. T.   20
They love Bill Cosby and Bob Marley
And some say to me "I love Spike Lee"
But they don't give a damn if we are free
They don't know a thing about our History
This History?   25
Yes.
It was a long a long a long a long a long long journey
And you don't stop
Everybody's rapping about money and sex
But nobody's rapping about Malcolm X: 30
El Hajj Malik was very unique
He came to I and I right off the street
But they shot him down in the Audubon Ballroom
Now they're just rapping and doing the wild thing on his
    tomb.   35

Boom boom boom boom
They shot him down
Boom boom
Shot him down because he wore the crown
Malcolm X?   40
He never played the clown
Now I'm not saying that we can't have no fun
That's not my idea of Revolution
But please don't forget about Paul Robeson:[1]
Big Paul   45
He was the king of them all y'all
All-American at playing ball
But that wasn't all y'all
He was Phi Beta Kappa, Shakespearean rapper
Big Paul stood tall y'all   50
Yes he was born in the USA
But in his heyday they took his passport away
Why?
Because they didn't like what he had to say:
"Here I stand, an African American   55
Son of a slave from cradle to the grave."
Are you now or have you ever been
aware of him?
Understood why they were scared of him?
This History?   60
Yes.
It was a long a long a long a long a long long journey
And you don't stop
Until the break of a new dawn
Like Marvin Gaye say: "Let's get it on"   65
You've got to be strong in this Babylon[2]
Because you'll never know yourself until you're back
        against the wall
Until you're Black
And you're under attack
Young and gifted and under attack   70
We must fight back
How we gonna do that?
We must learn to read and learn to write
And organize ourselves to fight
Fight for what?

---

[1] Paul Robeson (43)   An African American activist, actor, and singer popular from the 1920s through the 1940s.
[2] Babylon (65)   Any city or place of great luxury and corruption, often used to refer to the United States.

For our life   75
(That's the death)
Frederick Douglass will never run out of breath:
If there is not struggle there is not progress
Yes.

                                                                         80

Discussion Questions

1. What is the meaning of the word *Aparthate*?
2. In what ways does Smith urge African Americans to fight for their lives?
3. What does the speaker mean when he says that Frederick Douglass is still alive?
4. What does the speaker want the reader to realize about Douglass, Malcolm, and Robeson?
5. What examples does Smith use to support his choice of illustration as a rhetorical strategy?
6. How can you argue that the line, "If there is no struggle there is no progress," is the main idea of "The Rap on Frederick Douglass"?

Writing Assignments

1. Write a rap expressing your views on an issue.
2. Write an essay urging the importance of knowing one's history.
3. Think of an historical figure, and write an essay showing the extent to which that figure continues to influence today's society.

STUDENT ESSAY:
AFFIRMATIVE ACTION: THE CONTROVERSIAL TOPIC

James Mitchener

Vocabulary

blatant	(2)	completely obvious
equilibrium	(2)	a state of intellectual or emotional balance
quotas	(3)	proportional parts or shares

At the heart of the affirmative action issue is whether or not an attempt to ensure equal treatment for all racial and ethnic groups does not in fact result in reverse discrimination. By giving minorities advantages, some white males feel they are put at a disadvantage, which on the surface is an arguable point. 1

In assessing the need for affirmative action, one must try to think of another solution to blatant acts of discrimination. If there are solutions better than the one we have in affirmative action, most of us are unaware of them. One journalist made an interesting comparison concerning this very issue. He said, "Reverse racism is a correct description of affirmative action only if one considers the cancer racism to be morally and medically indistinguishable from the therapy we apply to it. A cancer is an invasion of the body's equilibrium, and so is chemotherapy; but we do not decline to fight the disease because the medicine we employ is also disruptive of normal functioning." In essence, regardless of how disruptive affirmative action may be, it is the only remedy to the problem of discrimination. 2

Another issue surrounding affirmative action is that some believe quotas take away from the quality of organizations. Some say that quality is lost when a person's race is more important than a person's talent. While this statement may be true, the painful truth is that talented minorities, who often are just as, if not more qualified than whites, must be given a chance to prove themselves. Such a chance is important, especially since many employers seem still to believe that white males are superior. Affirmative action is necessary because of this predominant idea. 3

I am sure that affirmative action will remain a very controversial topic for years to come. Until better solutions are found 4 to combat discrimination, Americans must endure affirmative action because for now it is the only sure way to break the race barrier.

Discussion Questions

1. Why is affirmative action a controversial topic?
2. What is the author's assessment of the effectiveness of affirmative action?
3. Why does Mitchener compare affirmative action to chemotherapy?
4. Why does the author argue the necessity of quotas?
5. How could Mitchener have used extended definition as an effective strategy to support his thesis statement?
6. How effective is the author's ending? Explain your answer.

Writing Assignments

1. In an essay, describe another remedy that may be regarded as problematic or disruptive, but necessary.
2. Write an essay in which you present opposing views to the Mitchener essay.

12

Arts • Sciences • Media

SHINING LIGHT OF A POET AND PIONEER

Earl Caldwell

Earl Caldwell (1941–   ) is a columnist with the New York Daily News. *Born in Clearfield, Pennsylvania, he attended the University of Buffalo. Caldwell has been a reporter for several newspapers: the* Clearfield Progress, *the* Intelligencer Journal *(Lancaster, Pennsylvania), the* Democrat and Chronicle *(Rochester, New York), the* Washington Star, *the* New York Post, *and the* New York Times. *He has the distinction of being the only reporter in Memphis with Dr. Martin Luther King, Jr., when King was assassinated in 1968. His account of the murder was headlined in newspapers across the country and abroad. The following article, which appeared in* The Amsterdam News *(1993), is a tribute to the life and career of African American journalist Robert C. Maynard.*

Vocabulary

piqued	(7)	aroused, exited
ombudsman	(9)	one who investigates citizens' complaints
formidable	(11)	awesome, powerful
lexicon	(12)	vocabulary
demystification	(13)	making less difficult to understand

"And yet do I marvel at this curious thing: To make a poet black,   1
and bid him sing!" (From "Yet Do I Marvel" by Countee Cullen.)

For the journalist Robert C. Maynard, the words of the   2
poet Countee Cullen made a perfect fit. More than anything
else, Bob Maynard was a newspaperman. He fell in love with
the craft as a kid growing up in the tough neighborhoods of the
Bedford-Stuyvesant section of Brooklyn. And in his life, which
spanned 56 years, that never changed, it never did.

In the world that he loved, Maynard did it all. He rose to   3
the top as a writer, reporter and editor. Eventually, he broke
through to become the first African-American to own and publish a major daily newspaper.

So large were his accomplishments that when he died two   4
days ago, his peers looked at the whole of what he had
achieved and they gave him the kind of acclaim rarely given in
the newspaper industry.

Bob Maynard made himself special. Much of the time,   5
what a newspaperman accomplishes gets measured almost entirely by the words he puts on paper. Maynard passed that
test—but for him that was just a starting place. He also possessed what Countee Cullen called "this curious thing."

He had a voice. It was a voice that was deep and rich and   6
full, and he coupled that with the enormous command he had
of the language. The combination of the two brought life to
Cullen's words: *"To make a poet black, and bid him sing."*

Maynard came of age in a newspaper industry that virtu-   7
ally held out a sign: "For white males only." That merely piqued
his determination. It only made him ready for battle. And he
did that. The New York City of his youth was a town filled with
newspapers, yet he couldn't get a start on any of the dailies. No
problem. He went out of town. After some breakthrough experience on some black weeklies, he wound up in southeastern
Pennsylvania in the town of York. When he was finished there,
he was managing editor and on the recommended list for a Nie-
man fellowship at Harvard.

He came away from that experience with so much going   8
for him that the door was opened. Editors at the Washington
Post—a newspaper with credentials that say "top of the line"—
beckoned him.

At the Post, Maynard did it all. There was nothing he   9
couldn't cover. He started on the streets working riots, and he
wound up at the White House covering former President Lyndon Johnson. Maynard wasn't finished. He showed a mind so
sharp that he was made an editorial writer, which meant he

was chosen to speak for the paper. Later, he was the readers' advocate as the newspaper's ombudsman.

All those experiences positioned Maynard for the work that was to change the industry. He set out to train young journalists, those who had been locked out because they were not white. He could have made some noise as a rabble-rouser. But that was not his way, not his style.   10

And Bob Maynard *had* style. It was in his voice; it was in his body language, and yes, it was in his soul. Together, it amounted to a formidable array of skills.   11

He stated the goal: "We want to remove from the lexicon of American journalism the words, 'We can't find any qualified minorities.'"   12

Just to train young people to get them into newsrooms was a major task. But for Maynard, that was only part of the job. He believed everybody, regardless of race or sex, had to know why it was important. So he brought a whole different language to the mission. These were his words: portrayal, diversity, demystification.   13

He was brilliant—spellbinding, too—in describing the damage that the media was inflicting in their portrayals of those who were not white.   14

He was eloquent in arguing the case for diversity in the newsroom—in detailing the ways diversity makes America better and stronger.   15

He demystified that which had been complicated, and he did it in a way that brought the publishers' association to embrace his "Year 2000 strategy" for a complete desegregation of the news business.   16

As it happened, Maynard didn't get all the years he should have had. So he will be buried this morning in Oakland, Calif., where he owned and published the daily paper until his health gave out. But for him, you say this: *My, how he used the time he had.*   17

Discussion Questions

1. How did Maynard open doors that had been closed to him as a journalist?
2. According to Caldwell, what was Maynard's primary goal as a journalist? How did he accomplish this goal?
3. What was Maynard's journalistic philosophy? How did this philosophy relate to his "Year 2000 strategy"?

4. How does Caldwell describe Maynard's "style"?

5. How does Caldwell use illustration to portray Maynard as both a poet and a pioneer?

6. Why is Caldwell's use of a famous quotation particularly effective in introducing his article?

Writing Assignments

1. Write an essay about someone considered a pioneer in his or her field.

2. Write an essay describing your particular style of doing something that may be different from others' style of doing it.

3. People confront problems differently. Write an essay showing two different approaches to the same problem.

CROSSOVER DREAMS AND RACIAL REALITIES

William Barlow

William Barlow (1943–) is associate professor of radio, television, and film at Howard University in Washington, D.C. He is the author of "Looking Up at Down": The Emergence of Blues Culture *(1989) and co-author of* Split Image: African Americans in the Mass Media *(1990), from which the following excerpt is taken. This excerpt describes the role and the dilemma of African American radio stations.*

Vocabulary

advocacy	(1)	actively supporting
lucrative	(1)	profitable
formidable	(2)	difficult to overcome
demographic	(2)	related to size and distribution of people
emulate	(3)	imitate

By the end of the 1980s, black radio in the United States had reached a new plateau. For the first time in its history there were both network and chain operations controlled by African American broadcasters. Furthermore, there now existed a bona fide national advocacy organization, the National Black Media Coalition, capable of coordinating on a national level the ongoing struggles against discrimination in radio employment and ownership. Consequently, the number of black-owned commercial broadcasting outlets has recently been increasing at its fastest rate ever. Moreover, it continued to be lucrative for advertisers to target the urban black consumer. Education and income levels for African Americans in the urban markets rose considerably in the 1970s, and the trend carried over into and lasted through the 1980s. In addition, research on black listeners during this period indicated that there were more of them as a group, and that they listened to more radio than their white counterparts. Ninety-seven percent of all African Americans listen to radio each week, and they listen to an average of thirty hours per week, 20 percent more than white listeners. This should give African American broadcasters a competitive edge in the urban markets with large black populations. Indeed, it appears that black commercial radio might be able to terminate, or at least minimize, its historical dependency on white broadcasters.

However, there still exist a number of structural factors   2
that are formidable obstacles to the goal of African American independence and self-sufficiency in radio broadcasting. For example, recent demographic patterns in the growing black middle-class population reveal a move to the suburbs, like that of the white middle class before them. The result is a significant fragmentation of the black urban audience, an event that has affected recent programming decisions. Fearing the loss of their most affluent listeners, even the leading black-controlled stations in the large urban markets have adopted crossover urban contemporary or urban adult formats. Some radio industry observers have heralded this as a breakthrough opening up the possibility of a new era of multiethnic commercial formats. But careful scrutiny of the airways reveals that, while the urban and adult contemporary formats have succeeded in allowing white artists greater access to black-controlled stations, African American artists have not gained corresponding exposure on white rock stations, except for crossover superstars like Michael Jackson and Prince. Urban contemporary and its spin-offs allow black broadcasters to anticipate the new demographic realities of the urban market, and in so doing to profit from these changes by converting them into higher ratings. However, this change also tends to undercut African American musicians and their music by narrowing their access to black radio outlets; moreover, those replaced by white crossover acts are invariably those with the least exposure in the first place. As has been the case so often in the past, the structure of the radio industry, its way of doing business, presents African Americans seeking an independent broadcast voice with a conflict of interest. The price of success all too often requires that the specific communication needs of the entire black community be forsaken.

On the other front, the upsurge in public radio in the   3
1970s and 1980s has opened up new terrain for African American broadcasters. They have responded by establishing over fifty college- and community-based public outlets. While some of the black college stations try to emulate successful commercial stations in their markets, most are engaged in promoting new African American musical talent, preserving African American musical traditions, and providing news and information for the local black populations within reach of their signals. In

general, the black public stations, in league with the more progressive black commercial outlets, are on the cutting edge of the movement to establish and maintain a self-sufficient African American presence on the radio airways. The white-controlled radio industry has been forced to open its doors to black employment and even ownership, no matter how reluctantly. Further, the negative images and stereotypes that characterized the portrayal of African Americans in the earlier years of broadcasting have all but vanished from radio's airways. These are important advances in the overall African American struggle to achieve racial equality and cultural self-determination. While black stations still only make up less than 2 percent of the total number of radio outlets broadcasting in the U.S.A. today, they are a crucial 2 percent, strategically located in all of the major black population centers in the country. Although they broadcast to local audiences, collectively they can also be quite effective in mobilizing black people on a national level for political campaigns like Jesse Jackson's bids for the presidency, or the more successful effort to have Martin Luther King, Jr.'s birthday declared a national holiday, or the ongoing campaign in the U.S.A. to end apartheid in South Africa. Black radio has played a vital role in furthering causes of this nature and no doubt will continue to do so in the future.

Discussion Questions

1. What accounts for the growth in the number of black-owned commercial broadcasting outlets by the end of the 1980s?
2. Why do you think African Americans listen to radio 20 percent more each week than whites?
3. How has the move to the suburbs, by the growing African American population, affected the African American broadcasting industry?
4. How have African American musicians been affected by not gaining corresponding exposure on white radio stations? How has this lack of exposure affected African American radio stations? What has been the effect on the African American community?
5. What seems to be the primary benefit of African American radio stations in major black population centers in the United States?
6. What is the meaning of the essay's title?
7. What is the cause-and-effect relationship described by Barlow?

8. The beginning and ending paragraphs of this essay are both considerably long. What effect, if any, does their length have on the quality of the essay?

Writing Assignments

1. Write an essay describing the kind of music played most often on your college radio station or on one of your favorite local stations. Why do you think this kind of music is played more often than other kinds?

2. Write a letter persuading your favorite radio station to omit or include a certain type of music or to provide a service that it currently does not provide.

3. Write an essay evaluating the effectiveness of a medium (other than radio) in shaping the image of African Americans.

TV'S BLACK WORLD

Henry Louis Gates, Jr.

*Henry Louis Gates, Jr. (1950–   ), leading literary critic
and Harvard professor of English, has written extensively
on issues of African American culture and race relations. He
has also edited several collections of African American literature. His* The Signifying Monkey: A Theory of African
American Literary Criticism *(1989) won an American Book
Award. The following excerpt, taken from "TV's Black World
Turns—But Stays Unreal," which first appeared in the* New
York Times *in 1989, gives a historical perspective on
African American television shows and the myths that have
been associated with them.*

Vocabulary

genre	(5)	kind, type
metaphorical	(7)	comparable, similar
purveyed	(8)	provided, offered
questing	(10)	searching, seeking
feisty	(10)	touchy, excitable
benevolent	(10	kind, helpful
paternalism	(10)	father-child relationship
motif	(11)	theme
fetish	(13)	object of excessive attention
subliminal	(13)	subconscious
sass	(16)	daring, recklessness
protocol	(20)	ceremonial courtesies
palatable	(21)	agreeable
militates	(21)	works (against)

In 1933, Sterling Brown, the great black poet and critic, di-   1
vided the full range of black character types in American literature into seven categories: the contented slave; the wretched freeman; the comic Negro; the brute Negro; the tragic mulatto; the
local color Negro, and the exotic primitive. It was only one small
step to associate our public negative image in the American mind
with the public negative social roles that we were assigned and to
which we were largely confined. "If only they could be exposed to
the *best* of the race," the sentiment went, "then they would see
that we were normal human beings and treat us better." . . .

What lies behind these sorts of arguments is a belief that 2
social policies affecting black Americans were largely determined by our popular images in the media. But the success of
The Cosby Show has put the lie to that myth: *Cosby* exposes
more white Americans than ever before to the most nobly idealized blacks in the history of entertainment, yet social and economic conditions for the average black American have not been
bleaker in a very long time.

To make matters worse, *Cosby* is also one of the most 3
popular shows in apartheid South Africa, underscoring the
fact that the relationship between how whites treat us and their
exposure to "the best" in us is far from straightforward. (One
can hear the Afrikaaner speaking to his black servants: "When
you people are like Cliff and Clair, *then* we will abandon
apartheid.")

There are probably as many reasons to like *The Cosby* 4
Show as there are devoted viewers—and there are millions of
them. I happen to like it because my daughters (ages nine and
seven) like it, and I enjoy watching them watch themselves in
the depictions of middle-class black kids, worrying about
school, sibling rivalries, and family tradition. But I also like
Cosby because its very success has forced us to rethink completely the relation between black social progress and the images of blacks that American society fabricates, projects, and
digests.

But the *Cosby* vision of upper-middle-class blacks and 5
their families is comparatively recent. And while it may have
constituted the dominant image of blacks for the last five years,
it is a direct reaction against the lower-class ghetto comedies of
the 70s, such as *Sanford and Son* (1972–77), *Good Times*
(1974–79), *That's My Mama* (1974–75), and *What's Happening!!* (1976–79). The latter three were single-mother-dominated
sitcoms. Although *Good Times* began with a nuclear family,
John Amos—who had succeeded marvelously in transforming
the genre of the black maternal household—was soon killed off,
enabling the show to conform to the stereotype of a fatherless
black family.

Even *The Jeffersons* (1975–85) conforms to this mold. 6
George and Louise began their TV existence as Archie Bunker's
working-class neighbors, saved their pennies, then "moved on
up," as the theme song says, to Manhattan's East Side. *The Jeffersons* also served as a bridge between sitcoms depicting the
ghetto and those portraying the new black upper class.

In fact, in the history of black images on television, char-   7
acter types have distinct pasts and, as is also the case with
white shows, series seem both to lead to other series and to
spring from metaphorical ancestors.

Pure Street in a Brooks Brothers Suit

Let's track the evolution of the *Cosby* type on television. While   8
social engineering is easier on the little screen than in the big
city, Sterling Brown's list of black stereotypes in American literature proves quite serviceable as a guide to the images TV has
purveyed for the last two decades. Were we writing a new sitcom using these character types, our cast might look like this—
contented slave: Andy, Fred Sanford, J. J. *(Good Times)*;
wretched freeman: George Jefferson; comic Negro: Flip Wilson;
brute Negro: Mr. T *(The A-Team)*, Hawk *(Spenser: for Hire)*;
tragic mulatto: *Julia*, Elvin *(Cosby)*, Whitley *(A Different World)*;
local color Negro: Meschach Taylor *(Designing Women)*; exotic
primitive: Link *(Mod Squad* 1968–73); most black characters
on MTV. If we add the category of Noble Negro (Cliff Huxtable,
Benson), our list might be complete.

We can start with George Jefferson, who we might think of   9
as a Kingfish *(Amos 'n' Andy)* or as a Fred Sanford *(Sanford and
Son)* who has finally made it. Jefferson epitomized Richard
Nixon's version of black capitalism, bootstrap variety, and all of
its terrifying consequences. Jefferson was anything but a man
of culture; unlike the *Cosby* living room, his East Side apartment had no painting by Jacob Lawrence or Charles White, Romare Bearden or Varnette Honeywood.[1] Despite his new-found
wealth, Jefferson was pure street, draped in a Brooks Brothers
suit. You did not want to live next to a George Jefferson, and
you most certainly did not want your daughter to marry one.

The Jeffersons was part of a larger trend in television in   10
the depiction of black men. We might think of this as their domestication, in direct reaction to the questing, macho images of
black males shown in the 60s news clips of the civil rights
movement, the Black Panthers, and the black power movement. While Jefferson (short, feisty, racist, rich, vulgar) repre-

---

[1] Jacob Lawrence   (9)   African American painters.
  Charles White
  Romare Bearden
  Varnette Honeywood

sents one kind of domestication, a more curious kind was the cultural dwarfism represented by *Diff'rent Strokes* (1978–86) and *Webster* (1983–87), in which small black "boys" (arrested adolescents who were much older than the characters they played) were adopted by tall, successful white males. These establishment figures represented the myth of the benevolent paternalism of the white upper class, an American myth as old as the abolitionist movement.

Indeed, one central motif of nineteenth-century American art is a sculpted tall white male (often Lincoln) towering above a crouched or kneeling adult or adolescent slave, in the act of setting them free. *Webster* and *Diff'rent Strokes* depict black orphans who are rescued from blackness and poverty; adopted, and raised just like any other upper-middle-class white kid, prep schools and all. These shows can be thought of as TV's fantasy of Lyndon Johnson's "Great Society" and the war on poverty rolled into one.

The formula was not as successful with a female character. An attempt to use the same format with a black woman, Shirley Hemphill (*One in a Million,* 1980) lasted only six months. *The White Shadow* (1978–1981) was a variation of this paternal motif, in which wild and unruly ghetto kids were tamed with a basketball.

These small black men signaled to the larger American audience that the very idea of the black male could be, and had been, successfully domesticated. Mr. T—whose 1983–87 *A-Team* run paralleled that of *Webster*—might appear to be an exception. We are forced to wonder, however, why such an important feature of his costume—and favorite fetish—was those dazzling gold chains, surely a subliminal suggestion of bondage.

This process of paternal domestication, in effect, made Cliff Huxtable's character a logical next step. In fact, I think of the evolution of the Huxtable character, generationally, in this way: imagine if George Jefferson owned the tenement building in which Florida and her family from *Good Times* lived. After John Amos dies, Jefferson evicts them for nonpayment of rent. Florida, destitute and distraught, tries to kill George. The state puts her children up for adoption.

They are adopted by Mr. Drummond *(Diff'rent Strokes)* and graduate from Dalton, Exeter, and Howard. Gary Coleman's grandson becomes an obstetrician, marries a lovely lawyer named Clair, and they move to Brooklyn Heights. And there you have it: the transformation of the character type of the black male on television.

And while Clair Huxtable is a refreshingly positive depic- 16
tion of an intelligent, successful black woman, she is clearly a descendant of *Julia* (1968–71), though a Julia with sensuality and sass. The extent of typecasting of black women as mammy figures, descended from the great Hollywood "Mammy" of *Gone with the Wind*, is astonishing; Beulah, Mama in *Amos 'n' Andy*, Geraldine (*Flip Wilson*, 1970–75), Florida, Nel in *Gimme a Break* (1981–88), Louise *(The Jeffersons);* Eloise (*That's My Mama*, 1974–75).

Is TV Depicting a Different World?

And what is the measure of the Huxtables' nobility? One of the 17
reasons *Cosby* and its spin-off, *A Different World*, are so popu-
lar is that the black characters in them have finally become, in most respects just like white people.

While I applaud *Cosby's* success at depicting (at long last) 18
the everyday concerns of black people (love, sex, ambition, generational conflicts, work and leisure) far beyond reflex responses to white racism, the question remains: has TV man-
aged to depict a truly "different world"? As Mark Crispin Miller puts it, "By insisting that blacks and whites are entirely alike, television denies the cultural barriers that slavery necessarily created; barriers that have hardened over years and years, and that still exist"—barriers that produced different cultures, distinct worlds.

And while *Cosby* is remarkably successful at introducing 19
most Americans to traditional black cultural values, customs, and norms, it has not succeeded at introducing America to a truly different world. The show that came closest—that presented the fullest range of black character types—was the 1987–88 series *Frank's Place*, starring Tim Reid and his wife Daphne Maxwell Reid and set in a Creole restaurant in New Orleans.

Unfortunately, Mr. Reid apparently has learned his lesson: 20
his new series, *Snoops*, in which his wife also stars, is a black detective series suggestive of *The Thin Man*. The couple is thoroughly middle class: he is a professor of criminology at George-
town; she is head of protocol at the State Department, "Drugs

and murder and psychotic people," Mr. Reid said in a recent interview. "I think we've seen enough of that in real life."

But it is also important to remember that the early 70s   21
ghetto sitcoms—(*Good Times* and *Sanford*) were no more realistic than *Cosby* is. In fact, their success made the idea of
ghetto life palatable for most Americans, robbing it of its reality
as a place of exile, a place of rage, and frustration, and death.
And perhaps with *Cosby*'s success and the realization that the
very structure of the sitcom (in which every character is a type)
militates against its use as an agent of social change, blacks
will stop looking to TV for our social liberation. As a popular
song in the early 70s put it, "The revolution will not be televised."

Discussion Questions

1. What is Gates's dissatisfaction with the portrayal of blacks on
   television?
2. According to Gates, what have been the negative consequences of
   The Cosby Show in terms of its presentation of black images?
   What positive contributions of the show does Gates cite?
3. How does Gates prove incorrect the belief that social policies affecting blacks were largely determined by popular black images
   in the media?
4. Why was it necessary in the 1960s and 1970s to present an image of "domesticated" black men on television?
5. What is the "myth of the benevolent paternalism" of the white
   upper class?
6. What is the "process of paternal domestication" to which Gates
   refers? How does this process relate to the evolution of the character of Cliff Huxtable?
7. What is the thesis of this excerpt?
8. How does Gates use illustration effectively to develop his thesis?

Writing Assignments

1. Write an essay that analyzes the character types on current
   African American television shows.
2. Write an essay describing how other ethnic groups are depicted
   on television or in the movies.
3. Write an essay about a particular stereotype that society holds
   about your ethnic group or culture.

THE SLAVE INVENTOR

Portia James

Portia P. James wrote The Real McCoy: African-American Invention and Innovation, 1619–1930 *(1989) for the Smithsonian Institution's exhibit on African American inventors. In this excerpt from Chapter 3, James discusses the dilemma of the slave inventor.*

Vocabulary

query	(2)	question, inquiry
affidavit	(6)	a written statement or oath
supererogation	(6)	act done beyond what is required
surplussage	(6)	quantity in excess of what is needed
culling	(10)	picking out

Although few written accounts fully identify slaves by name, reports of slaves inventing new devices and machines persisted. The slave inventor found himself in an unlikely position that must have strained the assumptions of slavery to the utmost. Nothing illustrates the slave inventor's dilemma more clearly than the story of "Ned," a slave mechanic in Pike County, Mississippi, and the manner in which the U.S. Patent Office, handled the question of patenting the cotton scraper he invented. Ned's situation provoked the federal government to draft legislation that specifically addressed the legal status of slave inventors. 1

Oscar J. E. Stuart, a prominent white planter and the proud owner of Ned, wrote to Secretary of the Interior Jacob Thompson on August 25, 1857, with a query about Ned and his valuable invention. Ned had constructed a new and innovative cotton scraper that local planters heralded as "a great labor-saving machine." With the assistance of one man and two horses it could, Stuart asserted, do the work of four men, four horses, two single scrapers, and two ploughs. Stuart wrote Thompson to request letters patent for himself as owner of Ned and therefore as owner of Ned's invention. 2

Ordinarily Stuart would have addressed his request to the U.S. Patent Office, but the commissioner of patents, Joseph Holt, was a northerner. Realizing that in the minds of those 3 uninitiated in the assumptions of slavery it might be problematic for one man to receive the patent for another's invention, Stuart appealed to Secretary Thompson as "a Mississippian, and southern man."

Although Stuart admitted that the concept for the invention came entirely from Ned, he reminded Thompson that in the tradition of southern law "the master is the owner of the fruits of the labor of the slave both intilectual [sic], and manual." Stuart went on to express his concern that there might be a question whether the patent should be awarded to the "servile race" rather than to the "political race," that is, to Ned as opposed to himself. Stuart concluded rather ironically that if this view were to prevail, "the value of the slave to his master is excluded, and the equal protection and benefit of government to all citizens . . . is subverted."   4

Such a request should not have been surprising given the numbers of first-rate slave craftsmen and the reports of their inventions, but the appearance of Stuart's letter in the secretary's office seemed to cause a certain amount of confusion. Secretary Thompson replied to Stuart that the question was a new one and would have to be forwarded to Attorney General Jeremiah Black for an opinion.   5

Meanwhile, Stuart wrote a letter to the commissioner of patents. Interestingly enough, he had Ned sign an "affidavit" stating that he had invented the machine and was indeed the slave of Stuart. The implications of the affidavit must have made Stuart extremely uncomfortable, for he explained: "The affidavit of the Negro I regarded as a matter of supererogation, mere surplussage, neither strengthening or diminishing whatever merits there might be in my application.". . .   6

The decision not to allow either slaves or their owners to receive patents for slave inventions meant that such inventions could not enjoy any legal protection, or, more important, any formal recognition. The attorney general's opinion stood until the end of the Civil War and the passage of the Thirteenth and Fourteenth Amendments.   7

After this historic exchange of letters about his invention, Ned disappeared from history, and nothing is known of what became of him. Ironically enough, in 1860 O. J. E. Stuart and his family went into the full-time business of manufacturing and marketing Ned's Double Cotton Scraper. Their advertising broadside includes this enthusiastic testimony: "I am glad to know that your implement is the invention of a Negro slave—   8 thus giving the lie to the abolition cry that slavery dwarfs the mind of the Negro. When did a free Negro ever invent anything?" After the end of the Civil War O. J. E. Stuart left Mississippi, because, it is said, of the "excesses" of Reconstruction. . . .

Largely because of the inability to identify slaves and the inventions they created, there has been speculation about the unacknowledged contributions of slaves to particular inventions. Two of the most persistent and widespread rumors are the stories that Eli Whitney's idea for the cotton gin came from slaves working on the plantation of General Nathaniel Greene and that Cyrus McCormick's harvester was primarily inspired by his slave assistant, Joe Anderson. While Anderson himself is not recorded as claiming any significant role in the conceptualization of the reaper, he worked closely with McCormick during its construction. Anderson does say that he served as "blower and striker" for the blacksmith who made the harvesters.   9

Another factor to keep in mind is the process of invention itself. Even though all applications for patents must meet a test of originality, most if not all inventions are based on previous discoveries of materials, formulas, principles, techniques, and mechanisms. In most cases a patented invention is merely an improvement on a current device or technique. Eli Whitney, for example, has been charged with borrowing the idea for the cotton gin from a simple comblike device that slaves used to clean the cotton. Whitney is said to have merely enlarged upon the idea of the comb to create the cotton gin, which works very much like an oversized comb culling the seeds and debris from the cotton. Whitney may have borrowed the idea, which though valuable was still incomplete. He may have used the principle behind the slaves' device and applied it to the broader problem—how to clean vast quantities of cotton. But this is the very essence of invention. In this sense, the process of invention can be seen as a kind of pyramid, with each new invention resting on a number of previous discoveries.   10

Discussion Questions

1. Before the passage of the Confederacy Patent Act of 1861, why could inventions by slaves not be patented? Why were most slaves not given credit for their inventions even after the act?

2. How did Ned's slavemaster, Stuart, justify his request to obtain a patent for Ned's invention?

3. To what extent did the unjust system of slavery have an ironic effect on Stuart's request for a patent?

4. How are most if not all inventions based on previous discoveries?

5. What is the thesis of this essay? Does the last paragraph of the essay strengthen or weaken the thesis? Explain your answer.

6. How is cause and effect used to show the problem of the slave inventor?

Writing Assignments

1. Write an essay illustrating how you, someone you know, or someone you have heard or read about has not been given credit for his or her contributions.

2. Write an essay describing other dilemmas that slaves experienced.

3. "One cannot enslave another without enslaving oneself." Write an essay in which you agree or disagree with this statement.

Student Essay:
THE EUGENICS STERILIZATION MOVEMENT

Karie Wermeling

Vocabulary

capitalist	(2)	pertaining to an economic system encouraging private ownership
encompassing	(2)	surrounding
impoverished	(3)	poor
recipients	(5)	receivers
mandates	(6)	laws
ideology	(6)	body of ideas or beliefs
diligence	(7)	attentive care

Eugenics is the movement devoted to improving the human 1
species by controlling heredity. Sterilization is a procedure that
makes one incapable of reproduction. When we couple the two
terms, *eugenics* and *sterilization,* we define a movement devoted
to improving the human species in an effort to control heredity
by making one incapable of reproducing. The eugenics sterilization movement has a long history within the United States, of
forcing the African American woman to become sterile.

In America, the eugenics sterilization movement was popu- 2
lar during the nineteenth century because it offered sound, justi-
fiable reasoning to the Anglo-Saxon Protestant communities for
controlling and/or ridding the United States of the African American race. Charles Darwin stated that God created all living beings with either a favorable variation or an unfavorable variation.
However, he did not define what either of these was. Francis Galton, another prominent natural scientist like Charles Darwin,
and many others in the Caucasian community took it upon
themselves to do the defining. They characterized low intelligence
and poor class status as unfavorable variations. The white capitalist society, to justify its enslavement of a whole race of people,
labeled the African American as an individual of extreme low intelligence—one incapable of obtaining and sustaining knowledge.
Racists, including those within the science fields, began to promote the idea that African Americans have a smaller brain and
encompassing skull. In 1840, Dr. Samuel Morton set out to prove
this true. White racists, especially those who were slaveholders,
used Morton's study to support their belief that African Ameri-

cans were inferior in intelligence. And because they were "proved" to be intellectually inferior, they were seen as unfavorably varied.

African Americans were also labeled unfavorable beings   3
because of their poor class status. At the time the eugenics sterilization movement was developing, legalized slavery flourished in the South. Black individuals were the ones who served the white community with their entire energy, yet received nothing in return. They were left impoverished. Because of this poverty, African Americans were the poorest of persons residing in the United States. Having such a characteristic, as well as being deemed people of low intelligence, the black race was defined as a race of people who were unfavorably varied. Francis Galton and his colleagues offered testimony before Congress, made political speeches, and wrote numerous books and articles that promoted the concept of white superiority and the need for race purity. These eugenic-minded scientists also promoted the idea that the lower races, African Americans being the lowest, would bring about the destruction of the white race.

Therefore, the two characteristics, low intelligence and   4
poor class status, became a racial factor in the eugenics sterilization movement. Racists were then justified in choosing the black race as the target for imposed sterilization policies.

Early in the history of the eugenics sterilization movement,   5
the need to sterilize those with undesirable variations was widely accepted. Also, it was widely believed that African Americans should be the majority targeted as the recipients of sterilization. However, it was never the intention to sterilize each and every black individual. Those in favor of sterilization knew it was only necessary to sterilize one gender of a given race in order to control or exterminate it. That gender, of course, was the female.

Therefore, the African American female was specifically,   6
forcefully targeted by sterilization mandates. There are two main reasons why this selection was made. First, the black female was regarded as the ultimate inferior being in American society. The white, male-dominated capitalist society defined any woman, white or black, as inferior. But if a woman was also an African American, she was regarded as a human being lower in status than all others—in body, mind, and soul. The flourishing ideology was that if one was going to sterilize a group, one should sterilize the group that resides at the bottom of the social ladder. So, in light of this, those who were sterilizing the black woman felt they were doing no wrong. Society felt justified because it believed, thanks to the proof offered by Francis Galton and other natural scientists, that inferior beings

deserved and required inferior treatment so the remaining society could reach a state of perfection and prosper forever.

The second reason for choosing the African American female for sterilization was that she was seen as a sexual delinquent. Her only concern in life was to satisfy her endless desire for sexual intercourse. This notion of being unintelligent and oversexed rendered the black woman as one incapable of utilizing birth control methods, methods that require intelligence and diligence. Because the American society believed the black female could not effectively control her sexual desires and/or pregnancies, it felt it had a right and a duty to regulate them for her. Infertility would allow her to maintain her sexually active life while society rested assured knowing that no undesirable offspring would result.   7

The design of the eugenics sterilization movement was complete. The white race understood what needed to be done, sterilization, in order to combat population and social problem growth. They also understood who should be the victims of forced sterilization: the African American woman. The design of the movement was regarded as perfect. And the widespread acceptance of the movement within nineteenth-century America caused it to be powerfully enforced.   8

Discussion Questions

1. Specifically, what was the eugenics sterilization movement?
2. How does Wermeling view scientists such as Francis Galton? Why do you think she perceives Galton and his colleagues as she does?
3. Why was the eugenics sterilization movement popular in the nineteenth century?
4. How did white racists support their beliefs that African Americans were inferior?
5. Why was the African American female selected for sterilization?
6. How important is Wermeling's use of definition to the reader's understanding of the topic? Explain your answer.
7. What transitions are particularly effective in helping the author achieve unity among paragraphs?

Writing Assignments

1. Write an essay in which you discuss the effect(s) that racial or sexist practices have on targeted people.
2. Write an essay justifying some action that may be (or may seem to be) unfair to others.

13

Religion • Church

SALVATION

Langston Hughes

Langston Hughes (1902–1967) was born in Joplin, Missouri. As an undergraduate, he attended both Columbia University and Lincoln University. In 1921, he published in the Crisis *his famous poem, "The Negro Speaks of Rivers." Later, he published his first book of poetry,* The Weary Blues, *in 1926 and his second volume,* Fine Clothes to the Jew, *in 1927. In the 1940s he created the memorable Jesse B. Semple, a humorous character who speaks straightforwardly about the African American experience. In the following selection from his autobiography,* The Big Sea *(1940), Hughes recounts a religious service at which he felt pressured to acknowledge a false salvation.*

Vocabulary

dire	(3)	terrible, frightful
rounder's son	(6)	son of a prodigal (or good-for-nothing) father
knickerbockered	(11)	gathered or banded just below the knee

I was saved from sin when I was going on thirteen. But not re- 1
ally saved. It happened like this. There was a big revival at my
Auntie Reed's church. Every night for weeks there had been
much preaching, singing, praying, and shouting, and some
very hardened sinners had been brought to Christ, and the
membership of the church had grown by leaps and bounds.
Then just before the revival ended, they held a special meeting
for children, "to bring the young lambs to the fold." My aunt
spoke of it for days ahead. That night I was escorted to the
front row and placed on the mourners' bench with all the other
young sinners, who had not yet been brought to Jesus.

My aunt told me that when you were saved you saw a 2
light, and something happened to you inside! And Jesus came
into your life! And God was with you from then on! She said
you could see and hear and feel Jesus in your soul. I believed
her. I had heard a great many old people say the same thing
and it seemed to me they ought to know. So I sat there calmly
in the hot, crowded church, waiting for Jesus to come to me.

The preacher preached a wonderful rhythmical sermon, all 3
moans and shouts and lonely cries and dire pictures of hell,
and then he sang a song about the ninety and nine safe in the
fold, but one little lamb was left out in the cold. Then he said:
"Won't you come? Won't you come to Jesus? Young lambs,
won't you come?" And he held out his arms to all us young sinners there on the mourners' bench. And the little girls cried.
And some of them jumped up and went to Jesus right away.
But most of us just sat there.

A great many old people came and knelt around us and 4
prayed, old women with jet-black faces and braided hair, old
men with work-gnarled hands. And the church sang a song
about the lower lights are burning, some poor sinners to be
saved. And the whole building rocked with prayer and song.

Still I kept waiting to *see* Jesus.   5

Finally all the young people had gone to the altar and were 6
saved, but one boy and me. He was a rounder's son named
Westley. Westley and I were surrounded by sisters and deacons
praying. It was very hot in the church, and getting late now. Finally Westley said to me in a whisper: "God damn! I'm tired o'
sitting here. Let's get up and be saved." So he got up and was
saved.

Then I was left all alone on the mourners' bench. My aunt 7
came and knelt at my knees and cried, while prayers and songs

swirled all around me in the little church. The whole congregation prayed for me alone, in a mighty wail of moans and voices. And I kept waiting serenely for Jesus, waiting, waiting—but he didn't come. I wanted to see him, but nothing happened to me. Nothing! I wanted something to happen to me, but nothing happened.

I heard the songs and the minister saying: "Why don't you   8
come? My dear child, why don't you come to Jesus? Jesus is waiting for you. He wants you. Why don't you come? Sister Reed, what is this child's name?"

"Langston," my aunt sobbed.   9

"Langston, why don't you come? Why don't you come and   10
be saved? Oh, Lamb of God! Why don't you come?"

Now it was really getting late. I began to be ashamed of   11
myself, holding everything up so long. I began to wonder what God thought about Westley, who certainly hadn't seen Jesus either, but who was now sitting proudly on the platform, swinging his knickerbockered legs and grinning down at me, surrounded by deacons and old women on their knees praying. God had not struck Westley dead for taking his name in vain or for lying in the temple. So I decided that maybe to save further trouble, I'd better lie, too, and say that Jesus had come, and get up and be saved.

So I got up.   12

Suddenly the whole room broke into a sea of shouting, as   13
they saw me rise. Waves of rejoicing swept the place. Women leaped in the air. My aunt threw her arms around me. The minister took me by the hand and led me to the platform.

When things quieted down, in a hushed silence, punctu-   14
ated by a few ecstatic "Amens," all the new young lambs were blessed in the name of God. Then joyous singing filled the room.

That night, for the last time in my life but one—for I was   15
a big boy twelve years old—I cried. I cried, in bed alone, and couldn't stop. I buried my head under the quilts, but my aunt heard me. She woke up and told my uncle I was crying because the Holy Ghost had come into my life, and because I had seen Jesus. But I was really crying because I couldn't bear to tell her that I had lied, that I had deceived everybody in the church, that I hadn't seen Jesus, and that now I didn't believe there was a Jesus any more, since he didn't come to help me.

Discussion Questions

1. What is the purpose of the "mourner's bench"?
2. In what way does Hughes's aunt unknowingly create his conflict?
3. Why does Westley decide to "get saved"?
4. Hughes confronts two disappointments that evening at the revival. What are they?
5. What is praiseworthy about Hughes's reluctance to go up to the altar and about his crying in bed?
6. In what way does Hughes's use of description enhance the reader's ability to see and feel the mounting pressure felt by both the narrator as well as members of the congregation?
7. How do the first two sentences of the story prepare the reader for the plot and theme?

Writing Assignments

1. In an essay describe a time when you were pressured to do something you did not want to do, and then regretted your action.
2. Write an essay in which you argue against conforming to someone else's habits, beliefs, or behavior.
3. Sometimes peer pressure can be positive. Write an essay illustrating this point.

THE CREATION

James Weldon Johnson

Poet, lyricist, fiction writer, government official, James Weldon Johnson (1871–1938) was born in Jacksonville, Florida. He received his B.A. degree from Atlanta University, attended Columbia University, and was admitted to the Florida bar in 1897. He served as U.S. consul to Venezuela and Nicaragua and as a prominent member of the NAACP. Primarily known for his poetry, he wrote God's Trombones: Seven Negro Sermons in Verse *(1927) from which the poem here is taken. He wrote a novel,* The Autobiography of an Ex-Colored Man *(1912), and in collaboration with his brother, composer J. Rosamond Johnson, he wrote the lyrics to several songs, the most popular of which is "Lift Every Voice and Sing," often referred to as the Negro national anthem. In "The Creation" Johnson retells the biblical story in verse.*

Vocabulary

cypress (2)   an evergreen tree that grows in swampy areas

And God stepped out on space,   1
And he looked around and said:
I'm lonely—
I'll make me a world.

And far as the eye of God could see   2
Darkness covered everything.
Blacker than a hundred midnights
Down in a cypress swamp.

Then God smiled,   3
And the light broke,
And the darkness rolled up on one side,
And the light stood shining on the other,
And God said: That's good!

Then God reached out and took the light in His hands,   4
And God rolled the light around in His hands
Until He made the sun;
And He set that sun a-blazing in the heavens.

And the light that was left from making the sun
God gathered it up in a shining ball
And flung it against the darkness,
Spangling the night with the moon and stars.
Then down between
The darkness and the light
He hurled the world;
And God said: That's good!

Then God himself stepped down—   5
And the sun was on His right hand,
And the moon was on His left;
The stars were clustered about His head,
And the earth was under His feet.
And God walked, and where He trod
His footsteps hollowed the valleys out
And bulged the mountains up.

Then He stopped and looked and saw   6
That the earth was hot and barren.
So God stepped over to the edge of the world
And He spat out the seven seas—
He batted His eyes, and the lightnings flashed—
He clapped His hands, and the thunders rolled—
And the waters above the earth came down,
The cooling waters came down.

Then the green grass sprouted,   7
And the little red flowers blossomed,
The pine tree pointed his finger to the sky,
And the oak spread out his arms,
The lakes cuddled down in the hollows of the ground,
And the rivers ran down to the sea;
And God smiled again,
And the rainbow appeared,
And curled itself around His shoulder.
Then God raised His arm and He waved His hand
Over the sea and over the land,
And He said: Bring forth! Bring forth!
And quicker than God could drop His hand,
Fishes and fowls
And beasts and birds
Swam the rivers and the seas,
Roamed the forests and the woods,
And split the air with their wings.
And God said: That's good!

Then God walked around,   8
And God looked around
On all that He had made.
He looked at His sun,
and He looked at His moon,
And He looked at His little stars;
He looked on His world
With all its living things,
And God said: I'm lonely still.

Then God sat down—   9
On the side of a hill where He could think;
By a deep, wide river He sat down;
With His head in His hands,
God thought and thought,
Till He thought: I'll make me a man!

Up from the bed of the river   10
God scooped the clay;
And by the bank of the river
He kneeled Him down;
And there the great God Almighty
Who lit the sun and fixed it in the sky,
Who flung the stars to the most far corner of the night,
Who rounded the earth in the middle of His hand;
This Great God,
Like a mammy bending over her baby,
Kneeled down in the dust
Toiling over a lump of clay
Till He shaped it in His own image;

Then into it He blew the breath of life,   11
And man became a living soul.
Amen. Amen.

Discussion Questions

1. In what way does Johnson use darkness and light to suggest positive and negative images? To what extent do these images affect African Americans today?

2. What image of the woman is conveyed by the use of the pronouns *His* and *He*? And what image is conveyed by the creation of *man*?

3. How does the account of creation found in Genesis, Chapter 1, differ from Johnson's?

4. How does the use of descriptive phrases such as "spat out the seven seas" and "hollowed the valleys out" help the reader see the process of creation?

5. What do you think is Johnson's purpose in this poem?

Writing Assignments

1. Describe a process you used in creating _____. Use as many strong action verbs as you can in describing this process.

2. "The Creation" gives us one of several theories regarding the beginning of our world. Write an essay in which you explore other theories.

3. Write an essay in which you speculate about the origin of something.

THE DYNAMIC TENSION IN THE BLACK CHURCH

Michael A. Battle, Sr.

Michael A. Battle (1950–   ), currently the chaplain at Hampton University, is a noted preacher, professor, lecturer, and author. He is a graduate of Trinity College, Hartford, Connecticut, Duke University Divinity School, and Howard University. Battle has authored and/or edited several books and articles, including Voices of Experience *(1985). In the following excerpt taken from his 1994 book,* The African-American Church at Work, *Battle discusses the challenges of today's black church.*

Vocabulary

transformation	(1)	change
prophetic	(2)	foretelling
repentant	(2)	regretful
existential	(4)	current
pietistic	(4)	hypocritical
proclamation	(5)	announcement
imperative	(5)	urgent
status quo	(7)	the existing condition or state of affairs

The Black Church is often misunderstood by those who are critical of her commitment to preach a gospel which sees social change as an inseparable part of the Gospel of Jesus Christ. There are some within the Black Church who suggest that the Church should be concerned exclusively with the condition of the soul, as if the soul of man exists in a vacuum separated from the rest of that which makes humans human. These voices of narrow view say that we should avoid and abandon the call to social transformation. The response of the Black Church is a response which correctly finds support in the ministry of Jesus. [1]

Jesus stood on the cutting edge of social transformation as a prophetic voice meeting people at the point of their need. His was a voice which called for the least to become the focus of attention, and for the greatest to become providers of service to others. Jesus stood at the crossroad between the despised and rejected on one hand, and the chosen and privileged on the other hand, and declared that each has equal access to the [2] promises of God. Where injustice was the daily practice of the law, Jesus called for an advanced understanding of the spirit of the law. The call to social transformation is inseparable from the message of the Christ who overthrew the money changers in the temple, ate with sinners, paid attention to beggars, heard the cries of the wounded, and was moved by the presence of a sick woman who, in a crowd, reached out to touch him. Social transformation was a part of the ministry of the Christ who found room in his heart and among his peers for a repentant tax collector, a Roman soldier's child, and for the rich Zacchees.[1] It is a gross error of interpretation to suggest that Jesus appealed only to the poor. His appeal was an universal appeal. "Whosoever will, let him come." This includes the rich and the powerful, for they are needed if social transformation is to occur.

In light of her commitment to social transformation, it is   3
not difficult to understand why much of the leadership in the Black community has come from the Black Church. Our Churches have been the greatest training ground for leadership skills because, in our churches, we have been afforded opportunity to assume responsibility in an environment which provides nurture.

Allan Boesak, in his book entitled *The Finger of God,*   4
states that it is the unenviable task of preachers to wrestle honestly with the Word of God to experience its critical power, for themselves and for the people they preach to—but always within the situation and the experience of their people, so that the preaching will be understandable and relevant. It is preaching that addresses their deepest existential problems, preaching that speaks to the whole of their existence, for Blacks, this means that the preacher must address not merely their 'being' in the world, but their 'being Black' in the world. Relevant preaching can not be a kind of preaching that is a pietistic pie-in-the-sky-when-you-die theology that passes for the gospel truth.

While holding on to the undeniable truth of the assured   5
hope for eternal life, the Black church has always seen the concerns of this earthly life to be of such tremendous importance that they are not to be ignored in a blind pursuit of heaven. Thus Black theology has always addressed the situation in life

---

[1] Zacchees   (2)   (Also known as Zaccheus) was a chief among the Publicans.

where Black people have been. In slavery, Black Theology, through the music of the spirituals, wrestled with the tension between sociology and theology. Listen carefully to the spirituals and you will discover what Wyatt Tee Walker,[2] in his analysis of the song tradition of Black People, describes as the political and religious message of the spirituals. *Go Down Moses* was a song which celebrated the hope of liberation from slavery as well as celebrated the theological hope of eternal life; *Swing Low Sweet Chariot* was as much about the underground railroad as it was about the life of the prophet Elijah. When Black folk sang "I got shoes, you got shoes, all God's children got shoes, when I get to heaven I'm gonna put on my shoes and shout all over God's heaven;" they were making a bold proclamation about the equality of man and about the temporary nature of man's authority over man. It is imperative to recognize the genius of our forefathers, who in the singing of the spirituals heard Jesus say, when I was captive you worked for my liberation. They also heard Him say, "I have come to set the captives free." . . .

Our neighborhoods will not be renewed if those who "make 6 it" continue to abandon them. Our businesses will not progress unless we support them; our children will not escape the threat of another generation lost unless we lead them. Our communities will not overcome the invasion of drugs unless we learn ourselves and teach our children the reality that drugs are destructive. The Black Church must stand in the gap with a relevant message and with relevant programs. Where families are disjointed, let the church become the extended family; when there are no places for youth to become involved in constructive activities, let the churches work together with each other and with the cities to provide places of refuge; where there is an absence of self-confidence, let the churches preach the message of a Christ who sees in the least of us value and goodness.

The Black Church must never be content to allow for the 7 preservation of the status quo. She must continue to be an agent of social transformation. When Blacks were not permitted to worship in freedom, the Black Church became the haven. When Blacks were not allowed access to educational opportunity, the Black Church started schools. When death benefits were not provided for black families through the non-black

[2] Wyatt Tee Walker   (5)   Prominent African American minister.

insurance companies, the Black Church started its own companies. When Blacks could not get loans in the financial institutions, the Black Church started credit unions. We must re-
vive that self-help mentality. We must nurture the dynamic
tension in the Black Church.

Discussion Questions

1. According to Battle, why do some people have a misconception
   regarding the mission of the "Black Church"?
2. How does Battle support his argument that "the call to social
   transformation" is inseparable from God's message?
3. For what particular audience is the essay intended? Support
   your answer.
4. What do you think Battle means when he says the church must
   nurture "dynamic tension"? What do you think is his definition of
   "tension"?
5. How does Battle's use of comparison and contrast strengthen his
   argument?
6. The introduction is an excellent beginning for the essay. Why is it
   particularly effective?

Writing Assignments

1. Write an essay in which you attempt to clarify a subject that has
   also been misunderstood.
2. Write an essay in which you explore those times when positive
   tension has been necessary.
3. Write an essay about a positive or negative condition concerning
   your church, school, local government, or community.

THE STUMBLING BLOCK

Paul Laurence Dunbar

Paul Laurence Dunbar (1872–1906) was a nationally known African American poet. He published six volumes of poetry. After making a name for himself as a poet, Dunbar remained a productive artist as he experimented with other genres. Between 1898 and 1904 he wrote four novels, four volumes of short stories, several dramatic sketches, lyrics for musical compositions, and even two plays for a friend, though neither play was actually published. In the short story here, from The Best Short Stories of Paul Laurence Dunbar *(1938), the main character is perceived by those around her as having a "stumblin' block" that threatens her salvation.*

Vocabulary

unflecked	(1)	unspotted
abashed	(3)	embarrassing
devoirs	(6)	respect, courtesy
rude	(6)	rural, unrefined
prostrated	(6)	kneeled down in adoration
torrent	(8)	overflow
exhortations	(9)	prayers
taper	(10)	something that gives off a feeble light
palate	(10)	sense of taste
irreverence	(11)	lack of respect or love
proselyte	(11)	a new religious convert
rogue	(12)	rascal, villain
skeptic	(12)	doubter
fervor	(12)	devotion, enthusiasm
asunder	(12)	apart

It was winter. The gray old mansion of Mr. Robert Selfridge, of Fayette County, Kentucky, was wrapped in its usual mantle of winter somberness, and the ample plantation stretching in every direction thereabout was one level plain of unflecked whiteness. At a distance from the house the cabins of the Negroes stretched away in a long, broken black line that stood out in bold relief against the extreme whiteness of their surroundings. 1

About the center of the line, as dark and uninviting as the   2
rest, with its wide chimney of scrap limestone turning clouds of
dense smoke into the air, stood a cabin.

There was nothing in its appearance to distinguish it from   3
the other huts clustered about. The logs that formed its sides
were just as seamy, the timbers of the roof had just the same
abashed, brow-beaten look; and the keenest eye could not have
detected the slightest shade of difference between its front and
the bare, unwhitewashed fronts of its scores of fellows. Indeed,
it would not have been mentioned at all, but for the fact that
within its confines lived and thrived the heroine of this story.

Of all the girls of the Selfridge estate, black, brown, or yel-   4
low, Anner 'Lizer was, without dispute, conceded to be the
belle. Her black eyes were like glowing coals in their sparkling
brightness; her teeth were like twin rows of shining ivories; her
brown skin was as smooth and soft as silk, and the full lips
that enclosed her gay and flexile tongue were tempting enough
to make the heart of any dusky swain throb and his mouth water.

Was it any wonder, then, that Sam Merritt—strapping, big   5
Sam, than whom there was not a more popular man on the
place—should pay devoted court to her?

Do not gather from this that it was Sam alone who paid   6
his *devoirs* to this brown beauty. Oh, no! Anner 'Lizer was the
"bright particular star" of that plantation, and the most desired
of all blessings by the young men thereabout. But Sam, with
his smooth but fearless ways, Sam with his lightsome foot, so
airy in the dance, Sam, handsome Sam, was the all-preferred.
If there was a dance to go to, a corn-husking to attend, a social
at the rude little log church, Sam was always the lucky man
who was alert and *able* to possess himself of Anner 'Lizer's
"comp'ny." And so, naturally, people began to connect their
names, and the rumor went forth, as rumors will, that the two
were engaged; and, as far as engagements went among the
slaves in those days, I suppose it was true. Sam had never exactly prostrated himself at his sweetheart's feet and openly declared his passion; nor had she modestly snickered behind her
fan and murmured Yes in the approved fashion of the present.
But he had looked his feelings, and she had looked hers, while
numerous little attentions bestowed on each other, too subtle
to be detailed, and the attraction which kept them constantly
together, were earnests of their intentions more weighty than
words could give. And so, let me say, without further explana-

tion, that Sam and Anner 'Lizer were engaged. But when did the course of true love ever run smooth?

There was never a time but there were some rocks in its channel around which the little stream had to glide or over which it had to bound and bubble; and thus it was with the loves of our young friends. But in this case the crystal stream seemed destined neither to bound over nor glide by the obstacle in its path, but rather to let its merry course be checked thereby. 7

It may, at first, seem a strange thing to say, but it was nevertheless true, that the whole sweep and torrent of the trouble had rise in the great religious revival that was being enthusiastically carried on at the little Baptist meeting-house. Interest, or perhaps, more correctly speaking, excitement ran high, and regularly as night came round, all the hands on the neighboring plantations flocked to the scene of their devotions. 8

There was no more regular attendant at these meetings, nor more deeply interested listener to the pastor's inflammatory exhortations, than Anner 'Lizer. The weirdness of the scene and the touch of mysticism in the services—though, of course, she did not analyze it thus—reached her emotional nature and stirred her being to its depths. Night after night found her in her pew, the third bench from the rude pulpit, her large eyes, dilated to their fullest capacity, following the minister through every motion, seeming at times in their steadiness to look him through and beyond to the regions he was describing—the harp-ringing heaven of bliss or the fire-filled home of the damned. 9

Now Sam, on the other hand, could not be induced to attend these meetings; and when his fellow-servants were at the little church praying, singing, and shouting, he was to be found sitting in one corner of his cabin, picking his banjo, or scouring the woods, carrying ax and taper, and, with a dog trotting at his heels, hunting for that venison of the Negro palate—'coon. 10

Of course this utter irreverence on the part of her lover shocked Anner 'Lizer; but she had not entered far enough into the regions of the ecstasy to be a proselyte; so she let Sam go his way, albeit with reluctance, while she went to church unattended. But she thought of Sam; and many a time when she secretly prayed to get religion she added a prayer that she might retain Sam. 11

He, the rogue, was an unconscious but pronounced skeptic; and day by day, as Anner 'Lizer became more and more 12 possessed by religious fervor, the breach between them widened; still widening gradually until the one span that connected the two hearts was suddenly snapped asunder on the night when Anner 'Lizer went to the mourners' bench. . . .

Night came, and with it the usual services. Anner 'Lizer   13 was one of the earliest of the congregation to arrive, and she went immediately to the mourners' bench. In the language of the congregation, "Eldah Johnson sholy did preach a powahful sermon" that night. More sinners were convicted and brought to their knees, and, as before, these recruits were converted and Anner 'Lizer left. What was the matter?

That was the question which everyone asked, but there   14 were none found who could answer it. The circumstance was all the more astounding from the fact that this unsuccessful mourner had not been a very wicked girl. Indeed, it was to have been expected that she might shake her sins from her shoulders as she would discard a mantle, and step over on the Lord's side. But it was not so.

But when a third night came and passed with the same   15 result, it became the talk of three plantations. To be sure, cases were not lacking where people had "mourned" a week, two weeks, or even a month; but they were woeful sinners and those were times of less spiritual interest; but under circumstances so favorable as were now presented, that one could long refrain from "gittin' religion" was the wonder of all. So, after the third night, everybody wondered and talked, and not a few began to lean to Phiny's explanation, that "de ole snek in de grass had been a-goin' on doin' all her dev'ment on de sly, so's *people* wouldn't know it; but de *Lawd* he did, an' he payin' her up fu' it now."

Sam Merritt alone did not talk, and seemed perfectly indif-   16 ferent to all that was said. When he was in Phiny's company and she rallied him about the actions of his "gal," he remained silent.

On the fourth night of Anner 'Lizer's mourning, the con-   17 gregation gathered as usual at the church. For the first half-hour all went on as usual, and the fact that Anner 'Lizer was absent caused no remark, for everyone thought she would come in later. But time passed and she did not come, "Eldah Johnsing's" flock became agitated. Of course there were other mourners, but the one particular one was absent; hence the dissatisfaction. Every head in the house was turned toward the door, whenever it was opened by some late comer; and around flew the whisper, "I wunner ef she's quit mou'nin'; you aint' heerd of her gittin' 'ligion, have you?" No one had.

Meanwhile the object of their solicitude was praying just 18 the same, but in a far different place. Grasping, as she was, at everything that seemed to give her promise of relief, somehow Uncle Eben's words had had a deep effect upon her. So, when night fell and her work was over, she had gone up into the woods to pray. She had prayed long without success, and now she was crying aloud from the very fullness of her heart, "O Lawd, sen' de light—sen' de light!" Suddenly, as if in answer to her prayer, a light appeared before her some distance away.

The sudden attainment of one's desires often shocks one; 19 so with our mourner. For a moment her heart stood still and the thought came to her to flee, but her mind flashed back over the words of one of the hymns she had heard down at church, "Let us walk in de light," and she knew that before she walked in the light she must walk toward it. So she rose and started in the direction of the light. How it flickered and flared, disappeared and reappeared, rose and fell, even as her spirits, as she stumbled and groped her way over fallen logs and through briers! Her limbs were bruised and her dress torn by the thorns. But she heeded it not; she had fixed her eye—physical and spiritual—on the light before her. It drew her with an irresistible fascination. Suddenly she stopped. An idea had occurred to her. Maybe this light was a Jack-o'-lantern! For a moment she hesitated, then promptly turned her pocket wrong side out, murmuring, "De Lawd'll tek keer o' me." On she started; but lo! the light had disappeared! What! had the turning of the pocket indeed worked so potent a charm?

But no! it reappeared as she got beyond the intervention 20 of a brush pile which had obscured it. The light grew brighter as she grew fainter; but she clasped her hands and raised her eyes in unwavering faith, for she found that the beacon did not recede, but glowed with a steady and stationary flame.

As she drew near, the sound of sharp strokes came to her 21 ears, and she wondered. Then, as she slipped into the narrow circle of light, she saw that it was made by a taper which was set on a log. The strokes came from a man who was chopping down a tree in which a 'coon seemed to have taken refuge. It needed no second glance at the stalwart shoulders to tell her that the man was—Sam. Her step attracted his attention, and he turned.

"Sam!" 22

"Anner 'Lizer!" 23

And then they both stood still, too amazed to speak. Fi-   24
nally she walked across to where he was standing, and said:
"Sam, I didn't come out heah to fin' you, but de Lawd has
'p'inted it so, 'ca'se he knowed I orter speak to you." Sam
leaned hopelessly on his ax; he thought she was going to ex-
hort him.

Anner 'Lizer went on: "Sam, you's my stumblin' block in   25
de highroad to salvation. I's been tryin' to git 'ligion fu' fo'
nights, an' I cain't do it jes' on you' 'count. I prays an' I prays,
an' jes as I's a'mos' got it, jes as I begin to heah de cha'iot
wheels a-rollin', yo' face comes right in 'tween an' drives it all
away. Tell me now, Sam, so's to put me out of my 'spense, does
you want to ma'y me, er is you goin' to ma'y Phiny? I jes' wants
you to tell me, not dat I keers pussonally, but so's my min' kin
be at res' spi'tu'lly, an' I kin git 'ligion. Jes' say yes er no; I
wants to be settled one way er t' other."

"Anner 'Lizer," said Sam, reproachfully, "you know I wants   26
to ma'y you jes' ez soon ez Mas' Rob'll let me."

"Dere now," said Anner 'Lizer, "bless de Lawd!" And some-   27
how Sam had dropped the ax and was holding her in his arms.

It boots not whether the 'coon was caught that night or   28
not, but it is a fact that Anner 'Lizer set the whole place afire by
getting religion at home early the next morning. And the same
night the minister announced that "de Lawd had foun' out de
sistah's stumblin' block an' removed it f'om de path."

Discussion Questions

1. Why do Anner 'Lizer and Sam Merritt grow apart?
2. How significant is it that the only person on the plantation who
doesn't talk about Anner 'Lizer's inability to "get religion" is Sam?
3. What is Anner 'Lizer's stumblin' block?
4. Why do you think Anner 'Lizer does not respond to the cries of
the church members? To what extent is it significant that she
"gets religion" at home and not at church?
5. How would you describe the church's method of taking in new
members?
6. To what extent does the author's use of cause and effect help the
reader better understand Anner 'Lizer's conversion?
7. What is the setting of the story? To what extent do you feel the
story is influenced by the setting?

Writing Assignments

1. Write an essay describing a time when you had a stumbling block.
2. Write an essay describing a time when you were pressed to do something you were not committed to doing.
3. Write an essay supporting your view on this statement: "We spend too much of our time living out others' expectations."

Student Essay:
THE TRADITION OF IFA

Karl Nichols

Vocabulary

paganism	(1)	beliefs or practices of those who have little or no religion
heathenism	(1)	beliefs of uncivilized or irreligious people
animism	(1)	the act of attributing conscious life to nature
repository	(2)	a storage place, room, or container
divination	(2)	the art or practice of foreseeing or foretelling future events
arbiter	(3)	someone who decides a disputed issue
natal	(3)	relating to or present at one's birth
derivative	(5)	something obtained or received from a specific source
deification	(6)	the act of making a god or of worshipping an object

Before the advent of Christianity and Islam, the continent of Africa possessed a multitude of religions that evolved and were honored by many Africans. Many of these African religions were commonly labeled as "traditional religions" and were wrongfully referred to by the West as paganism, heathenism, and even animism. However, today the ancient African religion of IFA is one of many systems that has survived and spread from the continent of Africa to areas in Cuba, Trinidad, Brazil, Haiti, and America. By properly understanding the origin of IFA, the purpose of orisha and ancestor worship and divination, African Americans may better appreciate traditional African religions.   1

The philosophy of IFA originated with the Yoruba peoples of West Africa in Nigeria. IFA mythology relates that the creation of humankind arose in the sacred city of Ile Ife just outside of Lagos (Nigeria). According to many anthropologists, the Yoruba created a highly sophisticated city-state empire that was comparable to ancient Athens. The Yoruba regard IFA as the repository of their beliefs and moral values. In fact, the IFA divination system and various poetic chants are used to validate important aspects of the Yoruba culture. Thus, IFA divination is performed during all important rites of passages: nam-   2

ing ceremonies, marriages, funerals, and installations of kings.
The Yoruba consider IFA the voice of the divinities and the wisdom of the ancestors. One of the central beliefs of IFA is that
only two events in our lives are predetermined: the day we are
born and the day we are supposed to die. Everything else can
be forecast and changed by performing ancestor worship and
divination and by worshiping the orisha.

The idea of ancestor and orisha worship pertains to com-   3
municating with higher energies of nature and with dead blood
relatives. The orisha are energies or deities that represent aspects of nature. Osun represents sweet waters, love, money,
and conception. Shango (a warrior) represents thunder and
lightning, strategy; Esu (messenger of Oludumare) is owner
of   roads   and   opportunities,   and   of   spiritual   energy;
Yemonja/Olukun (provider of wealth) represents the ocean and
mother; Obatala (arbiter of justice) represents the head, clarity;
Oya (female warrior) represents the marketplace, tornadoes,
and change of fortune; Ogun (owner of metals) represents the
fierce warrior, honor, and integrity. These various orishas make
up the universal body of God, which then constitutes the natal
personalities of humans. IFA teaches that each of us has a single orisha energy from the universe that is dominant within all
of us. This dominant energy is called our guardian orisha. For
instance, if someone were suffering from too much pressure
from work, he or she would find it helpful to tap into the energy
of Obatala, orisha of the head, justice, coolness, and clear
thinking.

In IFA, ancestor worship is a formalized structure for the   4
living to connect with the wisdom and knowledge of dead blood
relatives. The energy of deceased relatives is connected to the
family by the world's population. Ritual offerings and prayers
to deceased blood relatives are an integral part of everyday life.
Unlike the Jewish and Christian traditions, IFA sees life as a
continuum that enables one to actually communicate with departed family members. Ancestor worship is said to be the connection with the past and the road map to a better future.

Another basic belief of IFA is the use of divination to fore-   5
cast life events. Through information obtained through divination, a person is able to know something about the future and
the outcomes of all of his or her undertakings. The IFA system
of divination is based on 16 basic and 256 derivative figures
obtained either by the manipulation of sixteen palm nuts, or by
the toss of a chain of eight half seed shells. Each Odu contains

600 ese, or poems of IFA and range from short to long passages that rely on proverbs, stories, and allegories to pinpoint correct counsel for inquiring minds. Most of the poems in each Odu contain stories related to the character or theme in the Odu concerned. Some believe that IFA is the means through which Yoruba culture informs and regenerates itself and preserves all that is considered good and memorable in that society. IFA divination is practiced by the Yoruba and Benin Edo of Nigeria; the Fon of Dahomey; the Ewe, of Tog; and the Santeria of Cuba and Brazil.

IFA religion, which carries a strong tradition of culture   6 and spiritual conduct, is widely practiced all over the globe. Without a doubt the most powerful indication of the African American's rich African ancestry lies in spirituality. If religions are truly a deification of one's culture, African Americans should seek refuge in the black gods of the orisha.

Discussion Questions

1. What are the basic beliefs of IFA?
2. Why do you think this religion has been referred to as "paganistic" by those in Western culture?
3. Are there some IFA beliefs that may be present in African American culture today? Support your answer.
4. What does the author mean when he says each of us has a "guardian orisha"?
5. Why does the author say that African Americans should "seek refuge" in IFA?
6. Should Nichols have used the strategy of definition more extensively in this essay? Explain your answer.
7. What is the purpose of the last sentence in the essay?

Writing Assignments

1. Write an essay in which you show how your religion or personal beliefs reflect your culture.
2. In an essay, describe a religious or cultural ceremony celebrated by your family.

14

Heritage • Identity

TO KNOW ONE'S HISTORY IS TO KNOW ONESELF

John Henrik Clarke

One of the most important historians of Africa and African Americans, John Henrik Clarke (1915–   ) was born in Union Springs, Alabama. He studied at New York University, the New School for Social Research, the University of Ibadan (Nigeria), and the University of Ghana. He also has served as a writer for both the Pittsburgh Courier *and the* Ghana Evening News *(Accra, Ghana). Clarke has always urged African Americans to study their African heritage. In the summer of 1993, Clarke spoke before an audience of hundreds of African educators from throughout the world, teaching them the importance of placing Africa at the center of their lives. He has written and edited many books; one of his most recent publications is* Africans Away from Home *(1988). The following excerpt from "A Search for Identity" (1970) documents Clarke's belief that if African Americans do not know their history, they do not know themselves.*

During my first year in high school I was doing chores and, because the new high school did not even have a cloak room, I had to hold the books and papers of a guest lecturer. The speaker had a copy of a book called *The New Negro.* Fortunately I turned to an essay written by a Puerto Rican of African descent with a German-sounding name. It was called "The Negro Digs Up His Past," by Arthur A. Schomburg.[1] I knew then that I came from a people with a history older even than that of Europe. It was a most profound and overwhelming feeling—this great discovery that my people did have a place in history and that, indeed, their history is older than that of their oppressors.

The essay, "The Negro Digs Up His Past," was my intro-   2
duction to the ancient history of the black people. Years later when I came to New York, I started to search for Arthur A. Schomburg. Finally, one day I went to the 135th Street library and asked a short-tempered clerk to give me a letter to Arthur A. Schomburg. In an abrupt manner she said, "You will have to walk up three flights." I did so, and there I saw Arthur Schomburg taking charge of the office containing the Schomburg collection of books relating to African people the world over, while the other staff members were out to lunch. I told him impatiently that I wanted to know the history of my people, and I wanted to know it right now and in the quickest possible way. His patience more than matched my impatience. He said, "Sit down, son. What you are calling African history and Negro history is nothing but the missing pages of world history. You will have to know general history to understand these specific aspects of history." He continued patiently, "You have to study your oppressor. That's where your history got lost." Then I began to think that at last I will find out how an entire people— my people—disappeared from the respected commentary of human history.

It took time for me to learn that there is no easy way to   3
study history. (There is, in fact, no easy way to study anything.) It is necessary to understand all the components of history in order to recognize its totality. It is similar to knowing where the tributaries of a river are in order to understand the nature of what made the river so big. Mr. Schomburg, therefore, told me to study general history. He said repeatedly, "Study the history of your oppressor."

---

[1] Arthur A. Schomburg. "The Negro Digs Up His Past," in *The New Negro*, ed. Alain Locke (New York: Albert and Charles Boni, 1925), pp. 231–37.

I began to study the general history of Europe, and I dis-   4
covered that the first rise of Europe—the Greco-Roman period—was a period when Europe "borrowed" very heavily from
Africa. This early civilization depended for its very existence on
what was taken from African civilization. At that time I studied
Europe more than I studied Africa because I was following Mr.
Schomburg's advice, and I found out how and why the slave
trade started.

When I returned to Mr. Schomburg, I was ready to start a   5
systematic study of the history of Africa. It was he who is really
responsible for what I am and what value I have for the field of
African history and the history of black people the world over.

I grew up in Harlem during the depression, having come   6
to New York at the age of seventeen. I was a young depression
radical—always studying, always reading; taking advantage of
the fact that in New York City I could go into a public library
and take out books, read them, bring them back, get some
more, and even renew them after six weeks if I hadn't finished
them. It was a joyous experience to be exposed to books. Actually, I went through a period of adjustment because my illegiti-
mate borrowing of books from the Jim Crow library of Columbus, Georgia, had not prepared me to walk freely out of a
library with a book without feeling like a thief. It took several
years before I felt that I had every right to go there.

During my period of growing up in Harlem, many black   7
teachers were begging for black students, but they did not have
to beg me. Men like Willis N. Huggins, Charles C. Serfait, and
Mr. Schomburg literally trained me not only to study African
history and black people the world over but to teach this history.

My Teaching

All the training I received from my teachers was really set in   8
motion by my great grandmother's telling me the stories of my
family and my early attempts to search first for my identity as a
person, then for the definition of my family, and finally for the
role of my people in the whole flow of human history.

One thing that I learned very early was that knowing his-   9
tory and teaching it are two different things, and the first does
not necessarily prepare one for the second. At first I was an exceptionally poor teacher because I crowded too many of my

facts together and they were poorly organized. I was nervous, overanxious, and impatient with my students. I began my teaching career in community centers in Harlem. However, I learned that before I could become an effective teacher, I had to gain better control of myself as a human being. I had to acquire patience with young people who giggled when they were told about African kings. I had to understand that these young people had been so brainwashed by our society that they could see themselves only as depressed beings. I had to realize that they had in many ways adjusted to their oppression and that I needed considerable patience, many teaching skills, and great love for them in order to change their attitudes. I had to learn to be a more patient and understanding human being. I had to take command of myself and understand why I was blaming people for not knowing what I knew, and blaming students for not being so well versed in history. In effect, I was saying to them, "How dare you not know this?"

After learning what I would have to do with myself and 10 my subject matter in order to make it more understandable to people with no prior knowledge, I began to become an effective teacher. I learned that teaching history requires not only patience and love but also the ability to make history interesting to the students. I learned that the good teacher is partly an entertainer, and if he loses the attention of his class, he has lost his lesson. A good teacher, like a good entertainer, first must hold his audience's attention. Then he can teach his lesson.

I taught African history in community centers in the 11 Harlem neighborhood for over twenty years before I had any regular school assignment. My first regular assignment was as director of the Heritage Teaching Program at Haryou-Act, an antipoverty agency in Harlem. Here I had the opportunity after school to train young black persons in how to approach history and how to use history as an instrument of personal liberation. I taught them that taking away a people's history is a way to enslave them. I taught them that history is a two-edged sword to be used for oppression or liberation. The major point that I tried, sometimes successfully, to get across to them is that history is supposed to make one self-assured but not arrogant. It is not supposed to give one any privileges over other people, but it should make one see oneself in a new way in relation to other people.

After five years in the Haryou-Act project, I accepted my 12 first regular assignment at the college at which I still teach. I serve also as visiting professor at another university and as an instructor in black heritage during the summer program conducted for teachers by the history department of a third major university. I also travel to the extent that my classes will permit, training teachers how to teach about black heritage. The black power explosion and the black studies explosion have pushed men like me to the forefront in developing approaches to creative and well-documented black curricula. Forced to be in the center of this arena, I have had to take another inventory of myself and my responsibilities. I have found young black students eager for this history and have found many of them having doubts about whether they really had a history in spite of the fact that they had demanded it. I have had to learn patience all over again with young people on another level.

On the college level I have encountered another kind of   13
young black student—much older than those who giggled—the kind who does not believe in himself, does not believe in history, and who consequently is in revolt. This student says in effect, "Man, you're turning me on. You know that we didn't rule ancient Egypt." I have had to learn patience all over again as I learned to teach on a level where students come from a variety of cultural backgrounds.

In all my teaching, I have used as my guide the following   14
definition of heritage, and I would like to conclude with it.

> Heritage, in essence, is the means by which people have used their talents to create a history that gives them memories they can respect and that they can use to command the respect of other people. The ultimate purpose of heritage and heritage teaching is to use people's talents to develop awareness and pride in themselves so that they themselves can achieve good relationships with other people.

Discussion Questions

1. How did Arthur Schomburg motivate Clarke to learn about African American history?
2. How did Clarke discover that he came from a people whose history was older than that of Europe?
3. How does Clarke describe a people with a history?
4. According to Clarke, what is the ultimate purpose of heritage?
5. How has Clarke's learning about his history influenced his teaching?

6. How does Clarke use cause and effect to explain the significance of the title?

7. What do you think is Clarke's purpose for narrating his personal experiences both as a high school student and as a teacher?

Writing Assignments

1. In an essay, describe your introduction to your heritage.

2. Write an essay about some interesting person in your family's history.

3. Write an essay responding to the following statement: "Those who forget their history are destined to repeat it."

KUNTA KINTE IS BORN

Alex Haley

When he was fifty-four years old, Alex Haley (1920–1992) published his monumental book, Roots: The Saga of an American Family *(1976). Chronicling Haley's descent from the African named Kunta Kinte, this work (and the subsequent television miniseries) had a tremendous influence, especially on African Americans. It taught them to be proud of their heritage and to enthusiastically seek their roots. Haley was also the co-writer of* The Autobiography of Malcolm X. *According to Haley, this work "represents the best I could put on paper of what Malcolm said about his own life from his own mouth." The following selection, from Chapter 1 of* Roots, *documents the rich African culture in which Kunta Kinte is born.*

Vocabulary

presaged	(1)	warned of in advance, predicted
pestles	(2)	instruments used to pound, grind, or mash
couscous	(2)	African dish of steamed, crushed grain
mortars	(2)	bowls made of hard material in which substances are crushed with pestles
pungent	(3)	sharp, penetrating
calabash	(4)	a tropical tree; the fruit of this tree
sheathed	(4)	enclosed
savanna	(4)	a flat, treeless grassland of tropical regions

1 Early in the spring of 1750, in the village of Juffure, four days upriver from the coast of The Gambia, West Africa, a manchild was born to Omoro and Binta Kinte. Forcing forth from Binta's strong young body, he was as black as she was, flecked and slippery with Binta's blood, and he was bawling. The two wrinkled midwives, old Nyo Boto and the baby's Grandmother Yaisa, saw that it was a boy and laughed with joy. According to the forefathers, a boy firstborn, presaged the special blessings of Allah not only upon the parents but also upon the parents' families; and there was the prideful knowledge that the name of Kinte would thus be both distinguished and perpetuated.

2 It was the hour before the first crowing of the cocks, and along with Nyo Boto and Grandma Yaisa's clatterings, the first

sound the child heard was the muted, rhythmic *bomp-a-bomp-a-bomp* of wooden pestles as the other women of the village pounded couscous grain in their mortars, preparing the traditional breakfast of porridge that was cooked in earthen pots over a fire built among three rocks.

The thin blue smoke went curling up, pungent and pleasant, over the small dusty village of round mud huts as the nasal wailing of Kajali Demba, the village alimamo, began, calling men to the first of the five daily prayers that had been offered up to Allah for as long as anyone living could remember. Hastening from their beds of bamboo cane and cured hides into their rough cotton tunics, the men of the village filed briskly to the praying place, where the alimamo led the worship: *"Allahu Akbar! Ashadu an lailahailala!"* (God is great! I bear witness that there is only one God!) It was after this, as the men were returning toward their home compounds for breakfast, that Omoro rushed among them, beaming and excited, to tell them of his firstborn son. Congratulating him, all of the men echoed the omens of good fortune. 3

Each man, back in his own hut, accepted a calabash of porridge from his wife. Returning to their kitchens in the rear of the compound, the wives fed next their children, and finally themselves. When they had finished eating, the men took up their short, bent-handled hoes, whose wooden blades had been sheathed with metal by the village blacksmith, and set off for their day's work of preparing the land for farming of the groundnuts and the couscous and cotton that were the primary men's crops, as rice was that of the women, in this hot, lush savanna country of The Gambia. 4

By ancient custom, for the next seven days, there was but a single task with which Omoro would seriously occupy himself: the selection of a name for his firstborn son. It would have to be a name rich with history and with promise, for the people of his tribe—the Mandinkas—believed that a child would develop seven of the characteristics of whomever or whatever he was named for. 5

On behalf of himself and Binta, during this week of thinking, Omoro visited every household in Juffure, and invited each family to the naming ceremony of the newborn child, traditionally on the eighth day of his life. On that day, like his father and his father's father, this new son would become a member of the tribe. 6

When the eighth day arrived, the villagers gathered in the 7 early morning before the hut of Omoro and Binta. On their heads, the women of both families brought calabash containers of ceremonial sour milk and sweet munko cakes of pounded rice and honey. Karamo Silla, the jaliba of the village, was there with his tan-tang drums; and the alimamo, and the arafang, Brima Cesay, who would some day be the child's teacher; and also Omoro's two brothers, Janneh and Saloum, who had journeyed from far away to attend the ceremony when the drumtalk news of their nephew's birth had reached them.

As Binta proudly held her new infant, a small patch of his   8
first hair was shaved off, as was always done on this day, and all of the women exclaimed at how well formed the baby was. Then they quieted as the jaliba began to beat his drums. The alimamo said a prayer over the calabashes of sour milk and munko cakes, and as he prayed, each guest touched a calabash brim with his or her right hand, as a gesture of respect for the food. Then the alimamo turned to pray over the infant, entreating Allah to grant him long life, success in bringing credit and pride and many children to his family, to his village, to his tribe—and, finally, the strength and the spirit to deserve and to bring honor to the name he was about to receive.

Omoro then walked out before all of the assembled people   9
of the village. Moving to his wife's side, he lifted up the infant and, as all watched, whispered three times into his son's ear the name he had chosen for him. It was the first time the name had ever been spoken as this child's name, for Omoro's people felt that each human being should be the first to know who he was.

The tan-tang drum resounded again; and now Omoro   10
whispered the name into the ear of Binta, and Binta smiled with pride and pleasure. Then Omoro whispered the name to the arafang, who stood before the villagers.

"The first child of Omoro and Binta Kinte is named   11
Kunta!" cried Brima Cesay.

As everyone knew, it was the middle name of the child's   12
late grandfather, Kairaba Kunta Kinte, who had come from his native Mauretania into The Gambia, where he had saved the people of Juffure from a famine, married Grandma Yaisa, and then served Juffure honorably till his death as the village's holy man.

One by one, the arafang recited the names of the Maure-   13
tanian forefathers of whom the baby's grandfather, old Kairaba Kinte, had often told. The names, which were great and many,

went back more than two hundred rains. Then the jaliba pounded on his tan-tang and all of the people exclaimed their admiration and respect at such a distinguished lineage.

Out under the moon and the stars, alone with his son that eighth night, Omoro completed the naming ritual. Carrying little Kunta in his strong arms, he walked to the edge of the village, lifted his baby up with his face to the heavens, and said softly, *"Fend kiling dorong leh warrata ka iteh tee."* (Behold—the only thing greater than yourself.)   14

Discussion Questions

1. How was the news of the newborn infant communicated to other villages?
2. Why was selecting a meaningful historical name for one's son important to the Mandinka people?
3. Kunta Kinte was born into the Mandinka nation, rich in African tradition. What are some of the traditions that Haley records?
4. What does the story tell you about the role of the male in the Mandinka family?
5. What is the role of the women in the Juffure village?
6. What do you think were the jobs of the jaliba, the aragang, and the alimamo in the village?
7. What process is involved in naming a child?
8. How effective would it have been for Haley to begin his story with the last paragraph?

Writing Assignments

1. Write an essay in which you describe a ritual or ceremony that is a part of your family tradition or heritage.
2. Write an essay discussing a particular tradition of someone else's culture that you find interesting.
3. Write an essay describing any significant event of your birth, such as any special celebrations that took place or how you were named.

TO THOSE OF MY SISTERS
WHO KEPT THEIR NATURALS

NEVER TO LOOK A HOT COMB IN THE TEETH.

Gwendolyn Brooks

Gwendolyn Brooks (1917–   ) is still on the lecture circuit, conducting creative writing workshops at colleges and universities throughout the United States. Perhaps what is most remarkable about this African American poet is not her ability to learn and to grow from younger poets such as Haki R. Madhubuti (don l. lee), but her untiring, selfless efforts to spark young people to write creatively. Since the publication of her A Street in Bronzeville (1945), Ms. Brooks has published many volumes of poetry, including Annie Allen (1949), Riot (1969), Becomings (1975), Primer for Blacks (1980), and Blacks (1987). In all of her volumes, she offers snapshot descriptions of poor, frustrated, or troubled African Americans, living in urban areas in the North. In 1950, she became the first African American to receive the Pulitzer Prize for poetry. In 1994, she received the National Book Lifetime Achievement Award. Currently, she directs the Gwendolyn Brooks Center for Black Literature and Creative Writing in Chicago. The following selection celebrates those "sisters" who have proudly kept their hair in its natural state.

Sisters!   1
I love you.
Because you love you.
Because you are erect.
Because you are also bent.   5
In season, stern, kind.
Crisp, soft—in season.
And you withhold.
And you extend.
And you Step out.   10
And you go back.
And you extend again.
Your eyes, loud-soft, with crying and
        with smiles,

are older than a million years.
And they are young.   15
You reach, in season.
You subside, in season.
And ALL
below the richrough righttime of your hair.   20

You have not bought Blondine[1].
You have not hailed the hot-comb recently.
You never worshiped Marilyn Monroe.
You say: Farrah's hair[2] is hers.
You have not wanted to be white.
Nor have you testified to adoration of that   25
    state
with the advertisement of imitation
(*never* successful because the hot-comb is laughing too.)

Discussion Questions

1. What do the words *sisters* and *naturals* mean in the title?
2. What is the meaning of the subtitle?
3. Why does the persona (speaker) love sisters?
4. What is the significance of the references to "Blondine," Marilyn Monroe, and Farrah?
5. How does Brooks describe the "natural" woman?
6. What reason does Brooks offer for some women wanting to change their natural hair?
7. How does Brooks use cause and effect to convey her message?
8. At the beginning of the poem, how effective is Brooks's strategy of separating the main clause, "I love you," from the three subordinate clauses that follow it?

Writing Assignments

1. Write an essay celebrating some aspect of your culture or heritage.
2. Write an essay dedicated to someone or some group that has stood up for its convictions.
3. In an essay, discuss some seemingly insignificant habit or behavior that you have, or that someone else has, which actually suggests more than it does at first glance.

---

[1] Blondine (21)   Blond hair dye.
[2] Farrah's hair (24)   Straight blond hair like that of the actress, Farrah Fawcett.

MY BLACKNESS IS THE BEAUTY OF THIS LAND

Lance Jeffers

Lance Jeffers (1919–1985) was born in Nebraska and raised by his grandparents. He received his B. A. in English and his M. A. in English education at Columbia University. He taught at Howard University and North Carolina State University. Although he wrote short stories and a novel, Jeffers is most noted for his poetry. His books of poetry include When I Know the Power of My Black Hand *(1974),* O Africa, Where I Baked My Bread *(1977), and* Grandsire *(1979). The following selection is the title poem of Jeffers's first book of poetry,* My Blackness Is the Beauty of This Land *(1970). Strength, pride, and defiance in the face of oppression are the poem's subject.*

Vocabulary

drawling	(5)	natural speaking, characterized by lengthening or adding vowels as in a southern drawl
thrall	(8)	enslaved
gouging	(26)	deceiving
derision	(28)	ridicule; the act of making fun of someone or something

My blackness is the beauty of this land,   1
my blackness,
tender and strong, wounded and wise,
my blackness:
I, drawling black grandmother, smile muscular and sweet,   5
unstraightened white hair soon to grow in earth,
work-thickened hand thoughtful and gentle on
    grandson's head,
my heart is bloody-razored by a million memories' thrall:

    remembering the crook-necked cracker who spat
      on my naked body,   10
    remembering the splintering of my son's spirit
      because he remembered to be proud
    remembering the tragic eyes in my daughter's
      dark face when she learned her color's meaning.

and my own dark rage a rusty knife with teeth to gnaw   15
    my bowels,

my agony ripped loose by anguished shouts in Sunday's
    humble church,
my agony rainbowed to ecstasy when my feet oversoared
    Montgomery's slime,   20

ah, this hurt, this hate, this ecstasy before I die,
and all my love a strong cathedral!
My blackness is the beauty of this land!

Lay this against my whiteness, this land!
Lay me, young Brutus[1] stamping hard on the cat's tail,   25
gutting the Indian, gouging the nigger.
booting Little Rock's Minniejean Brown[2] in the buttocks
    and boast, my sharp white teeth derision-bared as I the
    conqueror crush!
Skyscraper-I, white hands burying God's human clouds
    beneath the dust!   30
Skyscraper-I, slim blond young Empire
   thrusting up my loveless bayonet to rape the sky,
then shrink all my long body with filth and in the gutter lie
as lie I will to perfume this armpit garbage,

While I here standing black beside   35
wrench tears from which the lies would suck the salt
to make me more American than America . . .
But yet my love and yet my hate shall civilize this land,
this land's salvation.

Discussion Questions

1. What is the meaning of the title?
2. What images of black are described in the poem?
3. Describe the image of white as it is used in the poem.
4. Historically, how have whites related to other racial or ethnic groups?
5. Why does Jeffers write that the black person is more "American than America"?
6. What is the meaning of the last two lines of the poem?
7. How does Jeffers's use of comparison and contrast help the reader to "see" the United States from the point of view of black people?

[1] Brutus (25)   Roman political and military leader who participated in the assassination of Julius Caesar.
[2] Minniejean Brown (27)   One of the "Little Rock Nine," students chosen in 1957 to desegregate the local high school in Little Rock, Arkansas.

8. Why do you think the poet chose to begin some of his lines with uppercase letters and some with lowercase letters?

Writing Assignments

1. Write an essay about what you perceive as the beauty of _____.

2. Write an essay describing the beauty and/or ugliness of America.

3. Write an essay responding to the following statement: "I see my _____ when I look at _____."

Student Essay:
KWANZAA: AN AFRICAN AMERICAN HOLIDAY

William Weir

As I grew into adulthood, I began to realize that for a religious 1
holiday, Christmas seemed to be nothing more than a commercial circus with little reference to its intended religious significance. Therefore, I was quite happy to find out about Kwanzaa,
an African American holiday that is celebrated around Christmas.

In 1966, Maulana Karenga, a scholar and professor, es- 2
tablished Kwanzaa for African Americans to better understand
their history and culture. Developed from the African tradition
of celebrating the harvest season, Kwanzaa is the only original
African American holiday and is ranked by some African Americans as important as Christmas, Easter, and Hanukkah are to
mainstream society.

Kwanzaa is divided into seven days beginning on Decem- 3
ber 26 and ending on January 1. Varying combinations of the
three red, one black, and three green candles are lit on each of
the seven days. Each candle represents the seven principles of
Kwanzaa, which are called the *Nguzo Saba*, the Swahili word
for principles. Each day begins with the greeting *Habari gani?*,
in Swahili, meaning, "What's new?" or "What's happening?" The
response given is the principle of the day. The seven principles
are as follows: *umoja* (unity), *kujichagulia* (self-determination),
ujima (collective work and responsibility), *ujamaa* (cooperative
economics), *nia* (purpose), *kuumba* (creativity), and *imani*
(faith). After lighting the candles, family, friends, and community discuss the principle of the day as it relates to the African
American experience.

A few other symbols are used in the celebration. The red, 4
black, and green flag, originally developed by Marcus Garvey
and his organization—the Universal Negro Improvement Association (UNIA)—is displayed in a prominent place. The color red
stands for the blood that African Americans shed throughout
their ordeal in the Western world; the black symbolizes the people; the green represents the motherland, Africa. Other symbols include the unity cup; the *kinara* (the candle holder); the
Kwanzaa mat; the *muhindi* (the corn representing the children

and their value to the life cycle of people of African descent); and the *zuwadi* (gifts given to children on January 1). These gifts should be educational, represent heritage, and/or be handcrafted.

Kwanzaa is not a religious holiday; it is a holiday during which African Americans celebrate their heritage. Therefore, even if you celebrate Christmas, you may still find it rewarding to celebrate Kwanzaa. 5

Discussion Questions

1. What is the author's view of Christmas?
2. What is Kwanzaa?
3. How is Kwanzaa celebrated?
4. What are some of the Kwanzaa symbols?
5. Why does the author say Kwanzaa can be celebrated by African Americans who celebrate Christmas?
6. Why do you think Weir chooses to use comparison and contrast in this essay?
7. How effective is the beginning and the ending of the essay?

Writing Assignments

1. In an essay, discuss a cultural tradition celebrated in your family.
2. Write an essay discussing a holiday that you think is negatively or positively observed.

15

Reading • Writing Education

DISCOVERING THE WRITER IN ME

Terry McMillan

Terry McMillan (1951–   ) was born in Port Huron, Michigan, graduated from the University of California at Berkeley, and briefly studied screenwriting at Columbia University. Her works include Mama *(1987);* Disappearing Acts *(1989);* Breaking Ice: An Anthology of Contemporary African-American Fiction *(1990); and* Waiting to Exhale *(1992), which appeared on the* New York Times *best-seller list for fourteen weeks and was made into a movie in 1995; and* How Stella Got Her Groove Back *(1996). In this excerpt from the introduction to* Breaking Ice, *McMillan describes how she discovered her abilities as a writer.*

Vocabulary

eccentric	(1)	odd, unconventional
horde	(2)	crowd
warrant	(5)	justify
provocative	(5)	exciting
verbose	(9)	wordy
vignettes	(11)	sketches, pictures
inherent	(12)	inborn, natural
philanthropy	(12)	love of humankind

As a child, I didn't know that African-American people wrote 1
books. I grew up in a small town in northern Michigan, where
the only books I came across were the Bible and required reading for school. I did not read for pleasure, and it wasn't until I
was sixteen when I got a job shelving books at the public library that I got lost in a book. It was a biography of Louisa May
Alcott. I was excited because I had not really read about poor
white folks before; her father was so eccentric and idealistic
that at the time I just thought he was crazy. I related to Louisa
because she had to help support her family at a young age,
which was what I was doing at the library.

Then one day I went to put a book away, and saw James 2
Baldwin's face staring up at me. "Who in the world is this?" I
wondered. I remember feeling embarrassed and did not read
his book because I was too afraid. I couldn't imagine that he'd
have anything better or different to say than Thomas Mann,
Henry Thoreau, Ralph Waldo Emerson, Nathaniel Hawthorne,
Ernest Hemingway, William Faulkner, etc. and a horde of other
mostly white male writers that I'd been introduced to in Literature 101 in high school. I mean, not only had there not been
any African-American authors included in any of those text-
books, but I'd never been given a clue that if we did have anything important to say that somebody would actually publish
it. Needless to say, I was not just naïve, but had not yet acquired an ounce of black pride. I never once questioned why
there were no representative works by us in any of those text-
books. After all, I had never heard of any African-American
writers, and no one I knew hardly read *any* books.

And then things changed. 3

It wasn't until after Malcolm X had been assassinated that 4
I found out who he was. I know I should be embarrassed about
this, but I'm not. I read Alex Haley's biography of him and it literally changed my life. First and foremost, I realized that there
was no reason to be ashamed of being black, that it was ridicu-
lous. That we had a history, and much to be proud of. I began
to notice how we had actually been treated as less than human; began to see our strength as a people whereas I'd only
been made aware of our inferiorities. I started thinking about
my role in the world and not just on my street. I started *thinking.* Thinking about things I'd never thought about before, and
the thinking turned into questions. But I had more questions
than answers.

So I went to college. When I looked through the catalog 5
and saw a class called Afro-American Literature, I signed up

and couldn't wait for the first day of class. Did *we* really have enough writers to warrant an entire class? I remember the textbook was called *Dark Symphony: Negro Literature in America* because I still have it. I couldn't believe the rush I felt over and over once I discovered Countee Cullen, Langston Hughes, Ann Petry, Zora Neale Hurston, Ralph Ellison, Jean Toomer, Richard Wright, and rediscovered and read James Baldwin, to name just a few. I'm surprised I didn't need glasses by the end of the semester. My world opened up. I accumulated and gained a totally new insight about, and perception of, our lives as "black" people, as if I had been an outsider and was finally let in. To discover that our lives held as much significance and importance as our white counterparts was more than gratifying, it was exhilarating. Not only had we lived diverse, interesting, provocative, and relentless lives, but during, through, and as a result of all these painful experiences, some folks had taken the time to write it down.

Not once, throughout my entire four years as an under-   6
graduate did it occur to me that I might one day *be* a writer. I mean, these folks had genuine knowledge and insight. They also had a fascination with the truth. They had something to write about. Their work was bold, not flamboyant. They learned how to exploit the language so that readers would be affected by what they said and how they said it. And they had talent.

I never considered myself to be in possession of many of   7
the above, and yet when I was twenty years old, the first man I fell in love with broke my heart. I was so devastated and felt so helpless that my reaction manifested itself in a poem. I did not sit down and say, "I'm going to write a poem about this." It was more like magic. I didn't even know I was writing a poem until I had written it. Afterward, I felt lighter, as if something had happened to lessen the pain. And when I read this "thing" I was shocked because I didn't know where the words came from. I was scared, to say the least, about what I had just experienced, because I didn't understand what had happened.

For the next few days, I read that poem over and over in   8
disbelief because *I* had written it. One day, a colleague saw it lying on the kitchen table and read it. I was embarrassed and shocked when he said he liked it, then went on to tell me that he had just started a black literary magazine at the college and he wanted to publish it. Publish it? He was serious and it found its way onto a typeset page.

Seeing my name in print excited me. And from that point on, if a leaf moved on a tree, I wrote a poem about it. If a crack in the sidewalk glistened, surely there was a poem in that. Some of these verbose things actually got published in various campus newspapers that were obviously desperate to fill up space. I did not call myself a poet; I told people I wrote poems. 9

Years passed. 10

Those poems started turning into sentences and I started getting nervous. What the hell did I think I was doing? Writing these little go-nowhere vignettes. All these beginnings. And who did I think I was, trying to tell a story? And who cared? Even though I had no idea what I was doing, all I knew was that I was beginning to realize that a lot of things mattered to me, things disturbed me, things that I couldn't change. Writing became an outlet for my dissatisfactions, distaste, and my way of trying to make sense of what I saw happening around me. It was my way of trying to fix what I thought was broken. It later became the only way to explore personally what I didn't understand. The problem, however, was that I was writing more about ideas than people. Everything was so "large," and eventually I had to find a common denominator. I ended up asking myself what I really cared about: it was people, and particularly African-American people. 11

The whole idea of taking myself seriously as a writer was terrifying. I didn't know any writers. Didn't know how you knew if you "had" it or not. Didn't know if I was or would ever be good enough. I didn't know how you went about the business of writing, and besides, I sincerely wanted to make a decent living. (I had read the horror stories of how so few writers were able to live off of their writing alone, many having lived like bohemians.[1]) At first, I thought being a social worker was the right thing to do, since I was bent on saving the world (I was an idealistic twenty-two years old), but when I found I couldn't do it that way, I had to figure out another way to make an impact on folks. A positive impact. I ended up majoring in journalism because writing was "easy" for me, but it didn't take long for me to learn that I did not like answering the "who, what, when, where, and why" of anything. I then—upon the urging of my mother and friends who had graduated and gotten "normal" jobs—decided to try something that would still allow me to 12

[1] bohemians (12)   Persons with artistic or literary interests who disregard conventional standards of behavior.

"express myself" but was relatively safer, though still risky: I went to film school. Of course what was inherent in my quest to find my "spot" in the world was this whole notion of affecting people on some grand scale. Malcolm and Martin caused me to think like this. Writing for me, as it's turned out, is philanthropy. It didn't take years for me to realize the impact that other writers' work had had on me, and if I was going to write, I did not want to write inconsequential, mediocre stories that didn't conjure up or arouse much in a reader. So I had to start by exciting myself and paying special attention to what I cared about, what mattered to me.

Film school didn't work out. Besides, I never could stop   13
writing, which ultimately forced me to stop fighting it. It took even longer to realize that writing was not something you aspired to be, it was something you did because you had to.

Discussion Questions

1. Why did McMillan feel embarrassed and afraid when she saw James Baldwin's picture on a book?
2. How did McMillan discover African American writers on a large scale?
3. When did McMillan first discover she might be a writer? What purpose did writing serve for her?
4. Of what significance was McMillan's discovery that "writing was not something that you aspired to be, it was something you did because you had to"?
5. How does McMillan use narration to trace her growth as a writer?
6. Why is the first sentence of the essay an effective one?

Writing Assignments

1. McMillan uses words such as "scared," "embarrassed," "shocked," "nervous," and "terrifying" to describe her early writing experiences. Write an essay in which you describe your early writing experiences.
2. Write an essay describing the impact on you of a particular reading, for example, a poem, a book, or an essay.
3. Write an essay in which you respond to the following: "Writing for me is _____."

SEND YOUR CHILDREN TO THE LIBRARIES

Arthur Ashe

Arthur Ashe (1943–1993), born in Richmond, Virginia, was a graduate of UCLA and the world's leading African American professional tennis player. Ranked twice as the number-one player in the world, he was captain of the U.S. Davis Cup team in 1981. After suffering a heart attack in 1979, he retired from competitive play and began writing articles for newspapers and magazines. His books include Portrait in Motion *(1976);* Mastering Your Tennis Strokes *(1978); and his autobiographies,* Off the Court *(1981) and* Days of Grace: A Memoir *(1993). He is also editor of* A Hard Road to Glory: A History of the African-American Athlete *(1988). In this article (1977), originally published in the* New York Times, *Ashe emphasizes the importance of education for African American children.*

Vocabulary

pretentious	(2)	showy
dubious	(3)	doubtful
emulate	(4)	imitate
lure	(4)	attraction
viable	(9)	practical

1   Since my sophomore year at University of California, Los Angeles, I have become convinced that we blacks spend too much time on the playing fields and too little time in the libraries.

2   Please don't think of this attitude as being pretentious just because I am a black, single professional athlete.

3   I don't have children, but I can make observations. I strongly believe the black culture expends too much time, energy and effort raising, praising and teasing our black children as to the dubious glories of professional sport.

4   All children need models to emulate—parents, relatives or friends. But when the child starts school, the influence of the parent is shared by teachers and classmates, by the lure of books, movies, ministers and newspapers, but most of all by television.

5   Which televised events have the greatest number of viewers?—Sports—The Olympics, Super Bowl, Masters, World

Series, pro basketball playoffs, Forest Hills. ABC-TV even has sports on Monday night prime time from April to December.

So your child gets a massive dose of O.J. Simpson, Kareem Abdul-Jabbar, Muhammad Ali, Reggie Jackson, Dr. J. and Lee Elder and other pro athletes. And it is only natural that your child will dream of being a pro athlete himself.   6

But consider these facts: For the major professional sports of hockey, football, basketball, baseball, golf, tennis and boxing, there are roughly only 3,170 major league positions available (attributing 200 positions to golf, 200 to tennis and 100 to boxing). And the annual turnover is small.   7

We blacks are a subculture of about 28 million. Of the $13\frac{1}{2}$ million men, 5 to 6 million are under 20 years of age, so your son has less than one chance in 1,000 of becoming a pro. Less than one in a thousand. Would you bet your son's future on something with odds of 999 to 1 against you? I wouldn't.   8

Unless a child is exceptionally gifted, you should know by the time he enters high school whether he has a future as an athlete. But what is more important is what happens if he doesn't graduate or doesn't land a college scholarship and doesn't have a viable alternative job career. Our high school dropout rate is several times the national average, which contributes to our unemployment rate of roughly twice the national average.   9

And how do you fight the figures in the newspapers every day. Ali has earned more than $30 million boxing, O.J. just signed for $2\frac{1}{2}$ million, Dr. J. for almost $3 million, Reggie Jackson for $2.8 million, Nate Archibald for $400,000 a year. All that money, recognition, attention, free cars, girls, jobs in the offseason—no wonder there is Pop Warner football, Little League baseball, National Junior Tennis League tennis, hockey practice at 5 A.M. and pickup basketball games in any center city at any hour.   10

There must be some way to assure that the 999 who try but don't make it to pro sports don't wind up on the street corners or in the unemployment lines. Unfortunately, our most widely recognized role models are athletes and entertainers— "runnin'" and "jumpin'" and "singin'" and "dancin.'" While we are 60 percent of the National Basketball Association, we are less than 4 percent of the doctors and lawyers. While we are about 35 percent of major league baseball we are less than 2 percent of the engineers. While we are about 40 percent of the National Football League, we are less than 11 per-   11 cent of construction workers such as carpenters and bricklayers.

Our greatest heroes of the century have been athletes— 12
Jack Johnson, Joe Louis and Muhammad Ali. Racial and economic discrimination forced us to channel our energies into athletics and entertainment. These were the two ways out of the ghetto, the ways to get that Cadillac, those alligator shoes, that cashmere sport coat.

Somehow, parents must instill a desire for learning along- 13
side the desire to be Walt Frazier. Why not start by sending black professional athletes into high schools to explain the facts of life.

I have often addressed high school audiences and my 14
message is always the same. For every hour you spend on the athletic field, spend two in the library. Even if you make it as a pro athlete, your career will be over by the time you are 35. So you will need that diploma.

Have these pro athletes explain what happens if you break 15
a leg, get a sore arm, have one bad year or don't make the cut for five or six tournaments. Explain to them the star system, wherein for every O.J. earning millions there are six or seven others making $15,000 or $20,000 or $30,000 a year.

But don't just have Walt Frazier or O.J. or Abdul-Jabbar ad- 16
dress your class. Invite a benchwarmer or a guy who didn't make it. Ask him if he sleeps every night. Ask him whether he was graduated. Ask him what he would do if he became disabled tomorrow. Ask him where his old high school athletic buddies are.

We have been on the same roads—sports and entertain- 17
ment—too long. We need to pull over, fill up at the library and speed away to Congress and the Supreme Court, the unions and the business world. We need more Barbara Jordans, Andrew Youngs, union card-holders, Nikki Giovannis and Earl Graveses. Don't worry: we will still be able to sing and dance and run and jump better than anybody else.

I'll never forget how proud my grandmother was when I 18
graduated from U.C.L.A. in 1966. Never mind the Davis Cup in 1968, 1969 and 1970. Never mind the Wimbledon title, Forest Hills, etc. To this day, she still doesn't know what those names mean.

What mattered to her was that of her more than 30 chil- 19
dren and grandchildren, I was the first to be graduated from college, and a famous college at that. Somehow, that made up for all those floors she scrubbed all those years.

Discussion Questions

1. Someone not reading this essay closely might mistakenly think that Ashe is discouraging young blacks from aspiring to be professional athletes. What is he really arguing?
2. What reasons does Ashe give to explain why blacks have historically entered the fields of athletics and entertainment?
3. What are the chances of a black child becoming a professional athlete? Does Ashe's use of statistics strengthen or weaken his argument?
4. What does Ashe propose as a means of giving students a realistic view of the world of professional sports?
5. Who is the audience for this essay?
6. Does it surprise you that as a professional athlete Ashe would take the position he does in this essay? Explain your answer.
7. How does Ashe use illustration to develop his argument?
8. How effective is the concluding paragraph of this essay? Explain your answer.

Writing Assignments

1. Ashe uses many examples of African American role models. Select one of these examples, or one of your own, and write an essay discussing his or her accomplishments.
2. Write an essay discussing your proposed career and the kind of education required for it.
3. Sometimes the glamour of a job may blind one to its many demands. Write an essay discussing a career that has been glamorized and some of the challenges associated with it.

MY SELF-EDUCATION

Malcolm X

Born Malcolm Little in Omaha, Nebraska, Malcolm X (1925–1965) was one of the most powerful and controversial African American leaders during the 1960s. While serving seven years in prison for burglary, he joined the Nation of Islam, headed by Elijah Muhammad, and later became the national spokesperson for the organization. Following a holy pilgrimage to Mecca in 1964, he took the name of El Hajj Malik El-Shabazz and separated himself from the Nation of Islam. At the time of his assassination, he had formed his own group, The Organization of Afro-American Unity. In this excerpt from his Autobiography *(1965), co-authored with Alex Haley, Malcolm X describes his self-education.*

Vocabulary

articulate	(2)	clearly spoken
emulate	(4)	imitate
riffling	(6)	shuffling
burrowing	(9)	digging a hole in the ground
engrossing	(16)	occupying one's complete attention
feigned	(18)	pretended
digressing	(27)	getting off the subject

1   It was because of my letters that I happened to stumble upon starting to acquire some kind of homemade education.

2   I became increasingly frustrated at not being able to express what I wanted to convey in letters that I wrote, especially those to Mr. Elijah Muhammad.[1] In the street, I had been the most articulate hustler out there—I had commanded attention when I said something. But now, trying to write simple English, I not only wasn't articulate, I wasn't even functional. How would I sound writing in slang, the way I would *say* it, something such as, "Look, daddy, let me pull your coat about a cat, Elijah Muhammad—"

[1] Elijah Muhammad   (2)   Leader of the Nation of Islam, 1935–1975.

Many who today hear me somewhere in person, or on tele- 3
vision, or those who read something I've said, will think I went
to school far beyond the eighth grade. This impression is due
entirely to my prison studies.

It had really begun back in the Charlestown Prison, when 4
Bimbi[2] first made me feel envy of his stock of knowledge.
Bimbi had always taken charge of any conversations he was in,
and I had tried to emulate him. But every book I picked up had
few sentences which didn't contain anywhere from one to
nearly all of the words that might as well have been in Chinese.
When I just skipped those words, of course, I really ended up
with little idea of what the book said. So I had come to the Norfolk Prison Colony still going through only book-reading motions. Pretty soon, I would have quit even these motions, unless
I had received the motivation that I did.

I saw that the best thing I could do was get hold of a dic- 5
tionary—to study, to learn some words. I was lucky enough to
reason also that I should try to improve my penmanship. It was
sad. I couldn't even write in a straight line. It was both ideas
together that moved me to request a dictionary along with some
tablets and pencils from the Norfolk Prison Colony school.

I spent two days just riffling uncertainly through the dic- 6
tionary's pages. I'd never realized so many words existed! I did-
n't know *which* words I needed to learn. Finally, just to start
some kind of action, I began copying.

In my slow, painstaking, ragged handwriting, I copied into 7
my tablet everything printed on that first page, down to the
punctuation marks.

I believe it took me a day. Then, aloud, I read back, to my- 8
self, everything I'd written on the tablet. Over and over, aloud,
to myself, I read my own handwriting.

I woke up the next morning, thinking about those words— 9
immensely proud to realize that not only had I written so much
at one time, but I'd written words that I never knew were in the
world. Moreover, with a little effort, I also could remember what
many of these words meant. I reviewed the words whose meanings I didn't remember. Funny thing, from the dictionary first
page right now, that "aardvark" springs to my mind. The dictionary had a picture of it, a long-tailed, long-eared, burrowing

[2] Bimbi (4)   A fellow inmate whose encyclopedic learning and verbal facility greatly impressed Malcolm X.

African mammal, which lives off termites caught by sticking out its tongue as an anteater does for ants.

I was so fascinated that I went on—I copied the diction- 10 ary's next page. And the same experience came when I studied that. With every succeeding page, I also learned of people and places and events from history. Actually the dictionary is like a miniature encyclopedia. Finally the dictionary's A section had filled a whole tablet—and I went on into the B's. That was the way I started copying what eventually became the entire dictionary. It went a lot faster after so much practice helped me to pick up handwriting speed. Between what I wrote in my tablet, and writing letters, during the rest of my time in prison I would guess I wrote a million words.

I suppose it was inevitable that as my word-base broad- 11 ened, I could for the first time pick up a book and read and now begin to understand what the book was saying. Anyone who has read a great deal can imagine the new world that opened. Let me tell you something: from then until I left that prison, in every free moment I had, if I was not reading in the library, I was reading on my bunk. You couldn't have gotten me out of books with a wedge. Between Mr. Muhammad's teachings, my correspondence, my visitors, . . . and my reading of books, months passed without my even thinking about being imprisoned. In fact, up to then, I never had been so truly free in my life.

The Norfolk Prison Colony's library was in the school 12 building. A variety of classes was taught there by instructors who came from such places as Harvard and Boston universities. The weekly debates between inmate teams were also held in the school building. You would be astonished to know how worked up convict debaters and audiences would get over subjects like "Should Babies Be Fed Milk?"

Available on the prison library's shelves were books on 13 just about every general subject. Much of the big private collection that Parkhurst[3] had willed to the prison was still in crates and boxes in the back of the library—thousands of old books. Some of them looked ancient: covers faded, old-time parchment-looking binding. Parkhurst . . . seemed to have been principally interested in history and religion. He had the money

---

[3] Parkhurst (13)   Charles Henry Parkhurst (1842–1933); U.S. clergyman, reformer, and president of the Society for the Prevention of Crime.

and the special interest to have a lot of books that you wouldn't have in a general circulation. Any college library would have been lucky to get that collection.

As you can imagine, especially in a prison where there was   14
heavy emphasis on rehabilitation, an inmate was smiled upon if he demonstrated an unusually intense interest in books. There was a sizable number of well-read inmates, especially the popular debaters. Some were said by many to be practically walking encyclopedias. They were almost celebrities. No university would ask any student to devour literature as I did when this new world opened to me, of being able to read and *understand*.

I read more in my room than in the library itself. An in-   15
mate who was known to read a lot could check out more than the permitted maximum number of books. I preferred reading in the total isolation of my own room.

When I had progressed to really serious reading, every   16
night at about ten P.M. I would be outraged with the "lights out." It always seemed to catch me right in the middle of something engrossing.

Fortunately, right outside my door was a corridor light   17
that cast a glow into my room. The glow was enough to read by, once my eyes adjusted to it. So when "lights out" came, I would sit on the floor where I could continue reading in that glow.

At one-hour intervals the night guards paced past every   18
room. Each time I heard the approaching footsteps, I jumped into bed and feigned sleep. And as soon as the guard passed, I got back out of bed onto the floor area of that light-glow, where I would read for another fifty-eight minutes—until the guard approached again. That went on until three or four every morning. Three or four hours of sleep a night was enough for me. Often in the years in the streets I had slept less than that.

The teachings of Mr. Muhammad stressed how history   19
had been "whitened"—when white men had written history books, the black man simply had been left out. Mr. Muhammad couldn't have said anything that would have struck me much harder. I had never forgotten how when my class, me and all of those whites, had studied seventh-grade United States history back in Mason, the history of the Negro had been covered in one paragraph, and the teacher had gotten a big laugh with his joke, "Negroes' feet are so big that when they walk, they leave a hole in the ground."

This is one reason why Mr. Muhammad's teachings spread   20
so swiftly all over the United States, among *all* Negroes,
whether or not they became followers of Mr. Muhammad. The
teachings ring true—to every Negro. You can hardly show me a
black adult in America—or a white one, for that matter—who
knows from the history books anything like the truth about the
black man's role. In my own case, once I heard of the "glorious
history of the black man," I took special pains to hunt in the library for books that would inform me on details about black
history.

I can remember accurately the very first set of books that   21
really impressed me. I have since bought that set of books and
I have it at home for my children to read as they grow up. It's
called *Wonders of the World.* It's full of pictures of archeological
finds, statues that depict, usually, non-European people.

I found books like Will Durant's[4] *Story of Civilization.* I   22
read H.G. Wells'[5] *Outline of History. Souls of Black Folk* by
W.E.B. Du Bois[6] gave me a glimpse into the black people's history before they came to this country. Carter G. Woodson's[7]
Negro History opened my eyes about black empires before the
black slave was brought to the United States, and the early Negro struggles for freedom.

J.A. Rogers'[8] three volumes of *Sex and Race* told about   23
race-mixing before Christ's time; and Aesop being a black man
who told fables; about Egypt's Pharaohs; about the great Coptic
Christian Empires;[9] about Ethiopia, the earth's oldest continuous black civilization, as China is the oldest continuous civilization. . . .

I have often reflected upon the new vistas that reading   24
opened to me. I knew right there in prison that reading had
changed forever the course of my life. As I see it today, the ability to read awoke inside me some long dormant craving to be
mentally alive. I certainly wasn't seeking any degree, the way a

[4] Will Durant   (22)   U.S. author and historian (1885–1981).
[5] H.G. Wells   (22)   English novelist and historian (1866–1946).
[6] W.E.B. Du Bois   (22)   William Edward Burghardt Du Bois, distinguished
black scholar, author, and activist (1868–1963). Du Bois was the first director of the
NAACP and was an important figure in the Harlem Renaissance; his best-known
book is *Souls of Black Folk.*
[7] Carter G. Woodson   (22)   distinguished African American historian
(1875–1950); considered the father of black history.
[8] J.A. Rogers   (23)   African American historian and journalist (1883–1965).
[9] Coptic Christian Empire   (23)   Territory of the Coptic Church, a native
Egyptian Christian church that maintains some of its African religious practices.

college confers a status symbol upon its students. My home-made education gave me, with every additional book that I read, a little bit more sensitivity to the deafness, dumbness, and blindness that was afflicting the black race in America. Not long ago, an English writer telephoned me from London, asking questions. One was, "What's your alma mater?" I told him, "Books." You will never catch me with a free fifteen minutes in which I'm not studying something I feel might be able to help the black man.

Yesterday I spoke in London, and both ways on the plane   25
across the Atlantic I was studying a document about how the United Nations proposes to insure the human rights of the op-pressed minorities of the world. The American black man is the world's most shameful case of minority oppression. What makes the black man think of himself as only an internal United States issue is just a catch-phrase, two words, "civil rights." How is the black man going to get "civil rights" before first he wins his *human* rights? If the American black man will start thinking about his *human* rights, and then start thinking of himself as part of one of the world's great peoples, he will see he has a case for the United Nations.

I can't think of a better case! Four hundred years of black   26
blood and sweat invested here in America, and the white man still has the black man begging for what every immigrant fresh off the ship can take for granted the minute he walks down the gangplank.

But I'm digressing. I told the Englishman that my alma   27
mater was books, a good library. Every time I catch a plane, I have with me a book that I want to read—and that's a lot of books these days. If I weren't out here every day battling the white man, I could spend the rest of my life reading, just satis-fying my curiosity—because you can hardly mention anything I'm not curious about. I don't think anybody ever got more out of going to prison than I did. In fact, prison enabled me to study far more intensively than I would have if my life had gone differently and I had attended some college. I imagine that one of the biggest troubles with colleges is there are too many dis-tractions, too much panty-raiding, fraternities, and boola-boola and all of that. Where else but in a prison could I have attacked my ignorance by being able to study intensely sometimes as much as fifteen hours a day?

Discussion Questions

1. What inspired Malcolm X to educate himself in prison?
2. What did he learn from his vast reading? What effect did it have on him?
3. How did copying the dictionary contribute to Malcolm X's education?
4. What examples does Malcolm X give to support his statement that history had been "whitened"?
5. Why does Malcolm X say that "I don't think anybody got more out of going to prison than I did"?
6. What is the tone of this excerpt?
7. How does Malcolm X use process to trace his self-education?
8. What is the purpose of this excerpt?

Writing Assignments

1. Write an essay explaining how knowledge gained from something you have recently read enlightened you on some issue.
2. Based on what you learned in your American history class, write an essay in which you agree or disagree with Malcolm X's statement that the "glorious history of the black man was omitted from history books."
3. Think of an activity other than reading that you feel has empowered you. Write an essay explaining why you feel empowered by this particular activity.

WHO I AM AND HOW I WRITE

Mari Evans

Poet Mari Evans was born in Toledo, Ohio, and studied at the University of Toledo. She has worked as a television producer-director and currently is a college professor. Her books of poetry include I Am a Black Woman *(1970),* Where Is All the Music? *(1968),* Nightstar: Poems From 1973–1978 *(1982), and* Black Women Writers (1950–1980): A Critical Evaluation *(1983), from which this excerpt is taken. Evans's works are noted for their powerful emphases on the beauty of blackness. In the following selection, Evans describes her father's influence on her development as a writer.*

Vocabulary

vulnerability	(2)	openness to criticism or attack
indomitable	(2)	not easily discouraged
inscribing	(3)	impressing deeply
caprice	(3)	impulse
aesthetically	(6)	with sensitivity to art and beauty
imbued	(6)	filled
pathos	(6)	quality to arouse emotions
diaspora	(7)	scattering of people outside their homeland
ergo	(11)	therefore
blatantly	(12)	with obvious offensiveness
remanded	(12)	sent back
internment	(12)	confinement or impoundment, especially during a war

> *. . . I cannot imagine a writer who is not continually reaching, who contains no discontent that what he is producing is not more than it is. . . .*

Who I am is central to how I write and what I write; and I am the continuation of my father's passage. I have written for as long as I have been aware of writing as a way of setting down feelings and the stuff of imaginings.

No single living entity really influenced my life as did my father, who died two Septembers ago. An oak of a man, his five feet eight loomed taller than Kilimanjaro.[1] He lived as if he were poured from iron, and loved his family with a vulnerability that was touching. Indomitable, to the point that one could not have spent a lifetime in his presence without absorbing something beautiful and strong and special.

He saved my first printed story, a fourth-grade effort accepted by the school paper, and carefully noted on it the date, our home address, and his own proud comment. By this action inscribing on an impressionable Black youngster both the importance of the printed word and the accessibility of "reward" for even a slight effort, given the right circumstances. For I knew from what ease and caprice the story had come.   3

Years later, I moved from university journalism to a by-lined column in a Black-owned weekly and, in time, worked variously as an industrial editor, as a research associate with responsibility for preparing curriculum materials, and as director of publications for the corporate management of a Job Corps installation.   4

I have always written, it seems. I have not, however, always been organized in my approach. Now, I find I am much more productive when I set aside a specific time and uncompromisingly accept that as commitment. The ideal, for me, is to be able to write for long periods of time on an eight-hour-a-day basis. That is, to begin to write—not to prepare to write, around eight-thirty, stop for lunch, resume writing around twelve-thirty and stop for the day around four-thirty when I begin to feel both fulfilled and exhausted by the effort. For most Black writers that kind of leisure is an unaccustomed luxury. I enjoyed it exactly once, for a two-week period. In that two weeks I came face to face with myself as a writer and liked what I saw of my productive potential. . . .   5

I originally wrote poems because certain things occurred to me in phrases that I didn't want to lose. The captured phrase is a joyous way to approach the molding and shaping of a poem. More often now, however, because my conscious direction is different, I choose the subject first, then set about the task of creating a work that will please me aesthetically and that will treat the subject with integrity. A work that is imbued with the urgency, the tenderness, the pathos, needed to transmit to readers my sense of why they should involve themselves with what it is I have to say.   6

[1] Kilimanjaro (2)   The highest mountain in Africa.

I have no favorite themes nor concerns except the overall   7
concern that Black life be experienced throughout the diaspora
on the highest, most rewarding, most productive levels. Hardly
chauvinistic, for when that is possible for our Black family/na-
tion it will be true and possible for all people.

My primary goal is to command the reader's attention. I   8
understand I have to make the most of the first few seconds his
or her eye touches my material. Therefore, for me, the poem is
structure and style as well as theme and content; I require
something of my poems visually as well as rhetorically. I work
as hard at how the poem "looks" as at crafting; indeed, for me
the two are synonymous.

I revise endlessly, and am not reluctant to consider a   9
poem "in process" even after it has appeared in print. I am not
often completely pleased with any single piece, therefore, I remember with great pleasure those rare "given" poems. "If There
Be Sorrow" was such a piece, and there were others, but I remember "Sorrow" because that was the first time I experienced
the exquisite joy of having a poem emerge complete, without
my conscious intervention.

The title poem for my second volume, *I Am a Black*   10
Woman, on the other hand, required between fifteen and twenty
revisions before I felt comfortable that it could stand alone.

My attempt is to be as explicit as possible while maintain-   11
ing the integrity of the aesthetic; consequently, I work so hard
for clarity that I suspect I sometimes run the risk of being, as
Ray Durem put it, "not sufficiently obscure." Since the Black
creative artist is not required to wait on inspiration nor to rely
on imagination—for Black life is drama, brutal and compelling—
one inescapable reality is that the more explicitly Black writers
speak their truths the more difficult it is for them to publish. My
writing is pulsed by my understanding of contemporary realities:
I am Afrikan first, then woman, then writer, but I have never had
a manuscript rejected because I am a woman: I have been rejected more times than I can number because the content of a
manuscript was, to the industry-oriented reader, more "Black"
ergo "discomforting" than could be accommodated.

Nevertheless, given the crisis nature of the Black position   12
at a time of escalating state-imposed repression and contain-
ment, in a country that has a history of blatantly genocidal
acts committed against three nonwhite nations (Native Americans, the Japanese of Hiroshima/Nagasaki, the inhabitants of
Vietnam), a country that has perfected the systematic destruc-

tion of a people, their land, foliage, and food supply; a country that at the stroke of a presidential pen not only revoked the rights and privileges of citizenship for 110,000 American citizens (identifiable, since they were nonwhite) for what they "could" do, but summarily remanded those citizens to American internment camps, I understand that Black writers have a responsibility to use the language in the manner it is and always has been used by non-Black writers and by the state itself: as a political force.

I think of myself as a political writer inasmuch as I am deliberately attempting the delivery of political concepts and premises through the medium of the Black aesthetic, seeing the various art forms as vehicles.   13

As a Black writer embracing that responsibility, approaching my Black family/nation from within a commonality of experience, I try for a poetic language that says, "This is *who* we are, where we have been, *where* we are. This, is where we must go. And *this*, is what we must do."   14

Discussion Questions

1. How did Evans's father influence her development as a writer?

2. What is Evans's approach to writing poems?

3. Evans implies that revision is an important part of the writing process. What does this idea reveal about the art of writing?

4. According to Evans, why is it more difficult for black writers to publish their works than it is for nonblack writers?

5. According to Evans, what is the responsibility of black writers?

6. How would you characterize Evans?

7. Evans uses a variety of rhetorical strategies in developing her essay. Identify as many strategies as you can. How is each used in the essay?

8. How does the opening quotation set the tone for the essay?

Writing Assignments

1. Write an essay in which you agree or disagree with the following statement: African American writers have a responsibility to use their writing to help other African Americans.

2. Write an essay discussing your views on writing or your writing habits.

3. Write an essay explaining how someone (a writer, a teacher, a parent, a friend, etc.) has influenced your writing development.

Student Essay:

PUBLIC SCHOOLS FOR AFRICAN AMERICAN MALES: ARE THEY NECESSARY?

Byron T. Thompson

Vocabulary

disproportionately	(2)	unequally
detrimental	(2)	causing damage or harm

America has a new endangered species: the African American   1
male. Usually, the term *endangered species* is used to refer to
animals that have their existence continually threatened. But
now, America has created a human endangered species. Statistics, research studies, and common knowledge serve as proof
that black males are one of the most threatened species on
earth.

America's public schools surface as the single largest con-   2
tributor of the many divisions of institutional racism that have
led black males to their current endangered state. The mis-
takes begin in elementary school, which is probably the most
critical period in the black male child's development. First of
all, teachers generally are white females who often do not understand black boys. Studies show that these teachers unjusti-
fiably and disproportionately place black children, especially
boys, in "special" classes. This unfair treatment is detrimental
to their future education.

Contrary to popular belief, black boys do have positive at-   3
titudes about school. One survey showed that nearly all black
boys expected to graduate, but almost half felt that their teachers did not set high enough standards for them.* The majority
of them felt that they should be pushed harder. Another survey, conducted by the same group of people who surveyed the
black boys, showed that six out of ten teachers believed that
black boys would not go to college.* In essence, black boys
have their academic potential substantially doubted before they
even set foot in the classroom.

---

* Garibaldi, Antoine M. "Educating and Motivating African-American Males to
Succeed." *Journal of Negro Education* 61 (1993):129–131.

It should be obvious that a change is needed in America's   4
public school systems. One option that has become a reality is
the development of public schools that are specifically designed
with the needs of black males in mind. But there is considerable opposition to the formation of such schools from both
African Americans and Caucasians. Parents, teachers, and administrators are among the opposition. Citing various reasons,
many feel that it is a step backward toward segregation, an im-
proper discriminatory use of public funds, and simply the
wrong answer to the problem.

Milwaukee's African American immersion schools[1] serve   5
as an example that refutes those opposing viewpoints. Founded
in 1991 after years of research and study, the Martin Luther
King Jr. Elementary School was opened in Milwaukee, Wisconsin, on a goal-oriented, developmental concept. It is open to all
students, but is specifically designed for black boys and promotes African American heritage. Besides having an open enrollment policy, this school was transformed from a school that
already had a greater than 90 percent black enrollment; therefore, it does not promote segregation, nor is it discriminatory.

The school's concept is to instill a notion of inclusion   6
through more accurate portrayals of black people in order to
eliminate feelings of exclusion that black youth currently face.
The common practice in today's schools is to eliminate or
strongly distort images that deal with African Americans. Other
than to mention the deeds of Dr. Martin Luther King, George
Washington Carver, and Harriet Tubman, there is virtually no
reference in texts or by teachers to the magnitude in which
African Americans contributed to the building and prosperity of
this country. When teachers discuss Jim Crow laws,[2] slavery,
and the like, the evils that were associated with them are not
adequately covered, nor are the negative effects that they had
on blacks. In short, blacks are portrayed as intruders to this
country, whereas the correct interpretation would be to tell
how Africans brought to America were intruded upon. An increase in self-esteem is certain to occur when the learning environment changes from one which promotes false images that
produce negativity to one which promotes true images that en-
courage positivity.

[1] African American immersion schools (5)   Schools for African Americans
that include African American history and culture as part of their curricula.
  [2] Jim Crow Laws   (6)   Legal and systematic practice of segregating, suppressing, and discriminating against African Americans.

Not only will schools for African American males change   7
attitudes, but also will help black males socially and academi-
cally. Since the goals of the African American immersion
schools focus on the development of social skills, communication, problem solving, and critical thinking (areas not often
stressed in regular public schools), a tremendous impact on
the boys will result because they will be receiving vital lessons
that would not be taught to them otherwise. Also included
within this curriculum is the promotion of true self-identity of
both males and females, since often their everyday environment is one that instills within them attitudes and beliefs that
will not enable them to properly function in society.

With so much potential for improvement, it must be con-   8
cluded that schools for African American males are necessary.
The long-term effects will benefit all of society. The number of
black male high school graduates will produce more black male
college graduates who will become productive members of society.

Discussion Questions

1. What reasons does Thompson give to support his view that
   African American males are an "endangered species"?
2. What happens in an African American immersion school that
   does not occur in a regular school?
3. What is the basis of Thompson's argument that the African
   American immersion schools are not a form of reverse discrimination? Do you agree or disagree with this argument?
4. How does Thompson argue that schools for African American
   males will benefit all of society?
5. What is the tone of this essay?
6. How does Thompson use comparison and contrast to develop his
   argument?
7. Thompson chose to predict outcomes in his conclusion. What
   other type of effective ending could he have chosen?

Writing Assignments

1. Write an essay in which you discuss the strengths or weaknesses
   of a public school education.
2. Write an essay describing improvements you would make in your
   former school(s) if you were principal.
3. Write an essay in which you discuss some things you wish you
   had learned earlier in school.

16

Political Philosophies

BOOKER T. AND W.E.B.

Dudley Randall

Poet, editor, and founder of Broadside Press, Dudley Randall (1914–) was influential in helping publish the poetry of artists such as Haki R. Madhubuti (don l. lee), Sonia Sanchez, Nikki Giovanni, and Etheridge Knight. In addition to editing and co-editing volumes of poems, he wrote "Poem Counterpoem" (1966) with Margaret Danner and "Cities Burning" (1970). In his well-known poetic dialogue between Booker T. Washington and W.E.B. DuBois, which follows, Randall reflects the historical philosophical controversy between the two political leaders.

Vocabulary

cheek	(1)	arrogance
grouse	(3)	informal word for "complain"
avail	(4)	to be of use

"It seems to me," said Booker T.,   1
"It shows a mighty lot of cheek
To study chemistry and Greek
When Mister Charlie[1] needs a hand
To hoe the cotton on his land,
And when Miss Ann[2] looks for a cook,
Why stick your nose inside a book?"

"I don't agree," said W. E. B.   2
"If I should have the drive to seek
Knowledge of chemistry or Greek,
I'll do it. Charles and Miss can look
Another place for hand or cook.
Some men rejoice in skill of hand,
And some in cultivating land,
But there are others who maintain
The right to cultivate the brain."

"It seems to me," said Booker T.,   3
"That all you folks have missed the boat
Who shout about the right to vote,
And spend vain days and sleepless nights
In uproar over civil rights.
Just keep your mouths shut, do not grouse,
But work, and save, and buy a house."

"I don't agree," said W. E. B.   4
"For what can property avail
If dignity and justice fail?
Unless you help to make the laws,
They'll steal your house with trumped-up clause.
A rope's as tight, a fire as hot,
No matter how much cash you've got.
Speak soft, and try your little plan,
But as for me, I'll be a man."

"It seems to me," said Booker T.—   5

"I don't agree,"   6
Said W. E. B.

---

[1] Mister Charlie and [2]Miss Ann (1)   Terms used to symbolize the slave
master and his wife; have been broadened to mean any white male or female authority figure.

Discussion Questions

1. Why does Randall choose to omit the last names in the title?
2. What are the two political philosophies presented in the poem? Discuss each one.
3. What do you think accounts for the differences in the men's philosophies?
4. Do you think that the poet communicates a strong preference for one of the views. What is his preference? Support your answer.
5. What rhetorical strategies are used to help the reader highlight the difference between Washington and Dubois?
6. What do the last three lines say about the argument?

Writing Assignments

1. Write an essay in which you support either Booker T. or W.E.B.'s philosophy.
2. Write an essay in which you contrast two views or strategies on abolishing racism.
3. Write an essay in which you contrast the views of a controversial issue, for example, health-care reform or prayer in public schools.

ATLANTA EXPOSITION ADDRESS

Booker T. Washington

Booker T. Washington (1856–1915) was born to a white slave-holding father and a black slave mother in Franklin County, Virginia. He was educated at Hampton Institute (now Hampton University) and went on to become founder and president of Tuskegee Institute, which emphasized the value of vocational education as a stepping-stone to economic empowerment for its students. Washington wrote twelve books. The most important of these are his autobiography Up from Slavery *(1901),* The Future of the American Negro *(1899), and* Life of Frederick Douglass *(1907). A controversial high point in Washington's career was his address to the Atlanta Cotton States and International Exposition in 1895. In that speech, excerpted here, he accepts social and legal segregation while promising racial cooperation.*

Vocabulary

injunction	(3)	command, order
gewgaws	(4)	knickknacks, trinkets
folly	(6)	nonsense
ostracized	(6)	shut out, ignored

Mr. President and Gentlemen of the Board of Directors and Citizens: One-third of the population of the South is of the Negro race. No enterprise seeking the material, civil, or moral welfare of this section can disregard this element of our population and reach the highest success. I but convey to you, Mr. President and Directors, the sentiment of the masses of my race when I say that in no way have the value and manhood of the American Negro been more fittingly and generously recognized than by the managers of this magnificent Exposition at every stage of its progress. It is a recognition that will do more to cement the friendship of the two races than any occurrence since the dawn of freedom. 1

Not only this, but the opportunity here afforded will awaken among us a new era of industrial progress. Ignorant and inexperienced, it is not strange that in the first years of our new life we began at the top instead of at the bottom; that a 2 seat in Congress or the State Legislature was more sought than real estate or industrial skill; that the political convention or stump speaking had more attractions than starting a dairy farm or truck garden.

A ship lost at sea for many days suddenly sighted a friendly vessel. From the mast of the unfortunate vessel was seen a signal, "Water, water; we die of thirst!" The answer from the friendly vessel at once came back: "Cast down your bucket where you are." A second time the signal, "Water, water; send us water!" ran up from the distressed vessel, and was answered: "Cast down your bucket where you are." The captain of the distressed vessel, at last heeding the injunction, cast down his bucket, and it came up full of fresh, sparkling water from the mouth of the Amazon River. To those of my race who depend upon bettering their condition in a foreign land, or who underestimate the importance of cultivating friendly relations with the Southern white man, who is his next door neighbor, I would say: "Cast down your bucket where you are"—cast it down in making friends in every manly way of the people of all races by whom we are surrounded.

Cast it down in agriculture, mechanics, in commerce, in domestic service, and in the professions. And in this connection it is well to bear in mind that whatever other sins the South may be called to bear, when it comes to business, pure and simple, it is in the South that the Negro is given a man's chance in the commercial world, and in nothing is this Exposition more eloquent than in emphasizing this chance. Our greatest danger is, that in the great leap from slavery to freedom we may overlook the fact that the masses of us are to live by the productions of our hands, and fail to keep in mind that we shall prosper in proportion as we learn to dignify and glorify common labor, and put brains and skill into the common occupations of life; shall prosper in proportion as we learn to draw the line between the superficial and the substantial, the ornamental gewgaws of life and the useful. No race can prosper till it learns that there is as much dignity in tilling a field as in writing a poem. It is at the bottom of life we must begin, and not at the top. Nor should we permit our grievances to overshadow our opportunities.

To those of the white race who look to the incoming of those of foreign birth and strange tongue and habits for the prosperity of the South, were I permitted I would repeat what I say to my own race, "Cast down your bucket where you are."

Cast it down among the 8,000,000 Negroes whose habits you know, whose fidelity and love you have tested in days when to have proved treacherous meant the ruin of your firesides. Cast down your bucket among these people who have, without strikes and labor wars, tilled your fields, cleared your forests, builded your railroads and cities, and brought forth treasures from the bowels of the earth, and helped make possible this magnificent representation of the progress of the South. Casting down your bucket among my people, helping and encouraging them as you are doing on these grounds, and, with education of head, hand and heart, you will find that they will buy your surplus land, make blossom the waste places in your fields, and run your factories. While doing this, you can be sure in the future, as in the past, that you and your families will be surrounded by the most patient, faithful, law-abiding, and unresentful people that the world has seen. As we have proved our loyalty to you in the past, in nursing your children, watching by the sick bed of your mothers and fathers, and often following them with tear-dimmed eyes to their graves, so in the future, in our humble way, we shall stand by you with a devotion that no foreigner can approach, ready to lay down our lives, if need be, in defense of yours, interlacing our industrial, commercial, civil, and religious life with yours in a way that shall make the interests of both races one. In all things that are purely social we can be as separate as the fingers, yet one as the hand in all things essential to mutual progress. . . .

6 The wisest among my race understand that the agitation of questions of social equality is the extremest folly, and that progress in the enjoyment of all the privileges that will come to us must be the result of severe and constant struggle rather than of artificial forcing. No race that has anything to contribute to the markets of the world is long in any degree ostracized. It is important and right that all privileges of the law be ours, but it is vastly more important that we be prepared for the exercise of those privileges. The opportunity to earn a dollar in a factory just now is worth infinitely more than the opportunity to spend a dollar in an opera house.

7 In conclusion, may I repeat that nothing in thirty years has given us more hope and encouragement, and drawn us so near to you of the white race, as this opportunity offered by the Exposition; and here bending, as it were, over the altar that represents the results of the struggles of your race and mine, both starting practically empty-handed three decades ago, I

pledge that, in your effort to work out the great and intricate problem which God has laid at the doors of the South, you shall have at all times the patient, sympathetic help of my race; only let this be constantly in mind that, while from representations in these buildings of the products of field, of forest, of mine, of factory, letters, and art, much good will come, yet far above and beyond material benefits will be the higher good, that let us pray God will come, in a blotting out of sectional differences and racial animosities and suspicions, in a determination to administer absolute justice, in a willing obedience among all classes to the mandates of law. This, coupled with our material prosperity, will bring into our beloved South a new heaven and a new earth.

Discussion Questions

1. In this address Washington presents his economic and social plan for southern blacks and whites. What is his message to each?
2. What does Washington mean in his "Cast-down-your-buckets-where-you-are" passage?
3. What does Washington mean when he says, "No race can prosper till it learns that there is as much dignity in tilling a field as in writing a poem"?
4. What image of African Americans does Washington present to "those of the white race"? Give examples. What is your response to that image?
5. What rhetorical strategies other than persuasion does Washington use?
6. What is the thesis of Washington's speech?

Writing Assignments

1. Write an essay in which you recount a situation when you or someone you know protested. Explain why the protest was memorable.
2. Using Washington's speech as a model, write your own speech to be addressed to _____ proposing _____.
3. Write an essay in which you or someone you know used one approach to solving a problem, but should have used another approach. Explain your response.

GARVEY SPEAKS AT MADISON SQUARE GARDEN

Marcus Garvey

Born in St. Ann's Bay, Jamaica, Marcus Garvey (1887–1940), perhaps more than any other leader, has had a far-reaching effect on African Americans as a result of his inspiring a revolution in black consciousness. He organized the Universal Negro Improvement Association (UNIA), aimed at uniting people of African descent throughout the world to establish "a country and government absolutely their own." Of all political organizations, the UNIA, still in existence today, has the record for having the largest worldwide membership of people of African descent. Finding color discrimination among Jamaicans a problem, Garvey moved his political base to the United States. Later, after a questionable prison conviction, he was deported but continued to carry his message throughout the world. He established a UNIA newspaper, The Negro World, *in 1918, and collections of his writings and speeches,* Philosophy and Opinions of Marcus Garvey, *were published in 1923 and 1926. In the following speech delivered at Madison Square Garden (1924), Garvey reflects much of the UNIA philosophy.*

Vocabulary

succored	(5)	supported
imperialism	(5)	economic or political domination of one nation over another
rancor	(10)	bitterness, grudge
encumbered	(11)	hindered

No Exclusive Right to the World

Let no black man feel that he has the exclusive right to the world, and other men none, and let no white man feel that way, either. The world is the property of all mankind, and each and every group is entitled to a portion. The black man now wants his, and in terms uncompromising he is asking for it.

The Universal Negro Improvement Association represents the hopes and aspirations of the awakened Negro. Our desire is for a place in the world; not to disturb the tranquillity of other men, but to lay down our burden and rest our weary backs and feet by the banks of the Niger, and sing our songs and chant our hymns to the God of Ethiopia. Yes, we want rest from the toil of centuries, rest of political freedom, rest of economic and indus- trial liberty, rest to be socially free and unmolested, rest from lynching and burning, rest from discrimination of all kinds.

Out of slavery we have come with our tears and sorrows,   3 and we now lay them at the feet of American white civilization. We cry to the considerate white people for help, because in their midst we can scarce help ourselves. We are strangers in a strange land. We cannot sing, we cannot play on our harps, for our hearts are sad. We are sad because of the tears of our mothers and the cry of our fathers. Have you not heard the plaintive wail? It is your father and my father burning at stake; but, thank God, there is a larger humanity growing among the good and considerate white people of this country, and they are going to help. They will help us to recover our souls.

As children of captivity we look forward to a new day and a   4 new, yet ever old, land of our fathers, the land of refuge, the land of the Prophets, the land of the Saints, and the land of God's crowning glory. We shall gather together our children, our treasures and our loved ones, and, as the children of Israel, by the command of God, faced the promised land, so in time we shall also stretch forth our hands and bless our country.

Good and dear America that has succored us for three   5 hundred years knows our story. We have watered her vegeta- tion with our tears for two hundred and fifty years. We have built her cities and laid the foundations of her imperialism with the mortar of our blood and bones for three centuries, and now we cry to her for help. Help us, America, as we helped you. We helped you in the Revolutionary War. We helped you in the Civil War, and, although Lincoln helped us, the price is not half paid. We helped you in the Spanish-American War. We died nobly and courageously in Mexico, and did we not leave behind us on the stained battlefields of France and Flanders[1] our rich blood to mark the poppies' bloom, and to bring back to you the glory of the flag that never touched the dust? We have no re- grets in service to America for three hundred years, but we pray that America will help us for another fifty years until we have solved the troublesome problem that now confronts us. We know and realize that two ambitious and competitive races

---

[1] Flanders   (5)   Refers to U.S. involvement in bitter and bloody trench war- fare during World War I.

cannot live permanently side by side, without friction and trouble, and that is why the white race wants a white America and the black race wants and demands a black Africa.

Let white America help us for fifty years honestly, as we 6
have helped her for three hundred years, and before the expiration of many decades there shall be no more race problem. Help us to gradually go home, America. Help us as you have helped the Jews. Help us as you have helped the Irish. Help us as you have helped the Poles, Russians, Germans and Armenians.

The Universal Negro Improvement Association proposes a 7
friendly co-operation with all honest movements seeking intelligently to solve the race problem. We are not seeking social equality; we do not seek intermarriage, nor do we hanker after the impossible. We want the right to have a country of our own, and there foster and reestablish a culture and civilization exclusively ours. Don't say it can't be done. The Pilgrims and colonists did it for America, and the new Negro, with sympathetic help, can do it for Africa.

Back to Africa

The thoughtful and industrious of our race want to go back 8
to Africa, because we realize it will be our only hope of permanent existence. We cannot all go in a day or year, ten or twenty years. It will take time under the rule of modern economics, to entirely or largely depopulate a country of a people, who have been its residents for centuries, but we feel that, with proper help for fifty years, the problem can be solved. We do not want all the Negroes in Africa. Some are no good here, and naturally will be no good there. The no-good Negro will naturally die in fifty years. The Negro who is wrangling about and fighting for social equality will naturally pass away in fifty years, and yield his place to the progressive Negro who wants a society and country of his own.

Negroes are divided into two groups, the industrious and adventurous, and the lazy and dependent. The industrious and 9
adventurous believe that whatsoever others have done it can do. The Universal Negro Improvement Association belongs to this group, and so you find us working, six million strong, to the goal of an independent nationality. Who will not help? Only the mean and despicable "who never to himself hath said, this is my own, my native land." Africa is the legitimate, moral and righteous home of all Negroes, and now, that the time is coming for all to assemble under their own vine and fig tree, we feel it our duty to arouse every Negro to a consciousness of himself.

White and black will learn to respect each other when they   10
cease to be active competitors in the same countries for the same
things in politics and society. Let them have countries of their
own, wherein to aspire and climb without rancor. The races can
be friendly and helpful to each other, but the laws of nature separate us to the extent of each and every one developing by itself.

We want an atmosphere all our own. We would like to gov-   11
ern and rule ourselves and not be encumbered and restrained.
We feel now just as the white race would feel if they were governed and ruled by the Chinese. If we live in our own districts,
let us rule and govern those districts. If we have a majority in
our communities, let us run those communities. We form a majority in Africa and we should naturally govern ourselves there.
No man can govern another's house as well as himself. Let us
have fair play. Let us have justice. This is the appeal we make
to white America.

Discussion Questions

1. What is the objective of the UNIA?
2. According to Garvey, what are some of the contributions that African Americans have made to the United States?
3. What is one of the reasons Garvey gives for reclaiming Africa for all people of African descent?
4. Why does Garvey say that the thoughtful and industrious Negro wants to return to Africa?
5. Why does Garvey think that white and black people should rule their own separate countries?
6. Why does Garvey appeal to the "considerate white people" for help with his plan?
7. To what extent does Garvey's use of classification help him clarify his point?
8. In paragraph 5, Garvey poses a series of questions. To what extent are these questions effective?

Writing Assignments

1. Based on what you know about African Americans in the United States, write an essay arguing for or against their returning to Africa.
2. Write an essay discussing the success or lack of success of integration in your neighborhood or school.
3. Write an essay discussing the different types of racial, ethnic, or social groups that exist in your school or community.

BECOMING A REPUBLICAN

Tony Brown

Tony Brown (1933–   ) was born in Charleston, West Virginia, and received his B.A. and M.S.W. degrees from Wayne State University. Currently, Brown is a very successful media personality. He is talk show host of Tony Brown's Journal, *a syndicated newspaper columnist, a film director, and a television and film producer. He is also a commentator for the National Public Radio program* All Things Considered. *In 1977, he founded Tony Brown Productions. A registered Republican, Brown wrote the following article, which appeared in the* Wall Street Journal *(August 1991). In it, he attempts to explain why he became a Republican.*

Vocabulary

fascism	(3)	a type of dictatorship
totalitarian	(3)	systematic, absolute control
demagoguery	(4)	power gained by appealing to people's emotions or prejudices
tacit	(4)	not spoken; understood from actions
polarization	(5)	two conflicting and contrasting views
insidious	(5)	harmful yet subtle
enclaves	(6)	distinct territorial, cultural, or social units

"A veteran black TV personality and longtime battler of racism is dropping a bombshell on his fans by ceremoniously joining the Republican Party," columnist Mary Papenfuss wrote in the *New York Post* last week after my announcement on July 8 that I was ceasing to be a political independent and was joining the party that was organized in 1854 to oppose the expansion of slavery. 1

Blacks responded after the end of slavery by voting for the party of the man who signed the Emancipation Proclamation, Abraham Lincoln. Blacks affiliated with the Republican Party, such as the remarkable Frederick Douglass, a former slave and an abolitionist who insisted that "power concedes nothing without a demand," emerged as national heroes. Republicans in Congress were the architects of Reconstruction, a 10-year pe- 2 riod of unprecedented political power for black people. They initiated the 13th Amendment, which outlawed slavery, the 14th Amendment, which guaranteed blacks citizenship, and the 15th Amendment, which extended the right to vote to former slaves, as well as the Civil Rights Act of 1866.

Independent Thinking

Ironically, it is the right of a black to be a member of the Republican Party that is being openly questioned in 1991. And unfortunately, the First Amendment's guarantee of free speech has not been taken seriously by some black intellectuals and leaders. Many of them perpetuate an intellectual fascism and foster a totalitarian environment in which any independent thinking black who breaks lock-step with their often self-serving Democratic worldview is severely condemned, and even ostracized.   3

How did blacks move from the party that gave them civil and political rights to a previously all-white Democratic Party with a history of racist demagoguery, support for slavery and Jim Crow, and tacit approval of lynching? The movement began during the Depression, when the social programs of Franklin Roosevelt severed the close ties that blacks had felt in the Republicans. But many blacks remained loyal to the party of Lincoln: 40% of black voters voted for Dwight Eisenhower in 1956, and 32% cast their ballots for Richard Nixon in 1960. The black middle class, eager to associate itself with a message of self-sufficiency, was even more Republican: In some prosperous areas, Republicans were getting nearly 50% of the black vote as late as 1960.   4

Then Lyndon Johnson—who accomplished more for blacks legislatively than any president in American history—enacted his historic civil rights acts. Disgruntled Southern whites defected to the Republicans in the 1961 election, enabling Barry Goldwater to win such once-solid Democratic states as Mississippi, Georgia, Louisiana, South Carolina and Alabama. Tempted by these votes, the Republicans adopted a "Southern strategy," which has carried them to the White House in all but one of the elections since then. The strategy, as expounded in "The Emerging Republican Majority" by Kevin Phillips, demonstrated how Republicans could profit from racial polarization with code words like "law and order." The   5 insidious idea behind this "Willie Hortonism"[1] was to gain anti-black votes without appearing racist in the old Deep South style.

Today's near-unanimous perception among blacks that all   6
white Republicans are racists is born out of that history—and the subsequent extension of the Southern strategy into Northern suburbs and ethnic enclaves. As a result, blacks have almost completely deserted the Republicans: In 1988, just 1% of the votes cast in the Republican presidential primaries were cast by blacks.

The absence of blacks from the Republican Party spells   7
disaster for the black community. Between 1936 and 1964, when blacks voted roughly 65% Democratic to 35% Republican, both parties had to compete for their votes. Today, however, because blacks vote overwhelmingly Democratic, the Democrats can offer lip service and still count on the black vote. And because blacks have become an almost nonexistent force in the GOP, Republicans can ignore them altogether.

But the absence of blacks from the Republican Party also   8
spells long-term economic ruin for our country. We must adapt to cultural diversity as the foundation of our economic competitiveness. And it spells long-term political danger for the Republicans themselves: What the GOP is doing, or not doing, in the black ghettoes can have consequences in the white suburbs. White suburbanites could defect from the Republican fold if the party becomes stigmatized as racist. That's what moves Republicans like Sen. John Danforth (R., Mo.) to criticize the way some Republicans are exploiting the quota issue. That's why the Ripon Republicans in the 1960s warned of the danger of a strategy of racial divisiveness and promoted racial inclusion instead.

So, no matter how great the risk to some of us personally,   9
we cannot allow black America to remain a one-party community in a two-party system. Nor can we permit the Republican Party to become a lily-white enclave in a heterogeneous country.

At one stage in history, the Democratic Party may have   10
been the best choice for blacks. However, the Democratic poli-

---

[1] Willie Hortonism   (5)   The act of creating conflicting views by distorting facts; named for a Massachusetts African American prison inmate, who committed a crime while on a weekend furlough. Distorting this story, Republicans were successful in polarizing voters and contributing to the Massachusetts governor (Michael Dukakis) losing the 1988 presidential race.

cies of exclusive reliance on government programs evidently has not brought economic success to black America. As Martin Luther King, Jr., said more than 20 years ago: "New laws are not enough. The emergency we now face is economic." Blacks have an abiding faith in the philosophy of self-sufficiency, but are stuck, out of perverse necessity, with the something-for-nothing entitlement dogma of the Democrats. But the problem with depending on government is that you cannot depend on it.

Racism is a problem, but poverty is the primary problem   11
facing blacks. Blacks need economic solutions. And self-help is a time-tested economic solution.

For example, the 350 black organizations that spend $16   12
billion in white-owned hotels each summer ($500 million at the Congressional Black Caucus meeting alone) discussing white racism and black poverty could cancel their 1992 conventions and use that $16 billion as a capital fund to buy hotels (at the moment, not one major hotel in America is owned by blacks) start new companies, create jobs for the poor and fund social programs in the black community.

In September, I am launching an effort to start 50,000   13
small companies in the next five years through a telephone-based loan program, using a state-of-the-art telecommunications system. Profits from calls to the businesses on the Buy Freedom 900 network will be used to provide the loans.

A community of 30 million people who emphasize civil   14
rights over economic power will never have equal rights. Both civil rights and economic power are equally necessary. Neither can a black community earning $300 billion a year, the equivalent of the GNP of the ninth-richest nation in the free world, spend 95% of its money with other groups and blame them for 100% of its problems.

The color of freedom is green. As Adam Smith taught in   15
"The Wealth of Nations," true freedom can come only from an intelligent and humane use of the free market system. And the party of free enterprise, despite all its potentially reversible shortcomings, is the Republican Party. If blacks want to return the Republican Party to its tradition of inclusion, they will have to join it and work from within.

Ideological Diversity

Since I announced my affiliation with the Republicans, a   16
surprising number of blacks have told me they will follow my

example. And all of the blacks who have spoken to me like the idea of greater ideological diversity within the black community. The statement that best typified the reaction to my becoming a Republican came from a woman at the Apollo Theater in Harlem, following my interview on WLIB, New York's black radio station.

"When I first heard the news, I thought you had sold out.   17 So I had to hear an explanation from you personally. After hearing you explain, I agree with you and admire your courage. We do have to rely on self-help and we do have to be involved in both parties. But I'm not ready to become a Republican yet. I don't trust the Republican Party, but I trust Tony Brown."

Discussion Questions

1. Why did Brown become a Republican?
2. After the abolition of slavery, why did blacks join the Republican Party? When did blacks begin to join the Democratic Party? Why?
3. According to Brown, why can we not allow "Black Americans to remain a one-party community in a two-party community"?
4. Brown feels that the color of freedom is green. What is the significance of this idea to blacks joining the Republican Party?
5. How does Brown prove that self-help is a time-tested economic solution?
6. To what extent do you agree or disagree with Brown's argument for becoming a Republican?
7. How does the use of comparison and contrast and cause and effect strengthen Brown's argument?
8. Does Brown provide sufficient examples to develop the thesis?

Writing Assignments

1. Write an essay in which you contrast your political viewpoint with that of someone you know.
2. If you disagree with Brown's view, write an essay arguing why African Americans should not join the Republican Party.
3. Write an essay in which you explain one of your philosophical, moral, or religious views.

Student Essay:
THE BLACK PANTHER PARTY

Khadijah A. Mayo

Vocabulary

turbulent   (1)   stormy
immeasurable (9)   unable to be determined

The civil rights era was a very turbulent period in the United   1
States. The country was battling over whether or not black people should receive racial equality. At the forefront of the movement in the early 1960s were Martin Luther King, Jr., and Malcolm X. After both of these black leaders were assassinated,
black people were left with a major sense of loss. The Black
Panther Party played a positive and greatly needed role in fulfilling this loss during the civil rights era.

In 1966, the Black Panther Party officially began in Oak-   2
land, California. Bobby Seale was the national chairman, Huey
P. Newton was the minister of defense, and Eldridge Cleaver
was the minister of information. The party was made up of a
wide cross section of individuals, including college graduates. It
was founded because the needs of the black community were
simply not being met. For instance, there was a lack of jobs,
and, as a result, the ghettos were saturated with sick, poor,
and hungry black people.

Although some of the party's ideas were not well planned,   3
many of them were positive and progressive. Most of its demands were related, directly and indirectly, to the economic
treatment of black people. These demands helped the Panthers
to awaken a consciousness in black people that made them realize there were problems in society. Unfortunately, many of
the people that opposed the Panthers were not familiar with the
positive work they did.

One of the most beneficial activities of the Panthers was   4
the Free Breakfast Program in Oakland, California. Many students were not eating breakfast and their hunger led to poor
progress in school. The goal of the program was to ensure that
black children did not go to school hungry. Parents and volunteers prepared and served the breakfasts, washed dishes, and
cleaned the facility. The Panthers solicited donations of food

and supplies from the community. These donations were the backbone of the program. Once the program began, teachers noted the improvement in the students' work. This program was the parent to the breakfast and lunch programs now in public and private schools.

To further aid the community, the Panthers founded Liberation Schools, which were open in the summer for students ages two to thirteen. The schools trained students to be revolutionary leaders. It also taught the students African and African American history.   5

Perhaps the most notable contribution of the Black Panthers was the People's Free Medical Care Center. The centers were located throughout the United States. They provided health care for people who would otherwise go without medical attention. The doctors and nurses volunteered their services. They went out into the community to look for people with illnesses. This service was a vital one because many could not afford medical care.   6

The Panthers did many other things for the black community that went unrecognized. For example, they registered blacks to vote and held community discussions. Huey Newton issued the "Pocket Lawyer," which informed people of their rights when arrested. It listed the number of the nearest Black Panther chapter so people could call for legal aid.   7

The *Black Panther* was a grassroots newspaper in which black people told news stories from a black person's perspective. The information for the paper was pooled from the various Black Panther Party chapters around the country. The first issue was printed in 1967 and was called the "Voice of the Party."   8

Regardless of the Panthers' shortcomings, their benefit to the black community was immeasurable. Black power was more than a phrase; it was an experience. Positive community activities may not have made the newspapers, but that omission was not necessary for the many people who benefited from the party's existence.   9

Discussion Questions

1. When was the Black Panther Party founded and why?

2. What were some of the positive programs started by the party?

3. Considering the type of contributions the Black Panther Party made, what assumptions can you make about the party's beliefs?

4. According to Mayo, why were some people opposed to the Panthers?

5. How effective is Mayo's use of illustration in her essay?

6. How effective is the writer's use of transitions?

Writing Assignments

1. Write an essay about the contributions made by some organization you know of or are affiliated with.

2. Write an essay about some of the improvements that are being made (or are needed) in the African American community. Discuss the source of these improvements and the significance of each.

17

Black Dialect • Language

PARAPOETICS

Eugene Redmond

Eugene Redmond (1937–   ), poet, editor, critic, and teacher, was born in St. Louis, Missouri, and graduated from Southern Illinois University and Washington University in St. Louis. He was a senior consultant to Katherine Dunham's Performing Arts Training Center at Southern Illinois University and has been writer-in-residence at Southern University, Oberlin College, and Sacramento State College. His works, which have appeared in a number of anthologies and journals, include A Tale of Two Toms *(1968),* Songs from an Afro/Phone *(1972),* In a Time of Rain and Desire *(1973), and* There's a Wiretap in My Soup *(1974). In the following poem, from* Sentry of the Four Golden Pillars *(1970), Redmond explores the process of poetry writing.*

Vocabulary

eloquented	(1)	vivid, forceful
cellular	(1)	having a small hollow space
gestate	(2)	to conceive and develop
lode	(5)	rich source or supply

(For my former students and writing friends in East St. Louis, Illinois)

Poetry is an *applied science:*   1
    Re-wrapped corner rap;
    Rootly-eloquented, cellular, soulular sermons.
    Grit reincarnations of
    Lady Day[1]
    Bird[2]
    & Otis;[3]
    Silk songs pitched on 'round and rhythmic rumps;
    Carved halos (for heroes) and asserted maleness:
    Sounds and sights of fire-tongues
    Leaping from lips of flame-stricken buildings in the night.

Directions: apply poetry as needed.   2
Envision.
Visualize.
Violate!
Wring minds.
Shout!
Right words.
Rite!!
Cohabitate.
Gestate.
Pregnate your vocabulary.
Dig, a parapoet!

[1] Lady Day (1)   Nickname of 1940s African American jazz singer Eleanor "Billie" Holiday.
[2] Bird (1)   Nickname of African American 1950s jazz alto saxophonist Charles Christopher "Charlie" Parker, Jr.
[3] Otis (1)   1960s African American rhythm and blues singer Otis Redding.

Parenthesis: Replace winter with spring, move Mississippi   3
to New York, Oberlin (Ohio) to East St. Louis, Harlem
to the summer whitehouse. Carve candles and flintstones
for flashlights.

Carry your poems.   4
Grit teeth. Bear labor-love pains.
Have twins and triplets.
Furtilize poem-farms with after-birth,
Before birth and dung [rearrange old words];
Study/strike tradition.

Caution to parapoets: 5
Carry the weight of your own poem.
. . . it's a *heavy lode.*

Discussion Questions

1. "Para" means "beyond" or "similar to." How significant is the poem's title to its message?

2. In what way does the second line suggest that poetry is not a new art form?

3. An applied science is one that is practiced or used. Why do you think Redmond writes that poetry is an applied science?

4. The "Parenthesis" section of the poem is a good example of the revising process. What do you think this section means?

5. How does Redmond convince the reader that writing in general and poetry writing in particular is hard work?

6. How does Redmond's use of process help the reader understand the definition of parapoetics?

7. Redmond uses interesting words to spark various reactions from the reader. Why do you think he uses unusual spellings of words such as *soulular* and *furtilize?*

Writing Assignments

1. Write an essay on a topic of your choice. Rewrite the essay several times, keeping in mind Redmond's suggestions for revision.
2. Write an essay that explains a familiar process.
3. A large part of writing is revision. Write an essay describing your process of revision.

AFRICAN AMERICAN YOUTH RESIST STANDARD ENGLISH

Felicia R. Lee

The following excerpt was first published in the New York Times *on January 5, 1994, under the title, "Grappling with How to Teach Young Speakers of Black Dialect." Its focus is the widespread and persistent use of black dialect, an occurrence that seems to be the result of the resistance of African American youth to those things associated with white people and white culture.*

Vocabulary

linguists	(2)	language specialists
diverged	(2)	departed from
assimilate	(3)	adapt, conform
cynicism	(3)	a distrustful attitude
exquisitely	(11)	very, intensely
vernacular	(11)	language commonly spoken by members of a particular group; language considered non-standard

More than a decade after educators first grappled with the issue, school districts in New York and elsewhere are still seeking the best way to teach standard English to students who usually use black dialect. A few districts have a policy to teach standard English like a second language, but in most, as in New York, the approach is scattershot, varying from school to school and classroom to classroom. 1

During this time, linguists say, the black vernacular has steadily diverged from standard English and become more widespread in poor, urban neighborhoods. Educators once predicted that as more black people entered the mainstream, the dialect would fade not only among the middle class, as it has, but also among the poor. Linguists say, however, that the current generation of inner-city youth rely more heavily on black vernacular than ever. 2

The persistence of the dialect reflects, in part, the growing resistance of some black young people to assimilate and their efforts to use language as part of a value system that prizes 3 cultural distinction. It also stems from the increasing isolation of black inner-city residents from both whites and middle-class blacks, and stems as well from a deep cynicism about the pay-offs of conforming.

While the dialect is used as a kind of in-group code among many black people of all stations, educators worry about those young people who never master standard English at all.   4

Some teachers say they are uncertain about how to in-struct students who use the dialect, and in the absence of clear policy, they are largely left to devise their own methods.   5

Mr. Halperin, who teaches at the Richard Green High School for Teaching, said that many of his students become fu-rious and shout "Who are you trying to be?" when a student uses standard English in class. His strategy is to work around the hostility with things like the bilingual dictionary, dramatic presentations and reading aloud.   6

In some neighborhoods, young people acknowledge an ele-ment of resistance, and even a stigma, to using standard Eng-lish or "talking proper."   7

"English is not our language," said Takiyah Hudson, a 17-year-old high school senior who lives in Harlem. She said her mother and sister correct her English when she slips into a black dialect, which she does not use in formal situations.   8

"Our language has more rhythmic tones," Ms. Hudson said. "To some people, 'she be going' just flows, it's just a nat-ural thing."   9

Ms. Hudson acknowledges that students have to use stan-dard English in some settings. "It's like going to France and speaking English and getting mad at them. Such and such cor-poration isn't going to hire me. That's realistic thinking."   10

The issue is exquisitely sensitive, going beyond nouns and verbs to questions of racial identity and class, as well as the politics of education. There is some sentiment among the black middle class that the vernacular legitimizes poor grammar. Others blame schools for not teaching standard English better because teachers have low expectations of black students. Lin-guists, having seen acknowledgement by educators of the di-alect, say it is time to become more sophisticated in the class-room.   11

"When we were in the 60's to the 80's, we were trying to get recognition for the language, that it had rules, it has a system, it has a pattern," said Geneva Smitherman, a Michigan State University linguist and English professor whose book on black   12 vernacular is to be published in June. "Now we are at the point where we need a multilingual policy that means that everybody would learn one other language or one other dialect. . . ."

Linguists say the dialect represents the remnants of West 13 African languages used by American slaves and the efforts of those slaves—denied formal education—to mimic white people. Ironically, the dialect has contributed richly to standard English, influencing everything from advertising to slang. The dialect has such features as dropping the verb "to be" or the lack of subject-verb agreement, resulting in "She sick" and "He like ice cream."

Jo-Ann Graham, chairwoman of the department of com- 14 munications at the Bronx Community College, said teaching standard English is not simply cleaning up grammatical lapses. "It is not just saying, 'You don't say "they is" you say "they are,"'" she said. "You have to teach the structure, the vocabulary, the sound system, the grammar just as if you were teaching another language."

The country's largest school system to use such an ap- 15 proach is Los Angeles. Its "Proficiency in English" program, started in 1978, uses methods like repetitive drills to teach standard English like a second language. Several other California school districts, including Oakland, Sacramento and Vallejo, use similar programs.

Individual school districts in cities with large black popu- 16 lations, like Baltimore, Detroit and Philadelphia, are using programs to teach students who use black vernacular.

Most programs use something called "contrastive analy- 17 sis," which attempts to get students to hear and see the differences between what they say and write and what is said and written in standard English.

There is also role-playing for different audiences, so stu- 18 dents learn the time and place for their vernacular and for formal speech.

"The problem is, this is not in any textbook," said Ms. 19 Wright-Lewis, a teacher at Boys and Girls High School in the Bedford-Stuyvesant section of Brooklyn. "I had to make up my own curriculum. No one asks teachers 'What would you put in a textbook?'"

Ms. Wright-Lewis has students write and rewrite assign- 20 ments. She makes them give oral presentations and participate in discussions that she privately assesses for syntax and grammar. She writes her own stories for students, in which characters switch back and forth between standard and non-standard English. And she corrects her students in private to help protect their fragile self-esteem.

Frank Mickens, the principal of Boys and Girls, believes   21
that the issue is not as pressing as other concerns, like the safety of his students, who come from some of the toughest housing projects in the nation. Most students, he said, already use both standard English and the vernacular.

Discussion Questions

1. What are the two reasons given for the persistence of the black vernacular?
2. What are some major features of black dialect?
3. Why is the use of black dialect considered a problem by educators?
4. Why has there been growing resistance by African American youth to using standard English?
5. What is the origin of black dialect?
6. How does Lee use cause and effect to explain the title of her essay?
7. How effective is the ending of Lee's essay? Explain your answer.

Writing Assignments

1. Write an essay discussing the use of dialect or slang in your family, group, or community.
2. In an essay, argue for or against the need for bilingual classes for African Americans.
3. Write an essay telling how teachers treat African American students who do not use standard English.

BLACK TALK

Geneva Smitherman

Geneva Smitherman (1940–) is University Distinguished Professor of English and director of the African-American Language and Literacy Programs at Michigan State University in East Lansing. She is also director of My Brother's Keeper Program in Detroit. Known for her passionate defense of black English, Smitherman was one of the expert witnesses in the so-called black English trial of 1977 in Ann Arbor, Michigan. Her works include Talkin and Testifyin: The Language of Black America *(1977),* Black English and the Education of Black Children and Youth *(1981),* Discourse and Discrimination *(1988), and* Black Talk: Words and Phrases from the Hood to the Amen Corner *(1994), from which this excerpt is taken. Here Smitherman discusses the crossover of black language into white America.*

Vocabulary

implicitly	(2)	by suggestion
sigged on	(3)	talked about
confrontational	(3)	face to face
adheres	(3)	sticks
deem	(3)	believe to be
dynamism	(4)	energy, force
potent	(4)	powerful
counterforce	(4)	opposition
generically	(5)	in general
wary	(5)	careful, cautious
Lexicon	(5)	vocabulary
exploitation	(6)	taking advantage of
sterile	(7)	uninteresting, lifeless
phenomenon	(7)	extremely unusual happening
deterioration	(7)	conditions becoming worse

A 1993 article by a European American used the title "A New Way to Talk that Talk" (small capitals added) to describe a new talk show. *The American Heritage Dictionary,* Third Edition, lists BUG and GRAPEVINE as just plain old words, with no label indicating "slang" or "Black." Merriam-Webster's latest (tenth) edition of its Collegiate Dictionary lists BOOM BOX the same way. A lengthy 1993 article in the *New York Times Maga-zine,* entitled "Talking Trash," discussed this ancient Black ver-bal tradition as the "art of conversation in the N.B.A." And in his first year in office, the nation's new "baby boomer" Presi-dent was taken to task for "terminal HIPness."

The absorption of African American English into Eurocen-tric culture masks its true origin and reason for being. It is a language born from a culture of struggle, a way of talking that has taken surviving African language elements as the base for self-expression in an alien tongue. Through various processes such as "Semantic Inversion" (taking words and turning them into their opposites), African Americans stake our claim to the English language, and at the same time, reflect distinct Black values that are often at odds with Eurocentric standards. "Fat," spelled *phat* in Hip Hop, refers to a person or thing that is excel-lent and desirable, reflecting the traditional African value that human body weight is a good thing, and implicitly rejecting the Euro-American mainstream, where skinny, not fat, is valued and everybody is on a diet. Senior Blacks convey the same value with the expression, "Don't nobody want no BONE." By the process of giving negative words positive meanings, BAD means "good," STUPID means "excellent," and even the word DOPE be-comes positive in Hip Hop, meaning "very good" or "superb."

The blunt, coded language of enslavement SIGGed on Christian slaveholders with the expression, "Everybody talkin bout Heaven ain goin there." Hip Hop language, too, is bold and confrontational. It uses obscenities, graphic depictions of the sex act, oral and otherwise, and it adheres to the pronunci-ation and grammar of African American English (which the un-informed deem "poor English") . . .

The dynamism and creativity in African American Lan-guage revitalizes and re-energizes bland Euro-talk. There's electricity and excitement in PLAYERS and FLY girls who wear GEAR. The metaphors, images, and poetry in Black Talk make the ordinary ALL THAT, AND THEN SOME. African American English is a dramatic, potent counterforce to verbal deadness and emptiness. One is not simply accepted by a group, one is IN LIKE FLIN. Fraternities and sororities don't merely march; they per-form a STEP SHOW. And when folk get AMP, they don't fight the feeling, they TESTIFY. For whites, there is a certain magnetism in the African American use of English because it seems to make the impossible possible. I bet you a FAT MAN AGAINST THE HOLE IN A DOUGHNUT. . . .

For *wiggas*[1] and other white folk latching onto Black   5
Talk, that's the good news. The bad news is that there's a reality check in African American English. Its terms and expressions keep you grounded, catch you just as you are taking
flight and bring you right back down to the NITTY GRITTY of
African American Life. There are rare flights of fancy in this poetry, no chance of getting so carried away that you don't know
yo ASS FROM A HOLE IN THE GROUND. Unh-unh. Words like NIGGA re-
inforce Blackness since, whether used positively, generically, or
negatively, the term can refer only to people of African descent.
DEVIL, a negative reference to the white man, reminds Blacks to
be on the lookout for HYPE. RUN AND TELL THAT, historically referring to Blacks who snitched to white folks, is a cultural caution
to those planning Black affairs to be wary of the Judases[2]
among them. Such words in the Black Lexicon are constant reminders of race and the Black Struggle. And when you TALK
THAT TALK, you must be loyal to Blackness, or as Ice Cube[3]
would say, be true to the GAME.

There are words and expressions in Black Talk like TWO-   6
MINUTE BROTHA, describing a man who completes the sex act in a
few seconds, and it's all over for the woman. Both in RAP and in
everyday talk, the words B (bitch) and HO (whore) are generic
references to Black women. GOT HIS/HER NOSE OPEN describes a
male or female so deeply in love that he or she is ripe for exploitation. Terms like these in Black Language are continuing
reminders that, despite all the talk about Black passion and
SOUL, despite all the sixty-minute-man myths, despite all the
WOOFin and TALKin SHIT, at bottom, the man-woman Thang
among African Americans is just as problematic as it is among
other groups.

Some African Americans see crossover as positive because   7
of its possibilities for reducing racial tension. Fashion journalist Robin D. Givhan, writing in the *Detroit Free Press* (June 21,
1993), asserts that she is "optimistic about wiggers":

> Appreciating someone else's culture is good. An increased level of
> interest among whites in what makes some African Americans
> groove can only be helpful to improved race relations.

[1] wiggas   (5)   Whites who adopt African American dress, language, and culture.
[1] Judas(es)   (5)   Disciple who betrayed Jesus; used here to refer to African
Americans who betray their race.
[3] Ice Cube   (5)   African American rapper.

Yet the reality of race, racism, and personal conflicts, which are often intensified by racism, does make crossover problematic. Whites pay no dues, but reap the psychological, social, and economic benefits of a language and culture born out of struggle and hard times. In his "We Use Words Like 'Mackadocious,'" Upski characterizes the "white rap audience" thus: "When they say they like rap, they usually have in mind a *certain* kind of rap, one that spits back what they already believe or lends an escape from their limited lives." And Ledbetter's "Imitation of Life" yields this conclusion: "By listening to rap and tapping into its extra-musical expressions, then, whites are attempting to bear witness to—even correct—their own often sterile, oppressive culture." Yet it is also the case that not only Rap, but other forms of Black Language and Culture, are attractive because of the dynamism, creativity, and excitement in these forms. However one accounts for the crossover phenomenon, one thing is certain: today we are witnessing a multi-billion-dollar industry based on this Language-Culture while there is continued underdevelopment and deterioration in the HOOD that produces it. In Ralph Wiley's collection of essays *Why Black People Tend to Shout*, which contains his *signifyin*[4] piece, "Why Black People Have No Culture," he states: "Black people have no culture because most of it is out on loan to white people. With no interest."

Discussion Questions

1. What are some characteristics of African American language described by Smitherman?

2. According to Smitherman, what is it about European Americans' lives that causes black language to cross over into mainstream use?

3. What is the "reality check" in African American English and what is its purpose?

4. What are some positive aspects of the crossover of African American English as seen by some African Americans?

5. According to Smitherman, what are some problems related to the crossover of African American English?

6. How does Smitherman use illustration to describe African American English?

7. What is the tone of this excerpt?

---

[4] signifyin (7)   African American verbal game of insults, usually played for fun and with humor.

Writing Assignments

1. Write an essay in which you illustrate some popular words or phrases used by you or your friends.
2. Write an essay in which you agree or disagree with the statement "Black people have no culture because most of it is out on loan to white people."
3. Write an essay illustrating and explaining the use of language in a particular rap song or in some other type of popular music.

IF BLACK ENGLISH ISN'T A LANGUAGE, THEN TELL ME, WHAT IS?

James Baldwin

James Baldwin (1924–1987) was born and raised in Harlem, New York. Most of his writings describe racial conflict and prejudice in the United States. His works include two books of autobiographical essays, Notes of a Native Son *(1955) and* Nobody Knows My Name *(1961); a nonfiction work,* The Fire Next Time *(1963); novels,* Go Tell It on the Mountain *(1953),* Another Country *(1962), and* Just Above My Head *(1979); and plays,* Blues for Mister Charlie *(1964) and* The Amen Corner *(1965). The following excerpt is from "If Black English Isn't a Language, Then Tell Me, What Is?" and was published in the* New York Times *in 1979. In it, Baldwin offers evidence to support the idea that black English, just like American English, is not a dialect but a language.*

Vocabulary

antecedents	(1)	ancestors
phenomenon	(2)	event
despairing	(2)	hopeless, desperate
skirmish	(4)	a minor dispute or fight
diaspora	(4)	areas where African Americans live outside of their homeland, Africa
chattel slavery	(4)	legal slavery
alchemy	(4)	process of changing from one form to another
unassailable	(6)	unquestionable
patronizingly	(7)	with an air of superiority
inarticulate	(7)	not able to express clearly
repudiate	(8)	refuse to recognize, reject
sustenance	(8)	nourishment, support
limbo	(8)	the state of being in between, neither here nor there
mediocrities	(9)	average abilities or achievements

It goes without saying, then, that language is also a political instrument, means, and proof of power. It is the most vivid and crucial key to identity: It reveals the private identity, and 1 connects one with, or divorces one from, the larger public, or communal identity. There have been, and are, times, and places, when to speak a certain language could be dangerous, even fatal. Or, one may speak the same language, but in such a way that one's antecedents are revealed, or (one hopes) hidden. This is true in France, and is absolutely true in England. The range (and reign) of accents on that damp little island make England coherent for the English and totally incomprehensible for everyone else. To open your mouth in England is (if I may use black English) to "put your business in the street": You have confessed your parents, your youth, your school, your salary, your self-esteem, and, alas, your future.

Now, I do not know what white Americans would sound   2
like if there had never been any black people in the United States, but they would not sound the way they sound. *Jazz*, for example, is a very specific sexual term, as in *jazz me, baby*, but white people purified it into the Jazz Age. *Sock it to me*, which means, roughly, the same thing, has been adopted by Nathaniel Hawthorne's descendants with no qualms or hesitations at all, along with *let it all hang out* and *right on! Beat to his socks*, which was once the black's most total and despairing image of poverty, was transformed into a thing called the Beat Generation, which phenomenon was, largely, composed of *uptight*, middle-class white people, imitating poverty, trying to *get down*, to get *with it*, doing their *thing*, doing their despairing best to be *funky*, which we, the blacks, never dreamed of doing—we *were* funky, baby, like *funk* was going out of style.

Now, no one can eat his cake, and have it, too, and it is   3
late in the day to attempt to penalize black people for having created a language that permits the nation its only glimpse of reality, a language without which the nation would be even more *whipped* than it is.

I say that this present skirmish is rooted in American his-   4
tory, and it is. Black English is the creation of the black diaspora. Blacks came to the United States chained to each other, but from different tribes: Neither could speak the other's language. If two black people, at that bitter hour of the world's history, had been able to speak to each other, the institution of chattel slavery could never have lasted as long as it did. Subsequently, the slave was given, under the eye, and the gun, of his master, Congo Square, and the Bible—or, in other words, and under these conditions, the slave began the formation of the black church, and it is within this unprecedented tabernacle

that black English began to be formed. This was not, merely, as in the European example, the adoption of a foreign tongue, but an alchemy that transformed ancient elements into new language: *A language comes into existence by means of brutal necessity, and the rules of the language are dictated by what the language must convey.*

There was a moment, in time, and in this place, when my brother, or my mother, or my father, or my sister, had to convey to me, for example, the danger in which I was standing from the white man standing just behind me, and to convey this with a speed, and in a language, that the white man could not possibly understand, and that, indeed, he cannot understand, until today. He cannot afford to understand it. This understanding would reveal to him too much about himself, and smash that mirror before which he has been frozen for so long.

Now, if this passion, this skill, this (to quote Toni Morrison) "sheer intelligence," this incredible music, the mighty achievement of having brought a people utterly unknown to, or despised by "history"—to have brought this people to their present, troubled, troubling, and unassailable and unanswerable place—if this absolutely unprecedented journey does not indicate that black English is a language, I am curious to know what definition of language is to be trusted.

A people at the center of the Western world, and in the midst of so hostile a population, has not endured and transcended by means of what is patronizingly called a "dialect." We, the blacks, are in trouble, certainly, but we are not doomed, and we are not inarticulate because we are not compelled to defend a morality that we know to be a lie.

The brutal truth is that the bulk of the white people in America never had any interest in educating black people, except as this could serve white purposes. It is not the black child's language that is in question, it is not his language that is despised: It is his experience. A child cannot be taught by anyone who despises him, and a child cannot afford to be fooled. A child cannot be taught by anyone whose demand, essentially, is that the child repudiate his experience, and all that gives him sustenance, and enter a limbo in which he will no longer be black, and in which he knows that he can never become white. Black people have lost too many black children that way.

And, after all, finally, in a country with standards so untrustworthy, a country that makes heroes of so many criminal

mediocrities, a country unable to face why so many of the nonwhite are in prison, or on the needle, or standing, futureless, in
the streets—it may very well be that both the child, and his elder, have concluded that they have nothing whatever to learn
from the people of a country that has managed to learn so little.

Discussion Questions

1. According to Baldwin, what is the role of language? How does it
   come into existence?
2. Why does Baldwin feel that black English is a language, not a dialect?
3. Why does Baldwin say that white Americans would not sound
   the way they do had there never been any black people in the
   United States?
4. What evidence does Baldwin offer to prove that black English developed as a result of the African American's attempt to retain a
   sense of identity and morality?
5. According to Baldwin, who cannot teach a child?
6. In the last paragraph, how does Baldwin describe the United
   States?
7. How does the title suggest the dominant rhetorical strategy that
   Baldwin uses in this essay?
8. How effective is Baldwin's technique of using the word *Now* to begin three of his paragraphs?

Writing Assignments

1. Certain words and expressions are peculiar to a particular experience or culture. Write an essay exploring a word or an expression that you feel few people know.
2. Write an essay classifying the various types of English dialects in
   the United States.
3. In an essay, argue the usefulness of slang.

Student Essay:
THE QUESTION OF NAME:
AFRICAN OR AFRICAN AMERICAN?

Cyril Austin Greene

Vocabulary

blatant   (5)   obvious
proscribe   (5)   to express disapproval of, to prohibit
goaded   (9)   urged

What's in a name? There are those who feel a name is just 1
a word; others feel a name defines who one is, and what he or
she stands for. Does a name have the power to mentally enslave an entire race of people? Or is a race, regardless of what
it is called, as strong as its members?

Since the early seventeenth century when Africans were 2
taken from their native land and placed into this foreign country, they have undergone an identity crisis. They could no
longer consider Africa their homeland, so could they call themselves Africans? They were in another world, which would soon
become known as America, but could they really call themselves Americans? They were here against their will, and they
were treated with total disregard for their humanity. Their enslavers took control of everything, even the right of these people
to define themselves. Hence, a 350-year history of an entire
race of people along with their identity was dictated by someone else.

Now, in the late twentieth century we as people of African 3
descent are breaking free of the hold that our enslavers have
had on us. Within the past fifty years, we people of color in
America have taken control of our destiny and part of that has
been a decision on what to call ourselves.

On the outside, the term *African American* seems so per- 4
fect. It acknowledges our current status of American citizenship and our former homeland of Africa. But why do we cling
so tightly to the idea of being American? Yes, according to our
birth certificates, we are American citizens, and we do reap certain benefits by living here, but we also went through slavery,

Jim Crow,[1] and civil rights, which are only giant umbrellas that enclose millions of personalized cases of hardships, torture, poverty, racism, and death. Maybe it is the fact that I do not forget the past as easily as others, but I refuse to associate myself with the name of a country that was built on exploitation, lies, rape, and murder.

To this day, Africans living here face discrimination, blatant and hidden. They must compete to survive, to attain human rights that were denied to them for so long. They were attacked by dogs, sprayed with hoses and shot in the streets a mere thirty years ago for trying to obtain the rights that were granted to them as human beings. Many lost their lives in a battle with the white majority, a battle for something that no one ever has the right to take from another: human rights. People died so that words could be printed on paper stating where our grandparents could eat and drink and sleep and walk. It still puzzles me the way in which one person can proscribe and prescribe the actions of another. Regardless of that fact, the battle against racism has been long and hard, and it is not over.   5

I believe this country will never accept me as it accepts the white majority. I am content with referring to myself as an African living in America. I have no desire to conform to this American culture and society; therefore, I choose not to recognize it in how I call myself.   6

Contrastingly, there are those who would argue that I cannot possibly call myself African, for I have never stepped foot on the continent of Africa. True, I am not an African citizen, nor have I ever been there. But does this mean that my heritage can be denied? I strongly feel that I am what my forefathers were. I doubt that Africans would be in this country were it not for the slave trade. It is unfortunate that some citizens of Africa look down on any attempts on the part of people of color from the United States to associate themselves with African citizenship, but I know where my heart lies.   7

Further opposition points out the fact that since this country was essentially built on slave labor, that gives us the right to call ourselves Americans, for in essence, we built this country. In theory, this sounds good, but the same people who forced us to build this country now own it, and they do not   8

---

[1] Jim Crow (4)   Legal and systematic practice of segregating, suppressing, and discriminating against African Americans.

plan to give up what is due to us. We may have the right to call ourselves American, but those in power will see to it that that is all we do, call ourselves American.

This society has a way of whitewashing situations so they   9 do not seem so bad. If one were not careful, he or she could be goaded into believing this is truly the land of the free. The virtue, strength, and freedom of America is propagandized to cover up the racism and the hate of this biased country, but the past is not easily forgotten.

The argument of being considered African or African   10 American continues. I believe the future holds other terms that we will use to define ourselves. I also see a split in our community. There will be those who try to refute their American heritage, as well as those who continue to search for a correct name to describe their mix of American and African backgrounds. As for me, I consider myself African. What do you consider yourself?

Discussion Questions

1. According to Greene, how long have African Americans experienced an identity crisis? Why have they experienced this crisis?
2. What are the major points presented to support Greene's position? Which do you think is his most convincing point?
3. What opposing points does Greene present? Can you think of others?
4. Why does Greene question the use of the term *African American?*
5. How does Greene address the following statement that some African Americans make: "Since this country was essentially built on slave labor, that gives us the right to call ourselves Americans"?
6. Does Greene use sufficient illustrations to make his argument convincing?
7. How effective is Greene's use of a question to end the essay?

Writing Assignments

1. Write an essay supporting the use of *African American* (or some other term) as an appropriate name for those we now call African Americans.
2. Write an essay examining the following question: Who is an American?

18

Folklore

I GET BORN

Zora Neale Hurston

Writer and folklorist Zora Neale Hurston (1907–1960) was born in Eatonville, Florida, and is the author of three novels: Jonah's Gourd Vine *(1934),* Their Eyes Were Watching God *(1937), and* Seraph on the Suwanee *(1948). Her works also include her autobiography,* Dust Tracks on the Road *(1943), from which this excerpt is taken, and several volumes of folklore. In this selection, Hurston recounts events surrounding her birth and early childhood.*

Vocabulary

shoat	(5)	young pig
gourd vine	(10)	vine of the bulb-shaped fruit of the squash, melon, and pumpkin family

This is all hear-say. Maybe some of the details of my birth   1
as told me might be a little inaccurate, but it is pretty well established that I really did get born.

The saying goes like this. My mother's time had come and my father was not there. Being a carpenter, successful enough to have other helpers on some jobs, he was away often on building business, as well as preaching. It seems that my father was away from home for months this time. I have never been told why. But I did hear that he threatened to cut his throat when he got the news. It seems that one daughter was all that he figured he could stand. My sister, Sarah, was his favorite child, but that one girl was enough. Plenty more sons, but no more girl babies to wear out shoes and bring in nothing. I don't think he ever got over the trick he felt that I played on him by getting born a girl, and while he was off from home at that. A little of my sugar used to sweeten his coffee right now. This is a Negro way of saying his patience was short with me. Let me change a few words with him—and I am of the word changing kind—and he was ready to change ends. Still and all, I looked more like him than any child in the house. Of course, by the time I got born, it was too late to make any suggestions, so the old man had to put up with me. He was nice about it in a way. He didn't tie me in a sack and drop me in the lake, as he probably felt like doing. 2

People were digging sweet potatoes, and then it was hog-killing time. Not at our house, but it was going on in general over the country like, being January and a bit cool. Most people were either butchering for themselves, or off helping other folks do their butchering, which was almost just as good. It is a gay time. A big pot of hasslits[1] cooking with plenty of seasoning, lean slabs of fresh-killed pork frying for the helpers to refresh themselves after the work is done. Over and above being neighborly and giving aid, there is the food, the drinks and the fun of getting together. 3

So there was no grown folks close around when Mama's water broke. She sent one of the smaller children to fetch Aunt Judy, the mid-wife, but she was gone to Woodbridge, a mile and a half away, to eat at a hog-killing. The child was told to go over there and tell Aunt Judy to come. But nature, being indifferent to human arrangements, was impatient. My mother had to make it alone. She was too weak after I rushed out to do anything for herself, so she just was lying there, sick in the body, and worried in mind, wondering what would become of 4

[1] hasslits (3)   Variety of leafy plants used as a vegetable.

her, as well as me. She was so weak, she couldn't even reach down to where I was. She had one consolation. She knew I wasn't dead, because I was crying strong.

Help came from where she never would have thought to   5
look for it. A white man of many acres and things, who knew the family well, had butchered the day before. Knowing that Papa was not at home, and that consequently there would be no fresh meat in our house, he decided to drive the five miles and bring a half of a shoat, sweet potatoes, and other garden stuff along. He was standing there a few minutes after I was born. Seeing the front standing open, he came on in, and hollered, "Hello, there! Call your dogs!" That is the regular way to call in the country because nearly everybody who has anything to watch has biting dogs.

Nobody answered, but he claimed later that he heard me   6
spreading my lungs all over Orange County, so he shoved the door open and bolted on into the house.

He followed the noise and then he saw how things were,   7
and, being the kind of man he was, he took out his Barlow Knife and cut the navel cord, then he did the best he could about other things. When the mid-wife, locally known as a granny, arrived about an hour later, there was a fire in the stove and plenty of hot water on. I had been sponged off in some sort of a way, and Mama was holding me in her arms.

As soon as the old woman got there, the white man un-   8
loaded what he had brought, and drove off cussing about some blankety-blank people never being where you could put your hands on them when they were needed. He got no thanks from Aunt Judy. She grumbled for years about it. She complained that the cord had not been cut just right, and the bellyband had not been put on tight enough. She was mighty scared I was going to have a weak back, and that I would have trouble holding my water until I reached puberty. I did.

The next day or so a Mrs. Neale, a friend of Mama's, came   9
in and reminded her that she had promised to let her name the baby in case it was a girl. She had picked up a name some-where which she thought was very pretty. Perhaps she had read it somewhere, or somebody back in those woods was smoking Turkish cigarettes. So I became Zora Neale Hurston.

There is nothing to make you like other human beings so   10
much as doing things for them. Therefore, the man who grannied me was back next day to see how I was coming along. Maybe it was a pride in his own handiwork, and his resource-

fulness in a pinch, that made him want to see it through. He remarked that I was a God-damned fine baby, fat and plenty of lung-power. As time went on, he came infrequently, but somehow kept a pinch of interest in my welfare. It seemed that I was spying noble, growing like a gourd vine, and yelling bass like a gator. He was the kind of man that had no use for puny things, so I was all to the good with him. He thought my mother was justified in keeping me.

But nine months rolled around, and I just would not get 11
on with the walking business. I was strong, crawling well, but showed no inclination to use my feet. I might remark in passing, that I still don't like to walk. Then I was over a year old, but still I would not walk. They made allowances for my weight, but yet, that was no real reason for my not trying.

They tell me that an old sow-hog taught me how to walk. 12
That is, she didn't instruct me in detail, but she convinced me that I really ought to try. It was like this. My mother was going to have collard greens for dinner, so she took the dishpan and went down to the spring to wash the greens. She left me sitting on the floor, and gave me a hunk of cornbread to keep me quiet. Everything was going along all right, until the sow with her litter of pigs in convoy came abreast of the door. She must have smelled the cornbread I was messing with and scattering crumbs about the floor. So, she came right on in, and began to nuzzle around.

My mother heard my screams and came running. Her 13
heart must have stood still when she saw the sow in there, because hogs have been known to eat human flesh.

But I was not taking this thing sitting down. I had been 14
placed by a chair, and when my mother got inside the door, I had pulled myself up by that chair and was getting around it right smart.

As for the sow, poor misunderstood lady, she had no inter- 15
est in me except my bread. I lost that in scrambling to my feet and she was eating it. She had much less intention of eating Mama's baby, than Mama had of eating hers. With no more suggestions from the sow or anybody else, it seems that I just took to walking and kept the thing a-going. The strangest thing about it was that once I found the use of my feet, they took to wandering. I always wanted to go. I would wander off in the woods all alone, following some inside urge to go places. This alarmed my mother a great deal. She used to say that she believed a woman who was an enemy of hers had sprinkled

"travel dust" around the doorstep the day I was born. That was the only explanation she could find. I don't know why it never occurred to her to connect my tendency with my father, who didn't have a thing on his mind but this town and the next one. That should have given her a sort of hint. Some children are just bound to take after their fathers in spite of women's prayers.

Discussion Questions

1. Why was Hurston's father disappointed in her birth?
2. Why does Hurston describe hog-killing time as a "gay time"?
3. Why did the white man take a special interest in Hurston?
4. According to Hurston, how did she learn to walk?
5. What are some of the folk sayings mentioned in the story? Explain each.
6. What are some of the folk myths surrounding Hurston's birth?
7. How does Hurston's use of cause and effect add to the interest of the story?
8. What is the main idea of this story?

Writing Assignments

1. Write an essay describing the circumstances of your birth and how you got your name.
2. Write an essay recounting a story about your early childhood, for example, speaking your first words, making your first steps, learning to ride a bike.
3. Write an essay about some of the sayings or superstitions you have heard in your family.

THE GHOST OF ORION

John Edgar Wideman

John Edgar Wideman (1941–   ) was born in Washington, D.C., and educated at the University of Pennsylvania, where he was an outstanding basketball player and scholar, and at Oxford University, where he was a Rhodes Scholar. He is professor of English at the University of Massachusetts at Amherst. Wideman has written several books, including Brothers and Keepers *(1984), about his brother who is serving a life term in prison, and* Philadelphia Fire *(1990). His* Homewood Trilogy *(named for the Homewood section of Pittsburgh where he grew up) consists of* Hiding Place *(1981),* Damballah *(1981), and* Sent for You Yesterday *(1983). His most recent work is* Fatheralong *(1994). This excerpt from* Damballah *is the story of a slave who maintains dignity and pride in his African heritage in spite of the consequences.*

Vocabulary

vaunted	(4)	boastful, extravagant
docility	(4)	obedience, submissiveness
tractability	(4)	ease with which one is managed or controlled
disparity	(4)	difference
accrued	(4)	accumulated
temporal	(4)	worldly
droning	(12)	humming

Damballah was the word. Said it to Aunt Lissy and she   1
went upside his head, harder than she had ever slapped him.
Felt like crumpling right there in the dust of the yard it hurt so
bad but he bit his lip and didn't cry out, held his ground and
said the word again and again silently to himself, pretending
nothing but a bug on his burning cheek and twitched and sent
it flying. Damballah. Be strong as he needed to be. Nothing
touch him if he don't want. Before long they'd cut him from the
herd of pickaninnies.[1] No more chasing flies from the table, no
more silver spoons to get shiny, no fat, old woman telling him

[1] pickaninnies   (1)   Negative term for African American children.

what to do. He'd go to the fields each morning with the men. Holler like they did before the sun rose to burn off the mist. Work like they did from can to caint. From first crack of light to dusk when the puddles of shadow deepened and spread so you couldn't see your hands or feet or the sharp tools hacking at the cane.

He was already taller than the others, a stork among 2 the chicks scurrying behind Aunt Lissy. Soon he'd rise with the conch horn[2] and do a man's share so he had let the fire rage on half his face and thought of the nothing always there to think of. In the spoon, his face long and thin as a finger. He looked for the print of Lissy's black hand on his cheek, but the image would not stay still. Dancing like his face reflected in the river. Damballah. "Don't you ever, you hear me, ever let me hear that heathen talk no more. You hear me, boy? You talk Merican, boy." Lissy's voice like chicken cackle. And his head a barn packed with animal noise and animal smell. His own head but he had to sneak round in it. Too many others crowded in there with him. His head so crowded and noisy lots of time don't hear his own voice with all them braying and cackling.

Orion squatted the way the boy had seen the other old 3 men collapse on their haunches and go still as a stump. Their bony knees poking up and their backsides resting on their ankles. Looked like they could sit that way all day, legs folded under them like wings. Orion drew a cross in the dust. Damballah. When Orion passed his hands over the cross the air seemed to shimmer like it does above a flame or like it does when the sun so hot you can see waves of heat rising off the fields. Orion talked to the emptiness he shaped with his long black fingers. His eyes were closed. Orion wasn't speaking but sounds came from inside him the boy had never heard before, strange words, clicks, whistles and grunts. A singsong moan that rose and fell and floated like the old man's busy hands above the cross. Damballah like a drum beat in the chant. Damballah a place the boy could enter, a familiar sound he began to anticipate, a sound outside of him which slowly forced its way inside, a sound measuring his heartbeat then one with the pumping surge of his blood.

[2] conch horn (2) A spiral one-piece seashell, often blown to call slaves to work.

The boy heard part of what Lissy saying to Primus in the
cooking shed: "Ryan he yell that heathen word right in the middle of Jim talking bout Sweet Jesus the Son of God. Jump up
like he snake bit and scream that word so everybody hushed,
even the white folks that came to hear Jim preach. Simple
Ryan standing there at the back of the chapel like a knot poked
out on somebody's forehead. Lookin like a nigger caught wid
his hand in the chicken coop. Screeching like some crazy hoot
owl while Preacher Jim praying the word of the Lord. They gon
kill that simple nigger one day."

4

> Dear Sir:
> The nigger Orion which I purchased of you in good faith
> sight unseen on your promise that he was of sound constitution
> "a full grown and able-bodied house servant who can read, write,
> do sums and cipher" to recite the exact words of your letter
> dated April 17, 1852, has proved to be a burden, a deficit to the
> economy of my plantation rather than the asset I fully believed I
> was receiving when I agreed to pay the price you asked. Of the
> vaunted intelligence so rare in his kind, I have seen nothing. Not
> an English word has passed through his mouth since he arrived.
> Of his docility and tractability I have seen only the willingness
> with which he bares his leatherish back to receive the stripes
> constant misconduct earn him. He is a creature whose brutish
> habits would shame me were he quartered in my kennels. I find
> it odd that I should write at such length about any nigger, but
> seldom have I have been so struck by the disparity between
> promise and performance. As I have accrued nothing but ex-
> pense and inconvenience as a result of his presence, I think it
> only just that you return the full amount I paid for this flawed
> *piece of the Indies.*
> You know me as an honest and fair man and my regard for
> those same qualities in you prompts me to write this letter. I am
> not a harsh master. I concern myself with the spiritual as well as
> the temporal needs of my slaves. My nigger Jim is renowned in
> this county as a preacher. Many say I am foolish, that the words
> of scripture are wasted on these savage blacks. I fear you have
> sent me a living argument to support the critics of my Christian-
> izing project. Among other absences of truly human qualities I
> have observed in this Orion is the utter lack of a soul.

She said it time for Orion to die. Broke half the overseer's
bones knocking him off his horse this morning and everybody
thought Ryan done run away sure but Mistress come upon the
crazy nigger at suppertime on the big house porch naked as
the day he born and he just sat there staring into her eyes till
Mistress screamed and run away. Aunt Lissy said Ryan ain't
studying no women, ain't gone near to woman since he been

5

here and she say his ain't the first black butt Mistress done seen all them nearly grown boys walkin round summer in the onliest shirt Master give em barely come down to they knees and niggers man nor woman don't get drawers the first. Mistress and Master both seen plenty. Wasn't what she saw scared her less she see the ghost leaving out Ryan's body.

The ghost wouldn't steam out the top of Orion's head. The 6 boy remembered the sweaty men come in from the fields at dusk when the nights start to cool early, remembered them with the drinking gourds[3] in they hands scooping up water from the wooden barrel he filled, how they throw they heads back and the water trickles from the sides of they mouth and down they chin and they let it roll on down they chests, and the smoky steam curling off they shoulders. Orion's spirit would not rise up like that but wiggle out of his skin and swim off up the river.

The boy knew many kinds of ghosts and learned the ways 7 you get round their tricks. Some spirits almost good company and he filled the nothing with jingles and whistles and took roundabout paths and sang to them when he walked up on a crossroads and yoo-hooed at doors. No way you fool the haunts if a spell conjured strong on you, no way to miss a beating if it your day to get beat, but the ghosts had everything in they hands, even the white folks in they hands. You know they there, you know they floating up in the air watching and counting and remembering them strokes Ole Master laying cross your back.

They dragged Orion across the yard. He didn't buck or 8 kick but it seemed as if the four men carrying him were struggling with a giant stone rather than a black bag of bones. His ashy nigger weight swung between the two pairs of white men like a lazy hammock but the faces of the men all red and twisted. They huffed and puffed and sweated through they clothes carrying Ryan's bones to the barn. The dry spell had layered the yard with a coat of dust. Little squalls of yellow spurted from under the men's boots. Trudging steps heavy as if each man carried seven Orions on his shoulders. Four grown men struggling with one string of black flesh. The boy had never seen so many white folks dealing with one nigger. Aunt Lissy had said it time to die and the boy wondered what Ryan's

[3] drinking gourds (6)   The dried, hollowed-out shells of the bulb-shaped fruit of the squash, melon, and pumpkin family, used as drinking cups or dippers.

ghost would think dropping onto the dust surrounded by the scowling faces of the Master and his overseers.

One scream that night. Like a bull when they cut off his   9
maleness. Couldn't tell who it was. A bull screaming once that night and torches burning in the barn and Master and the men coming out and no Ryan.

Mistress crying behind a locked door and Master messing   10
with Patty down the quarters.

In the morning light the barn swelling and rising and tee-   11
tering in the yellow dust, moving the way you could catch the ghost of something in a spoon and play with it, bending it, twisting it. That goldish ash on everybody's bare shins. Nobody talking. No cries nor hollers from the fields. The boy watched till his eyes hurt, waiting for a moment when he could slip un-seen into the shivering barn. On his hands and knees hiding under a wagon, then edging sideways through the loose boards and wedge of space where the weathered door hung crooked on its hinge.

The interior of the barn lay in shadows. Once beyond the   12
sliver of light coming in at the cracked door the boy stood still till his eyes adjusted to the darkness. First he could pick out the stacks of hay, the rough partitions dividing the animals. The smells, the choking heat there like always, but rising above these familiar sensations the buzz of flies, unnaturally loud, as if the barn breathing and each breath shook the wooden walls. Then the boy's eyes followed the sound to an open space at the center of the far wall. A black shape there. Orion there, floating in his own blood. The boy ran at the blanket of flies. When he stomped, some of the flies buzzed up from the carcass. Others too drunk on the shimmering blood ignored him except to join the ones hovering above the body in a sudden droning peal of annoyance. He could keep the flies stirring but they always re-turned from the recesses of the high ceiling, the dark corners of the building, to gather in a cloud above the body. The boy looked for something to throw. Heard his breath, heavy and threatening like the sound of the flies. He sank to the dirt floor, sitting cross-legged where he had stood. He moved only once, ten slow paces away from Orion and back again, near enough to be sure, to see again how the head had been cleaved from the rest of the body, to see how the ax and tongs, branding iron and other tools were scattered around the corpse, to see how one man's hat and another's shirt, a letter that must have

come from someone's pocket lay about in a helter-skelter way as if the men had suddenly bolted before they had finished with Orion.

Forgive him, Father. I tried to the end of my patience to re-   13
store his lost soul. I made a mighty effort to bring him to the Ark of Salvation but he had walked in darkness too long. He mocked Your Grace. He denied Your Word. Have mercy on him and forgive his heathen ways as you forgive the soulless beasts of the fields and birds of the air.

She say Master still down slave row. She say everybody   14
fraid to go down and get him. Everybody fraid to open the barn door. Overseer half dead and the Mistress still crying in her locked room and that barn starting to stink already with crazy Ryan and nobody gon get him.

And the boy knew his legs were moving and he knew they   15
would carry him where they needed to go and he knew the legs belonged to him but he could not feel them, he had been sitting too long thinking on nothing for too long and he felt the sweat running on his body but his mind off somewhere cool and quiet and hard and he knew the space between his body and mind could not be crossed by anything, knew you mize well try to stick the head back on Ryan as try to cross that space. So he took what he needed out of the barn, unfolding, getting his gangly crane's legs together under him and shouldered open the creaking double doors and walked through the flame in the center where he had to go.

Damballah said it be a long way a ghost be going and Jor-   16
dan chilly and wide and a new ghost take his time getting his wings together. Long way to go so you can sit and listen till the ghost ready to go on home. The boy wiped his wet hands on his knees and drew the cross and said the word and settled down and listened to Orion tell the stories again. Orion talked and he listened and couldn't stop listening till he saw Orion's eyes rise up through the back of the severed skull and lips rise up through the skull and the wings of the ghost measure out the rhythm of one last word.

Late afternoon and the river slept dark at its edges like it   17
did in the mornings. The boy threw the head as far as he could and he knew the fish would hear it and swim to it and welcome it. He knew they had been waiting. He knew the ripples would touch him when he entered.

Discussion Questions

1. What type of person is Orion? Why is he also called Ryan?
2. What effect does the word *Damballah* have on Aunt Lissy? Why does she want the boy to speak "Merican"?
3. Why is it significant that Orion could read and write but would not speak English?
4. Why does Orion's master decide to kill him?
5. Why is everyone afraid to bury Orion?
6. What are some of the mystical or supernatural occurrences in this story?
7. How does Wideman use classification to tell the story of Orion?
8. What is the main idea of this story?

Writing Assignments

1. Write an essay about someone you know who held on to his or her convictions in spite of the consequences.
2. Write an essay explaining the importance of maintaining one's heritage by observing its customs, traditions, or rituals.
3. Write an essay retelling one of your favorite ghost stories.

STRANGE THINGS OF 1923

Toni Morrison

Born Chloe Anthony Wofford in Lorain, Ohio, Toni Morrison (1931–) graduated from Howard University and Cornell University. She is the author of the following novels: The Bluest Eye *(1969),* Sula *(1973),* Song of Solomon *(1977),* Tar Baby *(1981),* Beloved *(1987), winner of the Pulitzer Prize in 1988, and being written into a screenplay by Oprah Winfrey's Harpo Productions, and* Jazz *(1992). Her work encompasses the total African American experience, from slavery to segregation to today. In 1993, Morrison won the Nobel Prize for Literature, becoming the first African American and only the second American woman so honored. She currently teaches creative writing at Princeton University. In this selection from* Sula, *set in 1923, Morrison describes supernatural events in the life of the Peace family.*

Vocabulary

splaying (29)   spreading out
spigot   (34)   faucet
trundled (41)   rolled along

1923

The second strange thing was Hannah's coming into her   1
mother's room with an empty bowl and a peck of Kentucky Wonders and saying, "Mamma, did you ever love us?" She sang the words like a small child saying a piece at Easter, then knelt to spread a newspaper on the floor and set the basket on it; the bowl she tucked in the space between her legs. Eva, who was just sitting there fanning herself with the cardboard fan from Mr. Hodges' funeral parlor, listened to the silence that followed Hannah's words, then said, "Scat!" to the deweys[1] who were playing chain gang near the window. With the shoelaces of each of them tied to the laces of the others, they stumbled and tumbled out of Eva's room.

---

[1] deweys   (1)   Three boys adopted by Eva.

"Now," Eva looked up across from her wagon at her daughter. "Give me that again. Flat out to fit my head." 2

"I mean, did you? You know. When we was little." 3

Eva's hand moved snail-like down her thigh toward her stump, but stopped short of it to realign a pleat. "No. I don't reckon I did. Not the way you thinkin'." 4

"Oh, well. I was just wonderin'." Hannah appeared to be through with the subject. 5

"An evil wonderin' if I ever heard one." Eva was not through. 6

"I didn't mean nothing by it, Mamma." 7

"What you mean you didn't *mean* nothing by it? How you gone not mean something by it?" 8

Hannah pinched the tips off the Kentucky Wonders and snapped their long pods. What with the sound of the cracking and snapping and her swift-fingered movements, she seemed to be playing a complicated instrument. Eva watched her a moment and then said, "You gone can them?" 9

"No. They for tonight." 10

"Thought you was gone can some." 11

"Uncle Paul ain't brought me none yet. A peck ain't enough to can. He say he got two bushels for me." 12

"Triflin'." 13

"Oh, he all right." 14

"Sho he all right. Everybody all right. 'Cept Mamma. Mamma the only one ain't all right. Cause she didn't *love* us." 15

"Awww, Mamma." 16

"Awww, Mamma? Awww, Mamma? You settin' here with your healthy-ass self and ax me did I love you? Them big old eyes in your head would a been two holes full of maggots if I hadn't." 17

"I didn't mean that, Mamma. I know you fed us and all. I was talkin' 'bout something else. Like. Like. Playin' with us. Did you ever, you know, play with us?" 18

"Play? Wasn't nobody playin' in 1895. Just 'cause you got it good now you think it was always this good? 1895 was a killer, girl. Things was bad. Niggers was dying like flies. Stepping tall, ain't you? Uncle Paul gone bring me *two* bushels. Yeh. And they's a melon downstairs, ain't they? And I bake every Saturday, and Shad brings fish on Friday, and they's a pork barrel full of meal, and we float eggs in a crock of vinegar . . ." 19

"Mamma, what you talkin' 'bout?" 20

"I'm talking 'bout 18 and 95 when I set in that house five 21 days with you and Pearl and Plum and three beets, you snake-eyed ungrateful hussy. What would I look like leapin' 'round that little old room playin' with youngins with three beets to my name?"

"I know 'bout them beets, Mamma. You told us that a million times."   22

"Yeah? Well? Don't that count? Ain't that love? You want   23
me to tinkle you under the jaw and forget 'bout them sores in your mouth? Pearl was shittin' worms and I was supposed to play rang-around-the-rosie?"

"But Mamma, they had to be some time when you wasn't   24
thinkin' 'bout . . . "

"No time. They wasn't no time. Not none. Soon as I got one   25
day done here come a night. With you all coughin' and me watchin' so TB wouldn't take you off and if you was sleepin' quiet I thought, O Lord, they dead and put my hand over your mouth to feel if the breath was comin' what you talkin' 'bout did I love you girl I stayed alive for you can't you get that through your thick head or what is that between your ears, heifer?"

Hannah had enough beans now. With some tomatoes and   26
hot bread, she thought, that would be enough for everybody, especially since the deweys didn't eat vegetables no how and Eva never made them and Tar Baby was living off air and music these days. She picked up the basket and stood with it and the bowl of beans over her mother. Eva's face was still asking her last question. Hannah looked into her mother's eyes.

"But what about Plum? What'd you kill Plum for,   27
Mamma?"

It was a Wednesday in August and the ice wagon was coming   28
and coming. You could hear bits of the driver's song. Now Mrs. Jackson would be tipping down her porch steps. "Jes a piece. You got a lil ole piece layin' 'round in there you could spare?" And as he had since the time of the pigeons, the iceman would hand her a lump of ice saying, "Watch it now, Mrs. Jackson. That straw'll tickle your pretty neck to death."

Eva listened to the wagon coming and thought about what   29
it must be like in the icehouse. She leaned back a little and closed her eyes trying to see the insides of the icehouse. It was a dark, lovely picture in this heat, until it reminded her of that winter night in the outhouse holding her baby in the dark, her fingers searching for his asshole and the last bit of lard scooped from the sides of the can, held deliberately on the tip

of her middle finger, the last bit of lard to keep from hurting him when she slid her finger in and all because she had broken the slop jar[2] and the rags had frozen. The last food staple in the house she had rammed up her baby's behind to keep from hurting him too much when she opened up his bowels to pull the stools out. He had been screaming fit to kill, but when she found his hole at last and struck her finger up in it, the shock was so great he was suddenly quiet. Even now on the hottest day anyone in Medallion could remember—a day so hot flies slept and cats were splaying their fur like quills, a day so hot pregnant wives leaned up against trees and cried, and women remembering some three-month-old hurt put ground glass in their lovers' food and the men looked at the food and wondered if there was glass in it and ate it anyway because it was too hot to resist eating it—even on this hottest of days in the hot spell, Eva shivered from the biting cold and stench of that outhouse.

Hannah was waiting. Watching her mother's eyelids. When Eva spoke at last it was with two voices. Like two people were talking at the same time, saying the same thing, one a fraction of a second behind the other.

"He give me such a time. Such a time. Look like he didn't even want to be born. But he come on out. Boys is hard to bear. You wouldn't know that but they is. It was such a carryin' on to get him born and to keep him alive. Just to keep his little heart beating and his little old lungs cleared and look like when he came back from that war he wanted to git back in. After all that carryin' on, just gettin' him out and keepin' him alive, he wanted to crawl back in my womb and well . . . I ain't got the room no more even if he could do it. There wasn't space for him in my womb. And he was crawlin' back. Being helpless and thinking baby thoughts and dreaming baby dreams and messing up his pants again and smiling all the time. I had room enough in my heart, but not in my womb, not no more. I birthed him once. I couldn't do it again. He was growed, a big old thing. Godhavemercy, I couldn't birth him twice. I'd be laying here at night and he be downstairs in that room, but when I closed my eyes I'd see him . . . six feet tall smilin' and crawlin' up the stairs quietlike so I wouldn't hear and opening the door soft so I wouldn't hear and he'd be creepin' to the bed trying to spread my legs trying to get back up in my womb. He was a man, girl, a big old growed-up man. I didn't have that

30

31

[2] slop jar (29)   A metal pot used as a toilet.

much room. I kept on dreaming it. Dreaming it and I knowed it was true. One night it wouldn't be no dream. It'd be true and I would have done it, would have let him if I'd've had the room but a big man can't be a baby all wrapped up inside his mamma no more; he suffocate. I done everything I could to make him leave me and go on and live and be a man but he wouldn't and I had to keep him out so I just thought of a way he could die like a man not all scrunched up inside my womb, but like a man."

Eva couldn't see Hannah clearly for the tears, but she looked up at her anyway and said, by way of apology or explanation or perhaps just by way of neatness, "But I held him close first. Real close. Sweet Plum. My baby boy."

32

Long after Hannah turned and walked out of the room, Eva continued to call his name while her fingers lined up the pleats in her dress.

33

Hannah went off to the kitchen, her old man's slippers plopping down the stairs and over the hardwood floors. She turned the spigot on, letting water break up the tight knots of Kentucky Wonders and float them to the top of the bowl. She swirled them about with her fingers, poured the water off and repeated the process. Each time the green tubes rose to the surface she felt elated and collected whole handfuls at a time to drop in twos and threes back into the water.

34

Through the window over the sink she could see the deweys still playing chain gang; their ankles bound one to the other, they tumbled, struggled back to their feet and tried to walk single file. Hens strutted by with one suspicious eye on the deweys, another on the brick fireplace where sheets and mason jars were boiled. Only the deweys could play in this heat. Hannah put the Kentucky Wonders over the fire and, struck by a sudden sleepiness, she went off to lie down in the front room. It was even hotter there, for the windows were shut to keep out the sunlight. Hannah straightened the shawl that draped the couch and lay down. She dreamed of a wedding in a red bridal gown until Sula came in and woke her.

35

But before the second strange thing, there had been the wind, which was the first. The very night before the day Hannah had asked Eva if she had ever loved them, the wind tore over the hills rattling roofs and loosening doors. Everything shook, and although the people were frightened they thought it meant rain and welcomed it. Windows fell out and trees lost arms. People waited up half the night for the first crack of

36

lightning. Some had even uncovered barrels to catch the rain water, which they loved to drink and cook in. They waited in vain, for no lightning no thunder no rain came. The wind just swept through, took what dampness there was out of the air, messed up the yards, and went on. The hills of the Bottom, as always, protected the valley part of town where the white people lived, and the next morning all the people were grateful because there was a dryer heat. So they set about their work early, for it was canning time, and who knew but what the wind would come back this time with a cooling rain. The men who worked in the valley got up at four thirty in the morning and looked at the sky where the sun was already rising like a hot white bitch. They beat the brims of their hats against their legs before putting them on and trudged down the road like old promises nobody wanted kept.

On Thursday, when Hannah brought Eva her fried tomatoes and soft scrambled eggs with the white left out for good luck, she mentioned her dream of the wedding in the red dress. Neither one bothered to look it up for they both knew the number was 522. Eva said she'd play it when Mr. Buckland Reed came by. Later she would remember it as the third strange thing. She had thought it odd even then, but the red in the dream confused her. But she wasn't certain that it was third or not because Sula was acting up, fretting the deweys and meddling the newly married couple. Because she was thirteen, everybody supposed her nature was coming down, but it was hard to put up with her sulking and irritation. The birthmark over her eye was getting darker and looked more and more like a stem and rose. She was dropping things and eating food that belonged to the newly married couple and started in to worrying everybody that the deweys needed a bath and she was going to give it to them. The deweys, who went wild at the thought of water, were crying and thundering all over the house like colts. 37

"We ain't got to, do we? Do we got to do what she says? It ain't Saturday." They even woke up Tar Baby, who came out of his room to look at them and then left the house in search of music. 38

Hannah ignored them and kept on bringing mason jars out of the cellar and washing them. Eva banged on the floor with her stick but nobody came. By noon it was quiet. The deweys had escaped, Sula was either in her room or gone off somewhere. The newly married couple, energized by their 39

morning lovemaking, had gone to look for a day's work happily
certain that they would find none.

The air all over the Bottom got heavy with peeled fruit and   40
boiling vegetables. Fresh corn, tomatoes, string beans, melon
rinds. The women, the children and the old men who had no
jobs were putting up for a winter they understood so well.
Peaches were stuffed into jars and black cherries (later, when it
got cooler, they would put up jellies and preserves). The greedy
canned as many as forty-two a day even though some of them,
like Mrs. Jackson, who ate ice, had jars from 1920.

Before she trundled her wagon over to the dresser to get   41
her comb, Eva looked out the window and saw Hannah bending to light the yard fire. And that was the fifth (or fourth, if you
didn't count Sula's craziness) strange thing. She couldn't find
her comb. Nobody moved stuff in Eva's room except to clean
and then they put everything right back. But Eva couldn't find
it anywhere. One hand pulling her braids loose, the other
searching the dresser drawers, she had just begun to get irri-
tated when she felt it in her blouse drawer. Then she trundled
back to the window to catch a breeze, if one took a mind to
come by, while she combed her hair. She rolled up to the window and it was then she saw Hannah burning. The flames from
the yard fire were licking the blue cotton dress, making her
dance. Eva knew there was time for nothing in this world other
than the time it took to get there and cover her daughter's body
with her own. She lifted her heavy frame up on her good leg,
and with fists and arms smashed the windowpane. Using her
stump as a support on the window sill, her good leg as a lever,
she threw herself out of the window. Cut and bleeding she
clawed the air trying to aim her body toward the flaming, dancing figure. She missed and came crashing down some twelve
feet from Hannah's smoke. Stunned but still conscious, Eva
dragged herself toward her firstborn, but Hannah, her senses
lost, went flying out of the yard gesturing and bobbing like a
sprung jack-in-the-box.

Mr. and Mrs. Suggs, who had set up their canning appara-   42
tus in their front yard, saw her running, dancing toward them.
They whispered, "Jesus, Jesus," and together hoisted up their
tub of water in which tight red tomatoes floated and threw it on
the smoke-and-flame-bound woman. The water did put out the
flames, but it also made steam, which seared to sealing all that
was left of the beautiful Hannah Peace. She lay there on the
wooden sidewalk planks, twitching lightly among the smashed

tomatoes, her face a mask of agony so intense that for years the people who gathered 'round would shake their heads at the recollection of it.

Somebody covered her legs with a shirt. A woman un- 43 wrapped her head rag and placed it on Hannah's shoulder. Somebody else ran to Dick's Fresh Food and Sundries to call the ambulance. The rest stood there as helpless as sunflowers leaning on a fence. The deweys came and stepped in the tomatoes, their eyes raked with wonder. Two cats sidled through the legs of the crowd, sniffing the burned flesh. The vomiting of a young girl finally broke the profound silence and caused the women to talk to each other and to God. In the midst of calling Jesus they heard the hollow clang of the ambulance bell struggling up the hill, but not the "Help me, ya'll" that the dying woman whispered. Then somebody remembered to go and see about Eva. They found her on her stomach by the forsythia bushes calling Hannah's name and dragging her body through the sweet peas and clover that grew under the forsythia by the side of the house. Mother and daughter were placed on stretchers and carried to the ambulance. Eva was wide awake. The blood from her face cuts filled her eyes so she could not see, could only smell the familiar odor of cooked flesh.

Hannah died on the way to the hospital. Or so they said. 44 In any case, she had already begun to bubble and blister so badly that the coffin had to be kept closed at the funeral and the women who washed the body and dressed it for death wept for her burned hair and wrinkled breasts as though they themselves had been her lovers.

When Eva got to the hospital they put her stretcher on the 45 floor, so preoccupied with the hot and bubbling flesh of the other (some of them had never seen so extreme a burn case before) they forgot Eva, who would have bled to death except Old Willy Fields, the orderly, saw blood staining his just-mopped floors and went to find out where it was coming from. Recognizing Eva at once he shouted to a nurse, who came to see if the bloody one-legged black woman was alive or dead. From then on Willy boasted that he had saved Eva's life—an indisputable fact which she herself admitted and for which she cursed him every day for thirty-seven years thereafter and would have cursed him for the rest of her life except by then she was already ninety years old and forgot things.

Lying in the colored ward of the hospital, which was a 46 screened corner of a larger ward, Eva mused over the perfection of the judgment against her. She remembered the wedding dream and recalled that weddings always meant death. And the red gown, well that was the fire, as she should have known. She remembered something else too, and try as she might to deny it, she knew that as she lay on the ground trying to drag herself through the sweet peas and clover to get to Hannah, she had seen Sula standing on the back porch just looking. When Eva, who was never one to hide the faults of her children, mentioned what she thought she'd seen to a few friends, they said it was natural. Sula was probably struck dumb, as anybody would be who saw her own mamma burn up. Eva said yes, but inside she disagreed and remained convinced that Sula had watched Hannah burn not because she was paralyzed, but because she was interested.

Discussion Questions

1. What seems to be the relationship between Hannah and her mother Eva?
2. What proof does Eva offer of her love for her children? How could you argue that Eva's killing of Plum was an act of love?
3. What are the five "strange things" that occur in 1923?
4. Why does Eva have trouble saving Hannah from the fire?
5. What is significant about Eva's thought that "Sula had watched Hannah burn not because she was paralyzed, but because she was interested"?
6. There are several examples of folk beliefs in this selection. One is that a dream of a wedding in a red bridal gown suggests death by fire. What are other examples of superstitions?
7. How is Morrison's use of description especially effective in this story?
8. Why do you think Morrison chose to begin her story with the second strange thing instead of the first?

Writing Assignments

1. Write an essay about some of the superstitions you have heard most of your life.
2. Write an essay about a time when you had a feeling or a dream that something good or bad was going to happen.
3. Write an essay about a time when you felt helpless in a situation.

Student Essay:
FOLKTALES: AN AFRICAN-AMERICAN TREASURE

Elizabeth Mitchell

Vocabulary

inexplicable	(2)	unexplainable
phenomena	(2)	events, circumstances
rites of passage	(2)	significant events in one's life that indicate a change from one stage to another (e.g., first car, marriage)
rivals	(3)	competitors, enemies

I can still remember how embarrassed I was when Aunt Jennie would corner my friends when they stopped by to see me and tell them one of her many folktales. Living with Aunt Jennie all of my life, I had taken her stories for granted and had come to resent her choosing inconvenient times to retell them to me and my friends. It took someone outside of my family to make me appreciate the value of her tales.

When I went away to summer camp school, I took a course entitled "African-American Folk Tradition." One day when I was only half listening to Mr. Dawson, he began talking about the value of African American folktales. He said that these tales, of unknown origin, have been passed from generation to generation. According to Mr. Dawson, they serve important functions: (1) to give encouragement, (2) to explain inexplicable phenomena, for example, why is the sky blue? (3) to teach moral lessons, (4) to help youth understand rites of passage, and (5) to provide entertainment. He said African American folktales are considered a cultural treasure.

After that afternoon session, I began to think about Aunt Jennie and all of the stories she had told me. I remembered an evening I had come home crying because my childhood rivals, who were bigger and stronger than I, were constantly picking on me. I remembered her telling me about a slave who learned to outsmart his master by being more clever. I also remembered how impatient I was then, having to listen to Aunt Jennie talk about slaves. Now I see that Aunt Jennie was giving me just what I needed, but I was too dumb to see it.

After summer camp school, I was anxious to share all that   4
I had learned about folktales with Aunt Jennie. "I don't know
nothing about all that stuff you're talking about," she grinned.
"I just know that my stories always make people feel better."

After finishing lunch, Aunt Jennie and I went into the   5
family room. Before she sank into her big Lazy Boy, she peered
out of the window to see the sun brightly beaming as the rain
continued to fall. "Do you know why the sun shines while it's
raining?" she asked.

"No," I smiled. "Tell me."   6

Then with a faraway look, Aunt Jennie began to explain.   7
"It all started a long, long time ago . . ." I inched closer to her
as she talked. And perhaps for the very first time, I heard her.

Discussion Questions

1. Why do you think that Mitchell was embarrassed by Aunt Jennie's tales before she left home?
2. How would you characterize Aunt Jennie?
3. According to Mitchell, what are the functions of African American folktales? Can you think of others?
4. Why do you think that Aunt Jennie did not try to explain the folktales to Mitchell?
5. What do you think the author means when she said, "And perhaps for the very first time, I heard her"?
6. How effective is Mitchell's use of the narrative within the narrative?
7. How effective is the conclusion?

Writing Assignments

1. Write an essay in which you discuss the significance of a folktale you have heard or read.
2. Write an essay in which you discuss how your exposure to other folk traditions, for example, music, medicine, or superstition influenced you or someone you know.

19

Racism • Discrimination

INCIDENT

Countee Cullen

Poet, editor, dramatist, Countee Cullen (1903–1946) was born in Baltimore, Maryland. He studied at New York University, where he earned the Phi Beta Kappa key, and completed his graduate work at Harvard. One of the best known of the artists of the Harlem Renaissance, Cullen wrote several volumes of poetry: Color *(1925),* Cooper Sun *(1927),* The Ballad of the Brown Girl *(1927), and* On These I Stand *(1947), published after his death. In the following poem, from his last collection, Cullen shares a memorable Baltimore experience with racism.*

(For Eric Walrond)

Once riding in old Baltimore,   1
   Heart-filled, head-filled with glee,
I saw a Baltimorean
   Keep looking straight at me.

Now I was eight and very small,   2
   And he was no whit bigger,

And so I smiled, but he poked out
  His tongue, and called me, "Nigger."

I saw the whole of Baltimore   3
  From May until December;
Of all the things that happened there
  That's all that I remember.

Discussion Questions

1. Why do you think that "the incident" is all the speaker remembers from his experience in Baltimore?

2. What assumption can the reader make about the young Baltimorean who called the speaker "nigger"?

3. Why do you think the author decided not to describe the speaker's immediate reaction to being called "nigger"?

4. What was the speaker's mood before the incident? What do you think it was after the incident?

5. How does Cullen use description and illustration to help the reader understand the differences between the two boys?

6. What is the tone of the poem?

Writing Assignments

1. Write an essay detailing your reaction to an incident when you were called an unpleasant name.

2. Write an essay about a childhood memory that is still vivid today.

3. Write an essay about something you did that you wish you could undo.

A DIFFERENCE OF OPINION

Toni Morrison

*Born Chloe Anthony Wofford, Toni Morrison (1931–), edi-
tor, dramatist, and Pulitzer Prize–winning novelist, is hailed
by many as having become the most accomplished African
American writer. She is the author of six critically acclaimed
novels:* The Bluest Eye *(1969),* Sula *(1973),* Song of
Solomon *(1977),* Tar Baby *(1981),* Beloved *(1987), and* Jazz
*(1992). In 1993, Morrison won the Nobel Prize for Literature,
becoming the first African American and only the second
American woman so honored. She currently teaches creative writing at Princeton University. In the following selection, first published in the* New York Times Magazine *in
1976, Morrison contrasts how her grandparents felt about
racism in the United States.*

Vocabulary

rancor	(1)	bitterness
lobotomized	(3)	deprived of sensitivity or intelligence
virility	(5)	manhood
irrevocable	(5)	unchangeable, binding

His name was John Solomon Willis, and when at age 5 he
heard from the old folks that "the Emancipation Proclamation
was coming," he crawled under the bed. It was his earliest recollection of what was to be his habitual response to the
promise of white people: horror and an instinctive yearning for
safety. He was my grandfather, a musician who managed to
hold on to his violin but not his land. He lost all 88 acres of his
Indian mother's inheritance to legal predators who built their
fortunes on the likes of him. He was an unreconstructed black
pessimist who, in spite of or because of emancipation, was convinced for 85 years that there was no hope whatever for black
people in this country. His rancor was legitimate, for he, John
Solomon, was not only an artist but a first-rate carpenter and
farmer, reduced to sending home to his family money he had
made playing the violin because he was not able to find work.
And this during the years when almost half the black male

1

population were skilled craftsmen who lost their jobs to white ex-convicts and immigrant farmers.

His wife, however, was of a quite different frame of mind   2
and believed that all things could be improved by faith in Jesus and an effort of the will. So it was she, Ardelia Willis, who sneaked her seven children out of the back window into the darkness, rather than permit the patron of their sharecropper's existence to become their executioner as well, and headed north in 1912, when 99.2 percent of all black people in the U.S. were native-born and only 60 percent of white Americans were. And it was Ardelia who told her husband that they could not stay in the Kentucky town they ended up in because the teacher didn't know long division.

They have been dead now for 30 years and more and I still   3
don't know which of them came closer to the truth about the possibilities of life for black people in this country. One of their grandchildren is a tenured professor at Princeton. Another, who suffered from what the Peruvian poet called "anger that breaks a man into children," was picked up just as he entered his teens and emotionally lobotomized by the reformatories and mental institutions specifically designed to serve him. Neither John Solomon nor Ardelia lived long enough to despair over one or swell with pride over the other. But if they were alive today each would have selected and collected enough evidence to support the accuracy of the other's original point of view. And it would be difficult to convince either one that the other was right.

Some of the monstrous events that took place in John   4
Solomon's America have been duplicated in alarming detail in my own America. There was the public murder of a President in a theater in 1865 and the public murder of another President on television in 1963. The Civil War of 1861 had its encore as the civil-rights movement of 1960. The torture and mutilation of a black West Point Cadet (Cadet Johnson Whittaker) in 1880 had its rerun with the 1970's murders of students at Jackson State College, Texas Southern and Southern University in Baton Rouge. And in 1976 we watch for what must be the thousandth time a pitched battle between the children of slaves and the children of immigrants—only this time, it is not the New York draft riots of 1863, but the busing turmoil in Paul Revere's home town, Boston.

Hopeless, he'd said. Hopeless. For he was certain that   5
white people of every political, religious, geographical and eco-

nomic background would band together against black people everywhere when they felt the threat of our progress. And a hundred years after he sought safety from the white man's "promise," somebody put a bullet in Martin Luther King's brain. And not long before that some excellent samples of the master race demonstrated their courage and virility by dynamiting some little black girls to death. If he were here now, my grandfather, he would shake his head, close his eyes and pull out his violin—too polite to say, "I told you so." And his wife would pay attention to the music but not to the sadness in her husband's eyes, for she would see what she expected to see— not the occasional historical repetition, but, *like the slow walk of certain species of trees from the flatlands up into the mountains,* she would see the signs of irrevocable and permanent change. She, who pulled her girls out of an inadequate school in the Cumberland Mountains, knew all along that the gentlemen from Alabama who had killed the little girls would be rounded up. And it wouldn't surprise her in the least to know that the number of black college graduates jumped 12 percent in the last three years: 47 percent in 20 years. That there are 140 black mayors in this country; 14 black judges in the District Circuit, 4 in the Court of Appeals and one on the Supreme Court. That there are 17 blacks in Congress, one in the Senate; 276 in state legislatures—223 in state houses, 53 in state senates. That there are 112 elected black police chiefs and sheriffs, 1 Pulitzer Prize winner; 1 winner of the Prix de Rome; a dozen or so winners of the Guggenheim; 4 deans of predominantly white colleges. . . .   Oh, her list would go on and on. But so would John Solomon's sweet sad music.

Discussion Questions

1. How would you characterize Morrison's grandfather and grandmother?
2. What was John Solomon Willis's view of life in the United States for African Americans? How did Willis's wife view life in the United States for African Americans?
3. What evidence does Morrison provide to support her grandfather's view? Her grandmother's?
4. Do you think Morrison's life was complicated or complemented by her grandparents' different views? Why or why not?

5. Why is comparison and contrast an ideal organization to use in developing the main idea of this essay?

6. What is the main idea that Morrison develops?

Writing Assignments

1. Write an essay contrasting two different views that your parents or grandparents had (or have) about race, religion, or culture.

2. Write an essay explaining what you would do if you received conflicting advice from two people who are both very close to you.

3. Write an essay exploring conflicting views on a subject that is both controversial and complex.

FOR MY PEOPLE

Margaret Walker

*Born in Birmingham, Alabama, Margaret Walker (1915–   )
completed her undergraduate work at Northwestern University in Evanston, Illinois. Perhaps Walker is best known for
her poem "For My People" (1942), which appears here, and
for her historical novel on slavery,* Jubilee *(1966). Her other
books include* Prophets for a New Day *(1970),* October
Journey *(1973), and* How I Wrote Jubilee and Other Essays on Life and Literature *(1990). In the following poem,
the narrator longs for "another world" that would relieve
blacks of racist oppression.*

Vocabulary

dirges	(1)	funeral hymns
ditties	(1)	simple songs
jubilees	(1)	celebrations
consumption	(5)	tuberculosis
omnisciently	(7)	with all knowledge
facile	(8)	effortless, simple
martial	(10)	military

For my people everywhere singing their slave songs repeatedly: 1
   their dirges and their ditties and their blues and jubilees,
   praying their prayers nightly to an unknown god, bending
   their knees humbly to an unseen power;

For my people lending their strength to the years: to the gone   2
   years and the now years and the maybe years, washing iron-
   ing cooking scrubbing sewing mending hoeing plowing digging planting pruning patching dragging along never gaining
   never reaping never knowing and never understanding;

For my playmates in the clay and dust and sand of Alabama   3
   backyards playing baptizing and preaching, and doctor and
   jail and soldier and school and mama and cooking and play-
   house and concert and store and Miss Choomby and hair
   and company;

For the cramped bewildered years we went to school to learn to   4
   know the reasons why and the answers to and the people
   who and the places where and the days when, in memory of
   the bitter hours when we discovered we were black and poor

and small and different and nobody wondered and nobody understood;

For the boys and girls who grew in spite of these things to be   5
Man and Woman, to laugh and dance and sing and play and drink their wine and religion and success, to marry their playmates and bear children and then die of consumption and anemia and lynching;

For my people thronging 47th Street in Chicago and Lenox Av-   6
enue in New York and Rampart Street in New Orleans, lost disinherited dispossessed and HAPPY people filling the cabarets and taverns and other people's pockets needing bread and shoes and milk and land and money and Something—Something all our own;

For my people walking blindly, spreading joy, losing time being   7
lazy, sleeping when hungry, shouting when burdened, drinking when hopeless, tied and shackled and tangled among ourselves by the unseen creatures who tower over us omnisciently and laugh;

For my people blundering and groping and floundering in the   8
dark of churches and schools and clubs and societies, associations and councils and committees and conventions, distressed and disturbed and deceived and devoured by money-hungry glory-craving leeches, preyed on by facile force of state and fad and novelty by false prophet and holy believer;

For my people standing staring trying to fashion a better way   9
from confusion from hypocrisy and misunderstanding, trying to fashion a world that will hold all the people all the faces all the adams and eves and their countless generations;

Let a new earth rise. Let another world be born. Let a bloody   10
peace be written in the sky. Let a second generation full of courage issue forth, let a people loving freedom come to growth, let a beauty full of healing and a strength of final clenching be the pulsing in our spirits and our blood. Let the martial songs be written, let the dirges disappear. Let a race of men now rise and take control!

Discussion Questions

1. Why was the speaker's discovery of being black and poor "bitter hours"?

2. In what geographical setting do the first five stanzas occur? Why do you think the setting changes in the sixth stanza?

3. What are some of the obstacles that Walker sees as preventing African Americans from taking control of their lives?
4. Why does Walker refer to her people as HAPPY people despite the unhappy and unpleasant aspects of their lives?
5. What is the speaker's attitude about prejudice and the hardships of growing up?
6. What is the significance of the last line?
7. Why is Walker's use of description important to the reader's recognition of blacks as victims and victors?
8. What is the tone of the poem?

Writing Assignments

1. Write an essay illustrating what you believe to be a current problem and propose a solution to it.
2. Write an essay in which you show how a popular solution to a social problem may not be a workable solution at all.
3. Write a letter to someone or to an organization in which you call for some type of action.

MY LIFE IN BLACK AND WHITE

Pauli Murray

Born in Baltimore, Maryland, Pauli Murray (1910–1985) was a writer, attorney, law professor, and the first African American woman ordained Episcopal priest. Murray graduated first in her Howard University law class, earning her a fellowship to Harvard Law School. Ironically, Harvard rejected her because of her gender. Refusing to be discouraged, she continued her studies and received her doctorate from Yale University in 1965. Her major works include Proud Shoes: The Story of an American Family *(1956), from which the following selection is taken, and* Dark Testament and Other Poems *(1970). In the following selection, Murray describes life growing up under segregation.*

Vocabulary

turrets	(4)	tower-shaped projections on a building
gables	(4)	triangular sections formed by two roof slopes
piazza	(4)	a roof or arcaded passageway
brickbat	(11)	piece of brick, especially one used as a weapon

As I look back on those years at Grandfather's house, I see that 1 I inhabited a world of unbelievable contradictions. There were the disciplines of study, of doing one's duty at all costs, of walking up to fear and conquering it. Against these were the imagined terrors of the cemetery and its dead and the equally disconcerting fear of the living—that unknown white world with which I had little or no contact but which surrounded and stifled me, a great amorphous mass without personality about which I had much curiosity but dared not investigate in the interests of maintaining my dignity and pride. There were the exhortations of Grandfather and my aunts as teachers to bring out the best in people and there were Grandmother's gloomy prophecies warning of the worst. There were competing prides and loyalties—Grandfather's loyalty to his Union cause and Grandmother's to her Smiths—and while each sprang from widely different sources, both, it seemed to me, in the long run ended up in near poverty and isolation between the Bottoms and the cemetery.

For me all this could only end in rebellion. I do not know 2
which generated the greater revolt in me: the talk I heard about
the Smiths or stories of the Fitzgeralds. Each played its part.
Listening to my elders tell of the old days in North Carolina, it
sometimes appeared that the world my aunts and mother grew
up in bore little resemblance to the one in which I lived only a
few decades later.

When the Fitzgeralds had gone south, there were no rigid 3
Jim Crow laws as I knew them in my time and there was still
room to breathe. Durham was a village without pre-Civil War
history or strong ante-bellum traditions. In some ways it was
like a frontier town. There was considerable prejudice, of
course, but there were recognition of individual worth and
bridges of mutual respect between the older white and colored
families of the town which persisted into the twentieth century.
Robert and Richard Fitzgerald were respected as builders of
this tobacco center and their families were held in high esteem.

Everyone knew the Fitzgerald daughters and what their 4
families stood for. Uncle Richard Fitzgerald was known as the
town's leading brick manufacturer and was considered
wealthy. He owned a great deal of property all over town and
was president of the first Negro bank organized in Durham. He
and his family lived in a fine eighteen-room slate-roofed house
of many turrets and gables and a wide piazza, set in a large
maple-and-magnolia grove and surrounded by white sandy
drives and terraced lawns. Grandfather lived in much humbler
surroundings but was equally respected for his integrity and
stubbornness in the face of many odds. People sometimes distinguished the two families as the "rich Fitzgeralds" and "poor
Fitzgeralds," but treated them all with deference and courtesy.
When my aunts went to town men of good breeding tipped their
hats and used courtesy titles in their business transactions.
They went where they pleased with little restraint and were all
grown women before the first law requiring separation on
trains and streetcars appeared in North Carolina.

They regarded these laws disdainfully as a temporary evil, 5
perhaps, and often ignored them, but they were never crushed
by them. They had known better times and were closer to the
triumphs of Grandfather's youth. I could only look
forward to a time when I could complete Grandfather's work,
which had been so violently interrupted during Reconstruction.

Mary Ruffin Smith had sown seeds of rebellion in dispos- 6
ing of her wealth. She had done what she thought was best ac-

Chapter 19

cording to her lights, but we thought differently. She gave the balance of her estate, which consisted mostly of heavily wooded land worth around $50,000, to the Western Diocese of the Protestant Episcopal Church in the state and the University of North Carolina. The University got the Jones's Grove tract with the stipulation that it be converted into a permanent trust fund in memory of her late brother who once owned it. The fund was to be used for the education of students at the University and is known as the Francis Jones Smith Scholarships.

Grandmother and her children owned property almost in the shadow of the University with whose history and traditions they were well acquainted. It did not take her daughters long to ask why she must pay taxes to support an institution which they could not attend. It was a burning issue in our family, kindled as much by feelings of personal injustice as by group discrimination. I heard it so often at home that it was only natural that I should be among the first to hammer on the doors of the University and demand the right to enter. 7

Then there was the fact of Grandfather's pension check and what it symbolized. I used to lead him to town each month when he went to cash it. He seemed to walk straighter on those days. He was the Robert Fitzgerald of old before blindness and infirmity had slowed his steps and interrupted his work. His check was his government's recognition of honored service and of the disability he had suffered in his country's cause. 8

But I saw the things which Grandfather could not see—in fact had never seen—the signs which literally screamed at me from every side—on streetcars, over drinking fountains, on doorways: FOR WHITE ONLY, FOR COLORED ONLY, WHITE LADIES, COLORED WOMEN, WHITE, COLORED. If I missed the signs I had only to follow my nose to the dirtiest, smelliest, most neglected accommodations or they were pointed out to me by a heavily armed, invariably mountainous red-faced policeman who to me seemed more a signal of calamity than of protection. I saw the names of telephone subscribers conspicuously starred "(C)" in the telephone directory and the equally conspicuous space given to crimes of Negroes by the newspapers, the inconspicuous space given to public recognition and always with the ignominious and insulting "negro" or "negress." 9

When Grandfather came south to teach, the little Negro freedmen and the poor white children were more or less on an equal footing, shared an abysmal ignorance and went to log cabin schools. A half century later the crusade against starving 10

the colored schools was a feeble whimper. Each morning I passed white children as poor as I going in the opposite direction on their way to school. We never had fights; I don't recall their ever having called me a single insulting name. It was worse than that. They passed me as if I weren't there! They looked through me and beyond me with unseeing eyes. Their school was a beautiful red-and-white brick building on a wide paved street. Its lawn was large and green and watered every day and flower beds were everywhere. Their playground, a wonderland of iron swings, sand slides, see-saws, crossbars and a basketball court, was barred from us by a strong eight-foot-high fence topped by barbed wire. We could only press our noses against the wire and watch them playing on the other side.

I went to West End where Aunt Pauline taught, on Ferrell   11
Street, a dirt road which began at a lumberyard and ended in a dump. On one side of this road were long low warehouses where huge barrels of tobacco shavings and tobacco dust were stored. All day long our nostrils sucked in the brown silt like fine snuff in the air. West End looked more like a warehouse than a school. It was a dilapidated, rickety, two-story wooden building which creaked and swayed in the wind as if it might collapse. Outside it was scarred with peeling paint from many winters of rain and snow. Inside the floors were bare and splintery, the plumbing was leaky, the drinking fountains broken and the toilets in the basement smelly and constantly out of order. We'd have to wade through pools of foul water to get to them. At recess we herded into a yard of cracked clay, barren of tree or bush, and played what games we could improvise like hopscotch or springboard, which we contrived by pulling rotted palings off the wooden fence and placing them on brickbats.

It was never the hardship which hurt so much as the con-   12
trast between what we had and what the white children had. We got the greasy, torn, dog-eared books; they got the new ones. They had field day in the city park; we had it on a furrowed stubbly hillside. They got wide mention in the newspaper; we got a paragraph at the bottom. The entire city officialdom from the mayor down turned out to review their pageantry; we got a solitary official.

Our seedy run-down school told us that if we had any   13
place at all in the scheme of things it was a separate place, marked off, proscribed and unwanted by the white people. We

were bottled up and labeled and set aside—sent to the Jim Crow car, the back of the bus, the side door of the theater, the side window of a restaurant. We came to know that whatever we had was always inferior. We came to understand that no matter how neat and clean, how law abiding, submissive and polite, how studious in school, how churchgoing and moral, how scrupulous in paying our bills and taxes we were, it made no essential difference in our place.

It seemed as if there were only two kinds of people in the world—*They* and *We*—*White* and *Colored*. The world revolved on color and variations in color. It pervaded the air I breathed. I learned it in hundreds of ways. I picked it up from grown folks round me. I heard it in the house, on the playground, in the streets, everywhere. The tide of color beat upon me ceaselessly, relentlessly.   14

Always the same tune, played like a broken record, robbing one of personal identity. Always the shifting sands of color so that there was no solid ground under one's feet. It was color, color, color all the time, color, features and hair. Folks were never just folks. They were white folks! Black folks! Poor white crackers! No-count niggers! Red necks! Darkies! Peckerwoods! Coons!   15

Two shades lighter! Two shades darker! Dead white! Coal black! High yaller! Mariny! Good hair! Bad hair! Stringy hair! Nappy hair! Thin lips! Thick lips! Red lips! Liver lips! Blue veined! Blue gummed! Straight nosed! Flat nosed!   16

Brush your hair, child, don't let it get kinky! Cold-cream your face, child, don't let it get sunburned! Don't suck your lips, child, you'll make them too niggerish! Black is evil, don't mix with mean niggers! Black is honest, you half-white bastard. I always said a little black and a little white sure do make a pretty sight! He's black as sin and evil in the bargain. The blacker the berry, the sweeter the juice!   17

Discussion Questions

1. How did the Jim Crow laws affect the life of blacks in North Carolina in 1956?
2. Why was color such a dominant issue for black people during that time?
3. How did the author's living conditions differ from those of her grandparents?

4. What do you think the author means by the expression, "the blacker the berry, the sweeter the juice"?

5. How does the author use illustration to show the extent of discrimination in the town?

6. What is the narrator's tone?

Writing Assignments

1. Write an essay comparing or contrasting your neighborhood with one that is significantly different from yours.

2. Write an essay recalling a childhood incident that led you to reach a new awareness of something.

3. Write an essay describing a time when you became stronger when confronting difficulty.

Student Essay:
POVERTY AND EDUCATION

Melinda Elaine Edmond

"One out of every twenty-one black American males will be murdered in their lifetime. Most will die at the hands of another black male." Many moviegoers and I first set eyes on that caption when watching John Singleton's *Boyz N The Hood* in July 1991. In August of that same year, my brother became a part of that statistic. Too often one opens the newspaper or turns on the nightly news and is informed about the death of another black male. Too often the victim of violence is also a victim of poverty. What can be done to stop it? Poverty is preventing America's ghetto youth from obtaining a decent education, and a lack of education is pulling the trigger of the guns that are murdering our black men.

Families living in poverty are deprived of a satisfactory education for several reasons. Schools in poor urban areas do not receive enough funding to compete with today's modern technology. These schools are not equipped with adequate materials to teach children about the changing world. For example, books and other learning aids are used and outdated; the word *computer* is almost foreign to students in these poor schools. If our children are not educated to use modern technology, they will be unable to compete in school, and as adults, unable to compete at work.

Along with inadequate resources in school, poor children face obstacles at home. For instance, poor families may not have enough food in the house; therefore, some children go to school on empty stomachs. When a child is hungry, he or she cannot focus and learn properly. His or her attention is on eating the free lunch the school provides, which, in some cases, is the only meal the child receives.

When children do not learn properly, the chances for their going on to higher education is almost impossible. Many of our black males think the only job available to them after graduation from high school (if they are lucky) is at a gas station or at McDonald's. Therefore, many turn to selling drugs for "fast cash." Desperate youths see the wealth gap between a legal and illegal job, and many choose the one that provides them

1

2

3

4

with the most money: drugs. As a result, black males are killing each other over drug money, trying to rob another drug dealer for his valuables, or over a deal gone wrong.

Lack of education can also lead to gang violence. Gang vio- 5 lence is another source of black-on-black crime. When black males are living in poverty, they often have no sense of family. They turn to gangs because of the unity and love they do not receive from home. Gangs provide young men with everything they feel they need to survive: family, money, and protection. The members' unity goes as far as killing for one another.

Youth today do not know enough about their own culture, 6 and do not know the contributions blacks have made to this society. Today's young blacks do not understand the struggle their grandparents and parents went through during the civil rights movement. They do not know the power of black people.

The key to understanding is in education—education that 7 the black poor in this country seldom achieve. Education provides an opportunity for blacks to compete for better jobs and, thus, to improve their economic condition, closing the gap that poverty has kept so wide for so long.

Discussion Questions

1. Why is poverty the enemy of the black male?
2. Why do you think the writer refers to poverty and education as being hopelessly linked?
3. Why is selling drugs a more attractive "job" for some young black males?
4. According to Edmond, why do young people turn to gangs?
5. How could knowledge of black history help solve some of the problems experienced by black youth?
6. What makes Edmond's argument an effective one?
7. The author chose to introduce her essay by using remarkable statistics. What other types of introductions might she have used?

Writing Assignments

1. Write an essay in which you discuss the "effects of _____."
2. Write an essay in which you show the positive contributions of today's African American youth.

20

Interracial Relationships

BECKY

Jean Toomer

Born Nathan Eugene Toomer in Washington, D.C., Jean Toomer (1894–1967) is best known for Cane *(1923), a book of poems, short stories, and a novella about African Americans frustrated by their conflicts in society and within themselves. This work established Toomer as a leading writer of the 1920s and inspired writers of the Harlem Renaissance. His other works include* Essentials *(1931) and* The Wayward and the Seeking, *published in 1980 after his death. In this short story from* Cane, *Toomer describes a tragic result of racial prejudice.*

Vocabulary

rustle	(1)	a soft whispering sound
mound	(1)	grave
listless	(4)	with a lack of energy or interest
snuff	(4)	powdered tobacco sniffed into the nose or applied to the gums
sullen	(5)	gloomy
cunning	(5)	sly

wraith	(5)	ghost
hant	(5)	ghost
stock-still	(6)	perfectly motionless
whinnied	(6)	whined
uncanny	(6)	mysterious, weird

Becky was the white woman who had two Negro sons. She's   1
dead; they've gone away. The pines whisper to Jesus. The Bible
flaps its leaves with an aimless rustle on her mound.

Becky had one Negro son. Who gave it to her? Damn buck   2
nigger, said the white folks' mouths. She wouldnt tell. Common, God-forsaken, insane white shameless wench, said the
white folks' mouths. Her eyes were sunken, her neck stringy,
her breasts fallen, till then. Taking their words, they filled her,
like a bubble rising—then she broke. Mouth setting in a twist
that held her eyes, harsh, vacant, staring . . . Who gave it to
her? Low-down nigger with no self-respect, said the black folks'
mouths. She wouldnt tell. Poor Catholic poor-white crazy
woman, said the black folks' mouths. White folks and black
folks built her cabin, fed her and her growing baby, prayed secretly to God who'd put His cross upon her and cast her out.

When the first was born, the white folks said they'd have   3
no more to do with her. And black folks, they too joined hands
to cast her out . . . The pines whispered to Jesus . . . The
railroad boss said not to say he said it, but she could live, if
she wanted to, on the narrow strip of land between the railroad
and the road. John Stone, who owned the lumber and the
bricks, would have shot the man who told he gave the stuff to
Lonnie Deacon, who stole out there at night and built the
cabin. A single room held down to earth . . . O fly away to Jesus . . . by a leaning chimney . . .

Six trains each day rumbled past and shook the ground   4
under her cabin. Fords, and horse- and mule-drawn buggies
went back and forth along the road. No one ever saw her.
Trainmen, and passengers who'd heard about her, threw out
papers and food. Threw out little crumpled slips of paper scrib-
bled with prayers, as they passed her eye-shaped piece of
sandy ground. Ground islandized between the road and railroad track. Pushed up where a blue-sheen God with listless
eyes could look at it. Folks from the town took turns, unknown, of course, to each other, in bringing corn and meat and
sweet potatoes. Even sometimes snuff . . . O thank y Jesus

. . . Old David Georgia, grinding cane and boiling syrup, never went her way without some sugar sap. No one ever saw her. The boy grew up and ran around. When he was five years old as folks reckoned it, Hugh Jourdon saw him carrying a baby. "Becky has another son," was what the whole town knew. But nothing was said, for the part of man that says things to the likes of that had told itself that if there was a Becky, that Becky now was dead.

The two boys grew. Sullen and cunning . . . O pines,   5
whisper to Jesus; tell Him to come and press sweet Jesus-lips against their lips and eyes . . . It seemed as though with those two big fellows there, there could be no room for Becky. The part that prayed wondered if perhaps she'd really died, and they had buried her. No one dared ask. They'd beat and cut a man who meant nothing at all in mentioning that they lived along the road. White or colored? No one knew, and least of all themselves. They drifted around from job to job. We, who had cast out their mother because of them, could we take them in? They answered black and white folks by shooting up two men and leaving town. "Godam the white folks; godam the niggers," they shouted as they left town. Becky? Smoke curled up from her chimney; she must be there. Trains passing shook the ground. The ground shook the leaning chimney. Nobody noticed it. A creepy feeling came over all who saw that thin wraith of smoke and felt the trembling of the ground. Folks began to take her food again. They quit it soon because they had a fear. Becky if dead might be a hant, and if alive—it took some nerve even to mention it . . . O pines, whisper to Jesus . . .

It was Sunday. Our congregation had been visiting at Pul-   6
verton, and were coming home. There was no wind. The autumn sun, the bell from Ebenezer Church, listless and heavy. Even the pines were stale, sticky, like the smell of food that makes you sick. Before we turned the bend of the road that would show us the Becky cabin, the horses stopped stock-still, pushed back their ears, and nervously whinnied. We urged, then whipped them on. Quarter of a mile away thin smoke curled up from the leaning chimney . . . O pines, whisper to Jesus . . . Goose-flesh came on my skin though there still was neither chill nor wind. Eyes left their sockets for the cabin. Ears burned and throbbed. Uncanny eclipse! fear closed my mind. We were just about to pass . . . Pines shout to Jesus! . . . the ground trembled as a ghost train rumbled by. The

chimney fell into the cabin. Its thud was like a hollow report, ages having passed since it went off. Barlo and I were pulled out of our seats. Dragged to the door that had swung open. Through the dust we saw the bricks in a mound upon the floor. Becky, if she was there, lay under them. I thought I heard a groan. Barlo, mumbling something, threw his Bible on the pile. (No one has ever touched it.) Somehow we got away. My buggy was still on the road. The last thing that I remember was whipping old Dan like fury; I remember nothing after that—that is, until I reached town and folks crowded round to get the true word of it.

> Becky was the white woman who had two Negro sons. She's   7
> dead; they've gone away. The pines whisper to Jesus. The Bible
> flaps its leaves with an aimless rustle on her mound.

Discussion Questions

1. Why was Becky abandoned by both the whites and the blacks?

2. What type of person do you think Becky was? Explain your answer.

3. What attitudes did Becky's sons have toward the whites and the blacks?

4. Why do you think the townspeople brought food to Becky and her sons "unknown to each other"? Why did they soon stop bringing food the second time?

5. How did Becky die?

6. What effect does the author's repetition of the phrase "O pines, whisper to Jesus" have on the reading of the story?

7. How does Toomer use cause and effect to illustrate the plight of Becky?

8. Toomer uses the same paragraph for both the opening and the ending of the story. What effect, if any, does this have on the tone of the story?

Writing Assignments

1. Write an essay about someone you know who died in a strange way.

2. Write an essay about a time when you or someone you know was treated badly because of prejudice.

3. Write an essay describing a situation in which you or someone you know learned something positive from an interracial relationship.

BETRAYAL? WHEN BLACK MEN DATE WHITE WOMEN

Bebe Moore Campbell

Bebe Moore Campbell (1950–) is a free-lance writer and novelist. She is a frequent contributor to Morning Edition *on National Public Radio (NPR) and has also contributed to the* New York Times, *the* Washington Post, *and the* Los Angeles Times. *She has written several books:* Successful Women, Angry Men: Backlash in the Two-Career Marriage *(1987),* Sweet Summer: Growing Up With and Without My Dad *(1989),* Your Blues Ain't Like Mine *(1992), and* Brothers and Sisters *(1994). In the following article, which appeared in the* New York Times Magazine *in 1992, Campbell expresses her feelings about interracial dating.*

Vocabulary

restrained	(2)	held back
surreptitiously	(2)	discreetly, without calling attention to
iota	(2)	very small amount
lamented	(5)	expressed deep sorrow
perfidy	(5)	betrayal of trust
fervor	(6)	intense feeling
rendition	(6)	performance
internecine	(11)	mutually destructive or deadly
proprietary	(15)	ownership
testosterone	(16)	male hormone
psyches	(33)	souls, spirits

Not long ago some friends and I, all African-American women, were sitting in a trendy Beverly Hills restaurant having lunch when a good-looking, popular black actor strolled in. 1

As an audible buzz of recognition traveled from table to table, my group, restrained stargazers all, managed to surreptitiously turn our heads toward the handsome celebrity without sacrificing one iota of our collective cool. 2

That is, until we saw the blonde trailing behind him. 3

Our forks hit the plates on the first beat. An invisible choir director only we could see raised her hands: All together now. In unison, we moaned, we groaned, we rolled our eyes heavenward. We gnashed our teeth in harmony and made ugly faces. 4

The altos sang, Umph! Umph! Umph!, then we all shook 5

our heads as we lamented for the 10,000th time the perfidy of black men and cursed trespassing white women who dared to "take our men."

The fact that I am married to my second black husband did-n't lessen the fervor of my rendition of this same old song one bit. 6

Had Spike Lee ventured in with a camera and recorder he would have had the footage and soundtrack for "Jungle Fever, Parts II, III and IV." 7

Before lunch was over I had a headache, indigestion and probably elevated blood pressure. In retrospect, I think I may have shortened my life considerably. 8

For many African-American women, the thought of black men, particularly those who are successful, dating or marrying white women is like being passed over for the prom by the boy we consider our steady date, causing us pain, rage and an overwhelming sense of betrayal and personal rejection. 9

When asked why they are with white women, most black men explain that they just happened to fall in love. Others say that they consider white women more docile and obedient than feisty black women. And some refuse to answer the question. 10

Whatever the real reasons may be, many black women perceive a hurtful mixture of blatant sexism and eerie in-ternecine racism: If you were good enough (if you looked like white women and didn't give me so much back talk) I wouldn't choose someone else. 11

For sisters, the message that we don't measure up is the nightmare side of integration. 12

We can't get even, so we get mad. 13

I once believed that if I could just lock my rolling eyes onto those of some wayward brothers, somehow I could will them to return to black women where they belong. 14

But as I drove home from lunch with my head pounding and my heart racing, I slowly came to a conclusion I've been avoiding for three decades, out of pride, sisterly solidarity and just plain stubbornness: In the multiracial society we Ameri-cans live in, to feel one has exclusive, proprietary rights to the members of the opposite sex of one's race is a one-way ticket to Migraine City. 15

Let me be clear: I'm not ashamed of my fury. The resent-ment and even hostility I harbor are perfectly normal, and I be-lieve my sisters and I have conducted ourselves with ladylike dignity and enormous restraint; we don't have enough testos-terone to do anybody harm. 16

I haven't slashed one brother's tire; I don't have any blond   17
ponytails hanging on my bedroom walls. I've just been obsessing.

And I'm in good company. Asian men, when their women   18
marry whites; Jewish women, when their men pick "shiksas";
and Latinas, when Latinos choose white women—all rant and
rave just as I do.

But if my anger is within the range of predictable and ac-   19
ceptable norms, it is increasingly uncomfortable for me personally. Anger has become an addiction.

There are, of course, black women who couldn't care less   20
about any man besides the man they are seeing. Still, almost
every time I get together with two or more African-American
women, the topic turns to "the problem."

We're disgusted; we're depressed. We're obsessing; we're   21
PMS-ing. I'm tired of putting my mood at the mercy of
strangers.

Yes, I want my people to date and marry each other and I   22
don't think it will ever give me pleasure to see black men with
white women, but my being angry isn't going to make these
couples stop choosing each other.

The only thing I can control regarding this phenomenon is   23
my response to it.

What I'm striving for is the same feeling I get whenever I   24
run into my ex-husband: neutrality. I can acknowledge the
man without giving up any negative energy or emotions. I
worked for years to achieve that kind of peace of mind; it is a
wonderful blessing.

Many sisters say black women's pain comes from black   25
men abandoning them for other women. I used to believe that,
but I no longer do.

I can't speak for other women, but when my thinking isn't   26
clouded by anger I am forced to recognize that my pain isn't
coming from black men and white women. It is coming from
within. Therein lies my healing.

I remember sitting in my bedroom in the dark with a hair   27
clip on my nose, trying to reduce the size of my wide nostrils.

When the teenage parties I attended grew hot and my   28
pageboy turned "nappy" I'd dash into the bathroom and attempt to comb it so the boys wouldn't see how ugly I was.

---

[1] "shiksas" (18)   Non-Jewish girls or young women.

While I was growing up I recall watching my grandmother 29
make pancakes and seeing Aunt Jemima's smiling face on the
box.

Aunt Jemima has a new, modern hairdo now, but she is 30
still on the pancake box, a sturdy, sensible woman, not unpleasant to look at, but clearly one who is meant for servitude
and not adoration.

And what I knew then, I know now: When some people 31
look at me, or any black woman, they see Aunt Jemima—a
mammy, built to serve, not to adore. A few of those people are
my men.

I can't change anyone's perception of me, but I can hold 32
all the facets of me in high esteem. The thing I like about Sister
Jemima is this: She's a survivor.

Some black men may need to ask themselves why they are 33
with white women, particularly those who use them as emotional props to soothe wounded psyches and maybe even those
who are truly in love. It isn't my responsibility to conduct the
interrogation.

I don't want to be held hostage by my own rage. Aunt 34
Jemima is a survivor. Like her, I want to endure through the
decades with a smile on my face, knowing that no one can reject me unless I give them permission to do so.

If, like me, my brothers need to embark upon the path 35
that leads to the resurrection of their damaged souls, then I
urge them to read the books, attend the seminars or choose the
therapists and begin their journey.

I forgive black men for hurting me; I forgive me for letting 36
them.

I am moving toward peace. 37

Discussion Questions

1. How would you describe Campbell's attitude toward black men who date white women?
2. According to Campbell, what reasons do most black men give for dating white women?
3. What is Campbell's attitude toward Aunt Jemima?
4. How has Campbell learned to soothe her anger and to heal her hurt?
5. What is the tone of this article?
6. What makes Campbell's argument a persuasive one?

7. Which sentence seems to state the thesis of this article? Explain your answer.

Writing Assignments

1. Write an essay expressing your feelings on interracial relationships.
2. Write an essay in which you explore reasons why some people have difficulty accepting interracial relationships.
3. Write an essay describing a positive or a negative interracial relationship that you have experienced or observed. Explain why you consider it positive or negative.

NOTES OF A NATIVE SON

James Baldwin

James Baldwin (1924–1987) was born and reared in Harlem, New York. Most of his writings describe racial conflict and prejudice in the United States. His works include two books of autobiographical essays, Notes of a Native Son *(1955) and* Nobody Knows My Name *(1961); a nonfiction work,* The Fire Next Time *(1963); novels,* Go Tell It on the Mountain *(1953),* Another Country *(1962), and* Just Above My Head *(1979); and plays,* Blues for Mister Charlie *(1964) and* The Amen Corner *(1965). This excerpt is taken from Baldwin's essay "Stranger in the Village," which was first published in* Notes of a Native Son. *Here Baldwin reflects on American black-white race relations.*

Vocabulary

sporadically	(2)	occassionally
ambivalence	(2)	conflicting feelings
subtle	(2)	hard to detect
sustenance	(2)	nourishment, food
estrangement	(3)	keeping apart
perpetual	(4)	continuing indefinitely

1   At the root of the American Negro problem is the necessity of the American white man to find a way of living with the Negro in order to be able to live with himself. And the history of this problem can be reduced to the means used by Americans—lynch law and law, segregation and legal acceptance, terrorization and concession—either to come to terms with this necessity, or to find a way around it, or (most usually) to find a way of doing both these things at once. The resulting spectacle, at once foolish and dreadful, led someone to make the quite accurate observation that "the Negro-in-America is a form of insanity which overtakes white men."

2   In this long battle, a battle by no means finished, the unforeseeable effects of which will be felt by many future generations, the white man's motive was the protection of his identity; the black man was motivated by the need to establish an identity. And despite the terrorization which the Negro in America endured and endures sporadically until today, despite the cruel

and totally inescapable ambivalence of his status in his country, the battle for his identity has long ago been won. He is not a visitor to the West, but a citizen there, an American; as American as the Americans who despise him, the Americans who fear him, the Americans who love him—the Americans who became less than themselves, or rose to be greater than themselves by virtue of the fact that the challenge he represented was inescapable. He is perhaps the only black man in the world whose relationship to white men is more terrible, more subtle, and more meaningful than the relationship of bitter possessed to uncertain possessors. His survival depended, and his development depends, on his ability to turn his peculiar status in the Western world to his own advantage and, it may be, to the very great advantage of that world. It remains for him to fashion out of his experience that which will give him sustenance, and a voice. . . .

Yet, if the American Negro has arrived at his identity by   3
virtue of the absoluteness of his estrangement from his past, American white men still nourish the illusion that there is some means of recovering the European innocence, of returning to a state in which black men do not exist. This is one of the greatest errors Americans can make. The identity they fought so hard to protect has, by virtue of that battle, undergone a change: Americans are as unlike any other white people in the world as it is possible to be. I do not think, for example, that it is too much to suggest that the American vision of the world—which allows so little reality, generally speaking, for any of the darker forces in human life, which tends until today to paint moral issues in glaring black and white—owes a great deal to the battle waged by Americans to maintain between themselves and black men a human separation which could not be bridged. It is only now beginning to be borne in on us— very faintly, it must be admitted, very slowly, and very much against our will—that this vision of the world is dangerously inaccurate, and perfectly useless. For it protects our moral high-mindedness at the terrible expense of weakening our grasp of reality. People who shut their eyes to reality simply invite their own destruction, and anyone who insists on remaining in a state of innocence long after that innocence is dead turns himself into a monster.

The time has come to realize that the interracial drama   4
acted out on the American continent has not only created a new black man, it has created a new white man, too. No road

whatever will lead Americans back to the simplicity of this European village where white men still have the luxury of looking on me as a stranger. I am not, really, a stranger any longer for any American alive. One of the things that distinguishes Americans from other people is that no other people has ever been so deeply involved in the lives of black men, and vice versa. This fact faced, with all its implications, it can be seen that the history of the American Negro problem is not merely shameful, it is also something of an achievement. For even when the worst has been said, it must also be added that the perpetual challenge posed by this problem was always, somehow, perpetually met. It is precisely this black-white experience which may prove of indispensable value to us in the world we face today. This world is white no longer, and it will never be white again.

Discussion Questions

1. According to Baldwin, what is the root of the "American Negro problem"?
2. Why does Baldwin say that "Americans are as unlike as any other white people in the world as it is possible to be"?
3. Why do you think Baldwin feels he is a stranger in Europe and not in America?
4. How does Baldwin use comparison and contrast, description, and illustration to develop his argument?
5. For what audience do you think this selection is written? Explain your answer.

Writing Assignments

1. Write an essay expressing your hope or lack of hope for improvement in race relations in America.
2. Write an essay describing a time when you felt like a stranger.
3. Write an essay responding to Baldwin's statement: "This world is white no longer, and it will never be white again."

WHAT'S AMERICAN ABOUT AMERICA?

Ishmael Reed

Ishmael Reed (1938–) was born in Chattanooga, Tennessee, but grew up in Buffalo, New York. He attended the University of Buffalo, was an activist in the Civil Rights Movement, and worked for several newspapers. Reed is best known for his many novels, which not only attack economic exploitation, racism, and sexism, but also poke fun at Western literary standards. Some of his novels include The Free-Lance Pallbearers *(1967),* Yellow Back Radio Broke-Down *(1971),* Mumbo Jumbo *(1972), and* Reckless Eye-balling *(1986). "What's American About America?" originally appeared as a longer version in Reed's collection of essays,* Writin' Is Fightin': Thirty-Seven Years of Boxing on Paper *(1988). This shortened version of the essay highlights the many serious social problems present in the United States and emphasizes that the nation has always been considered more like a bowl of stew or salad rather than a melting pot.*

Vocabulary

ostracism	(3)	exclusion from a group; rejection
mythological	(4)	imaginary
monolithic	(5)	always the same, unchanging
dissidents	(6)	those who disagree
patriarchs	(9)	father figures
razed	(9)	tore down, destroyed
meticulous	(11)	extremely careful and precise
repository	(14)	a place where things are put for safekeeping

On the day before Memorial Day, 1983, a poet called me to 1 describe a city he had just visited. He said that one section included mosques, built by the Islamic people who dwelled there. Attending his reading, he said, were large numbers of Hispanic people, 40,000 of whom lived in the same city. He was not talking about a fabled city located in some mysterious region of the world. The city he'd visited was Detroit.

A few months before, as I was visiting Texas, I heard the 2 taped voice used to guide passengers to their connections at the Dallas Airport announcing items in both Spanish and English. This trend is likely to continue; after all, for some southwestern states like Texas, where the largest minority is now Mexican-American, Spanish was the first written language and the Spanish style lives on in the western way of life.

Shortly after my Texas trip, I sat in a campus auditorium   3
at the University of Wisconsin at Milwaukee as a Yale professor—whose original work on the influence of African cultures upon those of the Americas has led to his ostracism from some intellectual circles—walked up and down the aisle like an old-time Southern evangelist, dancing and drumming the top of the lectern, illustrating his points before some Afro-American intellectuals and artists who cheered and applauded his performance. The professor was "white." After his lecture, he conversed with a group of Milwaukeeans—all who spoke Yoruban,[1] though only the professor had ever traveled to Africa.

One of the artists there told me that his paintings, which   4
included African and Afro-American mythological symbols and imagery, were hanging in the local McDonald's restaurant. The next day I went to McDonald's and snapped pictures of smiling youngsters eating hamburgers below paintings that could grace the walls of any of the country's leading museums. The manager of the local McDonald's said, "I don't know what you boys are doing, but I like it," as he commissioned the local painters to exhibit in his restaurant.

Such blurring of cultural styles occurs in everyday life in   5
the United States to a greater extent than anyone can imagine. The result is what the above-mentioned Yale professor, Robert Thompson, referred to as a cultural bouillabaisse.[2] Yet members of the nation's present educational and cultural elect still cling to the notion that the United States belongs to some vaguely defined entity they refer to as "Western civilization," by which they mean, presumably, a civilization created by people of Europe, as if Europe can even be viewed in monolithic terms. Is Beethoven's Ninth Symphony, which includes Turkish marches, a part of Western civilization? Or the late-nineteenth-and twentieth-century French paintings, whose creators were

[1] Yoruban (3)   An African language spoken in Nigeria.
[2] cultural bouillabaisse (5)   Refers to the coexistence of several cultures in one society; "bouillabaisse" is a stew made up of different types of fish and shellfish.

influenced by Japanese art? And what of the cubists,[3] through whom the influence of African art changed modern painting? Or the surrealists[4] who were so impressed with the art of the Pacific Northwest Indians that, in their map of North America, Alaska dwarfs the lower forty-eight states in size?

Are the Russians, who are often criticized for their adoption   6
of "Western" ways by Tsarist[5] dissidents in exile, members of Western civilization? And what of the millions of Europeans who have black African and Asian ancestry, black Africans having occupied several European countries for hundreds of years? Are these "Europeans" a part of Western civilization? Or the Hungarians, who originated across the Urals in a place called Greater Hungary? Or the Irish, who came from the Iberian Peninsula?

Even the notion that North America is part of Western civi-   7
lization because our "system of government" is derived from Europe is being challenged by Native American historians who say that the founding fathers, Benjamin Franklin especially, were actually influenced by the system of government that had been adopted by the Iroquois hundreds of years prior to the arrival of Europeans.

Western civilization, then, becomes another confusing cat-   8
egory—like Third World, or Judeo-Christian culture—as humanity attempts to impose its small-screen view of political and cultural reality upon a complex world. Our most publicized novelist recently said that Western civilization was the greatest achievement of mankind—an attitude that flourishes on the street level as scribbles in public restrooms: "White Power," "Niggers and Spics Suck," or "Hitler was a prophet." Where did such an attitude, which has caused so much misery and depression in our national life, which has tainted even our noblest achievements, begin? An attitude that caused the incarceration of Japanese-American citizens during World War II, the persecution of Chicanos and Chinese Americans, the near-extermination of the Indians, and the murder and lynchings of thousands of Afro-Americans.

---

[3] cubists   (5)   Those representing a school of painting and sculpture that reflects geometric shapes.
[4] surrealists   (5)   Those representing a literacy and artistic movement that proclaims the changing of social, scientific, and philosophical values through the freeing of the unconscious.
[5] Tsarist   (6)   Sometimes spelled *czarist;* characterized by a system of absolute authority or monarchy.

The Puritans of New England are idealized in our school-   9
books as the first Americans, "a hardy band" of no-nonsense
patriarchs whose discipline razed the forest and brought order
to the New World (a term that annoys Native American historians). Industrious, responsible, it was their "Yankee ingenuity"
and practicality that created the work ethic.

The Puritans, however, had a mean streak. They hated the   10
theater and banned Christmas. They punished people in a
cruel and inhuman manner. They killed children who dis-
obeyed their parents. They exterminated the Indians, who had
taught them how to survive in a world unknown to them. And
their encounter with calypso culture, in the form of a servant
from Barbados working in a Salem minister's household, resulted in the witchcraft hysteria.

The Puritan legacy of hard work and meticulous account-   11
ing led to the establishment of a great industrial society, but
there was the other side—the strange and paranoid attitudes
of that society toward those different from the elect.

The cultural attitudes of that early elect continue to   12
be voiced in everyday life in the United States; the president of
a distinguished university, writing a letter to the *Times,* belit-
tling the study of African civilizations; the television network
that promoted its show on the Vatican art with the boast that
this art represented "the finest achievements of the human
spirit."

When I heard a schoolteacher warn the other night about   13
the invasion of the American educational system by foreign
curricula, I wanted to yell at the television set, "Lady, they're
already here." It has already begun because the world is here.
The world has been arriving at these shores for at least 10,000
years from Europe, Africa, and Asia. In the late nineteenth and
early twentieth centuries, large numbers of Europeans arrived,
adding their cultures to those of the European, African, and
Asian settlers who were already here, and recently millions
have been entering the country from South America and the
Caribbean, making Robert Thompson's bouillabaisse richer and
thicker.

North America deserves a more exciting destiny than as a   14
repository of "Western civilization." We can become a place
where the cultures of the world crisscross. This is possible because the United States and Canada are unique in the world:
The world is here.

Discussion Questions

1. How does Reed show that the notion of Western civilization is not only confusing, but also leads to racist attitudes?
2. According to Reed, what mean streak did the Puritans possess? Give examples.
3. What does Reed mean when he says, "North America deserves a more exciting destiny than to be a repository of 'Western civilization'"?
4. According to Reed, what kind of place can North America become?
5. How effective is Reed's use of description? Support your answer.
6. Why do you think Reed chooses to use a question for the title of his essay? How effective is this choice?

Writing Assignments

1. Write an essay explaining the difference between the following two terms used to describe the United States: *melting pot* and *cultural bouillabaisse.*
2. Write an essay describing your culture's contribution to civilization.
3. Write an essay arguing for a North America that is better in some way.

Student Essay:
SOCIETY REJECTS MIXED CHILDREN

Mia Elliott

Though their numbers have significantly increased over 1
the past decade, interracial marriages still constitute only a
small percentage of the U.S. population. Until 1967, marriages
between whites and nonwhites were against the law. Though
these marriages are not illegal today, interracial couples and
their offspring still are often not accepted by society. Because
society is slow to accept them, many mixed children suffer psy-
chologically.

Many mixed children experience psychological problems 2
such as a loss of identity. For instance, children with one white
parent and one parent of color will generally be identified with
the parent of color; their biracial identity is ignored. Likewise,
children with one black parent and one parent of color from
another race are still perceived as black. Racial identity is influenced not only by the perceptions of white society, but also
by the tendency of cultures of color to be more accepting of
children of interracial unions than are those in white society.
Peer pressure is also a factor that contributes to psychological
problems. Names such as "zebra," "oreo," and "cream-in-coffee"
are often targeted at mixed children by their peers. Not surprisingly, mixed children, particularly during the teen years, face
many discomforts because they want to fit into their peer
group. For example, a young man, half black and half Chinese,
felt as if his mixed blood was a curse. He lived in a neighborhood where the majority was black, the group with whom he
seemed to relate. One day he met a Chinese girl in a store and
decided to get acquainted. As he began to approach her, his
black friends commented, "Don't tell me you're a chink lover."
Though the young man abandoned his intentions, he was hurt
that in doing so, he had rejected part of himself.

Despite many encounters with racism, mixed children are 3
learning to cope with it, to take pride in being themselves, and
to form friendships with people of diverse cultures. After all,
the world is changing and in order to survive, everyone must
learn to accept differences.

Discussion Questions

1. According to Elliott, what are some of the psychological problems suffered by mixed children?
2. What determines whether or not a mixed child is identified as belonging to one racial group or another?
3. The author says that society has difficulty in accepting mixed children. Why do you think this is the case?
4. Elliott has relied primarily on illustration in developing her essay. How does her use of narration and cause and effect also support her thesis?
5. Do you think this relatively short essay contains adequate details to support its thesis? Why or why not?

Writing Assignments

1. Write an essay in which you discuss another group that in your opinion has been rejected by society.
2. In an essay relate a time when you felt caught between two different groups, cultures, religions, or beliefs.

21

Intraracial Prejudice

IF YOU'RE LIGHT AND HAVE LONG HAIR

Gwendolyn Brooks

Gwendolyn Brooks (1917–   ) is still on the lecture circuit, conducting creative writing workshops at colleges and universities throughout the United States. Perhaps what is most remarkable about this African American poet is not her ability to learn and to grow from younger poets such as Haki R. Madhubuti (don l. lee), but her untiring, selfless efforts to spark young people to write creatively. Since the publication of her A Street in Bronzeville *(1945), Brooks has published many volumes of poetry, including* Annie Allen *(1949),* Riot *(1969),* Becomings *(1975),* Primer for Blacks *(1980), and* Blacks *(1987). In all of her volumes, she offers snapshot descriptions of poor, frustrated, or troubled African Americans living in urban areas in the North. In 1950, she became the first African American to receive the Pulitzer Prize for poetry. In 1994, she received the National Book Lifetime Achievement Award. Currently, she directs the Gwendolyn Brooks Center for Black Literature and Creative Writing in Chicago. The following selection is taken from Brooks's novel,* Maud Martha *(1953), and describes the problem that some African Americans face when they apply the beauty standards of white America to themselves.*

Vocabulary

elucidation	(1)	explanation
bid	(2)	invitation
supercilious	(10)	a feeling of contempt based on a sense of superiority
surreptitiously	(10)	secretly
superimposed	(10)	placed over something, covering
reeked	(21)	smelled strongly of

Came the invitation that Paul recognized as an honor of the   1
first water, and as sufficient indication that he was, at last, a
social somebody. The invitation was from the Foxy Cats Club,
the club of clubs. He was to be present, in formal dress, at the
Annual Foxy Cats Dawn Ball. No chances were taken: "Top hat,
white tie and tails" hastily followed the "Formal dress," and
that elucidation was in bold type.

    Twenty men were in the Foxy Cats Club. All were good-   2
looking. All wore clothes that were rich and suave. All "handled
money," for their number consisted of well-located barbers, policemen, "government men," and men with a lucky touch at the
tracks. Certainly the Foxy Cats Club was not a representative
of that growing group of South Side organizations devoted to
moral and civic improvements, or to literary or other cultural
pursuits. If that had been so, Paul would have chucked his bid
(which was black and silver, decorated with winking cat faces)
down the toilet with a yawn. "That kind of stuff" was hardly
understood by Paul, and was always dismissed with an airy
"dicty," "hincty," or "highfalutin." But no. The Foxy Cats devoted themselves solely to the business of being "hep," and
each year they spent hundreds of dollars on their wonderful
Dawn Ball, which did not begin at dawn, but was scheduled to
end at dawn. "Ball," they called the frolic, but it served also the
purposes of party, feast, and fashion show. Maud Martha,
watching him study his invitation, watching him lift his chin,
could see that he considered himself one of the blessed.

    Who—what kind soul had recommended him!   3

    "He'll have to take me," thought Maud Martha. "For the   4
envelope is addressed 'Mr. and Mrs.,' and I opened it. I guess
he'd like to leave me home. At the Ball, there will be only beautiful girls, or real stylish ones. There won't be more than a
handful like me. My type is not a Foxy Cat favorite. But he
can't avoid taking me—since he hasn't yet thought of words or
ways strong enough, and at the same time soft enough—for
he's kind; he doesn't like to injure—to carry across to me the

news that he is not to be held permanently by my type, and that he can go on with this marriage only if I put no ropes or questions around him. Also, he'll want to humor me, now that I'm pregnant."

She would need a good dress. That, she knew, could be a 5 problem, on his grocery clerk's pay. He would have his own expenses. He would have to rent his topper and tails, and he would have to buy a fine tie, and really excellent shoes. She knew he was thinking that on the strength of his appearance and sophisticated behavior at this Ball might depend his future admission (for why not dream?) to *membership,* actually, in the Foxy Cats Club!

"I'll settle," decided Maud Martha, "on a plain white 6 princess-style thing and some blue and black satin ribbon. I'll go to my mother's. I'll work miracles at the sewing machine.

"On that night, I'll wave my hair. I'll smell faintly of lily of 7 the valley."

The main room of the Club 99, where the Ball was held, 8 was hung with green and yellow and red balloons, and the thick pillars, painted to give an effect of marble, and stretching from floor to ceiling, were draped with green and red and yellow crepe paper. Huge ferns, rubber plants, and bowls of flowers were at every corner. The floor itself was a decoration, golden, glazed. There was no overhead light; only wall lamps, and the bulbs in these were romantically dim. At the back of the room, standing on a furry white rug, was the long banquet table, dressed in damask, accented by groups of thin silver candlesticks bearing white candles, and laden with lovely food: cold chicken, lobster, candied ham fruit combinations, potato salad in a great gold dish, corn sticks, a cheese fluff in spiked tomato cups, fruit cake, angel cake, sunshine cake. The drinks were at a smaller table nearby, behind which stood a genial mixologist, quick with maraschino cherries, and with lemon, ice, and liquor. Wines were there, and whisky, and rum, and eggnog made with pure cream.

Paul and Maud Martha arrived rather late, on purpose. 9 Rid of their wraps, they approached the glittering floor. Bunny Bates's orchestra was playing Ellington's "Solitude."

Paul, royal in rented finery, was flushed with excitement. 10 Maud Martha looked at him. Not very tall. Not very handsomely made. But there was that extraordinary quality of maleness. Hiding in the body that was not *too* yellow, waiting to spring, out at her, surround her (she liked to think)—that maleness. The Ball stirred her. The Beauties, in their gorgeous gowns, bustling, supercilious; the young men, who at other times most unpleasantly blew their noses, and darted surreptitiously into alleys to relieve themselves, and sweated and swore at their jobs, and scratched their more intimate parts, now smiling, smooth, overgallant; the drowsy lights; the smells of food and flowers, the smell of Murray's pomade, the body perfumes, natural and superimposed; the sensuous heaviness of the wine-colored draperies at the many windows; the music, now steamy and slow, now as clear and fragile as glass, now raging, passionate, now moaning and thickly gray. The Ball made toys of her emotions, stirred her variously. But she was anxious to have it end, she was anxious to be at home again, with the door closed behind herself and her husband. Then, he might be warm. There might be more than the absent courtesy he had been giving her of late. Then, he might be the tree she had a great need to lean against, in this "emergency." There was no telling what dear thing he might say to her, what little gem let fall.

But, to tell the truth, his behavior now was not very   11
promising of gems to come. After their second dance he escorted her to a bench by the wall, left her. Trying to look nonchalant, she sat. She sat, trying not to show the inferiority she did not feel. When the music struck up again, he began to dance with someone red-haired and curved, and white as a white. Who was she? He had approached her easily, he had taken her confidently, he held her and conversed with her as though he had known her well for a long, long time. The girl smiled up at him. Her gold-spangled bosom was pressed—was pressed against that maleness—

A man asked Maud Martha to dance. He was dark, too.   12
His mustache was small.

"Is this your first Foxy Cats?" he asked.   13

"What?" Paul's cheek was on that of Gold-Spangles.   14

"First Cats?"   15

"Oh. Yes." Paul and Gold-Spangles were weaving through   16
the noisy twisting couples, were trying, apparently, to get to the reception hall.

"Do you know that girl? What's her name?" Maud Martha   17
asked her partner, pointing to Gold-Spangles. Her partner looked, nodded. He pressed her closer.

"That's Maella. That's Maella."   18

"Pretty, isn't she?" She wanted him to keep talking about Maella. He nodded again.   19

"Yep. She has 'em howling along the stroll, all right, all right."   20

Another man, dancing past with an artificial redhead, threw a whispered word at Maud Martha's partner, who caught it eagerly, winked. "Solid, ol' man," he said. "Solid, Jack." He pressed Maud Martha closer. "You're a babe," he said. "You're a real babe." He reeked excitingly of tobacco, liquor, pinesoap, toilet water, and Sen Sen.[1]   21

Maud Martha thought of her parents' back yard. Fresh. Clean. Smokeless. In her childhood, a snowball bush had shone there, big above the dandelions. The snowballs had been big, healthy. Once, she and her sister and brother had waited in the back yard for their parents to finish readying themselves for a trip to Milwaukee. The snowballs had been so beautiful, so fat and startlingly white in the sunlight, that she had suddenly loved home a thousand times more than ever before, and had not wanted to go to Milwaukee. But as the children grew, the bush sickened. Each year, the snowballs were smaller and more dispirited. Finally a summer came when there were no blossoms at all. Maud Martha wondered what had become of the bush. For it was not there now. Yet she, at least, had never seen it go.   22

"Not," thought Maud Martha, "that they love each other. It oughta be that simple. Then I could like it. It oughta be that easy. But it's my color that makes him mad. I try to shut my eyes to that, but it's no good. What I am inside, what is really me, he likes okay. But he keeps looking at my color, which is like a wall. He has to jump over it in order to meet and touch what I've got for him. He has to jump away up high in order to see it. He gets awful tired of all that jumping."   23

Paul came back from the reception hall. Maella was clinging to his arm. A final cry of the saxophone finished that particular slice of the blues. Maud Martha's partner bowed, escorted her to a chair by a rubber plant, bowed again, left.   24

"I could," considered Maud Martha, "go over there and scratch her upsweep down. I could spit on her back. I could scream. 'Listen,' I could scream, 'I'm making a baby for this man and I mean to do it in peace.' "   25

[1] Sen Sen   (21)   Breath freshener.

But if the root was sour what business did she have up   26
there hacking at a leaf?

Discussion Questions

1. What kind of club is the Foxy Cats Club?
2. What is the meaning of the phrase, "trying not to show the inferiority she did not feel"?
3. What is the significance of the snowball bush?
4. What is the problem between Paul and Maud Martha?
5. What is the significance of the question at the end of the story?
6. How does Brooks use comparison and contrast in the story?
7. Why do you think Brooks uses a subordinate clause for the title of her story?

Writing Assignments

1. Write an essay relating an experience in which you felt embarrassed or ashamed.
2. Write an essay in which you discuss the types of people you have dated.
3. In an essay, compare and contrast two people you know who have different physical features, but who are both physically attractive.

THE REVOLT OF THE EVIL FAIRIES

Ted Poston

Theodore Roosevelt (Ted) Poston (1906–1974) was born in Hopkinsville, Kentucky, graduated from Tennessee State University, and did additional study at New York University. He was a pullman car porter before becoming a journalist with the New Amsterdam News *and the* Pittsburgh Courier. *Poston was among the first African American reporters to write for the* New York Post, *where he worked for over thirty-three years and demonstrated that an African American reporter could cover general stories. He won numerous awards for his coverage of World War II and was a member of Franklin Roosevelt's "Black Cabinet." Among Poston's most popular articles are "My Most Humiliating Jim Crow Experience" (1944), "New York Vs. Chicago: Which Is [the] Better Place for Negroes?" (1952), and "The Simple World of Langston Hughes" (1957). In this selection, which was first published in the* New Republic (1944), *Poston describes his experiences with intraracial prejudice as a student at the Booker T. Washington Colored Grammar School.*

Vocabulary

ferment	(5)	excitement
scion	(7)	descendant
skulking	(8)	moving in a sly, shifty manner
vanquished	(8)	conquered
inconsolable	(12)	not able to be comforted
fervent	(15)	with warm feelings, intense
purloined	(16)	stole
fettle	(22)	condition
slunk	(22)	moved in a sneaking manner

The grand dramatic offering of the Booker T. Washington Colored Grammar School was the biggest event of the year in our social life in Hopkinsville, Kentucky. It was the one occasion on which they let us use the old Cooper Opera House, and even some of the white folks came out yearly to applaud our presentation. The first two rows of the orchestra were always reserved for our white friends, and our leading colored citizens sat right behind them—with an empty row intervening, of course.

Mr. Ed Smith, our local undertaker, invariably occupied a   2
box to the left of the house and wore his cutaway coat and
striped breeches. This distinctive garb was usually reserved for
those rare occasions when he officiated at the funerals of our
most prominent colored citizens. Mr. Thaddeus Long, our colored mailman, once rented a tuxedo and bought a box too. But
nobody paid him much mind. We knew he was just showing
off.

The title of our play never varied. It was always Prince   3
Charming and the Sleeping Beauty but no two presentations
were ever the same. Miss H. Belle LaPrade, our sixth-grade
teacher, rewrote the script every season, and it was never like
anything you read in the storybooks.

Miss LaPrade called it "a modern morality play of conflict   4
between the forces of good and evil." And the forces of evil, of
course, always came off second best.

The Booker T. Washington Colored Grammar School was   5
in a state of ferment from Christmas until February, for this
was the period when parts were assigned. First there was the
selection of the Good Fairies and the Evil Fairies. This was very
important, because the Good Fairies wore white costumes and
the Evil Fairies black. And strangely enough most of the Good
Fairies usually turned out to be extremely light in complexion,
with straight hair and white folks' features. On rare occasions a
darkskinned girl might be lucky enough to be a Good Fairy, but
not one with a speaking part.

There was never any doubt about Prince Charming and   6
the Sleeping Beauty. They were always lightskinned. And
though nobody ever discussed those things openly, it was an
accepted fact that a lack of pigmentation was a decided advantage in the Prince Charming and Sleeping Beauty sweepstakes.

And therein lay my personal tragedy. I made the best   7
grades in my class. I was the leading debater, and the scion of
a respected family in the community. But I could never be
Prince Charming, because I was black.

In fact, every year when they started casting our grand   8
dramatic offering my family started pricing black cheesecloth at
Franklin's Department Store. For they knew that I would be
leading the forces of darkness and skulking back in the shadows—waiting to be vanquished in the third act. Mamma had
experience with this sort of thing. All my brothers had finished
Booker T. before me.

Not that I was alone in my disappointment. Many of my   9

classmates felt it too. I probably just took it more to heart. Rat Joiner, for instance, could rationalize the situation. Rat was not only black; he lived on Billy Goat Hill. But Rat summed it up like this:

"If you black, you black."   10

I should have been able to regard the matter calmly too.   11
For our grand dramatic offering was only a reflection of our daily community life in Hopkinsville. The yallers had the best of everything. They held most of the teaching jobs in Booker T. Washington Colored Grammar School. They were the Negro doctors, the lawyers, the insurance men. They even had a "Blue Vein Society," and if your dark skin obscured your throbbing pulse you were hardly a member of the elite.

Yet I was inconsolable the first time they turned me down   12
for Prince Charming. That was the year they picked Roger Jackson. Roger was not only dumb; he stuttered. But he was light enough to pass for white, and that was apparently sufficient.

In all fairness, however, it must be admitted that Roger   13
had other qualifications. His father owned the only colored saloon in town and was quite a power in local politics. In fact, Mr. Clinton Jackson had a lot to say about just who taught in the Booker T. Washington Colored Grammar School. So it was understandable that Roger should have been picked for Prince Charming.

My real heartbreak, however, came the year they picked   14
Sarah Williams for Sleeping Beauty. I had been in love with Sarah since kindergarten. She had soft light hair, bluish-gray eyes, and a dimple which stayed in her left cheek whether she was smiling or not.

Of course Sarah never encouraged me much. She never   15
answered any of my fervent love letters, and Rat was very scornful of my one-sided love affairs. "As long as she don't call you a black baboon," he sneered, "you'll keep on hanging around."

After Sarah was chosen for Sleeping Beauty, I went out for   16
the Prince Charming role with all my heart. If I had declaimed boldly in previous contests, I was matchless now. If I had bothered Mamma with rehearsals at home before, I pestered her to death this time. Yes, and I purloined my sister's can of Palmer's Skin Success.

I knew the Prince's role from start to finish, having played   17
the Head Evil Fairy opposite it for two seasons. And Prince

Charming was one character whose lines Miss LaPrade never varied much in her many versions. But although I never admitted it, even to myself, I knew I was doomed from the start. They gave the part to Leonardius Wright. Leonardius, of course, was yaller.

The teachers sensed my resentment. They were most   18
apologetic. They pointed out that I had been such a splendid Head Evil Fairy for two seasons that it would be a crime to let anybody else try the role. They reminded me that Mamma wouldn't have to buy any more cheesecloth because I could use my same old costume. They insisted that the Head Evil Fairy was even more important than Prince Charming because he was the one who cast the spell on Sleeping Beauty. So what could I do but accept?

I had never liked Leonardius Wright. He was a goody-   19
goody, and even Mamma was always throwing him up to me. But, above all, he too was in love with Sarah Williams. And now he got a chance to kiss Sarah every day in rehearsing the awakening scene.

Well, the show must go on, even for little black boys. So I   20
threw my soul into my part and made the Head Evil Fairy a character to be remembered. When I drew back from the couch of Sleeping Beauty and slunk away into the shadows at the approach of Prince Charming, my facial expression was indeed something to behold. When I was vanquished by the shining sword of Prince Charming in the last act, I was a little hammy perhaps—but terrific!

The attendance at our grand dramatic offering that year   21
was the best in its history. Even the white folks overflowed the two rows reserved for them, and a few were forced to sit in the intervening one. This created a delicate situation, but everybody tactfully ignored it.

When the curtain went up on the last act, the audience   22
was in fine fettle. Everything had gone well for me too—except for one spot in the second act. That was where Leonardius unexpectedly rapped me over the head with his sword as I slunk off into the shadows. That was not in the script, but Miss LaPrade quieted me down by saying it made a nice touch anyway. Rat said Leonardius did it on purpose.

The third act went on smoothly, though, until we came to   23
the vanquishing scene. That was where I slunk from the shadows for the last time and challenged Prince Charming to mortal combat. The hero reached for his shining sword—a bit un-

sportsmanlike, I always thought, since Miss LaPrade consistently left the Head Evil Fairy unarmed—and then it happened!

Later I protested loudly—but in vain—that it was a case of self-defense. I pointed out that Leonardius had a mean look in his eye. I cited the impromptu rapping he had given my head in the second act. But nobody would listen. They just wouldn't believe that Leonardius really intended to brain me when he reached for his sword. 24

Anyway, he didn't succeed. For the minute I saw that evil gleam in his eye—or was it my own?—I cut loose with a right to the chin, and Prince Charming dropped his shining sword and staggered back. His astonishment lasted only a minute, though, for he lowered his head and came charging in, fists flailing. There was nothing yellow about Leonardius but his skin. 25

The audience thought the scrap was something new Miss LaPrade had written in. They might have kept on thinking so if Miss LaPrade hadn't been screaming so hysterically from the sidelines. And if Rat Joiner hadn't decided that this was as good a time as any to settle old scores. So he turned around and took a sock at the male Good Fairy nearest him. 26

When the curtain rang down, the forces of Good and Evil were locked in combat. And Sleeping Beauty was wide awake and streaking for the wings. 27

They rang the curtain back up fifteen minutes later, and we finished the play. I lay down and expired according to specifications but Prince Charming will probably remember my sneering corpse to his dying day. They wouldn't let me appear in the grand dramatic offering at all the next year. But I didn't care. I couldn't have been Prince Charming anyway. 28

Discussion Questions

1. Why does Poston say that the Prince Charming presentation was only a reflection of the daily community life in Hopkinsville?
2. How would you characterize the narrator?
3. Why was the narrator not given the role of Prince Charming although he was qualified for the part?
4. From the context of the story, can you explain the meaning of the Blue Vein Society (paragraph 11) and Palmer's Skin Success (paragraph 16)?
5. What do you think led to the fight between the narrator and Prince Charming?

6. What does the casting of the roles reveal about the attitudes of the teachers, the students, and the parents?

7. How does Poston use cause and effect to illustrate the story's theme?

8. For what audience is this story written?

Writing Assignments

1. Write an essay analyzing the story's symbolic meanings of good and evil. Compare or contrast these meanings with society's view of them.

2. Write an essay about your experiences of discrimination because of ethnic, gender, or other differences.

3. Write an essay analyzing the causes and/or the effects of intraracial prejudice.

DEBUT

Kristin Hunter

Novelist Kristin Hunter (1931–) was born in Philadelphia and graduated from the University of Pennsylvania. She has worked as an elementary school teacher, an advertising copywriter, a television scriptwriter, and a professor of creative writing at the University of Pennsylvania. Her novels include God Bless the Child *(1964),* The Landlord *(1966),* The Survivors *(1975), and* The Lakestown Rebellion *(1978). She has also written several young adult books:* The Soul Brothers and Sister Lou *(1968),* Boss Cat *(1971), and* Lou in the Limelight *(1981). In this selection, which first appeared in* Negro Digest *(1968), a young girl examines her feelings while preparing for her debutante ball.*

Vocabulary

tattered	(9)	ragged, torn
ingratiated	(16)	brought into favor
precipitate	(19)	hasten
brazen	(23)	shameless, harsh
guffawed	(38)	laughed loudly
tapestry	(55)	a woven design
awe	(56)	wonder, respect
diffidence	(56)	lack of confidence, shyness
grating	(84)	irritating

"Hold *still*, Judy," Mrs. Simmons said around the spray of pins   1
that protruded dangerously from her mouth. She gave the thirtieth tug to the tight sash at the waist of the dress. "Now walk over there and turn around slowly."

The dress, Judy's first long one, was white organdy over   2
taffeta, with spaghetti straps that bared her round brown shoulders and a floating skirt and a wide sash that cascaded in a butterfly effect behind. It was a dream, but Judy was sick and tired of the endless fittings she had endured so that she might wear it at the Debutantes' Ball. Her thoughts leaped ahead to the Ball itself . . .

"*Slowly*, I said!" Mrs. Simmons' dark, angular face was al-   3
ways grim, but now it was screwed into an expression resembling a prune. Judy, starting nervously, began to revolve by moving her feet an inch at a time.

Her mother watched her critically. "No, it's still not right.   4
I'll just have to rip out that waistline seam again."

"Oh, Mother!" Judy's impatience slipped out at last. "No-   5
body's going to notice all those little details."

"They will too. They'll be watching you every minute, hop-   6
ing to see something wrong. You've got to be the *best*. Can't you
get that through your head?" Mrs. Simmons gave a sigh of despair. "You better start noticin' 'all those little details' yourself. I
can't do it for you all your life. Now turn around and stand up
straight."

"Oh, Mother," Judy said, close to tears from being made to   7
turn and pose while her feet itched to be dancing, "I can't stand
it any more!"

"You can't stand it, huh? How do you think *I* feel?" Mrs.   8
Simmons said in her harshest tone.

Judy was immediately ashamed, remembering the weeks   9
her mother had spent at the sewing machine, pricking her already tattered fingers with needles and pins, and the great
weight of sacrifice that had been borne on Mrs. Simmons'
shoulders for the past two years so that Judy might bare hers
at the Ball.

"All right, take it off," her mother said. "I'm going to take it   10
up the street to Mrs. Luby and let her help me. It's got to be
right or I won't let you leave the house."

"Can't we just leave it the way it is, Mother?" Judy pleaded   11
without hope of success. "I think it's perfect."

"You would," Mrs. Simmons said tartly as she folded the   12
dress and prepared to bear it out of the room. "Sometimes I
think I'll never get it through your head. You got to look just
right and act just right. That Rose Griffin and those other girls
can afford to be careless, maybe, but you can't. You're gonna
be the darkest, poorest one there."

Judy shivered in her new lace strapless bra and her old,   13
childish knit snuggies.[1] "You make it sound like a battle I'm
going to instead of just a dance."

"It is a battle," her mother said firmly. "It starts tonight   14
and it goes on for the rest of your life. The battle to hold your
head up and get someplace and be somebody. We've done all
we can for you, your father and I. Now you've got to start fighting some on your own." She gave Judy a slight smile; her voice

---

[1] snuggies   (13)   Thigh-length cotton underwear worn for extra warmth.

softened a little. "You'll do all right, don't worry. Try and get some rest this afternoon. Just don't mess up your hair."

"All right, Mother," Judy said listlessly.   15

She did not really think her father had much to do with   16
anything that happened to her. It was her mother who had in-
gratiated her way into the Gay Charmers two years ago, taking
all sorts of humiliation from the better-dressed, better-off,
lighter-skinned women, humbly making and mending their
dresses, fixing food for their meetings, addressing more mail and
selling more tickets than anyone else. The club had put it off as
long as they could, but finally they had to admit Mrs. Simmons
to membership because she worked so hard. And that meant, of
course, that Judy would be on the list for this year's Ball.

Her father, a quiet carpenter who had given up any other   17
ambitions years ago, did not think much of Negro society or his
wife's fierce determination to launch Judy into it. "Just keep
clean and be decent," he would say. "That's all anybody has to
do."

Her mother always answered, "If that's all *I* did we'd still   18
be on relief," and he would shut up with shame over the years
when he had been laid off repeatedly and her days' work and
sewing had kept them going. Now he had steady work but she
refused to quit, as if she expected it to end at any moment. The
intense energy that burned in Mrs. Simmons' large dark eyes
had scorched her features into permanent irony. She worked
day and night and spent her spare time scheming and planning. Whatever her personal ambitions had been, Judy knew
she blamed Mr. Simmons for their failure; now all her schemes
revolved around their only child.

Judy went to her mother's window and watched her stride   19
down the street with the dress until she was hidden by the
high brick wall that went around two sides of their house. Then
she returned to her own room. She did not get dressed because
she was afraid of pulling a sweater over her hair—her mother
would notice the difference even if it looked all right to Judy—
and because she was afraid that doing anything, even getting
dressed, might precipitate her into the battle. She drew a stool
up to her window and looked out. She had no real view, but
she liked her room. The wall hid the crowded tenement houses
beyond the alley, and from its cracks and bumps and depres-
sions she could construct any imaginary landscape she chose.
It was how she had spent most of the free hours of her dreamy
adolescence.

"Hey, can I go?"   20

It was the voice of an invisible boy in the alley. As another   21
boy chuckled, Judy recognized the familiar ritual; if you said
yes, they said, "Can I go with you?" It had been tried on her
dozens of times. She always walked past, head in the air, as if
she had not heard. Her mother said that was the only thing to
do; if they knew she was a lady, they wouldn't dare bother her.
But this time a girl's voice, cool and assured, answered.

"If you think you're big enough," it said.   22

It was Lucy Mae Watkins; Judy could picture her standing   23
there in a tight dress with bright, brazen eyes.

"I'm big enough to give you a baby," the boy answered.   24

Judy would die if a boy every spoke to her like that, but   25
she knew Lucy Mae could handle it. Lucy Mae could handle all
the boys, even if they ganged up on her, because she had been
born knowing something other girls had to learn.

"Aw, you ain't big enough to give me a shoe-shine," she   26
told him.

"Come here and I'll show you how big I am," the boy said.   27

"Yeah, Lucy Mae, what's happenin'?" another, younger boy   28
said. "Come here and tell us."

Lucy Mae laughed. "What I'm puttin' down is too strong   29
for little boys like you."

"Come here a minute, baby," the first boy said. "I got a cig-   30
arette for you."

"Aw, I ain't studyin' your cigarettes," Lucy Mae answered.   31
But her voice was closer, directly below Judy. There were the
sounds of a scuffle and Lucy Mae's muffled laughter. When she
spoke her voice sounded raw and cross. "Come on now, boy.
Cut it out and give me the damn cigarette." There was more
scuffling, and the sharp crack of a slap, and then Lucy Mae
said, "Cut it out, I said. Just for that I'm gonna take 'em all."
The clack of high heels rang down the sidewalk with a boy's
clumsy shoes in pursuit.

Judy realized that there were three of them down there.   32
"Let her go, Buster," one said. "You can't catch her now."

"Aw, hell, man, she took the whole damn pack," the one   33
called Buster complained.

"That'll learn you!" Lucy Mae's voice mocked from down   34
the street. "Don't mess with nothin' you can't handle."

"Hey, Lucy Mae. Hey, I heard Rudy Grant already gave you   35
a baby," a second boy called out.

"Yeah. Is that true, Lucy Mae?" the youngest one yelled.   36

There was no answer. She must be a block away by now.   37

For a moment the hidden boys were silent; then one of   38
them guffawed directly below Judy, and the other two joined in
the secret male laughter that was oddly high-pitched and femi-
nine.

"Aw, man, I don't know what you all laughin' about,"   39
Buster finally grumbled. "That girl took all my cigarettes. You
got some, Leroy?"

"Naw," the second boy said.   40

"Me neither," the third one said.   41

"What we gonna do? I ain't got but fifteen cent. Hell, man,   42
I want more than a feel for a pack of cigarettes." There was an
unpleasant whine in Buster's voice. "Hell, for a pack of cigarettes I want a bitch to come across."

"She will next time, man," the boy called Leroy said.   43

"She better," Buster said. "You know she better. If she   44
pass by here again, we gonna jump her, you hear?"

"Sure, man," Leroy said. "The three of us can grab her   45
easy."

"Then we can all three of us have some fun. Oh, *yeah,*   46
man," the youngest boy said. He sounded as if he might be
about 14.

Leroy said, "We oughta get Roland and J.T. too. For a   47
whole pack of cigarettes she oughta treat all five of us."

"Aw, man, why tell Roland and J.T.?" the youngest voice   48
whined. "They ain't in it. Them was *our* cigarettes."

"They was *my* cigarettes, you mean," Buster said with au-   49
thority. "You guys better quit it before I decide to cut you out."

"Oh, man, don't do that. We with you, you know that."   50

"Sure, Buster, we your aces, man."   51

"All right, that's better." There was a minute of silence.   52

Then, "What we gonna do with the girl, Buster?" the   53
youngest one wanted to know.

"When she come back we gonna jump the bitch, man. We   54
gonna jump her and grab her. Then we gonna turn her every
way but loose." He went on, spinning a crude fantasy that got
wilder each time he retold it, until it became so secretive that
their voices dropped to a low indistinct murmur punctuated by
guffaws. Now and then Judy could distinguish the word "girl"
or the other word they used for it; these words always produced the loudest guffaws of all. She shook off her fear with
the thought that Lucy Mae was too smart to pass there again
today. She had heard them at their dirty talk in the alley before

and had always been successful in ignoring it; it had nothing to
do with her, the wall protected her from their kind. All the ugliness was on their side of it, and this side was hers to fill with
beauty.

    She turned on her radio to shut them out completely and   55
began to weave her tapestry to its music. More for practice
than anything else, she started by picturing the maps of the
places to which she intended to travel, then went on to the
faces of her friends. Rose Griffin's sharp, Indian profile appeared on the wall. Her coloring was like an Indian's too and
her hair was straight and black and glossy. Judy's hair, naturally none of these things, had been "done" four days ago so
that tonight it would be "old" enough to have a gloss as nat-
ural-looking as Rose's. But Rose, despite her handsome looks,
was silly; her voice broke constantly into high-pitched giggles
and she became even sillier and more nervous around boys.

    Judy was not sure that she knew how to act around boys   56
either. The sisters kept boys and girls apart at the Catholic
high school where her parents sent her to keep her away from
low-class kids. But she felt that she knew a secret; tonight, in
that dress, with her hair in a sophisticated upsweep, she would
be transformed into a poised princess. Tonight all the college
boys her mother described so eagerly would rush to dance with
her, and then from somewhere *the boy* would appear. She did
not know his name; she neither knew nor cared whether he
went to college, but she imagined that he would be as dark as
she was, and that there would be awe and diffidence in his
manner as he bent to kiss her hand . . .

    A waltz swelled from the radio; the wall, turning blue in   57
deepening twilight, came alive with whirling figures. Judy rose
and began to go through the steps she had rehearsed for so
many weeks. She swirled with a practiced smile on her face,
holding an imaginary skirt at her side; turned, dipped, and
flicked on her bedside lamp without missing a fraction of the
beat. Faster and faster she danced with her imaginary partner,
to an inner music that was better than the sounds on the radio. She was "coming out," and tonight the world would discover what it had been waiting for all these years.

    "Aw, git it, baby." She ignored it as she would ignore the   58
crowds that lined the streets to watch her pass on her way to
the Ball.

    "Aw, do your number." She waltzed on, safe and secure on   59
her side of the wall.

"Can I come up there and do it with you?"   60

At this she stopped, paralyzed. Somehow they had come   61
over the wall or around it and into her room.

"Man, I sure like the view from here," the youngest boy   62
said. "How come we never tried this view before?"

She came to life, ran quickly to the lamp and turned it off,   63
but not before Buster said, "Yeah, and the back view is fine,
too."

"Aw, she turned off the light," a voice complained.   64

"Put it on again, baby, we don't mean no harm."   65

"Let us see you dance some more. I bet you can really do 66
it."

"Yeah, I bet she can shimmy on down."   67

"You know it, man."   68

"Come on down here, baby," Buster's voice urged softly   69
dangerously. "I got a cigarette for you."

"Yeah, and he got something else for you, too."   70

Judy flattened against her closet door, gradually lost her   71
urge to scream. She realized that she was shivering in her underwear. Taking a deep breath, she opened the closet door and
found her robe. She thought of going to the window and yelling
down, "You don't have a thing I want. Do you understand?" But
she had more important things to do.

Wrapping her hair in protective plastic, she ran a full   72
steaming tub and dumped in half a bottle of her mother's favorite cologne. At first she scrubbed herself furiously, irritating
her skin. But finally she stopped, knowing she would never be
able to get cleaner than this again. She could not wash away
the thing they considered dirty, the thing that made them pronounce "girl" in the same way as the other four-letter words
they wrote on the wall in the alley; it was part of her, just as it
was part of her mother and Rose Griffin and Lucy Mae. She relaxed then because it was true that the boys in the alley did not
have a thing she wanted. She had what they wanted, and the
knowledge replaced her shame with a strange, calm feeling of
power.

After her bath she splashed on more cologne and spent 40   73
minutes on her makeup, erasing and retracing her eyebrows
six times until she was satisfied. She went to her mother's
room then and found the dress, finished and freshly pressed,
on its hanger.

When Mrs. Simmons came upstairs to help her daughter   74
she found her sitting on the bench before the vanity mirror as

if it were a throne. She looked young and arrogant and beautiful and perfect and cold.

"Why, you're dressed already," Mrs. Simmons said in sur-   75
prise. While she stared, Judy rose with perfect, icy grace and
glided to the center of the room. She stood there motionless as
a mannequin.

"I want you to fix the hem, Mother," she directed. "It's still   76
uneven in back."

Her mother went down obediently on her knees muttering,   77
"It looks all right to me." She put in a couple of pins. "That better?"

"Yes," Judy said with a brief glance at the mirror. "You'll   78
have to sew it on me, Mother. I can't take it off now. I'd ruin my
hair."

Mrs. Simmons went to fetch her sewing things, returned,   79
and surveyed her daughter. "You sure did a good job on yourself, I must say," she admitted grudgingly. "Can't find a thing to
complain about. You'll look as good as anybody there."

"Of course, Mother," Judy said as Mrs. Simmons knelt and   80
sewed. "I don't know what you were so worried about." Her secret feeling of confidence had returned, stronger than ever, but
the evening ahead was no longer the vague girlish fantasy she
had pictured on the wall; it had hard, clear outlines leading up
to a definite goal. She would be the belle of the Ball because
she knew more than Rose Griffin and her silly friends; more
than her mother; more, even, than Lucy Mae, because she
knew better than to settle for a mere pack of cigarettes.

"There," her mother said, breaking the thread. She got up.   81
"I never expected to get you ready this early. Ernest Lee won't
be here for another hour."

"That silly Ernest Lee," Judy said, with a new contempt in   82
her young voice. Until tonight she had been pleased by the
thought of going to the dance with Ernest Lee; he was nice, she
felt comfortable with him, and he might even be the awe-struck
boy of her dream. He was a dark, serious neighborhood boy
who could not afford to go to college; Mrs. Simmons had reluctantly selected him to take Judy to the dance because all the
Gay Charmers' sons were spoken for. Now, with an undertone
of excitement, Judy said, "I'm going to ditch him after the first
dance, Mother. You'll see. I'm going to come home with one of
the college boys."

"It's very nice, Ernest Lee," she told him an hour later   83
when he handed her the white orchid, "but it's rather small. I'm

gong to wear it on my wrist, if you don't mind." And then, dazzling him with a smile of sweetest cruelty, she stepped back
and waited while he fumbled with the door.

"You know, Edward, I'm not worried about her any more," 84
Mrs. Simmons said to her husband after the children were
gone. Her voice became harsh and grating. "Put down that paper and listen to me! Aren't you interested in your child?—
That's better," she said as he complied meekly. "I was saying, I
do believe she's learned what I've been trying to teach her, after
all."

Discussion Questions

1. What type of person is Mrs. Simmons? What had she been trying
to teach Judy?
2. What are the Gay Charmers? Why was it so important for Mrs.
Simmons to join them?
3. What is Mrs. Simmons's relationship with her husband?
4. What effect does the boys' conversation with and about Lucy Mae
have on Judy? How does Lucy Mae differ from Judy?
5. What is the significance of the wall?
6. What are the intraracial prejudices reflected in the story? What
prejudice of her own does Judy acquire at the end of the story?
7. How does Hunter's use of comparison and contrast help the
reader understand Judy's change in attitude?
8. To what extent does Hunter's use of dialogue add to the reader's
understanding of the characters?

Writing Assignments

1. Write an essay describing a time when you gained a new awareness of something.
2. Write an essay comparing and/or contrasting your views on an
issue with those of your parent(s).
3. Write an essay about your experiences with intraracial prejudice.

TRUE LOVE LOST AND FOUND

Charles W. Chesnutt

Charles Waddell Chesnutt (1858–1932), born in Cleveland, Ohio, and primarily self-educated, was a teacher and a principal in the public schools of North Carolina. He was admitted to the Ohio bar in 1887 and worked as a court reporter and a commercial stenographer. Hailed as a master craftsman of the short story, Chesnutt's works consist of two collections of short stories: The Conjure Woman *(1899) and* The Wife of His Youth and Other Stories of the Color Line *(1899), from which this excerpt is taken. He also wrote three novels:* The House Behind the Cedars *(1900),* The Marrow of Tradition *(1901), and* The Colonel's Dream *(1905). Chesnutt, considered the first African American writer of fiction whose work was generally critiqued without regard to race, wrote about the complexities of class and color during the Reconstruction period. A major theme of Chesnutt's works, as illustrated in the following excerpt, is the tragic situation of intraracial prejudice.*

Vocabulary

affinity	(2)	similarity, likeness
assail	(3)	attack
bulwark	(3)	defense, protection
prerequisite	(3)	required beforehand
servile	(3)	like slaves or servants
grosser	(3)	more wrong, more obscene
irreproachable	(5)	faultless
vivacity	(6)	liveliness
epoch	(7)	period of time
laxity	(7)	slackness
nether	(8)	lower
buxom	(10)	healthily plump and ample
brooch	(12)	ornamental pin with a clasp
countenance	(28)	face
emphatically	(33)	forcibly
incredulously	(39)	disbelievingly
mincing	(45)	dainty, short

I

Mr. Ryder was going to give a ball. There were several reasons   1
why this was an opportune time for such an event.

Mr. Ryder might aptly be called the dean of the Blue   2
Veins. The original Blue Veins were a little society of colored
persons organized in a certain Northern city shortly after the
war. Its purpose was to establish and maintain correct social
standards among a people whose social condition presented almost unlimited room for improvement. By accident, combined
perhaps with some natural affinity, the society consisted of individuals who were, generally speaking, more white than black.
Some envious outsider made the suggestion that no one was eligible for membership who was not white enough to show blue
veins. The suggestion was readily adopted by those who were
not of the favored few, and since that time the society, though
possessing a longer and more pretentious name, had been
known far and wide as the "Blue Vein Society," and its members as the "Blue Veins."

The Blue Veins did not allow that any such requirement   3
existed for admission to their circle, but, on the contrary, declared that character and culture were the only things considered; and that if most of their members were light-colored, it
was because such persons, as a rule, had had better opportunities to qualify themselves for membership. Opinions differed,
too, as to the usefulness of the society. There were those who
had been known to assail it violently as a glaring example of
the very prejudice from which the colored race had suffered
most; and later, when such critics had succeeded in getting on
the inside, they had been heard to maintain with zeal and
earnestness that the society was a lifeboat, an anchor, a bul-
wark and a shield,—a pillar of cloud by day and of fire by night,
to guide their people through the social wilderness. Another al-
leged prerequisite for Blue Vein membership was that of free
birth; and while there was really no such requirement, it is
doubtless true that very few of the members would have been
unable to meet it if there had been. If there were one or two of
the older members who had come up from the South and from
slavery, their history presented enough romantic circumstances to rob their servile origin of its grosser aspects.

While there were no such tests of eligibility, it is true   4
that the Blue Veins had their notions on these subjects, and

that not all of them were equally liberal in regard to the things they collectively disclaimed. Mr. Ryder was one of the most conservative. Though he had not been among the founders of the society, but had come in some years later, his genius for social leadership was such that he had speedily become its recognized adviser and head, the custodian of its standards, and the preserver of its traditions. He shaped its social policy, was active in providing for its entertainment, and when the interest fell off, as it sometimes did, he fanned the embers until they burst again into a cheerful flame.

There were still other reasons for his popularity. While he was not as white as some of the Blue Veins, his appearance was such as to confer distinction upon them. His features were of a refined type, his hair was almost straight; he was always neatly dressed; his manners were irreproachable, and his morals above suspicion. He had come to Groveland a young man, and obtaining employment in the office of a railroad company as messenger had in time worked himself up to the position of stationery clerk, having charge of the distribution of the office supplies for the whole company. Although the lack of early training had hindered the orderly development of a naturally fine mind, it had not prevented him from doing a great deal of reading or from forming decidedly literary tastes. Poetry was his passion. He could repeat whole pages of the great English poets; and if his pronunciation was sometimes faulty, his eye, his voice, his gestures, would respond to the changing sentiment with a precision that revealed a poetic soul and disarmed criticism. He was economical, and had saved money; he owned and occupied a very comfortable house on a respectable street. His residence was handsomely furnished, containing among other things a good library, especially rich in poetry, a piano, and some choice engravings. He generally shared his house with some young couple, who looked after his wants and were company for him; for Mr. Ryder was a single man. In the early days of his connection with the Blue Veins he had been regarded as quite a catch, and young ladies and their mothers had manoeuvred with much ingenuity to capture him. Not, however, until Mrs. Molly Dixon visited Groveland had any woman ever made him wish to change his condition to that of a married man.

Mrs. Dixon had come to Groveland from Washington in the spring, and before the summer was over she had won Mr. Ryder's heart. She possessed many attractive qualities. She was much younger than he; in fact, he was old enough to have been her father, though no one knew exactly how old he was. She was whiter than he, and better educated. She had moved in the best colored society of the country, at Washington, and had taught in the schools of that city. Such a superior person had been eagerly welcomed to the Blue Vein Society, and had taken a leading part in its activities. Mr. Ryder had at first been attracted by her charms of person, for she was very good looking and not over twenty-five; then by her refined manners and the vivacity of her wit. Her husband had been a government clerk and at his death had left a considerable life insurance. She was visiting friends in Groveland, and, finding the town and the people to her liking, had prolonged her stay indefinitely. She had not seemed displeased at Mr. Ryder's attentions, but on the contrary had given him every proper encouragement; indeed, a younger and less cautious man would long since have spoken. But he had made up his mind, and had only to determine the time when he would ask her to be his wife. He decided to give a ball in her honor, and at some time during the evening of the ball to offer her his heart and hand. He had no special fears about the outcome, but, with a little touch of romance, he wanted the surroundings to be in harmony with his own feelings when he should have received the answer he expected.

Mr. Ryder resolved that this ball should mark an epoch in the social history of Groveland. He knew, of course,—no one could know better,—the entertainments that had taken place in past years, and what must be done to surpass them. His ball must be worthy of the lady whose honor it was to be given, and must, by the quality of its guests, set an example for the future. He had observed of late a growing liberality, almost a laxity, in social matters, even among members of his own set, and had several times been forced to meet in a social way persons whose complexions and callings in life were hardly up to the standard which he considered proper for the society to maintain. He had a theory of his own. 7

"I have no race prejudice," he would say, "but we people of mixed blood are ground between the upper and the nether millstone. Our fate lies between absorption by the white race and extinction in the black. The one doesn't want us yet, but may take us in time. The other would welcome us, but it would be for us a backward step. 'With malice towards none, with charity for all,' we must do the best we can for ourselves and those who are to follow us. Self-preservation is the first law of nature." 8

His ball would serve by its exclusiveness to counteract lev- 9
eling tendencies, and his marriage with Mrs. Dixon would help
to further the upward process of absorption he had been wishing and waiting for.

II

The ball was to take place on Friday night. The house had been 10
put in order, the carpets covered with canvas, the halls and
stairs decorated with palms and potted plants; and in the afternoon Mr. Ryder sat on his front porch, which the shade of a
vine running up over a wire netting made a cool and pleasant
lounging place. He expected to respond to the toast "The
Ladies" at the supper, and from a volume of Tennyson—his favorite poet—was fortifying himself with apt quotations. The volume was open at "A Dream of Fair Women." His eyes fell on
these lines, and he read them aloud to judge better of their effect:—

> At length I saw a lady within call,
>   Stiller than chisell'd marble, standing there;
> A daughter of the gods, divinely tall,
>   And most divinely fair.

He marked the verse, and turning the page read the stanza beginning,—

> O sweet pale Margaret,
> O rare pale Margaret.

He weighed the passage a moment, and decided that it would
not do. Mrs. Dixon was the palest lady he expected at the ball,
and she was of a rather ruddy complexion, and of lively disposition and buxom build. So he ran over the leaves until his eye
rested on the description of Queen Guinevere:—

> She seem'd a part of joyous Spring:
> A gown of grass-green silk she wore,
> Buckled with golden clasps before;
> A light-green tuft of plumes she bore
> Closed in a golden ring.

• • •

> She look'd so lovely, as she sway'd
> The rein with dainty finger-tips,
> A man had given all other bliss,
> And all his worldly worth for this,
> To waste his whole heart in one kiss
> Upon her perfect lips.

As Mr. Ryder murmured these words audibly, with an appreciative thrill, he heard the latch of his gate click, and a light footfall sounding on the steps. He turned his head, and saw a woman standing before his door. **11**

She was a little woman, not five feet tall, and proportioned to her height. Although she stood erect, and looked around her with very bright and restless eyes, she seemed quite old; for her face was crossed and recrossed with a hundred wrinkles, and around the edges of her bonnet could be seen protruding here and there a tuft of short gray wool. She wore a blue calico gown of ancient cut, a little red shawl fastened around her shoulders with an old-fashioned brass brooch, and a large bonnet profusely ornamented with faded red and yellow artificial flowers. And she was very black,—so black that her toothless gums, revealed when she opened her mouth to speak, were not red, but blue. She looked like a bit of the old plantation life, summoned up from the past by the wave of a magician's wand, as the poet's fancy had called into being the gracious shapes of which Mr. Ryder had just been reading. **12**

He rose from his chair and came over to where she stood. **13**

"Good-afternoon, madam," he said. **14**

"Good-evenin', suh," she answered, ducking suddenly with a quaint curtsy. Her voice was shrill and piping, but softened somewhat by age. "Is dis yere whar Mistuh Ryduh lib, suh?" she asked, looking around her doubtfully, and glancing into the open windows, through which some of the preparations for the evening were visible. **15**

"Yes," he replied, with an air of kindly patronage, unconsciously flattered by her manner. "I am Mr. Ryder. Did you want to see me?" **16**

"Yas, suh, ef I ain't 'sturbin' of you too much." **17**

"Not at all. Have a seat over here behind the vine, where it is cool. What can I do for you?" **18**

"'Scuse me, suh," she continued, when she had sat down on the edge of a chair, "'scuse me, suh. I's lookin' for my hus- **19**

ban'. I heerd you wuz a big man an' had libbed heah a long
time, an' I 'lowed you wouldn't min' ef I'd come roun' an' ax you
ef you'd ever heerd of a merlatter man by de name er Sam Taylor 'quirin' roun' in de chu'ches ermongs' de people fer his wife
'Liza Jane?"

    Mr. Ryder seemed to think for a moment.   20

    "There used to be many such cases right after the war," he   21
said, "but it has been so long that I have forgotten them. There
are very few now. But tell me your story, and it may refresh my
memory."

    She sat back farther in her chair so as to be more comfort-   22
able, and folded her withered hands in her lap.

    "My name's 'Liza," she began, "'Liza Jane. W'en I wuz   23
young I us'ter b'long ter Marse Bob Smif, down in ole Missoura.
I wuz bawn down dere. W'en I wuz a gal I wuz married ter a
man named Jim. But Jim died, an' after dat I married a merlatter man named Sam Taylor. Sam wuz free-bawn, but his
mammy and daddy died, an' de w'ite folks 'prenticed him ter
my marster fer ter work fer 'im 'tel he wuz growed up. Sam
worked in de fiel', an' I wuz de cook. One day Ma'y Ann, ole
miss's maid, came rushin' out ter de kitchen, an' says she,
''Liza Jane, ole marse gwine sell yo' Sam down de ribber.'

    "'Go way f'm yere,' says I; 'my husban' 's free!'   24

    "'Don' make no diff'ence. I heerd ole marse tell ole miss he   25
wuz gwine take yo' Sam 'way wid 'im ter-morrow, fer he needed
money, an' he knowed whar he could git a t'ousan' dollats fer
Sam an' no questions axed.'

    "W'en Sam come home f'm de fiel' dat night, I tole him   26
bout ole marse gwine steal 'im, an' Sam run erway. His time
wuz mos' up, an' he swo' dat w'en he wuz twenty-one he would
come back an' he'p me run erway, er else save up de money ter
buy my freedom. An' I know he'd 'a' done it, fer he thought a
heap er me, Sam did. But w'en he come back he didn' fin' me,
fer I wuzn' dere. Ole marse had heerd dat I warned Sam, so he
had me whip' an' sol' down de ribber.

    "Den de wah broke out, an' w'en it wuz ober de cullud   27
folks wuz scattered. I went back ter de ole home; but Sam
wuzn' dere, an' I could n' l'arn nuffin' 'bout 'im. But I knowed
he'd be'n dere to look fer me an' had n' foun' me, an' had gone
erway ter hunt fer me.

    "I's be'n lookin' fer 'im eber sence," she added simply, as   28
though twenty-five years were but a couple of weeks, "an' I
knows he's be'n lookin' fer me. Fer he sot a heap er sto' by me,

Sam did, an' I know he's be'n huntin' fer me all dese years,—
'less'n he's be'n sick er sump'n, so he could n' work er out'n his
head, so he could n' 'member his promise. I went back down de
ribber, fer I 'lowed he'd gone down dere lookin' for me. I's be'n
ter Noo Orleens, an' Atlanty an' Charleston, an' Richmon'; an'
w'en I'd be'n all ober de Souf I come ter de Norf. Fer I knows I'll
fin' 'im some er dese days," she added softly, "'er he'll fin' me,
an' den we'll bofe be as happy in freedom as we wuz in de ole
days befo' de wah." A smile stole over her withered counte-
nance as she paused a moment, and her bright eyes softened
into a faraway look.

This was the substance of the old woman's story. She had   29
wandered a little here and there. Mr. Ryder was looking at her
curiously when she finished.

"How have you lived all these years?" he asked.   30

"Cookin', suh. I's a good cook. Does you know anybody   31
w'at needs a good cook, suh? I's stoppin wid a cullud fam'ly
roun' de corner yonder 'tel I kin git a place."

"Do you really expect to find your husband? He may be   32
dead long ago."

She shook her head emphatically. "Oh no, he ain't dead.   33
De signs an' de token tells me. I dremp three nights runnin'
on'y dis las' week dat I foun' him."

"He may have married another woman. Your slave mar-   34
riage would not have prevented him, for you never lived with
him after the war, and without that your marriage doesn't
count."

"Wouldn' make no diff'ence wid Sam. He would n' marry   35
no yuther 'ooman 'tel he foun' out 'bout me. I knows it," she
added. "Sump'n 's be'n tellin' me all dese years dat I's gwine fin'
Sam 'fo' I dies."

"Perhaps he's outgrown you, and climbed up in the world   36
where he wouldn't care to have you find him."

"No, indeed, suh," she replied, "Sam ain' dat kin' er man.   37
He wuz good ter me, Sam wuz, but he wuzn' much good ter nobody e'se, fer he wuz one er de triflin'es' han's on de plantation.
I 'spec's ter haf ter suppo't 'im w'en I fin' 'im, fer he nebber
would work 'less'n he had ter. But den he wuz free, an' he didn'
git no pay fer his work, an' I don' blame 'im much. Mebbe he's
done better sence he run erway, but I ain' 'spectin' much."

"You may have passed him on the street a hundred times   38
during the twenty-five years and not have known him; time
works great changes."

She smiled incredulously. "I'd know 'im 'mongs' a hund'ed   39
men. Fer dey wuzn' no yuther merlatter man like my man Sam,
an' I couldn' be mistook. I's toted his picture roun' wid me
twenty-five years."

"May I see it?" asked Mr. Ryder. "It might help me to re-   40
member whether I have seen the original."

As she drew a small parcel from her bosom he saw that it   41
was fastened to a string that went around her neck. Removing
several wrappers, she brought to light an old-fashioned daguerreotype[1] in a black case. He looked long and intently at
the portrait. It was faded with time, but the features were still
distinct, and it was easy to see what manner of man it had represented.

He closed the case, and with a slow movement handed it   42
back to her.

"I don't know of any man in town who goes by that name,"   43
he said, "nor have I heard of any one making such inquiries.
But if you will leave me your address, I will give the matter
some attention, and if I find out anything I will let you know."

She gave him the number of a house in the neighborhood,   44
and went away, after thanking him warmly.

He wrote the address on the fly-leaf of the volume of Ten-   45
nyson, and, when she had gone, rose to his feet and stood looking after her curiously. As she walked down the street with
mincing step, he saw several persons whom she passed turn
and look back at her with a smile of kindly amusement. When
she had turned the corner, he went upstairs to his bedroom,
and stood for a long time before the mirror of his dressing-case,
gazing thoughtfully at the reflection of his own face.

Discussion Questions

1. What was the Blue Vein Society? Why do you think Chesnutt
   provides so much information about this society?
2. What type of person is Mr. Ryder?
3. What role did skin color play in the lives of African Americans
   during this time? Has this role changed today? Why or why not?
4. Is it significant that Liza Jane has searched for her husband for
   twenty-five years? Explain your answer.

[1] daguerreotype (41)   A photograph made by an early method on a plate of
chemically treated metal or glass, named for French inventor L.J.M. Daguerre
(1789–1851).

5. How does Liza Jane characterize Sam? Can you guess who Sam really is?

6. To what extent does Chesnutt use comparison and contrast to develop the theme of the story?

7. To what extent does black dialect help the reader understand the character of Liza Jane?

Writing Assignments

1. Write an essay that describes how you treated someone after a long separation or how someone treated you after a long separation.

2. Write an essay illustrating the existence or nonexistence of intraracial prejudice today.

3. Write an essay about an incident you viewed one way in the past and have come to view differently now. Explain why you think your views have changed.

Student Essay:
BLACK IS BEAUTIFUL—ALL SHADES

Andrea Providence Robinson

Vocabulary

preferential (3)   showing that one favors something or someone over another

illustrious (4)   brilliantly outstanding

Recently, while sitting in my doctor's waiting room, two dark-skinned sisters were engaged in conversation. I overheard one woman say, "I don't want my children to come out light." After hearing this statement, I swelled with so much anger that I could no longer bear to hear another word of their conversation. Without thinking, I immediately sprang up from my seat and walked away. I was upset over the ignorance that still exists within our culture.   1

It really puzzles me, how we have gone as far as to create stereotypes about one another—stereotypes that include making up such myths as "the blacker the berry, the sweeter the juice," or as some women would believe, "All that men are interested in is light skin and long hair."   2

Many of the stereotypes of today date back to slavery when the light-skinned slave children received preferential treatment over the dark-skinned slave children. In the 1940s anthropologists conducted studies to answer the question, "Why are African American men seeking to marry lighter complexioned women?" Well, times have certainly changed. We are now more culturally aware of our history and have more pride in it. Also, color barriers have become less a factor in entertainment, sports, and the workplace. But I ask, if times have changed so much, then why is dark-skinned vs. light-skinned still an issue? In today's black music videos, for example, the love interest is usually a fair-skinned, long-haired, hazel-eyed black woman. We watch these videos and subconsciously allow them to arouse resentment against each other's skin color.   3

We cannot allow the media and others to have such a profound impression on our feelings about one another. Instead of indulging ourselves in insignificant concerns such as skin color, we must embrace our rich and illustrious culture and   4 celebrate the beauty of the variety of shades our culture has to offer—like that little chocolate-complexioned boy who lives down the street, that caramel cream–colored teenage girl who works at the mall, or that eggshell-complexioned woman who watches the neighborhood children.

Let us not engage in name calling, such as "high-yellow," "redbone," "jiggaboo," and "wannabee." These names, whether we choose to realize it or not, can be degrading. Put simply, they can hurt. 5

We must educate our children that no matter what shade their skin is, they are beautiful, because "black is beautiful." Let us teach them to be proud of their culture and to show respect for one another, regardless of complexion. Let us teach them love, instead of hate; for it is this love that will unite our communities and make them stand strong. 6

So now I would ask that woman in the doctor's waiting room, "Would you sell yourself short by passing up a nice light-skinned brother who would love you and respect you just as a dark-skinned brother would? If it happens that you have a light-skinned child, would you love him or her any less than if he or she were dark-skinned?" Well, my sister, I can answer that question, for in the final analysis, color makes no difference because "black *is* beautiful—all shades." 7

Discussion Questions

1. What is the author's primary argument?
2. What are some stereotypes that exist concerning African American skin color?
3. According to the author, where do these stereotypes originate?
4. Why is skin color still an issue among African Americans?
5. What solution does the author propose?
6. What rhetorical strategies does Robinson use in this essay? Support your answer.
7. Why is the title an effective one for this essay?

Writing Assignments

1. Write an essay describing an incident of color discrimination that happened to you or to someone you know.
2. In an essay, explain your own observations regarding color prejudice.

22

Supplemental Readings

FREEDOM • EQUALITY • UNITY • PROTEST

LETTER TO THOMAS JEFFERSON

Benjamin Banneker

The son of ex-slave parents, Benjamin Banneker (1731–1806) was born free in Baltimore County, Maryland. His grandmother taught him to read, and he went on to become a mathematician, naturalist, astronomer, inventor, poet, and urban planner. With his knowledge of astronomy, Banneker compiled an almanac for the year 1792. Because of his knowledge of civil engineering, President George Washington appointed him to a commission to lay out the city of Washington, D.C. Despite all of his accomplishments, and those of other African Americans, there were prominent white statesmen and philosophers who spoke and wrote about the African American's intellectual inferiority. One of these statesmen was Thomas Jefferson, who in his "Notes on Virginia" wrote that "in reason" African Americans were "much inferior." It is in response to Jefferson's "Notes" that Banneker wrote the following letter to Jefferson on August 19, 1791.

Vocabulary

prepossession	(1)	attitude
attested	(2)	affirmed, proven to be true
censure	(2)	an expression of blame or disapproval
calamities	(3)	disasters
eradicate	(4)	erase
concurrent	(4)	in agreement with
solicitous	(6)	anxious and concerned
diffusion	(6)	the act of pouring out or scattering about
degradation	(6)	disgrace
thraldom	(7)	enslavement
fruition	(7)	pleasure
fortitude	(8)	endurance or courage
abhorrence	(9)	hatred
benevolence	(10)	goodwill
impartial	(10)	unprejudiced
imbibed	(11)	absorbed into the mind
ardently	(12)	eagerly, enthusiastically
assiduous	(13)	hardworking, devoted

Maryland, Baltimore County
Near Ellicotts' Lower Mills, August 19th, 1791

Thomas Jefferson, Secretary of State,

Sir:—I am fully sensible of the greatness of that freedom,   1
which I take with you on the present occasion, a liberty which
seemed to me scarcely allowable, when I reflected on that distinguished and dignified station in which you stand, and the
almost general prejudice and prepossession which is so prevalent in the world against those of my complexion.

I suppose it is a truth too well attested to you, to need a   2
proof here, that we are a race of beings who have long laboured
under the abuse and censure of the world, that we have long
been considered rather as brutish than human, and scarcely
capable of mental endowments.

Sir, I hope I may safely admit, in consequence of that re-   3
port which hath reached me, that you are a man far less inflex-
ible in sentiments of this nature than many others, that you
are measurably friendly and well disposed towards us, and that
you are willing and ready to lend your aid and assistance to
our relief, from those many distresses and numerous calami-
ties, to which we are reduced.

Now, sir, if this is founded in truth, I apprehend you will   4
readily embrace every opportunity to eradicate that train of

absurd and false ideas and opinions, which so generally pre-
vails with respect to us, and that your sentiments are concur-
rent with mine, which are that one universal Father hath given
Being to us all, and that he hath not only made us all of one
flesh, but that he hath also without partiality afforded us all
the same sensations, and endued us all with the same facul-
ties, and that however variable we may be in society or religion,
however diversified in situation or colour, we are all of the same
family, and stand in the same relation to him.

Sir, if these are sentiments of which you are fully per-   5
suaded, I hope you cannot but acknowledge, that it is the indispensable duty of those who maintain for themselves the
rights of human nature, and who profess the obligations of
christianity, to extend their power and influence to the relief of
every part of the human race, from whatever burden or oppression they may unjustly labour under, and this I apprehend a
full conviction of the truth and obligation of these principles
should lead all to.

Sir, I have long been convinced that if your love for your-   6
selves and for those inesteemable laws, which preserve to you
the rights of human nature, was found on sincerity, you could
not but be solicitous that every individual of whatever rank or
distinction, might with you equally enjoy the blessings thereof,
neither could you rest satisfied, short of the most active diffu-
sion of your exertions in order to their promotions from any
state of degradation, to which the unjustifiable cruelty and bar-
barism of men have reduced them.

Sir, I freely and cheerfully acknowledge that I am of the   7
African race, and in that colour which is natural to them of the
deepest dye, and it is under a sense of the most profound grati-
tude to the Supreme Ruler of the universe that I now confess to
you that I am not under that state of tyrannical thraldom and
inhuman captivity to which too many of my brethren are
doomed; but that I have abundantly tasted of the fruition of
those blessings which proceed from that free and unequalled
liberty with which you are favoured and which, I hope you will
willingly allow you have received from the immediate hand of
that Being, from whom proceedeth every good and perfect gift.

Sir, suffer me to recall to your mind that time in which the   8
arms and tyranny of the British Crown were exerted with every
powerful effort in order to reduce you to a State of Servitude,
look back I entreat you on the variety of dangers to which you
were exposed; reflect on that time in which every human aid

appeared unavailable, and in which even hope and fortitude wore the aspect of inability to the conflict and you cannot but be led to a serious and grateful sense of your miraculous and providential preservation; you cannot but acknowledge that the present freedom and tranquility which you enjoy you have mercifully received and that it is the peculiar blessing of Heaven.

This sir, was a time in which you clearly saw into the injustice of a state of slavery and in which you had just apprehensions of the horrors of its condition, it was now, sir, that your abhorrence thereof was so excited, that you publicly held forth this true and valuable doctrine, which is worthy to be recorded and remembered in all succeeding ages. "We hold these truths to be self-evident, that all men are created equal, and that they are endowed by their creator with certain unalienable rights, that among these are life, liberty and the pursuit of happiness."   9

Here, sir, was a time in which your tender feelings for yourselves had engaged you thus to declare, you were then impressed with proper ideas of the great valuation of liberty and the free possession of those blessings to which you were entitled by nature; but, sir, how pitiable is it to reflect that although you were so fully convinced of the benevolence of the Father of mankind and of his equal and impartial distribution of those rights and privileges which he had conferred upon them, that you should at the same time counteract his mercies in detaining by fraud and violence so numerous a part of my brethren under groaning captivity and cruel oppression, that you should at the same time be found guilty of that most criminal act which you professedly detested in others with respect to yourselves.   10

Sir, I suppose that your knowledge of the situation of my brethren is too extensive to need a recital here; neither shall I presume to prescribe methods by which they may be relieved, otherwise than by recommending to you and all others to wean yourselves from those narrow prejudices which you have imbibed with respect to them and as Job proposed to his friends, "put your souls in their souls stead," thus shall your hearts be enlarged with kindness and benevolence towards them, and thus shall you need neither the direction of myself or others, in what manner to proceed herein.   11

And now, sir, although my sympathy and affection for my brethren hath caused my enlargement thus far, I ardently hope that your candour and generosity will plead with you in my   12 behalf when I make known to you that it was not originally my design; but that having taken up my pen in order to direct to you as a present, a copy of an almanac, which I have calculated for the succeeding year, I was unexpectedly and unavoidably led thereto.

This calculation, sir, is the production of my arduous   13
study in this my advanced stage of life; for having long had unbounded desires to become acquainted with the secrets of nature, I have had to gratify my curiosity herein through my own assiduous application to astronomical study, in which I need not to recount to you the many difficulties and disadvantages which I have had to encounter.

And although I had almost declined to make my calcula-   14
tion for the ensuing year, in consequence of that time which I had allotted therefor being taken up at the Federal Territory by the request of Mr. Andrew Ellicott, yet finding myself under several engagements to printers of this state, to whom I had communicated my design, on my return to my place of residence I industriously applied myself thereto which I hope I have accomplished with correctness and accuracy, a copy of which I have taken the liberty to direct to you and which I humbly request you will favorably receive. Although you may have the opportunity of perusing it after its publication yet I chose to send it to you in manuscript previous thereto that you might not only have an earlier inspection but that you might also view it in my own handwriting.

And now, sir, I shall conclude and subscribe myself, with   15
the most profound respect, your most obedient humble servant.

B. Banneker

Discussion Questions

1. What is the purpose of Benjamin Banneker's letter to Thomas Jefferson?
2. Why does Banneker ask Jefferson to remember the time when Jefferson and the other colonists were considered British subjects?
3. Why does Banneker remind Jefferson that all humankind is created by God?
4. Why did Banneker give Jefferson an almanac that Banneker had written?

5. Why does Banneker make reference to the Declaration of Independence?

6. What is the tone of Banneker's letter?

7. How does Banneker's use of illustration and comparison and contrast help strengthen his argument?

8. What do you think of the letter format as a structural device for conveying Banneker's ideas?

Writing Assignments

1. Write an essay arguing that intelligence is determined primarily by opportunities and environment, not by one's race.

2. Write a letter to a friend, group, or newspaper editor voicing your concern about a particular issue.

3. In an essay, discuss the ways in which racism is rationalized or accepted.

RLACK COMEDY, WHITE REALITY

Jannette Dates

Jannette Dates (1939–   ) is associate dean of the Howard University School of Communications. She is co-author of Split Image: African-Americans in the Mass Media *(1990), from which this excerpt is taken. In this selection, Dates analyzes African American television shows of the 1970s and how white Americans perceived them.*

Vocabulary

frugal	(1)	thrifty
vignette	(2)	sketch, picture
outlandish	(3)	absurd, bizarre
racy	(3)	coarse, suggestive
satirical	(3)	sarcastic, mocking
infused	(4)	filled
nuances	(4)	subtle changes
nouveau riche	(5)	the recent rich
acumen	(5)	mental sharpness
redressing	(5)	making up for
palatable	(5)	acceptable
jaded	(5)	tired, worn out
protagonists	(6)	main characters
aberration	(6)	departure from the normal
innocuous	(7)	harmless
emasculated	(7)	weak, powerless
subversive	(7)	intending to overthrow
quintessential	(7)	ultimate
apex	(7)	peak
culmination	(7)	highest point
subliminal	(8)	subconscious
peripheral	(9)	outside, external

1

Television viewers' perceptions about African Americans changed during the 1960s as the civil rights story unfolded at dinnertime each day. Moreover, law and order and the "silent" majority were much discussed by those in the Nixon White House of the late 1960s and early 1970s. Then, between 1972 and 1979, Richard Nixon was forced to resign as president of the country, Gerald Ford served out Nixon's term, and Jimmy Carter was elected to a single term in office. When "Good Times" first aired at this point, the civil rights era was drawing to a close. The series was introduced to American viewers by its producers as a sympathetic, "authentic," and realistic portrayal of the black man's plight. The setting in the series established the environment as a lower-class, housing projects apartment, where the frugal, conscientious mother, Florida (played by Esther Rolle, who was formerly the maid on "Maude"), used curtains behind which she hid clothes and household items. One room served this family as the entrance area, living room, and the dining-kitchen area. The three bedrooms were out of most camera shots, as large windows allowed suggestions of daylight or nighttime into the living room-kitchen area. A desk and chair in one corner were surrounded by boxes, probably used to store family belongings. When the series premiered, Esther Rolle was the star. As the scripts developed, however, Jimmie Walker (J.J.), the older son, eclipsed Rolle (Florida) and John Amos (James), as he caught on with teenage viewers who often influenced their parents' viewing patterns.

Though the setting was a lower-class, poor neighborhood, the values and beliefs expressed in "Good Times" were from middle America. In the segment "J.J.'s Eighteenth Birthday," for example, the worldly character Willona, with snapping fingers and "I know the score" glances, stated, "When I was twenty-five, I decided to blow out the candles, freeze the cake, and stop the clock," as J.J.'s parents manipulated their plastic money to try to give him a worthy eighteenth-birthday celebration. Willona, established as good-hearted, represented a lower-class figure, but in her the writers created a contradictory image. Viewers were never quite sure whether she was a swinger or a middle-class striver fallen on bad times, who was forced to live in "the projects." The "J.J.'s Eighteenth Birthday" episode could have evolved into an authentic vignette about black culture at the lower socioeconomic level, but instead the plot developed in the "usual" (white, middle-class) style. For example, for this celebration everyone came in changed clothes, "dressed up" for the occasion, and helped prepare J.J's favorite foods. After eating, they "moved to the living room," which was two steps from the kitchen table, for coffee and cake. Few people would act this way in this setting. **2**

The comedy of "Sanford and Son" was based on the assumption that the characters lacked intelligence. It was a modern version of "Amos 'n' Andy," featuring outlandish (though **3** often funny) plots and one-dimensional clown characters. Redd Foxx was a well-known stand-up comedian from the nightclub circuit. He had built up a strong following among black audiences. His material often featured racy, off-color humor with much profanity. Like Nipsey Russell, a comedian who played minor roles in other television programs and was Foxx's contemporary, and Richard Pryor, another major comedian from television and film, Foxx had used racial incidents as a basis for much of his satirical humor. When he was signed to play Fred on "Sanford and Sons," black viewers anticipated and received the type of performances from Foxx that they expected, with some important alterations.

Fred Sanford was a stubborn bully who dominated others   4
with his sharp tongue and ever-present anger. Sanford seemed to be angry at anyone who intruded on his turf, from his dead wife's sister to any nonblack who entered his domain, a junkyard where he and his son acquired and recycled society's discards. This series was not original to America, however. The story concept was imported from a popular British series entitled "Steptoe and Son." The American story lines were sometimes infused with African American cultural nuances, but the basic themes were created by white producers and writers, based on the British model. Again, viewers saw African American characters whose values and outlook were shaped and designed by outsiders to their culture.

"The Jeffersons" began as a spinoff from "All in the Fam-   5
ily." George Jefferson was cast in the mold of the freed, corrupt, black legislators of the film "Birth of a Nation," who were depicted as arrogant and idiotic. The audience is asked to laugh at Jefferson's antics and his basic insecurity without unconsciously making an association with his blackness. Obviously this is a difficult feat to accomplish. "The Jeffersons" dealt with middle-class strivers who happened to be black. When it was originally broadcast, the theme celebrated the arrival of the nouveau riche black middle class. George Jefferson, characterized by producers as a loudmouthed braggart, spoke a great deal about "honkies" and "whities" while Louise, his wife, tried to appease him and smooth the ruffled feathers of others. Usually, the plots centered on George's attempts to climb the social ladder or make more money, with some note made of how difficult it was for those of African descent to move up in American society. The humor and warmth of the show often came from Louise's methods of controlling George

and the problems he caused. Louise Jefferson, though submissive to a degree, exercised great influence over George because, no matter what the conflict, George was never right. Even in the early episodes, though George was recognized as having exceptional business acumen, those skills were never transferred into his personal family relationships. This family was seldom portrayed as engaging in group activities or working toward a collective goal. In a 1983 article in the journal *Channels*, columnist William Henry noted that "The Jeffersons" appealed to white Americans because they represented African Americans who had "made it." "The Jeffersons" was the fulfillment of the American dream. Henry thought that viewers "yearned to believe that a social revolution had been won," and that this somehow freed white Americans from redressing any more grievances which African Americans might have said were due. He went on to argue that though George Jefferson was a counterpart to Archie Bunker, the distinct difference between the two men's situations made George a palatable character to white viewers. He noted that Archie was the master in his own home while George was not ("George's wife outmaneuvered, out foxed and out whoofed him, constantly"). Archie was taken seriously whereas George was not (other characters tried to reason with Archie about his bigotry, while George was ignored or laughed at), and Archie had the respect of his household, while George did not. For example, George constantly battled with his maid over who was really master. In the early years of "The Jeffersons," Lear developed George's character in the manner described above in an attempt to bring to viewers' consciousness some of the same social issues generated by the Archie Bunker character, seen this time through the eyes of a counterpart in the black community—George Jefferson. The Jefferson character, like Bunker, was a flawed person who tried to live life on his own terms, marching to his own drummer and subject to insecurities and human frailties. Lear thus attempted to make viewers empathize and identify with a black person similar in human strengths and failings to themselves. He succeeded with both characters, by touching the pulse of an America that had become jaded by post-Vietnam blues—partially because of ambivalent feelings about the conflict itself and partially because of their loss of faith in the country's leadership. Americans were no longer idealistic about the nation. Thus, Lear's comedies reflected a "tell it like it is" philosophy of life that featured imperfect characters and realistic problems.

A 1974 article by Eugenia Collier, a college professor and   6
writer, entitled "Black Shows for White Viewers," compared two
of the highly rated television series featuring African Americans
in prime time. She concluded that "Sanford and Son" was ap-
pealing because viewers could laugh *at* weak people in order to
feel good about themselves, whereas viewers of "Good Times"
laughed *with* strong survivors. She argued that "Good Times"
had appeal because of the universal attractiveness of protago-
nists pitted against strong outside forces that make courage,
resourcefulness, and intelligence essential to survival. She believed that viewers were enriched, made wiser and more humane, by their experiences with "Good Times" but were diminished by their experiences with "Sanford and Son" because the
latter program focused on the baser instincts—trickery, ignorance, naïveté, and mental aberration.

"Benson" fit the pattern that scripted African American   7
male characters as innocuous true-believers in the system,
who supported, defended, and nurtured mainstream, middle-
class American values, interests, concerns, and even faults.
Benson was thus an emasculated, nonthreatening, "acceptable" black male. A spinoff from the highly successful series of
the seventies, "Soap," the "Benson" series featured Robert Guillaume as Benson Dubois, a witty and quietly subversive but
dependable confidant of the governor of some mythical state.
Benson began the series as the head housekeeper but was later
promoted to a position of Lieutenant Governor. According to sociologist Herman Gray, Robert Guillaume was "attractive and
likeable, cool under pressure, and perhaps the quintessential
black middle class professional." The Benson character was the
apex of all the servant and helping roles that black actors had
played historically in television and the movies. There was,
however, one major qualification—"Benson was uniquely modern—sophisticated, competent and arrogant! He openly maintained his integrity and his pride week after week [though] . . .
the posture of servitude was maintained." In this sense, Gray
believed, Benson represented the culmination of a white view of
acceptable African American males.

The adoption of black male children into middle-class   8
white American homes on television allowed creators opportunities to send conscious and subconscious messages to viewers
about molding and controlling the minds and hearts of young
African American males, possibly to make them more acceptable to whites. In the situation comedy "Webster," Emmanuel

Lewis played the black adopted son of a white couple in a cross between a kid show and a family comedy. Like "Different Strokes," the hit NBC series with a similar theme, the subliminal message the "Webster" series sent out was that black people did not involve themselves with their own people's children when their parents died. This circumstance could be seen as an advantage since white foster parents could then socialize the youngsters into the "real" American way. Even visits from grandparents or cousins, or any evidence of their concern about the youngsters' welfare, were not central to the theme of either of these two series during their first season. Beginning with the second season, Ben Vereen was featured as Webster's uncle, who vainly attempted to adopt the youngster and visited him on occasion. In reality, however, the black extended family often had black women who reared generation after generation of other people's children—grandchildren, cousins, nephews and nieces, and so on—"because their own folks were gone or dead."

"The White Shadow," an earlier series that had aired from 1979 to 1981, had featured a white basketball coach/physical education teacher and his predominantly black high-school team. "The White Shadow," "Webster," and "Different Strokes" each treated the issue of race as peripheral, as the frame of reference for addressing other issues where race was simply another individual difference rather than a social or public issue. Race as a central theme of concern in American society was ignored or broken down into simplified components and then resolved with ease. Like early television series such as "East Side, West Side," usually the problems raised on television, even those involving African Americans and particularly evident in these programs, were resolved by a white male problem-solver.

9

Discussion Questions

1. Why did television viewers' perceptions of African Americans change during the 1960s?
2. According to Dates, how did *Good Times* represent middle-class values, even though it featured a poor, lower-class family?
3. What was the assumption on which the comedy of *Sanford and Son* was based?
4. According to Dates, what was the appeal of *The Jeffersons* to white America?

5. Why does Dates describe Benson as "an emasculated, nonthreatening, 'acceptable' black male"?

6. What was the subliminal message sent out by *Webster* and *Different Strokes*?

7. How does Dates use classification to discuss the various television shows?

8. Dates chose not to write a formal conclusion to this essay. What type of ending would you suggest for this essay?

Writing Assignments

1. Write an essay in which you disagree with one of Dates's theories about one or more of the television shows discussed in the essay.

2. Write an essay comparing one of the shows discussed in the essay with a current African American television show.

3. Write an essay analyzing one or more current African American television shows, and discuss the basis for your analysis.

REQUIEM BEFORE REVIVAL

Gwendolyn Brooks

At seventy-seven, Gwendolyn Brooks (1917–   ) is still on the lecture circuit, conducting creative writing workshops at colleges and universities throughout the United States. Perhaps what is most remarkable about the African American poet is not her ability to learn and to grow from younger poets such as Haki R. Madhubuti (don l. lee), but her untiring, selfless efforts to spark young people to write creatively. Since the publication of her A Street in Bronzeville *(1945),* Brooks has published many volumes of poetry, including Annie Allen *(1949),* Riot *(1969),* Becomings *(1975),* Primer for Blacks *(1980), and* Blacks *(1987). In all of her volumes, she offers snapshot descriptions of poor, frustrated, or troubled African Americans living in urban areas in the North. In 1950, she became the first African American to receive the Pulitzer Prize for poetry. Currently, she directs the Gwendolyn Brooks Center for Black Literature and Creative Writing in Chicago. In the following selection, Brooks attempts to persuade African Americans that they must reclaim their identity as a proud and powerful people.*

Vocabulary

assimilationist	(1)	one who adapts himself or herself to a particular society without any protest
inarticulate	(1)	unable to express oneself
befuddles	(3)	thoroughly confuses
mesmerized	(6)	fascinated or hypnotized by something or someone
fervently	(6)	eagerly, intensely
iterated	(6)	repeated
efficacy	(6)	effectiveness; the power to bring about a desired result
vertigo	(6)	confusion

We still need the essential Black statement of defense and   1
definition. Of course, we are happiest when that statement is
not dulled by assimilationist urges, secret or overt. However,

there is in "the souls of Black Folk"—even when inarticulate and crippled—a yearning toward Black validation.

To be Black is rich, is subtle, is nourishing and a nutrient   2
in the universe. What could be nourishing about aiming against your nature?

I give whites big credit. They have never tried to be any-   3
thing but what they are. They have been and will be everlast-ingly proud proud proud to be white. It has never occurred to them that there has been or ever will be ANYthing better than, nor one zillionth as good as, being white. They have an over-whelming belief in their validity. Not in their "virtue," for they are shrewdly capable of a very cold view of *that*. But their valid-ity they salute with an amazing innocence—yes, a genuine in-nocence, the brass of which befuddles most of the rest of us in the world because we have allowed ourselves to be hypnotized by its shine.

In the throat of the Town Crier throbs the Power.   4

If you yell long enough and shrilly enough "I'M GREAT!,"   5
ultimately you will convince your listeners. Or you will be thrown into the insane asylum. The scant Caucasian race has escaped the insane asylum and has gone on to *virtually* un-questioned "glory"—has achieved virtually unchallenged italics.

Swarms of Blacks have not understood the mechanics of   6
the proceeding, and they trot along to the rear of Pied Piper whites, their strange gazes fixed on, and worshiping, each switch of the white rear, their mesmerized mentalities fervently and firmly convinced that there is nothing better than quaking in that tail's wake. They do not see that the secret of Su-premacy success is—you just go ahead and impress yourself on the world whether the world wants you or not. They have not seen some Announcements register just *because* they are iterated and iterated and iterated—the oppressed conscious-ness finally sinking back and accepting the burden of relent-less assault. Though eager to imitate any other property of the white compulsion, much of the Black swarm has refused to im-itate the efficacy of Iteration; and the fruit of that Black refusal is chaos, is vertigo, is self-swallow, or self-shrivel and decline.

I continue my old optimism. In spite of all the disappoint-   7
ment and disillusionment and befuddlement out there, I go on believing that the Weak among us will, finally, perceive the im-pressiveness of our numbers, perceive the quality and legiti-macy of our essence, and take sufficient, indicated steps to-ward definition, clarification.

Discussion Questions

1. How does Brooks describe African Americans?
2. What do you think is the meaning of the following line: "In the throat of the Town Crier throbs the Power"?
3. Why do you think Brooks capitalizes words such as "Power" and "Folk"? Why do you think some words are in all capital letters?
4. What does Brooks see as the main strength of white America?
5. What does Brooks say is the secret of supremacy?
6. What is the meaning of the title?
7. How does Brooks use comparison and contrast to strengthen her argument?
8. What is thesis? Is it stated or implied?

Writing Assignments

1. Write an essay describing what it means to be a part of your racial or ethnic group.
2. There is an old proverb: "As one thinks, so is he [or she]." Write an essay in which you agree or disagree with the proverb. Explain why or why not.
3. Write an essay discussing a particular strength you have observed in some racial or ethnic group other than your own.

WITHOUT DAD

Bebe Moore Campbell

Bebe Moore Campbell (1950–   ) is an essayist, novelist, and free-lance writer. She is a frequent contributor to Morning Edition *on National Public Radio (NPR) and has also contributed to the* New York Times, *the* Washington Post *and the* Los Angeles Times. *She has written the following books:* Successful Women, Angry Men: Backlash in the Two-Career Marriage *(1987);* Sweet Summer: Growing Up With and Without My Dad *(1989), from which the following excerpt was taken;* Your Blues Ain't Like Mine *(1992); and* Brothers and Sisters *(1994). The following selection shows how deeply a young girl is affected by the absence of a father in her home.*

Vocabulary

allure	(5)	charm, glamour
cajoled	(6)	urged
distaff	(6)	female, maternal
hapless	(9)	unfortunate, pitiful
cootie	(10)	slang for lice
buttressed	(11)	reinforced
hordes	(11)	crowds
unremitting	(12)	constant, unending
nonplussed	(35)	amazed, dumbfounded

The red bricks of 2239 North 16th Street melded into the uniformity of look-alike doors, windows, and brownstone-steps. From the outside our rowhouse looked the same as any other. When I was a toddler, the similarity was unsettling. The family story was that my mother and I were out walking on the street one day when panic rumbled through me. "Where's our house? Where's our house?" I cried, grabbing my mother's hand. 1

My mother walked me to our house, pointed to the numbers painted next to the door. "Twenty-two thirty-nine," she said, slapping the wall. "This is our house." 2

Much later I learned that the real difference was inside.   3

In my house there was no morning stubble, no long johns   4
or Fruit of the Loom on the clothesline, no baritone hollering
for keys that were sitting on the table. There was no beer in the
refrigerator, no ball game on TV, no loud cussing. After dark
the snores that emanated from the bedrooms were subtle, ladylike, little moans really.

Growing up, I could have died from overexposure to femi-   5
ninity. Women ruled at 2239. A grandmother, a mother, occasionally an aunt, grown-up girlfriends from at least two generations, all the time rubbing up against me, fixing my food,
running my bathwater, telling me to sit still and be good in
those grown-up, girly-girl voices. Chanel and Prince Matcha-
belli wafting through the bedrooms. Bubble bath and Jergens
came from the bathroom, scents unbroken by aftershave, macho beer breath, a good he-man funk. I remember a house full
of 'do rags and rollers, the soft, sweet allure of Dixie peach and
bergamot;[1] brown-skinned queens wearing pastel housecoats
and worn-out size six-and-a-half flip-flops that slapped softly
against the wood as the royal women climbed the stairs at
night carrying their paperbacks to bed.

The outside world offered no retreat. School was taught by   6
stern, old-maid white women with age spots and merciless gray
eyes; ballet lessons, piano lessons, Sunday school, and choir
were all led by colored sisters with a hands-on-their-hips attitude who cajoled and screeched in distaff tongues.

And what did they want from me, these Bosoms? Achieve-   7
ment! This desire had nothing to do with the pittance they collected from the Philadelphia Board of Education or the few dollars my mother paid them. Pushing little colored girls forward
was in their blood. They made it clear: a life of white picket
fences and teas was for other girls to aspire to. I was to *do*
something. And if I didn't climb willingly up their ladder, they'd
drag me to the top. Rap my knuckles hard for not practicing.
Make me lift my leg until I wanted to die. Stay after school and
write "I will listen to the teacher" five hundred times. They were
not playing. "Obey them," my mother commanded.

When I entered 2B—the Philadelphia school system di-   8
vided grades into A and B—in September 1957, I sensed immediately that Miss Bradley was not a woman to be challenged.

---

[1]Dixie peach and bergamot   (5)   Refers to African American hair condi-
                                          tioning products.

She looked like one of those evil old spinsters Shirley Temple[2] was always getting shipped off to live with; she was kind of hefty, but so tightly corseted that if she happened to grab you or if you fell against her during recess, it felt as if you were bouncing into a steel wall. In reality she was a sweet lady who was probably a good five years past her retirement age when I wound up in her class. Miss Bradley remained at Logan for one reason and one reason only: she was dedicated. She wanted her students to learn! learn! learn! Miss Bradley was halfway sick, hacking and coughing her lungs out through every lesson, spitting the phlegm into fluffy white tissues from the box on her desk, but she was *never* absent. Each day at three o'clock she kissed each one of her "little pupils" on the cheek, sending a faint scent of Emeraude home with us. Her rules for teaching children seemed to be: love them; discipline them; reward them; and make sure they are clean.

Every morning she ran a hygiene check on the entire   9
class. She marched down the aisle like a stormtrooper, rummaging through the ears of hapless students, checking for embedded wax. She looked under our fingernails for dirt. Too bad on you if she found any. Once she made David, a stringy-haired white boy who thought Elvis Presley was a living deity and who was the most notorious booger-eater in the entire school, go the the nurse's office to have the dirt cleaned from under his fingernails. Everybody knew that what was under David's fingernails was most likely dried-up boogies and not dirt, but nobody said anything.

If she was death on dirt and earwax, Miss Bradley's spe-   10
cialty was head-lice patrol. Down the aisles she stomped in her black Enna Jettick shoes,[3] stopping at each student to part strands of blond, brown, or dark hair, looking for cooties. Miss Bradley would flip through plaits, curls, kinks—the woman was relentless. I always passed inspection. Nana put enough Nu Nile in my hair to suffocate any living creature that had the nerve to come tipping up on my scalp. Nu Nile was the official cootie killer. I was clean, wax-free, bug-free, and smart. The folder inside my desk contained a stack of spelling and arithmetic papers with A's emblazoned across the top, gold stars in

---

[2]Shirley Temple   (8)   Famous child actor of the 1930s and 1940s.
[3]Enna Jettick shoes   (10)   Brand name of women's shoes.

the corner. Miss Bradley always called on me. She sent me to run errands for her too. I was her pet.

When Mrs. Clark, my piano teacher and my mother's good friend, told my mother that Logan Elementary School was accepting children who didn't live in the neighborhood, my mother immediately enrolled Michael and later me. "It's not crowded and it's mixed," she told a nodding, smiling Nana. The fact that Logan was integrated was the main reason Michael and I were sent there. Nana and Mommy, like most upwardly mobile colored women, believed that to have the same education as a white child was the first step up the rocky road to success. This viewpoint was buttressed by the fact that George Washington Carver, my neighborhood school, was severely overcrowded. Logan was just barely integrated, with only a handful of black kids thrown in with hordes of square-jawed, pale-eyed second-generation Ukrainians whose immigrant parents and grandparents populated the neighborhood near the school. There were a few dark-haired Jews and aristocratic-looking WASPs too. My first day in kindergarten it was Nana who enthusiastically grabbed Michael's and my hands, pulling us away from North Philly's stacked-up rowhouses, from the hucksters whose wagons bounced down the streets with trucks full of ripe fruits and vegetables, from the street-corner singers and jitterbugs who filled my block with all-day doo-wahs. It was Nana who resolutely walked me past the early-morning hordes of colored kids heading two blocks away to Carver Elementary School, Nana who pulled me by the hand and led me in another direction.

11

We went underground at the Susquehanna and Dauphin subway station, leaving behind the unremitting asphalt and bricks and the bits of paper strewn in the streets above us. We emerged at Logan station, where sunlight, brilliant red and pink roses and yellow chrysanthemums, and neatly clipped lawns and clean streets startled me. There were robins and blue jays flying overhead. The only birds in my neighborhood were sparrows and pigeons. Delivering me at the schoolyard, Nana firmly cupped my chin with her hand as she bent down to instruct me. "Your mother's sending you up here to learn, so you do everything your teacher tells you to, okay?" To Michael she turned and said, "You're not up here to be a monkey on a stick." Then to both of us: "Don't talk. Listen. Act like you've got some home training. You've got as much brains as anybody

12

up here. Do you know that? All right now. Make Nana proud of you."

A month after I returned from Pasquotank County,[4] I sat   13
in Miss Bradley's classroom on a rainy Monday watching her
write spelling words on the blackboard. The harsh sccurr,
sccurr of Miss Bradley's chalk and the tinny sound the rain
made against the window took my mind to faraway places. I
couldn't get as far away as I wanted. Wallace, the bane of the
whole class, had only moments earlier laid the most gigunda[5]
fart in history, one in a never-ending series, and the air was
just clearing. His farts were silent wonders. Not a hint, not the
slightest sound. You could be in the middle of a sentence and
then wham! bam! Mystery Funk would knock you down.

Two seats ahead of me was Leonard, a lean colored boy   14
from West Philly who always wore suits and ties to school, waving his hand like a crazy man. A showoff if ever there was one.

I was bored that day. I looked around at the walls. Miss   15
Bradley had decorated the room with pictures of the ABCs in
cursive. Portraits of the presidents were hanging in a row on
one wall above the blackboard. On the bulletin board there was
a display of the Russian satellite, *Sputnik I*, and the American
satellite, *Explorer I.* Miss Bradley was satellite-crazy. She
thought it was just wonderful that America was in the "space
race" and she constantly filled our heads with space fantasies.
"Boys and girls," she told us, "one day man will walk on the
moon." In the far corner on another bulletin board there was a
Thanksgiving scene of turkeys and pilgrims. And stuck in the
corner was a picture of Sacajawea.[6] Sacajewea, Indian Woman
Guide. I preferred looking at Sacajawea over satellites any day.

Thinking about the bubble gum that lay in my pocket, I   16
decided to sneak a piece, even though gum chewing was
strictly forbidden. I rarely broke the rules. Could anyone hear
the loud drumming of my heart, I wondered, as I slid my hand
into my skirt pocket and felt for the Double Bubble? I peeked
cautiously to either side of me. Then I managed to unwrap it
without even rustling the paper; I drew my hand to my lips,

[4]Pasquotank County	(13)	North Carolina county where Campbell's father lived.
[5]gigunda	(13)	Slang for gigantic.
[6]Sacajawea	(15)	a Shoshone Native American woman (1786–1812) who was captured and sold to a white man. She became a famous guide of the 1804 Lewis and Clark expedition.

coughed, and popped the gum in my mouth. Ahhh! Miss Bradley's back was to the class. I chomped down hard on the Double Bubble. Miss Bradley turned around. I quickly packed the gum under my tongue. My hands were folded on top of my desk. "Who can give me a sentence for 'birthday'?" Leonard just about went nuts. Miss Bradley ignored him, which she did a lot. "Sandra," Miss Bradley called.

A petite white girl rose obediently. I liked Sandra. She had   17
shared her crayons with me once when I left mine at home. I remember her drawing: a white house with smoke coming out of the chimney, a little girl with yellow hair like hers, a mommy, a daddy, a little boy, and a dog standing in front of the house in a yard full of flowers. Her voice was crystal clear when she spoke. There were smiles in that voice. She said, "My father made me a beautiful dollhouse for my birthday."

The lump under my tongue was suddenly a stone and   18
when I swallowed, the taste was bitter. I coughed into a piece of tablet paper, spit out the bubble gum, and crumpled up the wad and pushed it inside my desk. The center of my chest was burning. I breathed deeply and slowly. Sandra sat down as demurely as a princess. She crossed her ankles. Her words came back to me in a rush. "Muuuy fatha made me a bee-yoo-tee-ful dollhouse." Miss Bradley said, "Very good," and moved on to the next word. Around me hands were waving, waving. Pick me! Pick me! Behind me I could hear David softly crooning, "You ain't nothin' but a hound dog, cryin' all the time." Sometimes he would stick his head inside his desk, sing Elvis songs, and pick his boogies at the same time. Somebody was jabbing pins in my chest. Ping! Ping! Ping! I wanted to holler, "Yowee! Stop!" as loud as I could, but I pressed my lips together hard.

"Now who can give me a sentence?" Miss Bradley asked. I   19
put my head down on my desk and when Miss Bradley asked me what was wrong I told her that I didn't feel well and that I didn't want to be chosen. When Leonard collected the homework, I shoved mine at him so hard all the papers he was carrying fell on the floor.

Bile was still clogging my throat when Miss Bradley sent   20
me into the cloakroom to get my lunchbox. The rule was, only one student in the cloakroom at a time. When the second one came in, the first one had to leave. I was still rummaging around in my bookbag when I saw Sandra.

"Miss Bradley said for you to come out," she said. She was   21
smiling. That dollhouse girl was always smiling. I glared at her.

"Leave when I get ready to," I said, my words full of   22
venom.

Sandra's eyes darted around in confusion. "Miss Bradley   23
said . . . " she began again, still trying to smile as if she expected somebody to crown her Miss America or something and
come take her picture any minute.

In my head a dam broke. Terrible waters rushed out. "I   24
don't care about any Miss Bradley. If she messes with me I'll,
I'll . . . I'll take my butcher knife and stab her until she
bleeds." What I lacked in props I made up for in drama. My
balled-up hand swung menacingly in the air. I aimed the invisible dagger toward Sandra. Her Miss America smile faded in-
stantly. Her eyes grew round and frightened as she blinked
rapidly. "Think I won't, huh? Huh?" I whispered, enjoying my
meanness, liking the scared look on Sandra's face. Scaredy cat!
Scaredy cat! Muuuy fatha made me a bee-yoo-tee-full dollhouse. "What do you think about that?" I added viciously, looking into her eyes to see the total effect of my daring words.

But Sandra wasn't looking at me. Upon closer inspection,   25
I realized that she was looking *over* me with sudden relief in
her face. I turned to see what was so interesting, and my chin
jammed smack into the Emeraude-scented iron bosom of Miss
Bradley. Even as my mind scrambled for an excuse, I knew I
was lost.

Miss Bradley had a look of horror on her face. For a   26
minute she didn't say anything, just stood there looking as
though someone had slapped her across the face. Sandra didn't
say anything. I didn't move. Finally, "Would you mind repeating
what you just said, Bebe."

"I didn't say anything, Miss Bradley." I could feel my dress   27
sticking to my body.

"Sandra, what did Bebe say?"   28

Sandra was crying softly, little delicate tears streaming   29
down her face. For just a second she paused, giving a tiny shudder. I rubbed my ear vigorously, thinking, "Oh, please . . ."

"She said, she said, if you bothered with her she would   30
cut you with her knife."

"Unh unh, Miss Bradley, I didn't say that. I didn't. I didn't   31
say anything like that."

Miss Bradley's gray eyes penetrated mine. She locked me   32
into her gaze until I looked down at the floor. Then she looked
at Sandra.

"Bebe, you and I had better go see the principal." 33

The floor blurred. The principal! Jennie G., the students 34
called her with awe and fear. As Miss Bradley wrapped her
thick knuckles around my forearm and dutifully steered me
from the cloakroom and out the classroom door, I completely
lost what little cool I had left. I began to cry, a jerky hiccuping,
snot-filled cry for mercy. "I didn't say it. I didn't say it," I
moaned.

Miss Bradley was nonplussed. Dedication and duty over- 35
ruled compassion. Always. "Too late for that now," she said
grimly.

Jennie G.'s office was small, neat, and dim. The principal 36
was dwarfed by the large brown desk she sat behind, and when
she stood up she wasn't much bigger than I. But she was big
enough to make me tremble as I stood in front of her, listening
to Miss Bradley recount the sordid details of my downfall. Jennie G. was one of those pale, pale vein-showing white women.
She had a vocabulary of about six horrible phrases, designed to
send chills of despair down the spine of any young transgres-
sor. Phrases like "We'll just see about that" or "Come with me,
young lady," spoken ominously. Her face was impassive as she
listened to Miss Bradley. I'd been told that she had a six-foot
paddle in her office used solely to beat young transgressors.
Suppose she tried to beat me? My heart gave a lurch. I tugged
rapidly at my ears. I longed to suck my thumb.

"Well, Bebe, I think we'll have to call your mother." 37

My mother! I wanted the floor to swallow me up and take 38
me whole. My mother! As Jennie G. dialed the number, I envi-
sioned my mother's face, clouded with disappointment and
shame. I started crying again as I listened to the principal
telling my mother what had happened. They talked for a pretty
long time. When she hung up, ole Jennie G. flipped through
some paper on her desk before looking at me sternly.

"You go back to class and watch your mouth, young lady." 39

As I was closing the door to her office I heard her say to 40
Miss Bradley, "What can you expect?"

Discussion Questions

1. Why does the narrator feel she was "overexposed to femininity"
when she was growing up?

2. Who are the "Bosoms" to whom Campbell refers?

3. Do you think Bebe's feelings about a household of women are generally shared by other young girls who grow up in a similar situation? Why or why not?

4. Why did Bebe get angry at Sandra?

5. Why is Bebe taken to the principal's office?

6. What does the principal mean when she says "What do you expect"?

7. To what extent does Campbell's use of cause and effect support the theme of the story?

8. How would this story be different if it were told by a character other than the main character?

Writing Assignments

1. Write an essay describing an incident in which you took out your frustration on someone who didn't deserve it.

2. Write an essay describing your childhood relationship with a person or persons who had a major influence on your life.

3. Write an essay in which you explore some stereotypic beliefs about the roles of men and women.

Student Essay:
FEMALE GENITAL MUTILATION AND CASTRATION

Anika Yetunde

Vocabulary

genital	(1)	of, relating to, or being a sexual organ
mutilated	(1)	cut off or crippled
retention	(3)	the act of keeping
obsolete	(6)	no longer useful

African women throughout the world have a common op- 1
pressor: female genital mutilation and castration. The woman
suffers from this oppression because of racism, sexism, and
classism. Because she suffers from all of these forms of oppression, the woman of African descent has been the one most affected by this practice throughout the world. For example,
6,000 young girls are mutilated daily, many of them African
women. Since the early 1980s, over 100 million young girls and
women have been mutilated. Yet organizations such as
UNICEF[1] have only recently acknowledged that this practice
still exists. How can you ignore 100 million mutilated women?
It has a lot to do with the fact that the majority of these women
are poor and African.

Female genital mutilation is the collective name given to the 2
several different traditional practices that involve the cutting and
mutilating of female genitals. There are many different forms of
female genital mutilation, and they vary from region to region
and continent to continent, but they all fall into three broad categories. The first is called "sunna" circumcision and is the
mildest type. It consists of removing only the tip of the prepuce[2]
of the clitoris.[2] The next type is called "clitoridectomy" which

---

[1]UNICEF	(1)	United Nations International Children's Emergency Fund founded in 1946.
[2]prepuce, clitoris, labia minora, labia majora	(2)	Biological names for parts of the female genital or-gan.

consists of the removal of the entire clitoris, usually together with the adjacent parts of the labia minora.[2] The last type is called "infibulation," which includes removing the entire clitoris, some or all of the labia minora, and making incisions on the labia majora[2] to create raw surfaces. These raw surfaces are either stitched together or kept in contact by pressure until they heal as a "hood of skin" that covers the urethra[3] and most of the vagina. Since a physical barrier to sexual intercourse is created as a result, a small hole must be reconstructed for the flow of urine and menstrual blood. Also, recutting and stitching is performed after each childbirth. This means a woman may average six to eight reinfibulations in her lifetime!

Many complications are associated with female genital   3
mutilation: excessive bleeding, infection, continuous pain, urine retention, damage to the urethra, and stress. In the infibulation case, there is an excessive growth of scar tissue and severe complications during childbirth. The majority of these practices are performed in rural areas where anesthesia is difficult to obtain. Despite these complications, the psychological and emotional side effects of female genital mutilation have never been investigated and recorded.

Myths concerning the origin of the practice are numerous.   4
Most of the myths trace the practice to Africa, others to ancient Rome. Some believe it is associated with Islam; others say it predates Islam.

Why does the practice persist? Many women have said   5
that female genital mutilation represents a spiritual bond that they share with their ancestors; in other words, it is a custom or a tradition. Many also have stated that they fear the ancestors would seek vengeance if they abandon this practice. The vast majority who are Islamic believe it is a requirement. Moreover, African men in Islamic societies place a great deal of emphasis on women being virgins upon marriage, so the majority of the men will not marry a woman if she is not circumcised. In the societies where female genital mutilation is allowed, there is an obsession with controlling a woman's virginity. Many people in these societies believe that if a woman is not circumcised she will become a sex delinquent. Then, too, many myths and superstitions surround this practice, such as circumcision increases fertility; an uncircumcised woman is dirty and masculine; and an uncircumcised woman will kill her firstborn.

---

[3]urethra   (3)   The body part through which urine is eliminated.

Female genital mutilation and male circumcision used to have one similarity. Both of these practices were performed on boys and girls in the same age group and were a part of the rites of passage into adulthood. Today, these rites of passage are almost obsolete, yet the mutilation continues. It appears as if female genital mutilation has only continued to be practiced, on women of African descent in particular, because of the triple oppression that they confront. This practice must be abolished.   3

Discussion Questions

1. How does the author account for the reluctance of some health organizations to acknowledge the practice of female genital mutilation?
2. What are the three types of circumcision? How are they different?
3. Why does the practice persist?
4. Of the many reasons given by the author to discontinue female circumcision, which do you consider the most convincing? Why?
5. How effective is Yetunde's use of classification in educating the reader on female genital mutilation and castration?
6. How can you argue that the last sentence of the essay is Yetunde's thesis statement?

Writing Assignments

1. In an essay, offer reasons why you think female (or male) circumcision should (or should not) be abolished.
2. Write an essay in which you argue that some type of other societal or environmental practice should be abolished.

Literary and Writing Terms

audience   person or group to whom a piece of writing is addressed

body   in writing, the central part of an essay where ideas supporting the thesis are presented

brainstorming   prewriting strategy whereby words or phrases are listed as quickly as they come to mind

cause and effect   organizing strategy that examines the reasons for a certain condition or event (causes) or examines the results a certain condition or event has had on something or someone else (effects)

central idea   main point of a piece of writing; thesis

character   person in a story, poem, or play

classification   method of defining whereby one places various people, ideas, or things into separate and distinct categories

climax   highest or most dramatic point of a story

comparison and contrast   technique of analyzing two topics or works in order to determine similarities and/or differences

complex sentence   consisting of only one independent clause and at least one dependent clause
　　Example: Since traffic was so heavy, Rashida walked to the park.

compound-complex sentence   consisting of at least two independent clauses and at least one dependent clause
　　Example: Since traffic was so heavy, Rashida walked to the park, but she took the bus home.

compound sentence   consisting of two independent clauses and no dependent clauses
　　Example: Rashida walked to the park, but she took the bus home.

conflict   clash between or within characters and/or society

connotation what a word suggests beyond its dictionary meaning

Example: I was impressed by her *childlike* behavior. [Whereas *child-like* connotates positive behavior, *childish* connotates negative behavior.]

denotation the dictionary meaning of a word

definition organizing strategy that emphasizes the meanings of word(s) to develop a major point

description organizing strategy that focuses on sensory details (sight, sound, touch, taste, smell)

dialect speech of a particular region or social group

dialogue speech between two (or more) characters

diction choice and/or use of words in an essay

dilemma choices a character faces in resolving a problem

drama a play

editing process of correcting spelling, grammar, punctuation, or changing sentence structure and word choice; also see *revising*

essay group of paragraphs that develops a single idea

explication detailed analysis of a literary work

fiction writing based on an author's imagination

figurative language words and expressions that often attempt to compare unlike things

first-person narrator when a character in the story narrates it, using first-person singular (*I*) and plural (*we*) pronouns

flashback part in a story, play, or film, showing events that happened at an earlier time

folklore songs, stories, myths, and proverbs of a people or cultural group with no known origin that are handed down from generation to generation

freewriting process of writing down your thoughts on paper, freely and continuously for a set period of time

genre type of literature, for example, fiction, nonfiction, drama, or poetry

hyperbole exaggerated speech

Example: Her heart is as big as Texas.

idiom phrase (particularly to a group, race, nation, or class) that does not make sense taken literally

Example: *green thumb* or *sweet tooth*

illustration organizing strategy that relies on specific examples or reasons to develop an idea

imagery vivid language that appeals to the senses of sight, sound, taste, smell, and touch

irony something said or done, but something else meant or expected

jargon language characteristic of a particular profession or activity

Example: Kwame has downloaded the file he received from Jamal.

journal notebook in which one writes on a regular basis; unlike a diary in which one records the day's events, a journal reflects the writer's feelings on a given subject

loose sentence   sentence in which the main idea comes at the beginning
> Example: *Carolyn had played her best although she lost the triathlon.*

metaphor   comparison of two things by substituting one for the other
> Example: Dante, the smart new reporter, thinks he is a *firecracker* of the well-known national newspaper.

mood   writer's attitude in a piece of writing

narrative   organizing strategy that tells a story to make a point

narrator   the one who tells the story; sometimes referred to as the speaker

nonfiction   writing that is factual rather than imaginary

nonstandard English   language that does not conform to standards of American edited English

novel   long work of fiction

onomatopoeia   consonant and vowel sounds used to imitate or suggest the activity being described
> Example: The mother grew tired of listening to the *bangs* and *booms* of her six-year-old son.

parable   story designed to illustrate a truth, often associated with the stories of Jesus

paradox   statement that is seemingly contradictory yet true
> Example: The weary parent said she had just about loved her young teenage daughter to death.

paraphrase   rewording of someone else's ideas in a piece of writing to fit the style of the writer

periodic sentence   sentence in which the main idea comes at the end of the sentence
> Example: Although she tried her best, *Carolyn lost the triathlon.*

persona   speaker of a poem

personification   expression that gives human qualities to nonhuman things
> Example: The *tree's branches danced* in the wind.

persuasion   organizing strategy designed to convince readers to accept or seriously consider the writer's viewpoint

plot   sequence of incidents in a story or play

poetry   literature characterized by rhythmic language

point of view   perspective from which a story is told, for example, first-person or third-person narrator

précis   *in literature,* a short paraphrased summary of a narrative; *in writing,* a summary that captures the overall style and tone of the source

process   organizing strategy that focuses on how something works or is done

proofreading   reviewing an essay for both revision and editing concerns

prose   the ordinary form of written language, not arranged in verse

protagonist   main character in a story or play

pun   play on words

   Example: The owner of the butcher shop *cut* his losses by laying off two workers.

purpose   writer's chief reason for communicating something about a topic, for example, to inform, to persuade, to express feelings

resolution   final stage of a story in which conflicts are resolved

revising   reconsidering the whole paper as well as its individual parts, including assessing purpose, audience, main idea, and perhaps reordering supporting paragraphs and sentences

rhetorical strategies   methods used to organize an essay (See section on "Planning Your Essay.")

setting   time and place in which a story occurs

sexist language   language that excludes or offends men or women

short story   short fictional work

simile   comparison of unlike objects using "like" or "as"

   Example: His eyes twinkled *like* the stars.

simple sentence   consisting of only one independent clause and no dependent clauses

   Example: Rashida walked to the park.

slang   informal language that is short lived and used by those within a particular group

speaker   See *persona* and *narrator.*

stanza   In a poem, lines that are grouped together

structure   arrangement of material in a story

style   overall characteristic of a writer's work that gives the work its particular flavor

symbol   word or object that stands for something other than itself

syntax   word order and sentence structure

theme   main idea of a piece of writing

thesis   generally, a specific sentence that reflects the central point of an essay; however, a thesis may also be implied.

third-person narrator   speaker who tells the story, but is not a character in it

tone   writer's attitude toward his or her ideas and toward the audience

topic sentence   sentence that reflects the main idea of a paragraph

understatement   sentence that by design undervalues something

writing process   mental and physical activities that go into producing a piece of writing

Suggested Bibliography

SLAVERY

COOPER, J. CALIFORNIA. *Family: A Novel.* New York: Doubleday, 1991.

HARRIS, MIDDLETON. *The Black Book.* New York: Random House, 1974.

HAYDEN, ROBERT. "Middle Passage." In Arthur P. Davis, J. Saunders Redding and Joyce Ann Joyce (eds), *The New Cavalcade.* 2 vols. Washington, DC: Howard University Press, 1991. 1:846–851.

HORTON, MOSES. "On Liberty and Slavery." In Arthur P. Davis, J. Saunders Redding and Joyce Ann Joyce (eds.), *The New Cavalcade.* 2 vols. Washington, DC: Howard University Press, 1991. 1:50–51.

JOHNSON, CHARLES. *Middle Passage.* New York: Atheneum, 1990.

MORRISON, TONI. *Beloved.* New York: Knopf, 1987.

"Raise a Ruckus Tonight." In Richard K. Barksdale and Keneth Kinnamon (eds.), *Black Writers of America.* New York: Macmillan, 1972.

"Swapping Dreams." In Richard K. Barksdale and Keneth Kinnamon (eds.), *Black Writers of America.* New York: Macmillan, 1972.

WALKER, DAVID. *Appeal.* New York: Hill and Wang, 1965.

WALKER, MARGARET. *Jubilee.* New York: Bantam, 1975.

WILLIAMS, SHERLEY ANNE. *Dessa Rose.* New York: Berkley, 1987.

AFRICAN AMERICAN WOMEN

ANGELOU, MAYA. *I Know Why the Caged Bird Sings.* New York: Random House, 1969.

CLIFTON, LUCILLE. "for her." In Amiri and Amina Baraka (eds.), *Confirmation: An Anthology of African American Women.* New York: Quill, 1983.

CORTEZ, JAYNE. "Rape." In Amiri and Amina Baraka (eds.), *Confirmation: An Anthology of African American Women.* New York: Quill, 1983.

HUDSON-WEEMS, CLENORA. *Africana Womanism.* Troy, MI: Bedford, 1993.

JONES, GAYL. "Asylum." In Mary Helen Washington (ed.), *Midnight Birds.* New York: Anchor Press/Doubleday, 1980.

LEWIS-THORNTON, RAE. "Facing AIDS." *Essence,* December 1994: 62–64, 124, 126, 130.

NAYLOR, GLORIA. *The Women of Brewster Place.* New York: Penguin, 1983.

NELSON, JILL. "Doing Time: Our Women in Prison." *Essence,* May 1994: 83–84, 86, 158, 160.

MORRISON, TONI. *The Bluest Eye.* New York: Holt, Rinehart & Winston, 1970.

TRUTH, SOJOURNER. "And Arn't I a Woman?" In Arthur P. Davis, J. Saunders Redding and Joyce Ann Joyce (eds.), *The New Cavalcade.* 2 vols. Washington, DC: Howard University Press, 1991. 1:101–104.

WALKER, ALICE. *The Color Purple.* New York: Harcourt, 1982.

WHETSTONE, MURIEL L. "New AIDS Scare for Heterosexuals: The Increasing Threat to Black Women." *Ebony,* April 1994: 118, 120.

AFRICAN AMERICAN MEN

BROWN, CLAUDE. *Manchild in the Promised Land.* New York: Macmillan, 1965.

BROWN, WILLIAM WELLS. "from *The Negro in the American Rebellion: His Heroism and His Fidelity.*" Richard K. Barksdale and Keneth Kinnamon (eds.), *Black Writers of America.* New York: Macmillan, 1972.

DANIELS, LEE. "Targeting Black Boys for Failure." *Emerge,* May 1994: 58–61.

HODGES, FRENCHY. "Requiem for Willie Lee." In Mary Helen Washington (ed.), *Midnight Birds.* New York: Anchor Press/Doubleday, 1980.

KILLENS, JOHN. *And Then We Heard the Thunder.* Washington, DC: Howard University Press, 1982.

MORRISON, TONI. *Song of Solomon.* New York: Knopf, 1977.

WIDEMAN, JOHN EDGAR. "Tommy." In *Damballah.* New York: Vintage, 1988.

WILLIAMS, JOHN. *The Man Who Cried I Am.* New York: Little, Brown, 1967.

WRIGHT, RICHARD. *Black Boy.* New York: Harper, 1945.

CHILDHOOD • ADOLESCENCE • GROWING UP

BALDWIN, JAMES. *Go Tell It on the Mountain.* New York: Dell, 1953.

CHILDRESS, ALICE. *A Hero Ain't Nothin But a Sandwich.* New York: Coward, McCann and Geoghegan, 1973.

DEVEAUX, ALEXIS. "The Riddles of Egypt Brownstone." In Mary Helen Washington (ed.), *Midnight Birds.* New York: Anchor Press/Doubleday, 1980.

JOHNSON, KIRK. "Alive and Well." *Essence,* December 1993: 74, 83.

MERIWETHER, LOUISE. *Daddy Was a Number Runner.* New York: Feminist Press, 1986.

MORRISON, TONI. *The Bluest Eye.* New York: Holt, Rinehart & Winston, 1970.

PARKS, GORDON. *The Learning Tree.* New York: Fawcett Crest, 1963.

FAMILY

BALDWIN, JAMES. *Go Tell It on the Mountain.* New York: Dell, 1953.

"The Black Family Nobody Knows." *Ebony,* August 1993: 28, 30–31.

COOPER, J. CALIFORNIA. "Swimming to the Top of the Rain." *Homemade Love.* New York: St. Martin's Press, 1987.

JEWELL, K. SUE. *Survival of the Black Family.* New York: Praeger, 1989.

MALCOLM X. "Nightmare." In *The Autobiography of Malcolm X.* New York: Grove Press, 1965.

MORRISON, TONI. *The Bluest Eye.* New York: Holt, Rinehart & Winston, 1970.

MURRAY, PAULI. *Proud Shoes.* New York: Harper, 1956.

RUSSELL, SANDI. "Sister." In Margaret Bugsby (ed.), *Daughters of Africa.* New York: Pantheon Books, 1992.

SCOTT-JONES, DIANE, A. DAVIS, M. FOSTER, and P. HUGHES. "Sexual Activity, Pregnancy and Childbearing Among African-American Youth." In Ronald L. Taylor. *African-American Youth: Their Social and Economic Status in the U.S.* New York: Praeger, 1994.

SHANGE, NTOZAKE. *Sassafrass, Cypress & Indigo.* New York: St. Martin's Press, 1982.

TAYLOR, MILDRED. *Roll of Thunder, Hear My Cry.* New York: Dial, 1976.

MALE-FEMALE RELATIONSHIPS

"Date Rape: The Tyson Syndrome." *Emerge,* May 1992: 43–44.

DOVE, RITA. "The Zulus." In Margaret Bugsby (ed.), *Daughters of Africa.* New York: Pantheon Books, 1992.

GRIMES, NIKKI. "Fragments: Mousetrap." Amiri and Amina Baraka (eds.), *Confirmation.* New York: Quill, 1983.

HURSTON, ZORA NEALE. "The Gilded Six-Bits." John Henrik Clarke (ed.), In *American Negro Short Stories.* New York: Hill and Wang, 1966.

———. *Their Eyes Were Watching God.* Urbana: University of Illinois Press, 1978.

KARENGA, MAULANA. "Black Male-Female Relationships." In *Introduction to Black Studies.* Los Angeles: University of Sankore Press, 1992.

McMILLAN, TERRY. *Disappearing Acts.* New York: Washington Square Press, 1989.

———. *Waiting to Exhale.* New York: Viking, 1992.

MORRISON, TONI. *Tar Baby.* New York: Knopf, 1981.

SHANGE, NTOZAKE. "comin to terms." Mary Helen Washington (ed.), In *Midnight Birds.* New York: Anchor Press/Doubleday, 1980.

CIVIL RIGHTS

BALDWIN, JAMES. "Blues for Mister Charlie." Clinton F. Oliver and Stephanie Sills (eds.), *Contemporary Black Drama.* New York: Scribner's, 1971.

CAMPBELL, BEBE MOORE. *Your Blues Ain't Like Mine.* New York: Ballantine, 1992.

GAINES, ERNEST J. *The Autobiography of Miss Jane Pittman.* New York: Doubleday, 1987.

KING, MARTIN LUTHER, JR. *Stride Toward Freedom: The Montgomery Story.* New York: Harper & Row, 1958.

LOWE, WALTER, JR. "Civil Rights: 25 Years After Martin's Death." *Emerge,* April 1993: 32–39.

WALKER, ALICE. *Meridian.* New York: Harcourt, 1976.

ZINN, HOWARD. *SNCC: The New Abolitionists.* Boston: Beacon Press, 1964.

FREEDOM • EQUALITY • UNITY • PROTEST

APTHEKER, HERBERT. *American Negro Slave Revolts.* New York: International, 1963.

BARAKA, AMINA. "Soweto Song." Amiri and Amina Baraka (eds.), *Confirmation.* New York: Quill, 1983.

"Beyond Rodney King: Unequal Justice in America." *Emerge,* December 1992: 38–40.

GIOVANNI, NIKKI. "For Saundra." Dudley Randall (ed.), *The Black Poets.* New York: Bantam, 1971.

GREENLEE, SAM. *The Spook Who Sat by the Door.* New York: Kayode Publishers, 1991.

HARDING, VINCENT. "Power from Our People." *The Black Scholar* 18(1) Jan./Feb. 1987, pp. 41–51.

ISMAILI, RASHIDAH. "Dialogue." Amiri and Amina Baraka (eds.), *Confirmation.* New York: Quill, 1983.

SANCHEZ, SONIA. *The Bronx Is Next. The Drama Review* 12(4) (T40), Summer 1968.

WHEATLEY, PHILLIS. "To the Right Honorable William, Earl of Dartmouth." Margaret Bugsby (ed.), *Daughters of Africa.* New York: Pantheon Books, 1992.

ARTS • SCIENCES • MEDIA

BARAKA, AMIRI. "Black Art." *The Black Scholar* 18(1), Jan./Feb. 1987, pp. 23–30.

"Guinea Pigs: Secret Medical Experiments on Blacks." *Emerge,* October 1994: 24–35.

JEWELL, K. SUE. *From Mammy to Miss America and Beyond: Cultural Images and the Shaping of U.S. Social Policy.* New York: Routledge, 1993.

KENNEDY, SHAWN. "Prime-Time Sister." *Emerge,* April 1994: 46–49.

NEAL, LARRY. "The Social Background of the Black Arts Movement." *The Black Scholar* 18(1), Jan./Feb. 1987, pp. 11–22.

WALKER, ALICE. "In Search of Our Mother's Gardens." In *In Search of Our Mother's Gardens.* New York: Harcourt Brace Jovanovich, 1983.

RELIGION • CHURCH

BALDWIN, JAMES. *Go Tell It on the Mountain.* New York: Dell, 1953.

——. *The Amen Corner.* New York: Dial, 1968.

BATTLE, V. DuWAYNE. "The Influence of Al-Islam in America on the Black Community." *The Black Scholar* 19(1), Jan./Feb. 1988, pp. 33–41.

CLARKE, JOHN HENRIK. "The Boy Who Painted Christ Black." In *American Negro Short Stories.* New York: Hill and Wang, 1966.

HAYNES, REV. LEMUEL B. "Universal Salvation—A Very Ancient Doctrine." In Richard K. Barksdale and Keneth Kinnamon (eds.), *Black Writers of America.* New York: Macmillan, 1972.

HUGHES, LANGSTON. *Tambourines to Glory.* New York: Hill and Wang, 1958.

JONES, LISA. "Blacks in the Bible." *Ebony,* February 1994: 60, 62, 66.

MONROE, SYLVESTER. "The Fruits of Islam: Muslim Faith Grows in Followers and Respect." *Emerge,* March 1994: 38–43.

WHEATLEY, PHILLIS. "On Being Brought from Africa to America." Richard K. Barksdale and Keneth Kinnamon (eds.), *Black Writers of America.* New York: Macmillan, 1972.

HERITAGE • IDENTITY

CARMICHAEL, STOKELY. "From Black Power Back to Pan-Africanism." In *Stokely Speaks.* New York: Vintage, 1971.

CULLEN, COUNTEE. "Heritage." In Richard K. Barksdale and Keneth Kinnamon (eds.), *Black Writers of America.* New York: Macmillan, 1972.

DuBois, W.E.B. *The World and Africa.* New York: International, 1965.

DUNBAR, PAUL LAURENCE. "Ode to Ethiopia." In Arthur P. Davis, J. Saunders Redding, and Joyce Ann Joyce (eds.), *The New Cavalcade.* 2 vols. Washington, DC: Howard University Press, 1991. 1: 304–305.

ELLISON, RALPH. *Invisible Man.* New York: Vintage, 1972.

HALEY, ALEX. *Roots.* New York: Doubleday, 1976.

KILLENS, JOHN. "Yoruba." In Arthur P. Davis, J. Saunders Redding, and Joyce Ann Joyce (eds.), *The New Cavalcade.* 2 vols. Washington, DC: Howard University Press, 1991. 2: 29–44.

MARSHALL, PAULE. *Praisesong for the Widow.* New York: Putnam, 1983.

VAN SERTIMA, IVAN. *They Came Before Columbus: The African Presence in Ancient America.* New York: Random House, 1976.

WILLIAMS, CHANCELLOR. *The Destruction of Black Civilization.* Chicago: Third World Press, 1987.

READING • WRITING • EDUCATION

IRVINE, JACQUELINE J. *Black Students and School Failure.* New York: Praeger, 1991.

MADGETT, NAOMI LONG. "Writing a Poem." In Arthur P. Davis, J. Saunders Redding, and Joyce Ann Joyce (eds.), *The New Cavalcade.* 2 vols. Washington, DC: Howard University Press, 1991. 2: 175.

"Separate and Unequal: The Education of Blacks 40 Years After Brown." *Emerge,* May 1994: 25–52.

"Toni Morrison," In Claudia Tate (ed.), *Black Women Writers at Work.* New York: Continuum, 1985.

WILLIE, CHARLES V. (ed.). *The Education of African-Americans.* New York: Praeger, 1991.

WOODSON, CARTER G. *The Mis-Education of the Negro.* Nashville, TN: Winston-Derek, 1940.

POLITICAL PHILOSOPHIES

AKADE, MAURICE. "A New Call: Reparations for Africa." *Emerge,* October 1992: 20.

CARMICHAEL, STOKELY, and CHARLES V. HAMILTON. *Black Power: The Politics of Liberation in America.* New York: Vintage, 1967.

CRUMMELL, ALEXANDER. "The Relations and Duties of Free Colored Men in America to Africa." In Richard K. Barksdale and Keneth Kinnamon (eds.), *Black Writers of America.* New York: Macmillan, 1972.

DAVIS, ANGELA Y. *Angela Davis: An Autobiography.* New York: International Publishers, 1988.

DOUGLASS, FREDERICK. "Oration, Delivered in Corinthian Hall, Rochester, July 5, 1852." In Richard K. Barksdale and Keneth Kinnamon (eds.), *Black Writers of America.* New York: Macmillan, 1972.

DuBois, W.E.B. *The Souls of Black Folk.* A.C. McClurg, 1903. Mattituck, New York: Amereon Ltd.

GARVEY, MARCUS. *The Philosophy and Opinions of Marcus Garvey.* 2 vols. Amy Jacques Garvey (ed.), New York: Atheneum, 1973.

KING, MARTIN LUTHER, JR. *Why We Can't Wait.* New York: Harper & Row, 1964.

MALCOLM X. *Malcolm X Speaks.* New York: Grove Press, 1965.

MUHAMMAD, ELIJAH. *Message to the Black Man in America.* Chicago: Muhammad Mosque of Islam No. 2, 1965.

SHAKUR, ASSATA. *Assata: An Autobiography.* Westport, CT: Lawrence Hill, 1987.

WASHINGTON, BOOKER T. *Up from Slavery.* New York: Doubleday, 1901.

BLACK ENGLISH • DIALECT

CHESNUTT, CHARLES W. *The Conjure Woman.* New York: Houghton Mifflin, 1969.

DANIEL, JACK L., and GENEVA SMITHERMAN. "How I Got Over: Communication Dynamics in the Black Community." *Quarterly Journal of Speech* 62, 1976, pp. 26–39.

DILLARD, JOEY L. *Black English: Its History and Usage in the U.S.* New York: Random House, 1972.

DUNBAR, PAUL Laurence "The Party." In Richard K. Barksdale and Keneth Kinnamon (eds.), *Black Writers of America.* New York: Macmillan, 1972.

HOLT, GRACE SIMS. "Stylin' Outta the Black Pulpit." In Thomas Kochman (ed.), *Rappin' and Stylin' Out.* Urbana: University of Illinois Press, 1972.

MAJOR, CLARENCE (ed.). *Juba to Jive: A Dictionary of African-American Slang.* New York: Penguin, 1994.

SMITHERMAN, GENEVA. *Talkin and Testifyin: The Language of Black America.* Boston: Houghton Mifflin, 1977.

——. *Black Talk: Words and Phrases from the Hood to the Amen Corner.* Boston: Houghton-Mifflin, 1994.

FOLKLORE

BUTLER, OCTAVIA. *Wild Seed.* New York: Doubleday, 1980.

——. *Kindred.* New York: Beacon Press, 1988.

CAMPBELL, JAMES EDWIN. "De Cunjah Man." In Arthur P. Davis, J. Saunders Redding, and Joyce Ann Joyce (eds.), *The New Cavalcade.* 2 vols. Washington, DC: Howard University Press, 1991. 1:287–288.

CHESNUTT, CHARLES W. *The Conjure Woman.* New York: Houghton Mifflin, 1969.

HURSTON, ZORA NEALE. *Mules and Men.* Bloomington: Indiana University Press, 1978.

——. *Their Eyes Were Watching God.* Urbana: University of Illinois Press, 1978.

MARSHALL, PAULE. "Ibo Landing." In Chapter 3, *Praisesong for the Widow.* New York: Plume, 1983.

MORRISON, TONI. *Song of Solomon.* New York: Knopf, 1977.

NAYLOR, GLORIA. *Mama Day.* New York: Vintage, 1989.

REED, ISHMAEL. *Yellow Back Radio Broke-Down.* New York: Doubleday, 1971.

RACISM • DISCRIMINATION

DULA, ANNETTE (ed.). *"It Just Ain't Fair": The Ethics of Health Care for African Americans.* New York: Praeger, 1994.

DUMAS, HENRY. *Ark of Bones, and Other Stories.* Carbondale: Southern Illinois University Press, 1974.

KILLENS, JOHN OLIVER. *Black Man's Burden.* New York: Simon & Schuster, 1965.

KING, MARTIN LUTHER, JR. *Why I Can't Wait.* New York: Harper & Row, 1964.

McKAY, CLAUDE. "America." In Richard K. Barksdale and Keneth Kinnamon (eds.), *Black Writers of America.* New York: Macmillan, 1972.

NICHOLS, CHARLES H. *Many Thousand Gone: The Ex-Slaves' Account of Their Bondage and Freedom.* Bloomington: Indiana Univ. Press, 1969.

WELLS, IDA B. *Crusade for Justice.* Chicago: University of Chicago Press, 1970.

WHITE, WALTER. "I Investigate Lynchings." In Richard K. Barksdale and Keneth Kinnamon (eds.), *Black Writers of America.* New York: Macmillan, 1972.

WRIGHT, RICHARD. *Uncle Tom's Children.* New York: Harper, 1969.

INTERRACIAL RELATIONSHIPS

ANGELOU, MAYA. "The Reunion." In Amiri and Amina Baraka (eds.), *Confirmation.* New York: Quill, 1983.

BALDWIN, JAMES. "Going to Meet the Man." In *Going to Meet the Man.* New York: Doubleday, 1965.

CAMPBELL, BEBE MOORE. *Your Blues Ain't Like Mine.* New York: Ballantine, 1992.

DUMAS, HENRY. "Double Nigger." In *Goodbye, Sweetwater.* New York: Thunder's Mouth Press, 1988.

FAUSET, JESSIE. *There Is Confusion.* New York: Boni & Liveright, 1924.

JONES, LEROI. "Dutchman." Clinton F. Oliver and Stephanie Sills (eds.), *Contemporary Black Drama.* New York: Scribner's, 1971.

JONES, LISA, and HETTIE JONES. "Mama's White." *Essence,* May 1994: 78–80, 150–152, 154, 158.

KILLENS, JOHN OLIVER. "God Bless America." John Henrik Clarke (ed.), In *American Negro Short Stories.* New York: Hill and Wang, 1966.

INTERRACIAL PREJUDICE

BATES, KAREN GRIGSBY. "The Color Thing." *Essence,* September 1994: 79–30, 132, 134–135.

BROOKS, GWENDOLYN. *Maud Martha.* New York: Farrar, Straus & Giroux, 1969.

CHESNUTT, CHARLES. *The Wife of His Youth, and Other Stories of the Color Line.* New York: Houghton Mifflin, 1899.

FAUSET, JESSIE. *Comedy: American Style.* Stokes, 1933.

LARSEN, NELLA. *Passing.* New York: Collier, 1971.

MORRISON, TONI. "Geraldine." *The Bluest Eye.* New York: Holt, Rinehart and Winston, 1970.

THURMAN, WALLACE. *The Blacker the Berry.* New York: Macaulay, 1929.

Video List to Supplement Readings

(Unless otherwise noted, all video cassettes may be rented from your local video store or borrowed from your local public library. Where film length and ratings were available, they have been provided.)

Slavery

Skin Game. 102 min. 1971 (Color) (PG).
Roots. 540 min. 1977 (Color).
Roots: The Next Generation. 480 min. 1978 (Color).
Presenting Mr. Frederick Douglass: "The Lesson of the Hour." 60 min. (Color) Films for the Humanities and Sciences.
Unearthing the Slave Trade. 28 min. (Color) Films for the Humanities and Sciences.
Race to Freedom: The Underground Railroad. 90 min. 1993 (Color).
Brother Future. A Wonderworks Family Movie. 60 min.
Half Slave, Half Free (a.k.a. *Solomon Northrop's Odyssey*). 113 min. 1984.
Half Slave, Half Free 2 (a.k.a. *Charlotte Forten's Mission: Experiment in Freedom*). 120 min. 1985.
Sankofa. 120 min. 1993 (Color).

African American Women

Lady Sings the Blues. 144 min. 1972 (Color) (R).
Happy Birthday, Mrs. Craig. 55 min. Filmakers Library.
Two Dollars and A Dream: Madame C.J. Walker. 56 min. Filmakers Library.
Freedom Bags. 32 min. Filmakers Library.
Ida B. Wells: A Passion for Justice. 60 min.
The Women of Brewster Place. 180 min. 1988 (Color).
Fundi: The Story of Ella Baker. 45 min. 1986 (Color). First Run/Icarus Films.

Wilma: The Wilma Rudolph Story. 100 min. (Color) (PG-13).
Mrs. Fannie Lou Hamer. 52 min. 1983 (Color).

African American Men

Jo Jo Dancer, Your Life Is Calling. 97 min. 1986 (Color) (R).
Native Son. 111 min. 1987 (Color).
Black Boy. 86 min. 1994. The African-American Video Library.
Almos' A Man. 51 min. (Color).
Tuskegee Airmen. 23 min.
The "Rodney King" Case: What The Jury Saw in California v. Powell. 1992 (Color).
Menace II Society. 104 min. 1993 (Color) (R).
Negro Soldier. 49 min. 1943.
Glory. 122 min. 1989 (Color) (R).

Childhood • Adolescence • Growing Up

I Know Why the Caged Bird Sings. 96 min. 1979 (Color).
The Learning Tree. 107 min. 1969 (Color) (PG).
Bustin' Loose. 94 min. 1981 (Color) (R).
The Kid from Left Field. 99 min. 1979 (Color) (G).
The Breeding of Impotence. 55 min. 1993 (Color). The Cinema Guild, Inc.
Hardwood Dreams. 47 min. 1993 (Color).
Tell Them Who We Are: African-American Drill Teams. 29 min. New Day Film Library.
A Hero Ain't Nothin' But a Sandwich. 1977 (PG).
South Central. 99 min. 1992 (Color) (R).
Runaway. 58 min. (Color).
Fresh. 112 min. 1994 (Color) (R).

Family

A Raisin in the Sun. 128 min. 1961 (B & W).
The River Niger. 104 min. 1978 (Color) (R).
Sounder. 105 min. 1972 (Color) (G).
Crooklyn. 112 min. 1994 (Color) (PG-13).
In Search of Our Fathers. 55 min. Filmakers Library.
Goin Back to T-Town: African-Americans in Oklahoma. 60 min.
Go Tell It on the Mountain. 100 min. 1985 (Color).
The River Niger. 104 min. 1978 (R).
The Sky Is Gray. 46 min. 1980.

Male-Female Relationships

Mahogany. 110 min. 1975 (Color) (PG).
Pipe Dreams. 89 min. 1976 (Color).
Poetic Justice. 109 min. (Color) (R).
The Color Purple. 154 min. 1985 (Color) (PG-13).
What's Love Got to Do with It. 118 min. (Color) (R).
The Honorable Louis Farrakhan: The Role of Women and Their Relationship with God and Man. 1990.
Jawanza Kunjufu on Black Male-Female Relationships. 1992.
Porgy and Bess. 138 min. 1959.
Waiting to Exhale. 127 min. 1996 (Color) (R).

Civil Rights

King. 245 min. 1978 (Color).
The Autobiography of Miss Jane Pittman. 110 min. 1974 (Color).
The Freedom Train. 28 min. Filmakers Library.
Last Breeze of Summer. (bussing).
The Ernest Green Story. (desegregation).
For Us the Living: The Story of Medgar Evers. 84 min. 1984 (Color).
Mississippi Burning. 127 min. 1988 (Color) (R).

Freedom • Equality • Unity • Protest

Eyes on the Prize, Pts. I and II. 50 min. segments.
Roll of Thunder, Hear My Cry. 115 min. 1978 (Color) (PG).
Freedom on My Mind. 115 min. (Color). Clarity Educational Productions, Inc.
Words by Heart. A Wonderworks Family Movie.
Dark Exodus. 28 min. (B & W).
The Spook Who Sat by the Door. 102 min. 1973 (Color) (PG).
Attica. 97 min. 1980.
Cornbread, Earl and Me. 95 min. 1975 (PG).
Meteor Man. 99 min. 1993 (Color) (PG).
A Gathering of Old Men. 100 min. 1987 (Color).
Heat Wave. 94 min. 1990 (Color).

Arts • Sciences • Media

The Deadly Deception: The Tuskegee Study of Untreated Syphilis in the Negro Male. 58 min. (Color). Films for the Humanities and Sciences.
Jessye Norman, Singer. 74 min. Filmakers Library.
Didn't We Ramble On: The Black Marching Band. 14 min. Filmakers Library.
African-American Art: Past and Present. 90 min. Reading & O'Reilly, Inc.
Race Against Prime Time. 58 min. 1985. California Newsreel.
Color Adjustment. 88 min. 1991. California Newsreel.

Religion • Church

God's Alcatraz. 36 min. (B & W). Filmakers Library.
Saturday Night, Sunday Morning. 70 min. 1992. California Newsreel.
Let the Church Say Amen. 60 min. 1973 (Color). First Run/Icarus Films.
King James Version. 91 min. 1988 (Color). First Run/Icarus Films.
Religion and Race in America: Martin L. King's Lament. 60 min. (Color). Films for the Humanities and Sciences.
Go Down Death. 54 min. 1944.
Africentric Spirituality: A Lecture by Dr. Akbar. 1993.
Say Amen Somebody. 120 min. (Color). GTN Productions.

Heritage • Identity

Roots. 540 min. 1977 (Color).
Speak It! From the Heart Nova Scotia. 29 min. Filmakers Library.
Kwanzaa: A Cultural Celebration. 29 min. (Color). Films for the Humanities and Sciences.

Black Is . . . Black Ain't. 87 min. 1995. California Newsreel.
Bernice Johnson Reagon: The Songs Are Free. 58 min. 1991 (Color).
Daughters of the Dust. 113 min. 1991 (Color).

Reading • Writing • Education

Something with Me. 55 min. 1992. Filmakers Library.
Toni Morrison: A Writer's Work. 52 min. (Color). Films for the Humanities
and Sciences.
Facing the Facade. 60 min. 1994 (Color). The Cinema Guild.
Clarence and Angel. 75 min. 1980 (Color) (G).
The George McKenna Story. 95 min. 1993 (Color).
Cooley High. 107 min. 1975 (PG).
The Marva Collins Story. 100 min. 1981 (Color).
The Mighty Pawns. 58 min. 1987 (Color).
To Be Popular or Smart: The Black Peer Group. (Jawanza Kunjufu) 1988.

Political Philosophies

Malcolm X. 201 min. 1992 (Color) (PG-13).
Marcus Garvey: Toward Black Nationhood. 42 min. (Color). Films for the Hu-
manities and Sciences.
Ida B. Wells: A Passion for Justice. 60 min. Public Broadcasting System.
King: A Filmed Record . . . Montgomery to Memphis. 153 min. 1970.
Black Conservatives. 28 min. (Color). Films for the Humanities and Sci-
ences.
Paul Robeson. 118 min. 1977.

Black Dialect • Language

The Darker Side of Black. 59 min. 1966. Filmakers Library.
Straight Up Rappin'. 29 min. Filmakers Library.
Rap, Race and Equality. 58 min. Filmakers Library.
The Story of English: Black on White. Public Broadcasting System.

Folklore

Aesop's Fables. 30 min. (Color).
Zajota and the Boogie Spirit. 20 min. Filmakers Library.
When the Animals Talked. 28 min. 1982.
Juba: How Stories Came to Be. 15 min. (Color).
Juba: Brer Rabbit Stories. 15 min. (Color).
Juba: Why Stories. 15 min. (Color).

Racism • Discrimination

To Kill a Mockingbird. 129 min. 1962 (B & W).
The Watermelon Man. 97 min. 1970 (Color) (R).
Black Like Me. 110 min. 1964 (B & W).
Ethnic Notions. 56 min. 1987. California Newsreel.
The Road to Brown. 56 min. 1990. California Newsreel.
The Klansman. 112 min. 1974 (Color) (R).

Tarzan, the Ape Man. 104 min. 1932.
Jawanza Kunjufu: From Miseducation to Education: The Psychological Effects of Racism on African-Americans. 1992.

Interracial Relationships

In the Heat of the Night. 111 min. 1967 (Color).
Guess Who's Coming to Dinner. 108 min. 1967 (Color).
The Adventures of Huckleberry Finn. 74 min. 1975 (Color) (G).
Are We Different? 27 min. Filmakers Library.
Just Black? 57 min. Filmakers Library.
Dutchman. 55 min. 1967. Insight Media.
Separate But Equal. 193 min. 1991 (Color) (PG).
Do the Right Thing. 120 min. 1989 (Color) (R).
The Sky Is Gray. 46 min. 1980.

Intraracial Prejudice

School Daze. 114 min. 1987 (Color) (R).
A Question of Color. 56 min. 1993. California Newsreel.
I Passed for White. 93 min. 1960.
Imitation of Life. 124 min. 1959.
The Colored Museum. 60 min. (Color). Public Broadcasting System.

Additional Videos

Fire Eyes: Female Circumcision. 60 min. Filmakers Library. (African-American Women).
The Defiant Ones. 97 min. 1958 (B & W). (Interracial).
The Call of the Jitterbug. 30 min. Filmakers Library. (Arts/Sciences/Media).
South Central. 99 min. 1992 (Color) (R). (Childhood/Adolescence/ Growing Up).
Wild Women Don't Have the Blues. 58 min. 1989. California Newsreel. (Racism/Discrimination).
Kindred Spirits: Contemporary African-American Artists. 30 min. 1992 (Color). (Arts/Sciences/Media).
A Patch of Blue. 106 min. 1965 (Interracial Relationships).
To Sir With Love. 105 min. 1967 (Color). (Reading/Writing/Education).

Acknowledgments

ELIJAH ANDERSON, "Respect of the Streets" (editors' title), excerpt from "The Code of the Streets" from *The Code of the Streets*. Originally in *The Atlantic Monthly* 273, no. 5 (May 1994). Copyright © 1994 by Elijah Anderson. Reprinted with the permission of W.W. Norton & Company, Inc.

MAYA ANGELOU, "Marguerite's Graduation" (editors' title) from *I Know Why the Caged Bird Sings*. Copyright © 1969 by Maya Angelou. Reprinted with the permission of Random House, Inc.

ARTHUR ASHE, "Send Your Children to the Libraries," *The New York Times* (February 6, 1977). Copyright © 1977 by The New York Times Company. Reprinted with the permission of *The New York Times*.

JAMES BALDWIN, "If Black English Isn't a Language, Then Tell Me, What Is?," *The New York Times* (July 29, 1979). Copyright © 1979 by The New York Times Company. Reprinted with the permission of *The New York Times*.

JAMES BALDWIN, "The Stranger in the Village" from *Notes of a Native Son*. Copyright © 1953, 1955 by James Baldwin. Reprinted with the permission of Beacon Press.

TONI CADE BAMBARA, "Gorilla, My Love" from *Gorilla, My Love*. Copyright © 1972 by Toni Cade Bambara. Reprinted with the permission of Random House, Inc.

MICHAEL A. BATTLE, SR., "The Dynamic Tension in the Black Church" from *The African-American Church at Work*. Reprinted with the permission of Hodale Press, Inc.

ARNA BONTEMPS, "A Summer Tragedy" from *The Old South: "A Summer Tragedy" and Other Stories of the Thirties* (New York: Dodd, Mead, 1973). Copyright 1933 by Arna Bontemps. Reprinted with the permission of Harold Ober Associates, Inc.

GWENDOLYN BROOKS, "To Those Of My Sisters Who Kept Their Naturals" from *Blacks* (Chicago: Third World Press, 1987). Copyright © 1991 by Gwendolyn Brooks. Reprinted with the permission of the author. "Requiem

Before Revival" from *Primer for Blacks* (Chicago: Third World Press, 1991). Copyright © 1991 by Gwendolyn Brooks. Reprinted with the permission of the author. "if you're light and have long hair" from *Maud Martha*, reprinted in *Blacks* (Chicago: Third World Press, 1987). Copyright © 1991 by Gwendolyn Brooks. Reprinted with the permission of the author.

TONY BROWN, "Becoming a Republican," *The Wall Street Journal* (August 5, 1991). Copyright © 1991 by Dow Jones & Company, Inc. Reprinted with the permission of *The Wall Street Journal.*

EARL CALDWELL, "Shining light of a poet & pioneer," *Amsterdam News* (August 21, 1993). Reprinted by permission.

BEBE MOORE CAMPBELL, "Without Dad" (editors' title) from *Sweet Summer: Growing Up With and Without My Dad.* Copyright © 1989 by Bebe Moore Campbell. Reprinted with the permission of The Putnam Publishing Group. "Betrayal? When black men date white women," The New York Times Magazine (August 29, 1992). Copyright © 1992 by Bebe Moore Campbell. Reprinted with the permission of *The New York Times.*

JOHN HENRIK CLARKE, "To Know One's History Is To Know Oneself" (editors' title, originally titled and excerpted from "A Search for Identity"), *Social Casework* (May 1970). Copyright © 1970 by Family Services Association of America. Reprinted with the permission of Families International, Inc.

BILL COSBY, "A Fling on the Track" from *Love and Marriage.* Copyright © 1989 by William H. Cosby, Jr. Reprinted with the permission of Doubleday, a division of Bantam Doubleday Dell Publishing Group, Inc.

COUNTEE CULLEN, "Incident" from *On These I Stand* (New York: Harper & Brothers, 1925). Copyright 1925 by Harper & Brothers, renewed 1953 by Ida M. Cullen. Reprinted with the permission of GRM Associates as agents for the Estate of Ida M. Cullen.

JANNETTE LAKE DATES and WILLIAM BARLOW, "Crossover Dreams and Racial Realities" (editors' title, originally titled "Conclusion: Crossover Dreams and Racial Realities") and "Black Comedy, White Reality" (editors' title, originally titled "Commercial Television"), both from *Split Image: African Americans in the Mass Media.* Copyright © 1990 by Janette Lake Dates and William Barlow. Reprinted with the permission of Howard University Press.

ANGELA DAVIS, "Slavery and Womanhood" (editors' title) from *Women, Race and Class.* Copyright © 1983 by Angela Carter. Reprinted with the permission of Random House, Inc.

MELINDA ELAINE EDMOND, "Poverty and Education" (previously unpublished student essay). Reprinted with the permission of the author.

MIA ELLIOTT, "Society Rejects Mixed Children" (previously unpublished student essay). Reprinted with the permission of the author.

MARI EVANS, "Who I Am and How I Work" (editors' title, originally titled "My Father's Passage") from *Black Women Writers (1950–1980): A Critical Evaluation,* edited by Mari Evans. Copyright © 1983 by Mari Evans. Reprinted with the permission of Doubleday, a division of Bantam Doubleday Dell Publishing Group, Inc. "I Am a Black Woman" from *I Am A Black Woman* (New York: William Morrow & Company, 1970). Copyright © 1970 by Mari Evans. Reprinted with the permission of the author.

ERNEST GAINES, "The Sky is Gray" (excerpt) from *Bloodline.* Copyright © 1963 by Ernest Gaines. Reprinted with the permission of Doubleday, a division of Bantam Doubleday Dell Publishing Group, Inc.

MARCUS GARVEY, "Garvey Speaks at Madison Square Garden" (editors' title, originally titled "Speech Delivered at Madison Square Garden, March 1924"). Reprinted by permission.

HENRY LOUIS GATES, JR., "TV's Black World," (editors' title, originally titled "TV's Black World Turns—But Stays Unreal"), *The New York Times* (November 12, 1989). Copyright © 1989 by Henry Louis Gates, Jr. Reprinted with the permission of Brandt & Brandt Literary Agents, Inc.

CAMILLE GRAY, "The Positive Environment in Black Female-Headed Families" (previously unpublished student essay). Reprinted with the permission of the author.

CYRIL AUSTIN GREENE, "The Question of Name: African or African-American?" (previously unpublished student essay). Reprinted with the permission of the author.

HAKIMAH A. GREGORY, "Fruits of Labor, Fruits of Sorrow, Fruits of Love" (previously unpublished student essay). Reprinted with the permission of the author.

DWAYNE GRIFFIN, "Are Black Males Becoming An Endangered Species?" (previously unpublished student essay). Reprinted with the permission of the author.

ALEX HALEY, "Kunta Kinte Is Born" (editors' title) from *Roots.* Copyright © 1976 by Alex Haley. Reprinted with the permission of Doubleday, a division of Bantam Doubleday Dell Publishing Group, Inc.

VIRGINIA HAMILTON, "The People Could Fly" from *The People Could Fly: American Black Folktales.* Copyright © 1985 by Virginia Hamilton. Reprinted with the permission of Alfred A. Knopf, Inc.

LORRAINE HANSBERRY, "A Raisin in the Sun" (excerpt). Copyright © 1958, 1959, 1966, 1984 by Robert Nemiroff. Reprinted with the permission of Random House, Inc.

ROBERT HAYDEN, "Those Winter Sundays" from *Angle of Ascent: New and Selected Poems.* Copyright © 1966 by Robert Hayden. Reprinted with the permission of Liveright Publishing Corporation.

LANGSTON HUGHES, "Mother to Son" and "The Negro Speaks of Rivers" from *Selected Poems.* Copyright 1926 by Alfred A. Knopf, Inc., renewed 1954 by Langston Hughes. Reprinted with the permission of the publisher. "Salvation" from *The Big Sea.* Copyright 1940 by Langston Hughes, renewed © 1968 by Arna Bontemps and George Houston Bass. Reprinted with the permission of Hill & Wang, a division of Farrar, Straus & Giroux, Inc.

KRISTIN HUNTER, "Debut," *Negro Digest* 17 (June 1968). Copyright © 1968 by Kristin Hunter. Reprinted with the permission of the author, c/o Jane Dystel Literary Management.

ZORA NEALE HURSTON, "Tea Cake and Janie" (editors' title) from *Their Eyes Were Watching God.* Copyright 1937 by Zora Neale Hurston, renewed © 1965 by John C. Hurston and Joel Hurston. Reprinted with the permission of HarperCollins Publishers, Inc. "I Get Born" from *Dust Tracks on a Road* (New York: J.B. Lippincott, 1971). Copyright 1942 by Zora Neale Hurston, renewed © 1970 by John C. Hurston. Reprinted with the permission of HarperCollins Publishers, Inc.

PORTIA P. JAMES, "The Slave Inventors" (editors' title, originally titled "Enslaved Inventors: Hidden Contributions") from *The Real McCoy: African American Invention and Innovation 1619–1930.* Copyright © 1989. Reprinted with the permission of Smithsonian Institution Press.

JOYCE M. JARRETT, "Freedom" from *Between Worlds* (1988). Reprinted in *Pathways: A Text for Developing Writers* by Joyce Jarrett, Doreatha Mbalia and Margaret Lee (New York: Macmillan Publishing Company, 1990). Copyright © 1988 by Joyce Jarrett. Reprinted with the permission of the author.

LANCE JEFFERS, "My Blackness is the Beauty of this Land" from *My Blackness is the Beauty of this Land.* Copyright © 1970 by Lance Jeffers. Reprinted with the permission of Broadside Press.

JAMES WELDON JOHNSON, "The Creation" from *God's Trombones.* Copyright 1927 by The Viking Press, Inc., renewed © 1955 by Grace Nail Johnson. Reprinted with the permission of Viking Penguin, a division of Penguin Books USA Inc.

JAMAICA KINCAID, "The Circling Hand" from *Annie John.* Copyright © 1985 by Jamaica Kincaid. Reprinted with the permission of Farrar, Straus & Giroux, Inc.

MARTIN LUTHER KING, JR., "I Have a Dream." Copyright © 1962 by Martin Luther King, Jr., renewed 1990 by Coretta Scott King, Dexter King, Martin Luther King III, Yolanda King and Bernice King. Reprinted with the permission of the Joan Daves Agency.

FELICIA R. LEE, "African-American Youth Resist Using Standard English" (editors' title, originally titled "Grappling With How to Teach Young Speakers of Black Dialect"), *The New York Times* (January 5, 1994). Copyright © 1994 by The New York Times Company. Reprinted with the permission of *The New York Times.*

JEROME MASON, "Stone City" (previously unpublished student essay). Reprinted with the permission of the author.

KHADIJAH A. MAYO, "The Black Panther Party" (previously unpublished student essay). Reprinted with the permission of the author.

CLAUDE MCKAY, "If We Must Die" from *Home to Harlem* (New York: Harper & Brothers, 1928). Copyright 1928 by Harper & Brothers, Inc., renewed © 1956 by Hope McKay Virtue. Reprinted with the permission of Carl Cowl, Administrator, The Archives of Claude McKay.

TERRY MCMILLAN, "Discovering the Writer In Me" (editors' title) from "Introduction" to *Breaking Ice.* Copyright © 1990 by Terry McMillan. Reprinted with the permission of Viking Penguin, a division of Penguin Books USA Inc.

MARSHALL MERCY, "The Criminal Justice System and Poor Blacks" (previously unpublished student essay). Reprinted with the permission of the author.

JAMES MITCHENER, "Affirmative Action: The Controversial Topic" (previously unpublished student essay). Reprinted with the permission of the author.

ANNE MOODY, Chapter X from *Coming of Age in Mississippi.* Copyright © 1968 by Anne Moody. Reprinted with the permission of Doubleday, a division of Bantam Doubleday Dell Publishing Group, Inc.

TONI MORRISON, "A Difference of Opinion" (editors' title, originally titled "A Slow Walk of Trees"), *The New York Times Magazine* (July 4, 1976). Copyright © 1976 by Toni Morrison. Reprinted with the permission of International Creative Management, Inc. "1923" from *Sula* (New York: Alfred A. Knopf, 1974). Copyright © 1973 by Toni Morrison. Reprinted with the permission of International Creative Management, Inc.

ROBERT W. MULLEN, "Blacks in Vietnam" (editors' title) from *Blacks in America's Wars.* Copyright © 1973 by Dr. Robert W. Mullen. Reprinted with the permission of the author.

VERNELL MUNADI, "Islam and African-American Women" (previously unpublished student essay). Reprinted with the permission of the author.

PAULI MURRAY, "My Life in Black and White" (editors' title) from *Proud Shoes:*

The Story of An American Family. Copyright © 1956 and renewed 1984 by Pauli Murray. Reprinted with the permission of HarperCollins Publishers, Inc.

KARL NICHOLS, "The Tradition of IFA" (previously unpublished student essay). Reprinted with the permission of the author.

JASON ORR, "Positive Affirmations Among African-American Men and Women" (previously unpublished student essay). Reprinted with the permission of the author.

ANN PETRY, "Like a Winding Sheet," *The Crisis* (November 1945). Copyright 1945 and renewed © 1974 by Ann Petry. Reprinted with the permission of *The Crisis.*

TED POSTON, "The Revolt of the Evil Fairies" from *The Dark Side of Hopkinsville,* edited by Kathleen A. Hauke (Athens: The University of Georgia Press, 1991). Reprinted with the permission of Mrs. Ersa Hines Poston and Mrs. Ruth Banks for The Estate of Ted Poston.

DUDLEY RANDALL, "Booker T. and W.E.B." from *Poem Counterpoem.* Copyright © 1966 by Margaret Danner and Dudley Randall. Reprinted with the permission of Broadside Press.

EUGENE REDMOND, "Parapoetics" from *The Eye in the Ceiling: Selected Poems* (New York: Harlem River Press, 1991). Originally in *Sentry of the Four Golden Pillars.* Copyright © 1991 by Eugene Redmond. Reprinted with the permission of the author.

ISHMAEL REED, "What's American About America?" (editors' title, originally titled "America: The Multicultural Society") from *Writin' is Fightin'* (New York: Atheneum Publishers, 1988). Originally in *San Francisco Focus* (1983). Copyright © 1983 by Ishmael Reed. Reprinted with the permission of Barbara Lowenstein Literary Agency.

ANDREA L. PROVIDENCE ROBINSON, "Black is Beautiful - ALL Shades" (previously unpublished student essay). Reprinted with the permission of the author.

DAVID RUBEL, "Working for SNCC" from *Fannie Lou Hamer: From Sharecropper to Politics.* Reprinted by permission.

SONIA SANCHEZ, "Just Don't Never Give Up On Love" from *Homegirls and Handgrenades.* Copyright © 1984 by Sonia Sanchez. Reprinted with the permission of Thunder's Mouth Press.

Cleveland Sellers, "Howard University: A Rude Awakening" (editors' title, originally titled "Howard University: The Beginning of Total Commitment") from *The River of No Return.* Copyright © 1973 by Cleveland Sellers. Reprinted with the permission of William Morrow and Company, Inc.

ROGER GUENVEUR SMITH, "The Rap on Frederick Douglass" from *The New York Times* (February 19, 1990). Copyright © 1990 by The New York Times Company. Reprinted with the permission of *The New York Times.*

GENEVA SMITHERMAN, excerpt from "Introduction" from *Black Talk: Words and Phrases from the Hood to the Amen Corner.* Copyright © 1994 by Geneva Smitherman. Reprinted with the permission of Houghton Mifflin Company.

BRENT STAPLES, "Just Walk On By: A Black Man Ponders His Power to Alter Public Space," *Ms.* (September 1986). Copyright © 1986 by Brent Staples. Reprinted with the permission of the author.

TANSEY THOMAS, "Those 'Super Strong' Black Women." Reprinted by permission.

BRIAN THOMPSON, "Public Schools for African-American Males: Are They Necessary?" (previously unpublished student essay). Reprinted with the permission of the author.

JEAN TOOMER, "Becky" from *Cane.* Copyright 1923 by Boni & Liveright, renewed 1951 by Jean Toomer. Reprinted with the permission of Liveright Publishing Corporation.

MALCOLM X, "Learning to Read" (editors' title, originally titled "Learning To Read") from *The Autobiography of Malcolm X* by Malcolm X with the assistance of Alex Haley. Copyright © 1964 by Alex Haley and Malcolm X. Copyright © 1965 by Alex Haley and Malcolm X, copyright © 1965 by Alex Haley and Betty Shabazz. Reprinted with the permission of Random House, Inc.

MARGARET WALKER, "For My People" from *This is My Century: New and Collected Poems.* Copyright 1942 by Margaret Walker Alexander. Reprinted with the permission of The University of Georgia Press.

WILLIAM WEIR, "Kwanzaa" (previously unpublished student essay). Reprinted with the permission of the author.

KARIE WERMELING, "The Eugenics Sterilization Movement" (previously unpublished student essay). Reprinted with the permission of the author.

PAULETTE CHILDRESS WHITE, "Alice" from *Essence* (January 1977). Copyright © 1977 by Paulette Childress White. Reprinted by permission.

JOHN EDGAR WIDEMAN, "The Ghost of Orion" (editors' title) from *Damballah.* Copyright © 1988 by John Edgar Wideman. Reprinted with the permission of Vintage Books, a Division of Random House, Inc.

RICHARD WRIGHT, "Living Jim Crow" (editors' title, originally titled "The Ethics of Living Jim Crow: An Autobiographical Sketch," parts I-III), from *Uncle Tom's Children* (New York: Harper, 1937). Copyright 1937 by Richard Wright, renewed © 1965 by Ellen Wright. Reprinted with the permission of HarperCollins Publishers, Inc.

ANIKA YETUNDE, "Female Genital Mutilation and Castration" (previously unpublished student essay). Reprinted with the permission of the author.

Index